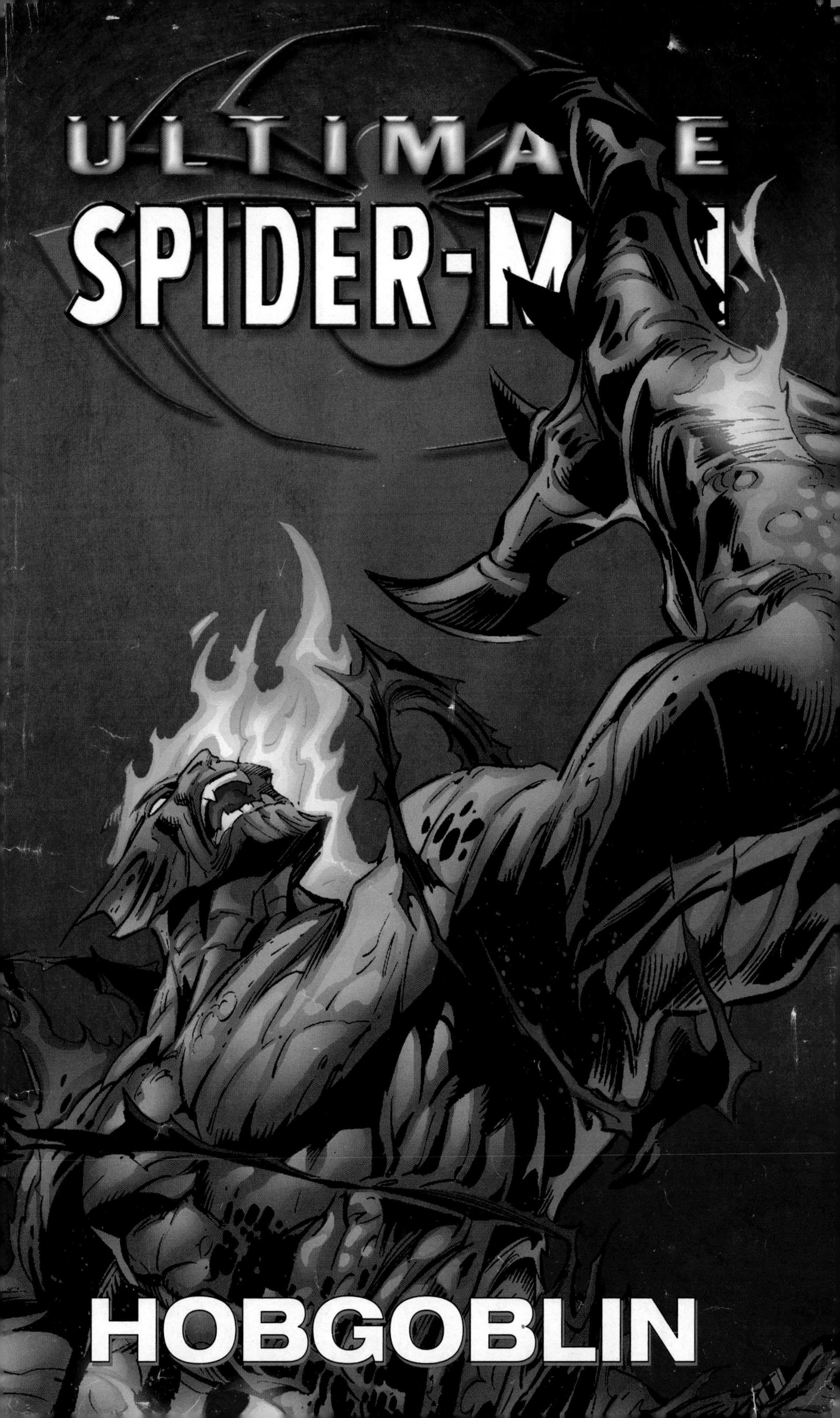

ULTIMATE SPIDER-MAN

HOBGOBLIN

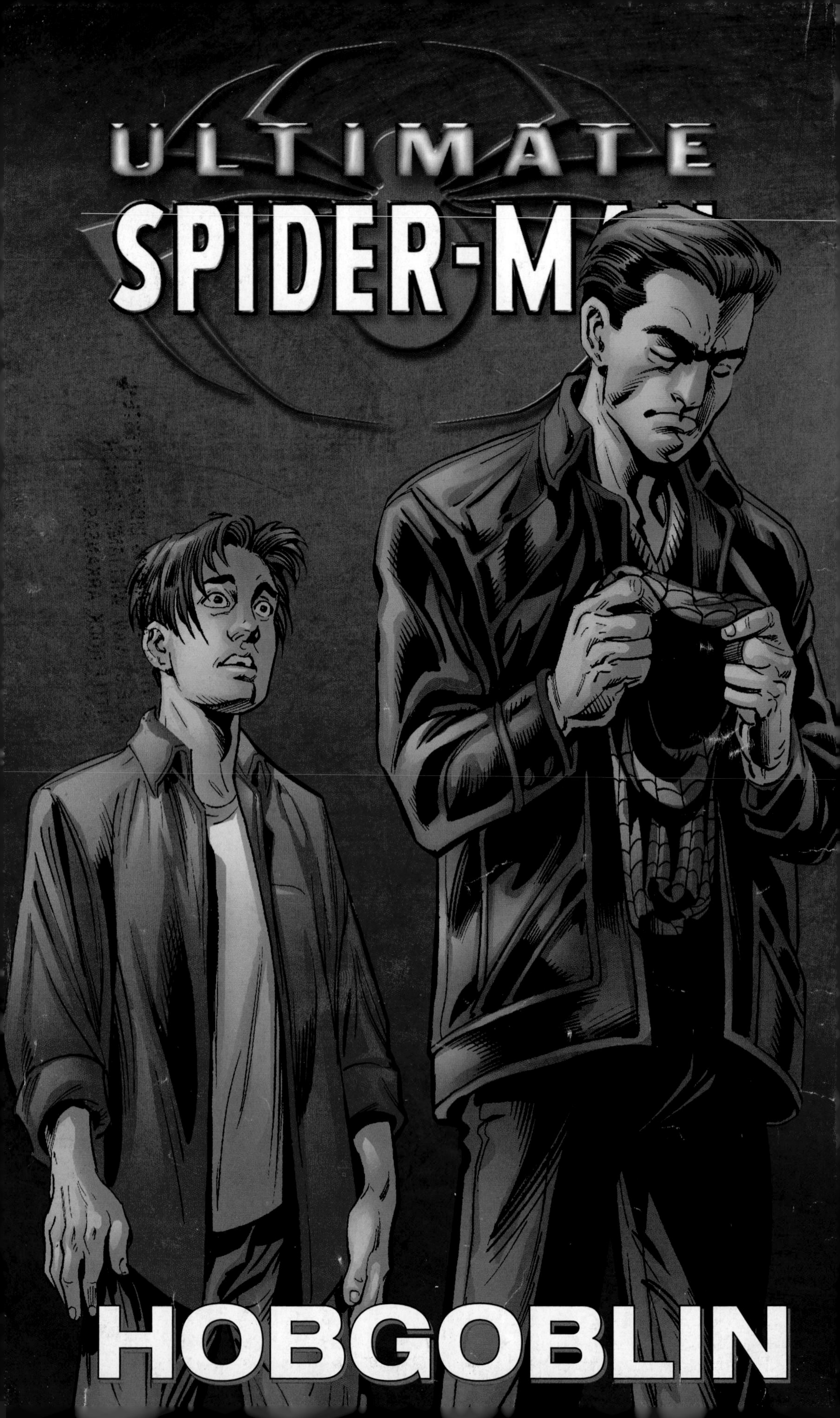
ULTIMATE
SPIDER-MAN
HOBGOBLIN

writer
BRIAN MICHAEL BENDIS

pencils
MARK BAGLEY

inks
SCOTT HANNA

colors
J.D. SMITH

letters
CHRIS ELIOPOULOS

covers by
MARK BAGLEY & RICHARD ISANOVE

assistant editors
JOHN BARBER & NICOLE WILEY

associate editor
NICK LOWE

editor
RALPH MACCHIO

collections editor
JENNIFER GRÜNWALD

senior editor, special projects
JEFF YOUNGQUIST

director of sales
DAVID GABRIEL

production
LORETTA KROL

book designer
JEOF VITA

creative director
TOM MARVELLI

editor in chief
JOE QUESADA

publisher
DAN BUCKLEY

PREVIOUSLY IN ULTIMATE SPIDER-MAN ...

Recent battles with villains Carnage and Nightmare have put Peter in an awful mental state, especially since the death of his friend Gwen Stacy at the hands of Carnage. He is doubting his role as Spider-Man and is unable to communicate with his girlfriend and confidante, Mary Jane Watson.

Norman Osborn, the father of Peter's best friend, Harry, was developing a wonder drug called Oz. Testing of the mystery drug created the genetically altered spider that accidentally created Spider-Man.

In an attempt to repeat the process on himself, Osborn destroyed his life. He mutated himself into a hulking goblin figure. Driven mad by the mutation, he set out to erase any memory of his existence. He killed his wife and attempted to kill his own son.

In fact, one of Spider-Man's first tests of mettle was fighting the mysterious Goblin.

Harry Osborn has been witness to all of his father's shocking and violent Goblin outbursts. Norman Osborn recently escaped from S.H.I.E.L.D. custody and tried to use Peter as part of a commando brigade against the White House. Nick Fury led the Ultimates and Spider-Man to a successful defeat of Osborn, but was forced to use Harry Osborn as a decoy.

A dumbstruck Harry witnessed the violent defeat of his father. Peter tried to comfort his old friend. The only words Harry could mutter were: "I'll kill you all."

That was the last time Peter, or anyone, saw Harry.

72

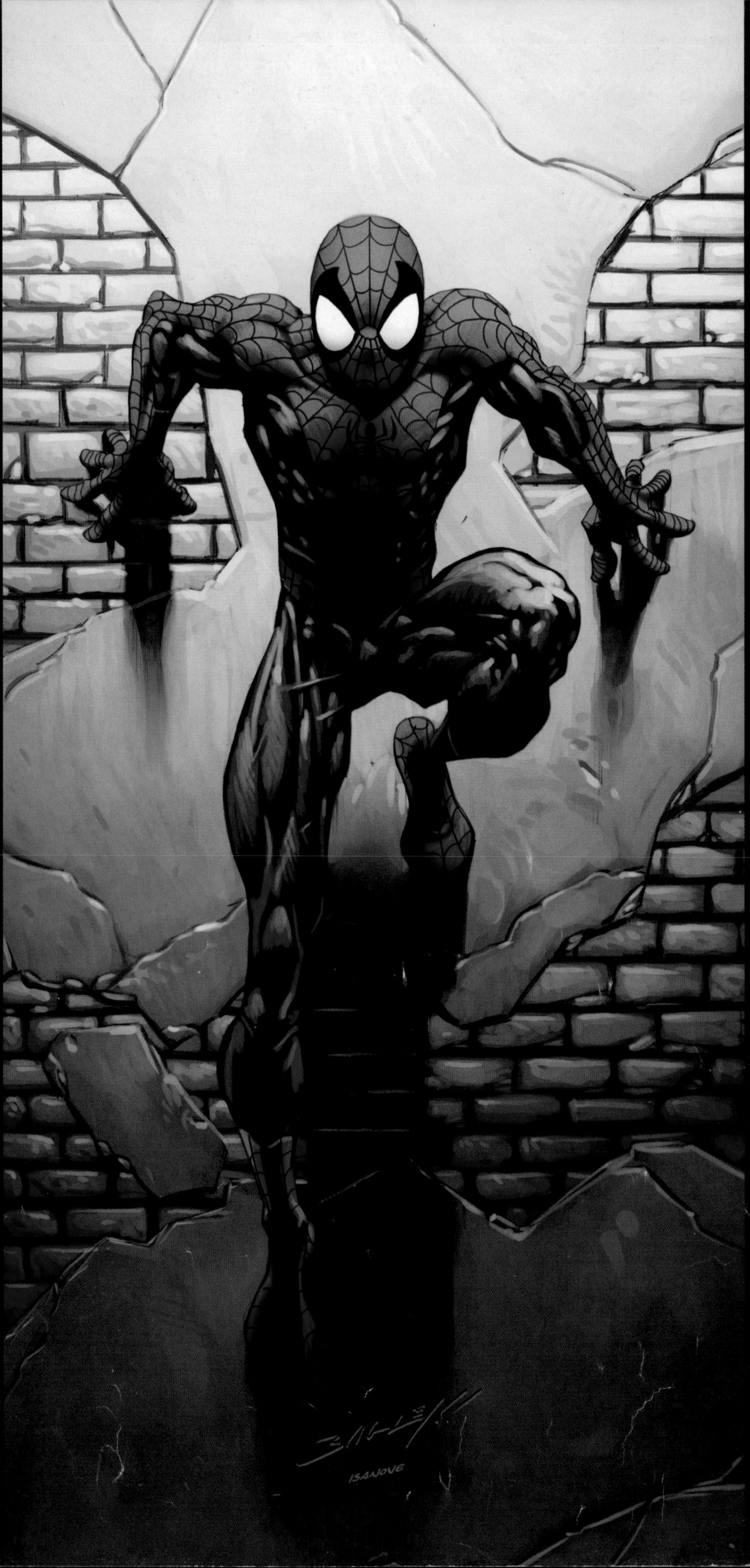

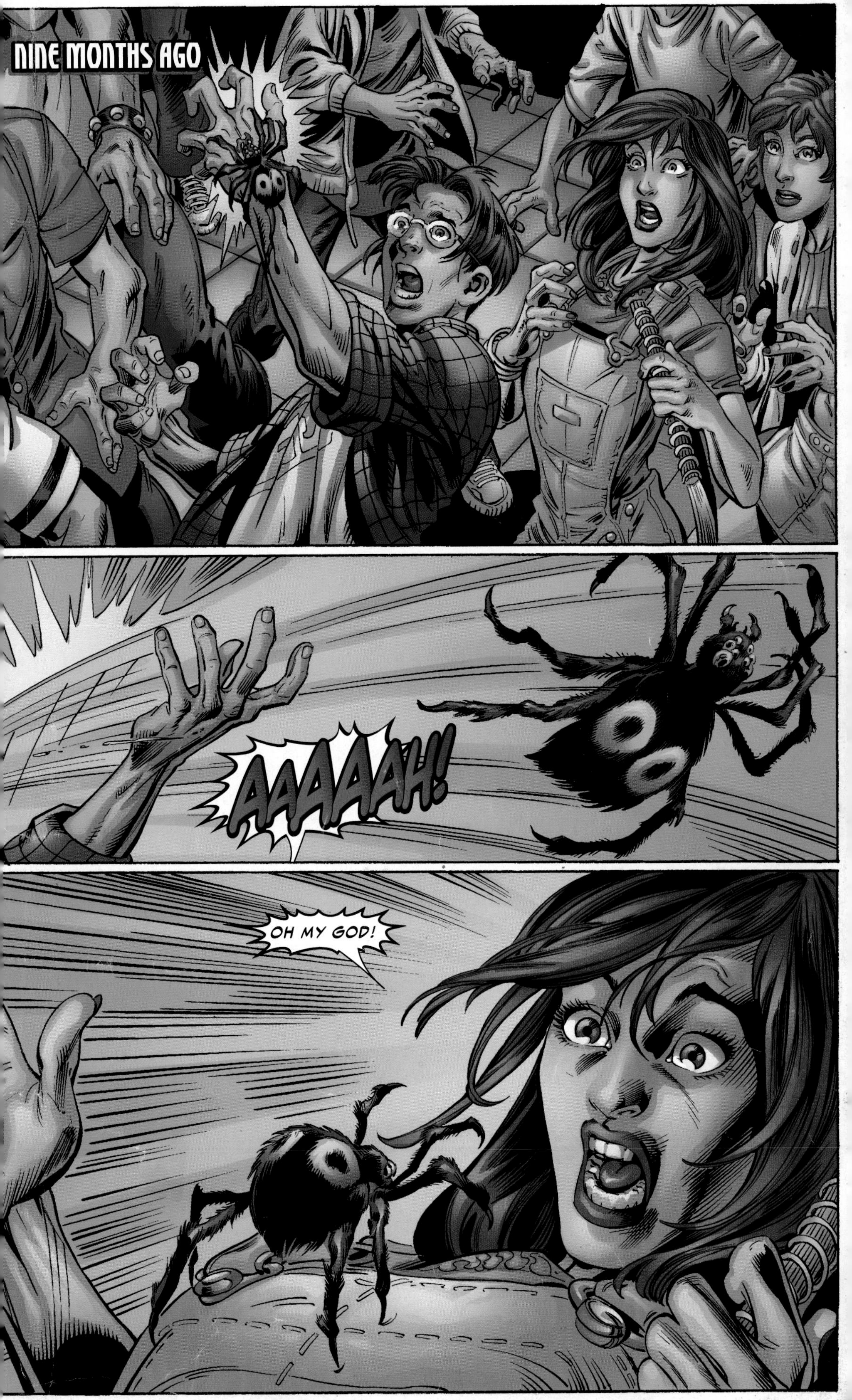
NINE MONTHS AGO
AAAAAH!
OH MY GOD!

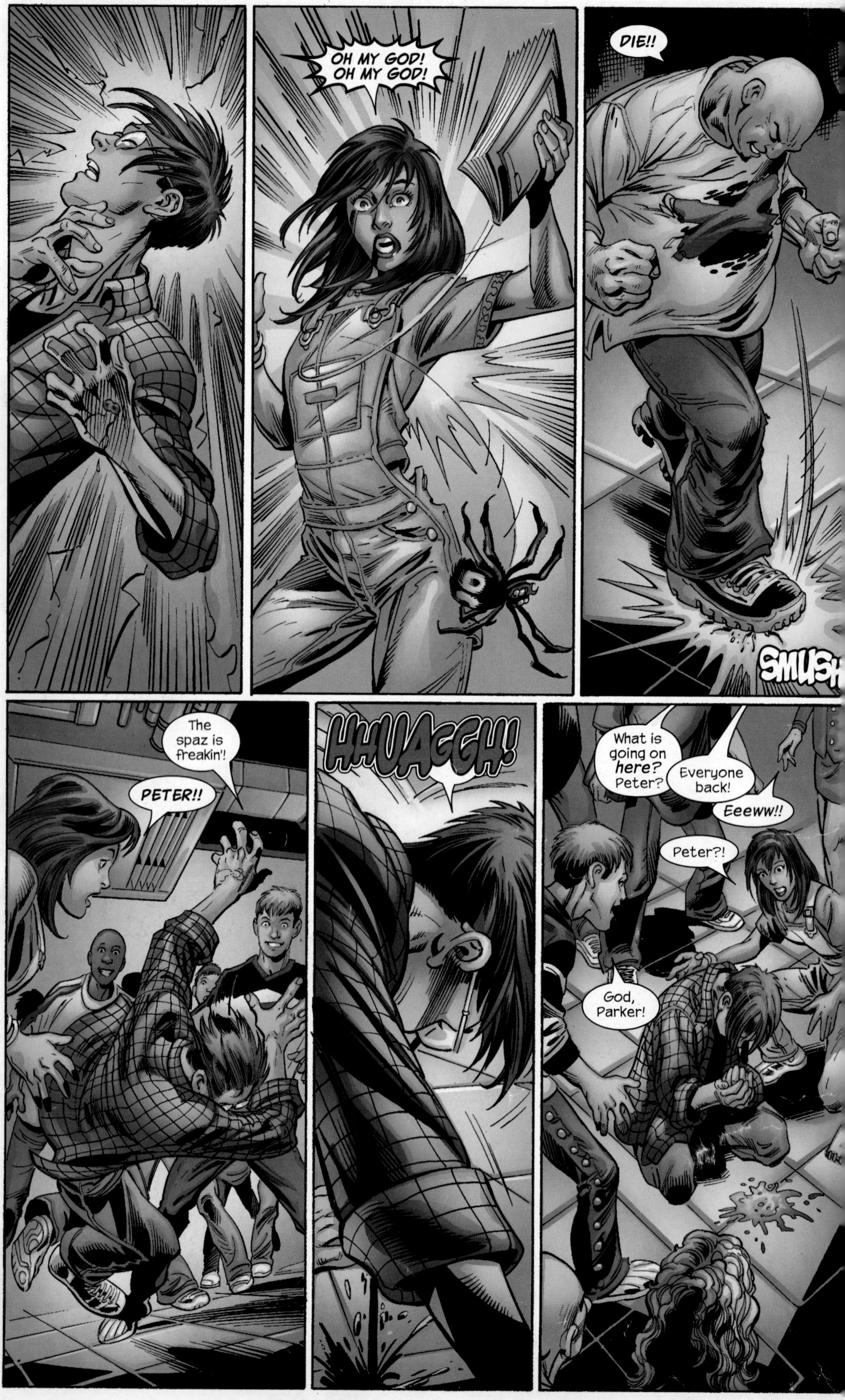
OH MY GOD! OH MY GOD!
DIE!!
SMUSH
The spaz is freakin'!
PETER!!
HHUAGGH!
What is going on here? Peter?
Everyone back!
Eeeww!!
Peter?!
God, Parker!

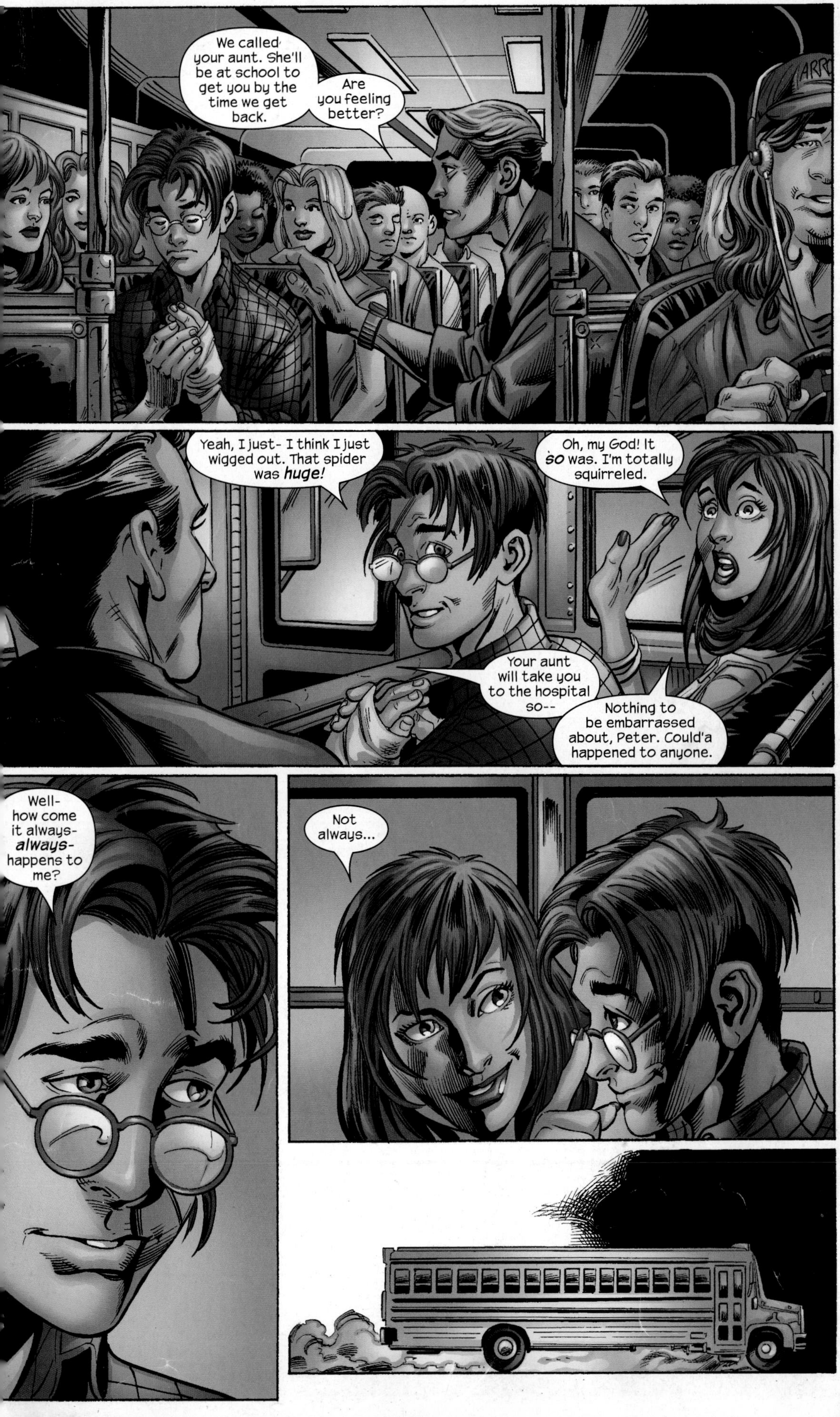
We called your aunt. She'll be at school to get you by the time we get back.
Are you feeling better?
Yeah, I just- I think I just wigged out. That spider was *huge!*
Oh, my God! It *so* was. I'm totally squirreled.
Your aunt will take you to the hospital so--
Nothing to be embarrassed about, Peter. Could'a happened to anyone.
Well- how come it always- *always-* happens to me?
Not always...

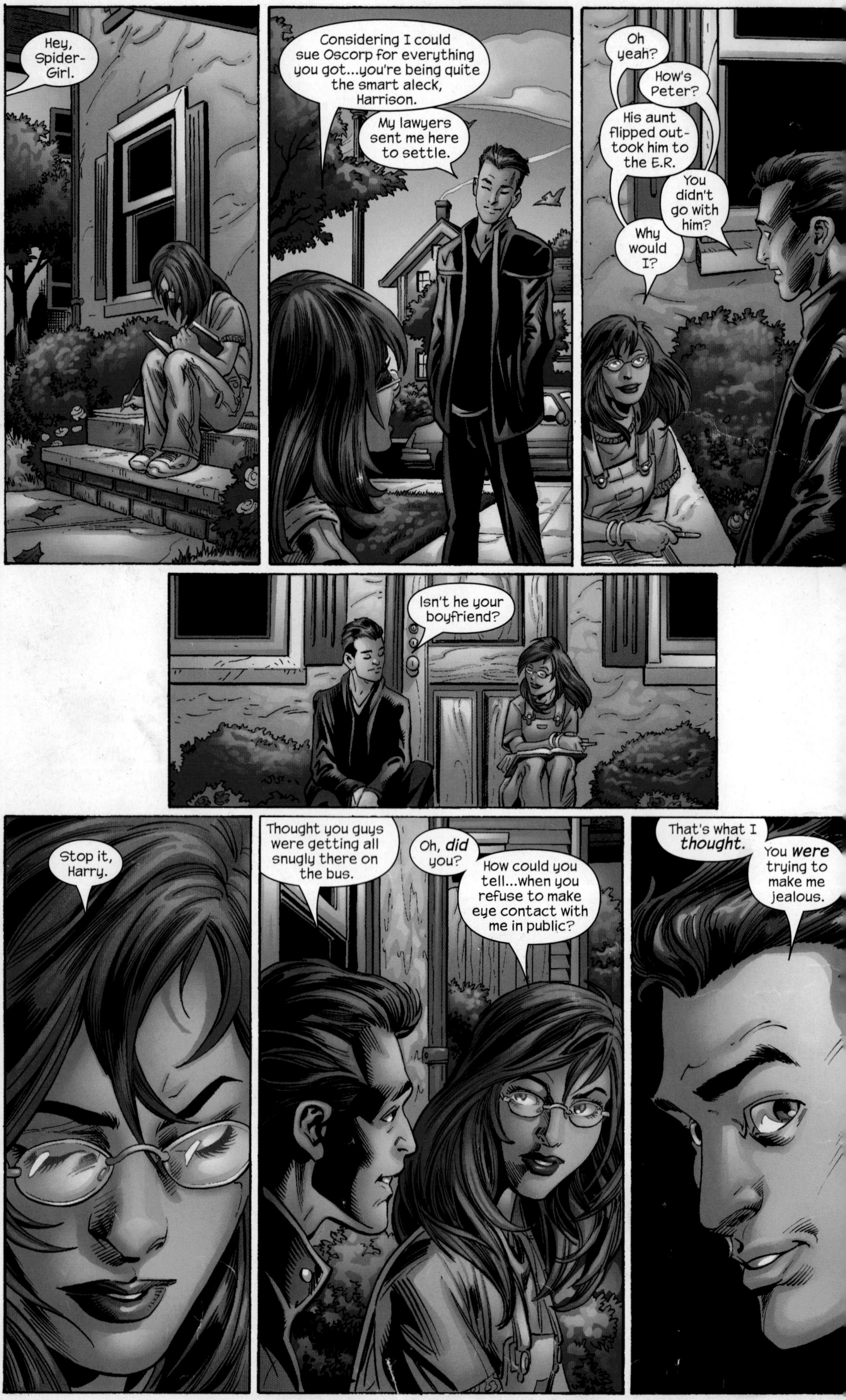
Hey, Spider-Girl.
Considering I could sue Oscorp for everything you got...you're being quite the smart aleck, Harrison.
My lawyers sent me here to settle.
Oh yeah?
How's Peter?
His aunt flipped out-took him to the E.R.
You didn't go with him?
Why would I?
Isn't he your boyfriend?
Stop it, Harry.
Thought you guys were getting all snugly there on the bus.
Oh, *did* you?
How could you tell...when you refuse to make eye contact with me in public?
That's what I *thought.*
You *were* trying to make me jealous.

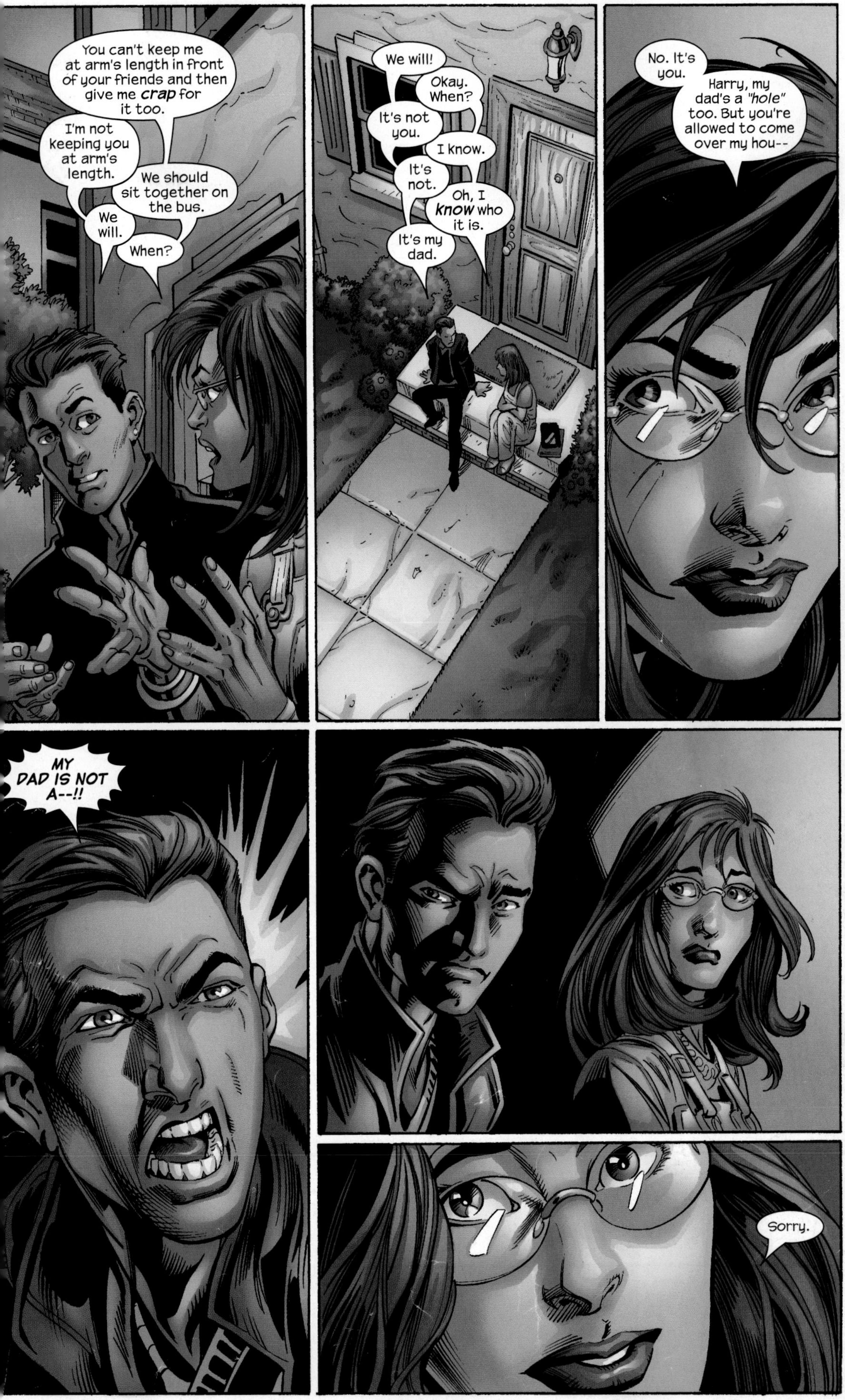
You can't keep me at arm's length in front of your friends and then give me *crap* for it too.
I'm not keeping you at arm's length.
We should sit together on the bus.
We will.
When?
We will!
Okay. When?
It's not you.
I know.
It's not.
Oh, I *know* who it is.
It's my dad.
No. It's you.
Harry, my dad's a "*hole*" too. But you're allowed to come over my hou--
MY DAD IS NOT A--!!
Sorry.

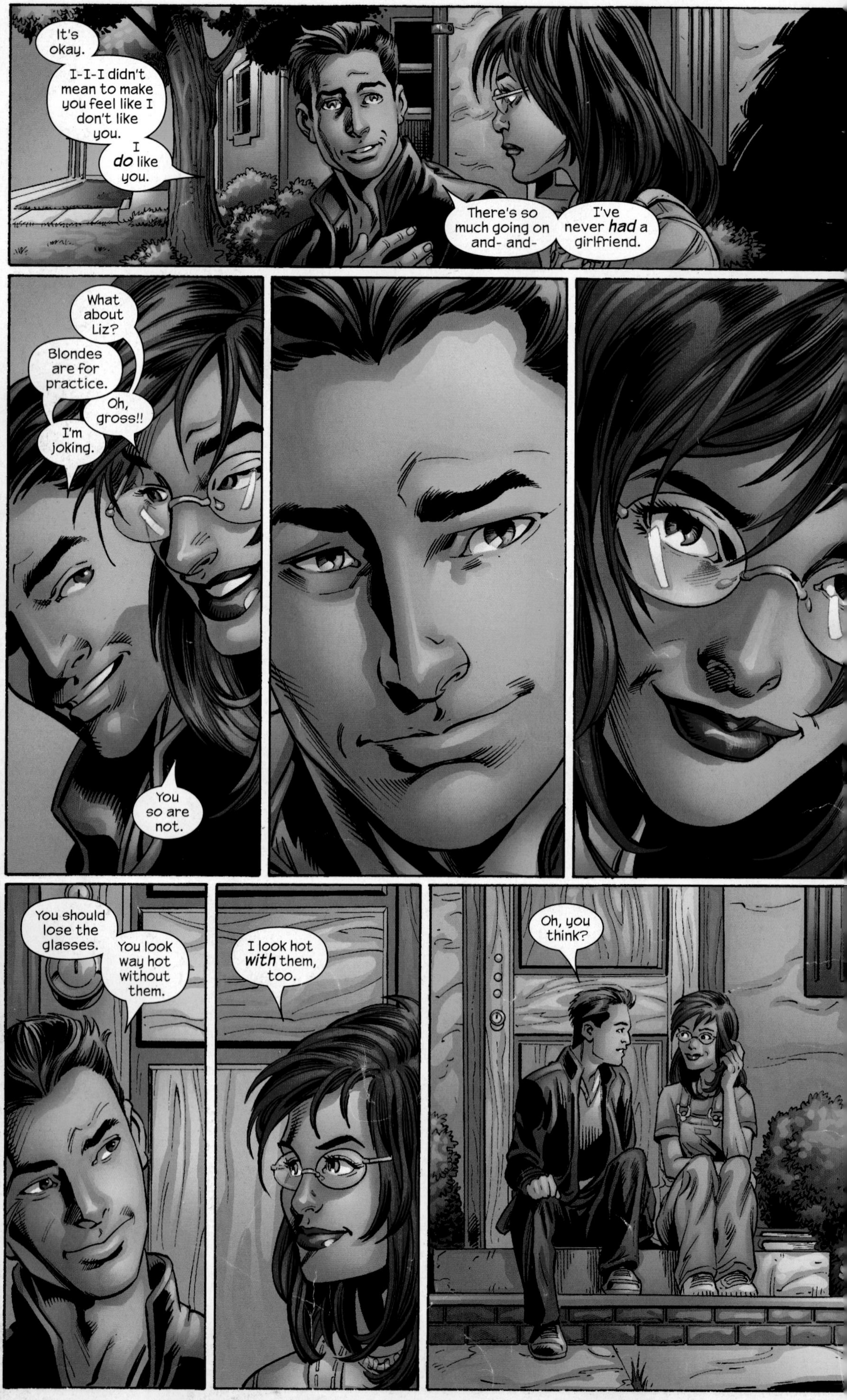
It's okay.
I-I-I didn't mean to make you feel like I don't like you.
I *do* like you.
There's so much going on and- and-
I've never *had* a girlfriend.
What about Liz?
Blondes are for practice.
Oh, gross!!
I'm joking.
You so are not.
You should lose the glasses.
You look way hot without them.
I look hot *with* them, too.
Oh, you think?

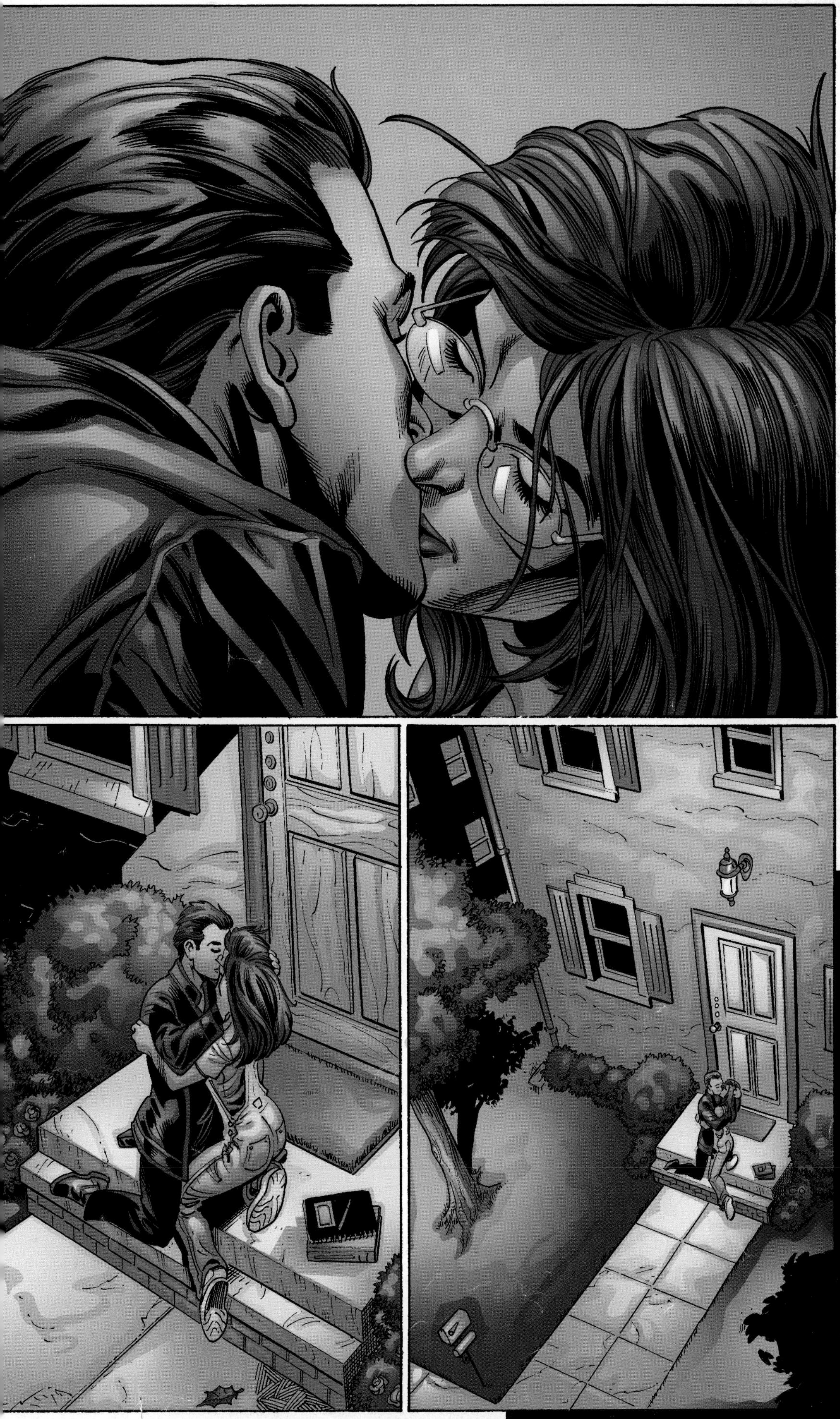

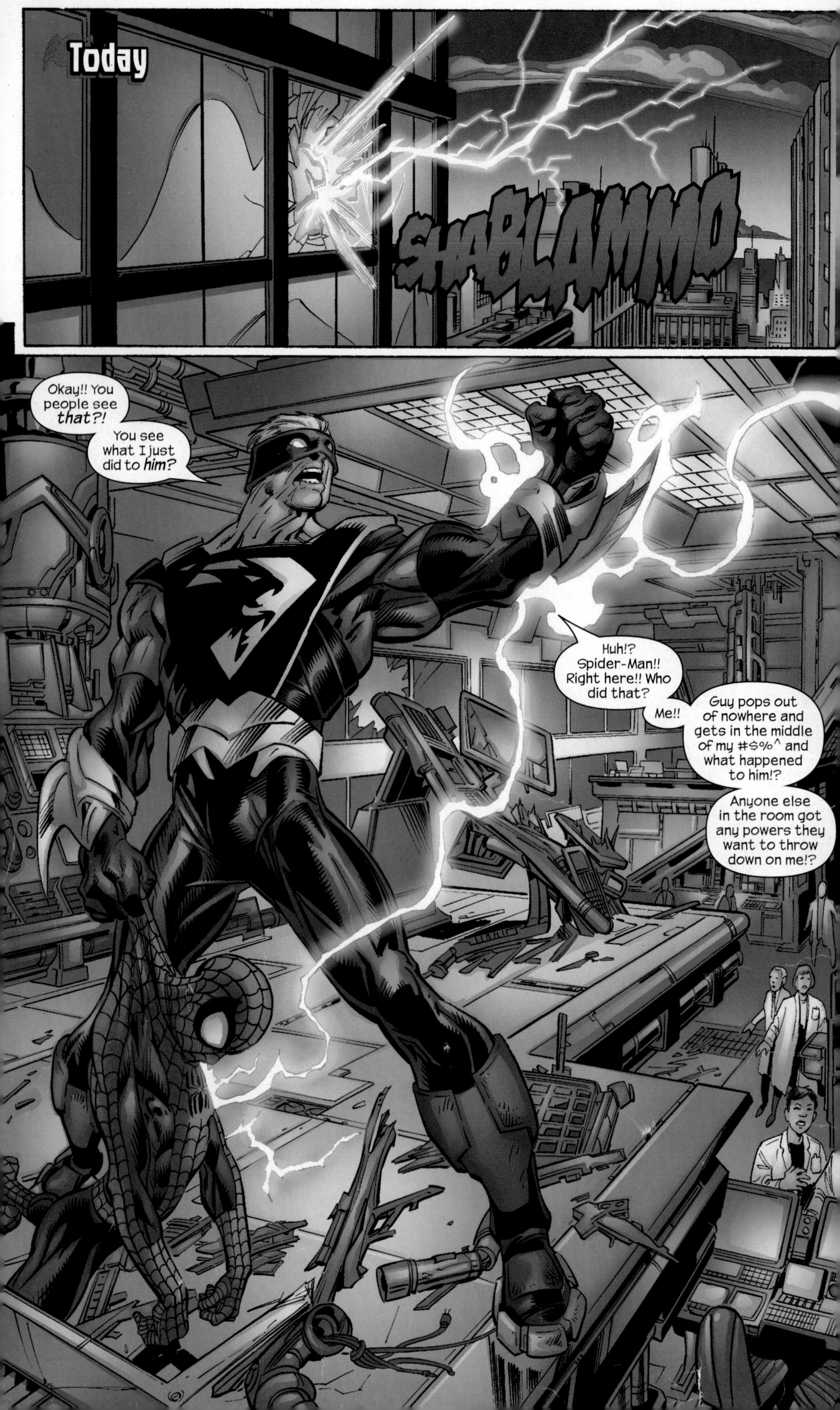

Today
SHABLAMMO
Okay!! You people see *that*?!
You see what I just did to *him*?
Huh!? Spider-Man!! Right here!! Who did that?
Me!!
Guy pops out of nowhere and gets in the middle of my #$%^ and what happened to him!?
Anyone else in the room got any powers they want to throw down on me!?

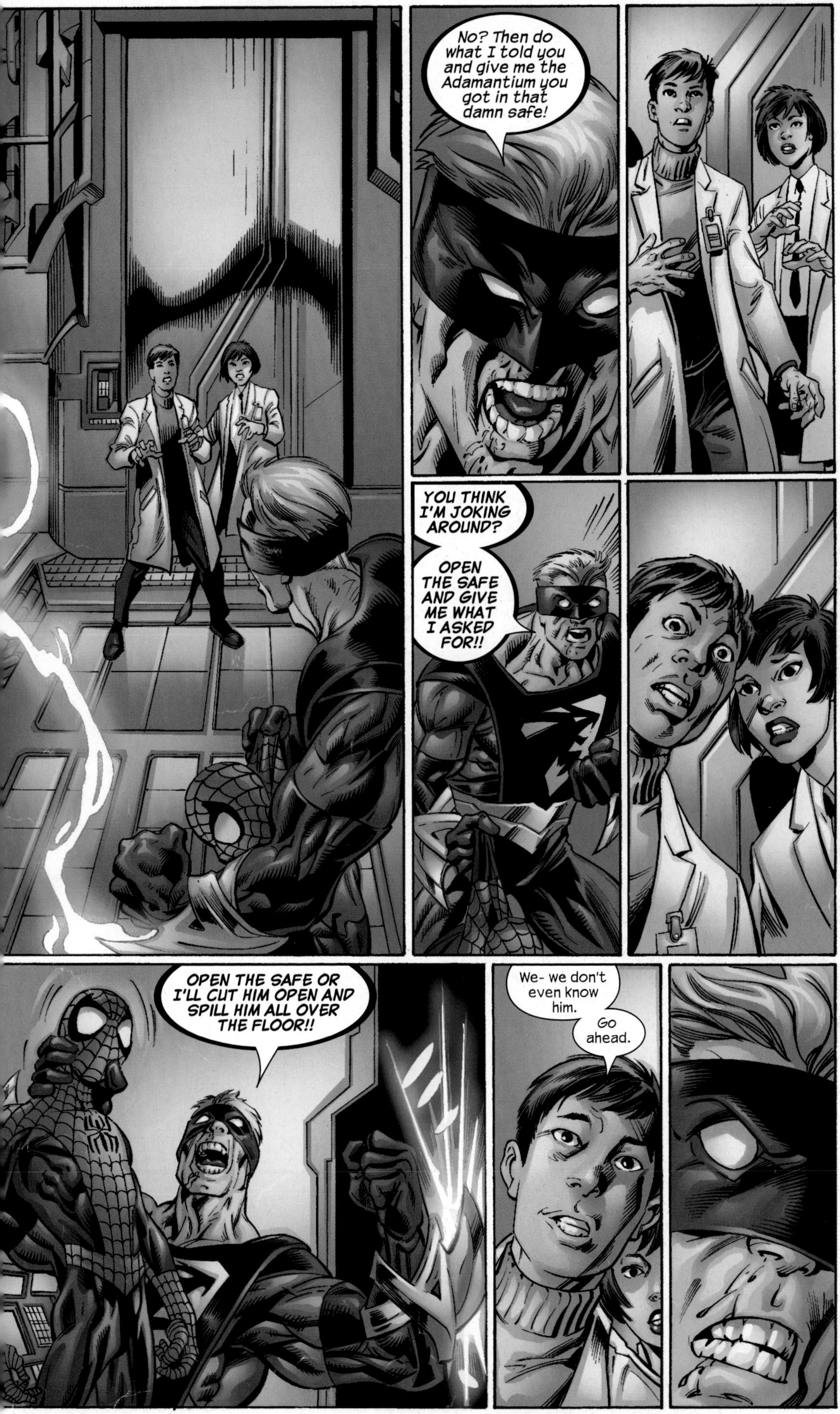
No? Then do what I told you and give me the Adamantium you got in that damn safe!
YOU THINK I'M JOKING AROUND?
OPEN THE SAFE AND GIVE ME WHAT I ASKED FOR!!
OPEN THE SAFE OR I'LL CUT HIM OPEN AND SPILL HIM ALL OVER THE FLOOR!!
We- we don't even know him.
Go ahead.

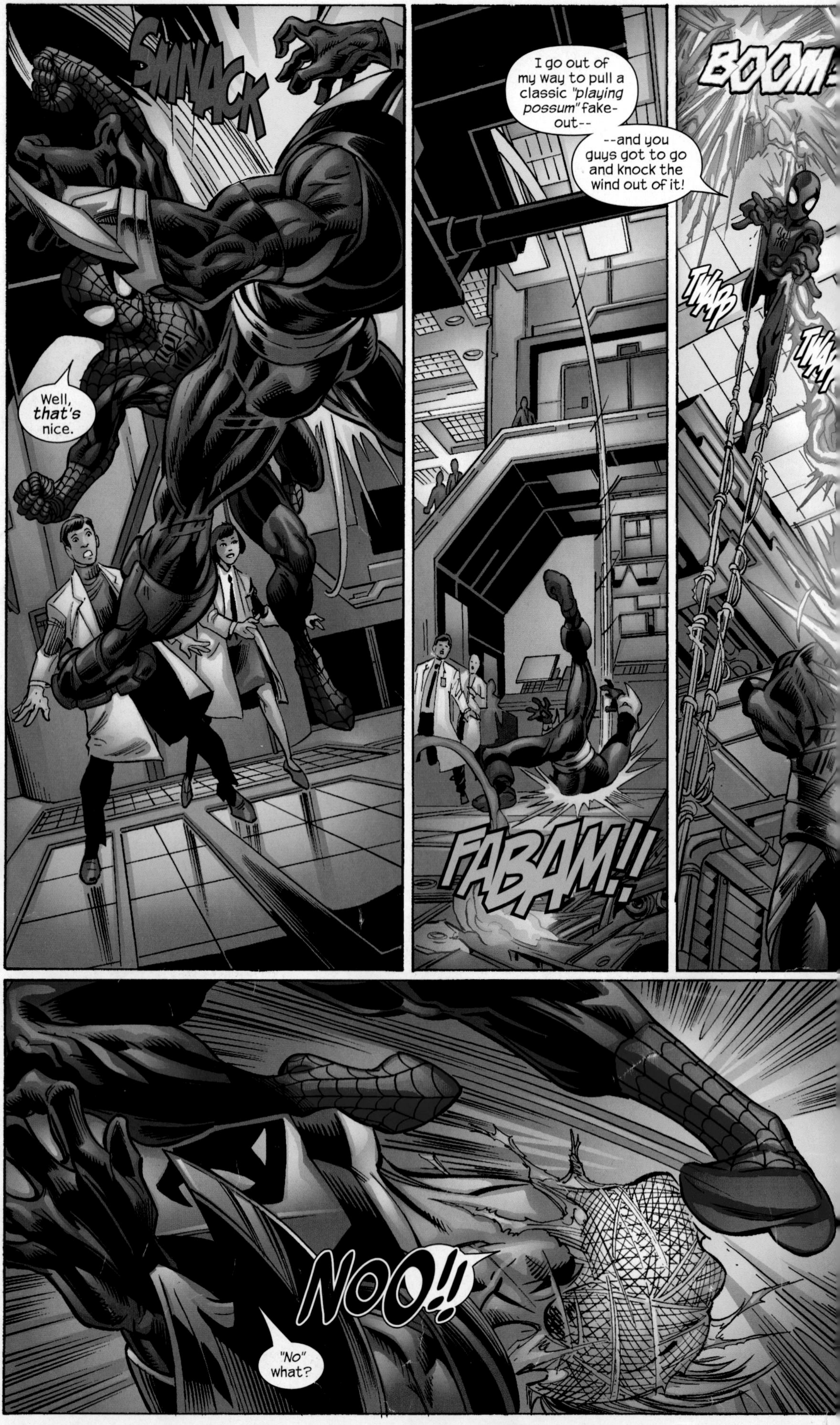
SMNACK
Well, *that's* nice.
I go out of my way to pull a classic *"playing possum"* fake-out--
--and you guys got to go and knock the wind out of it!
FABAM!!
BOOM
TWAP
NOO!!
"No" what?

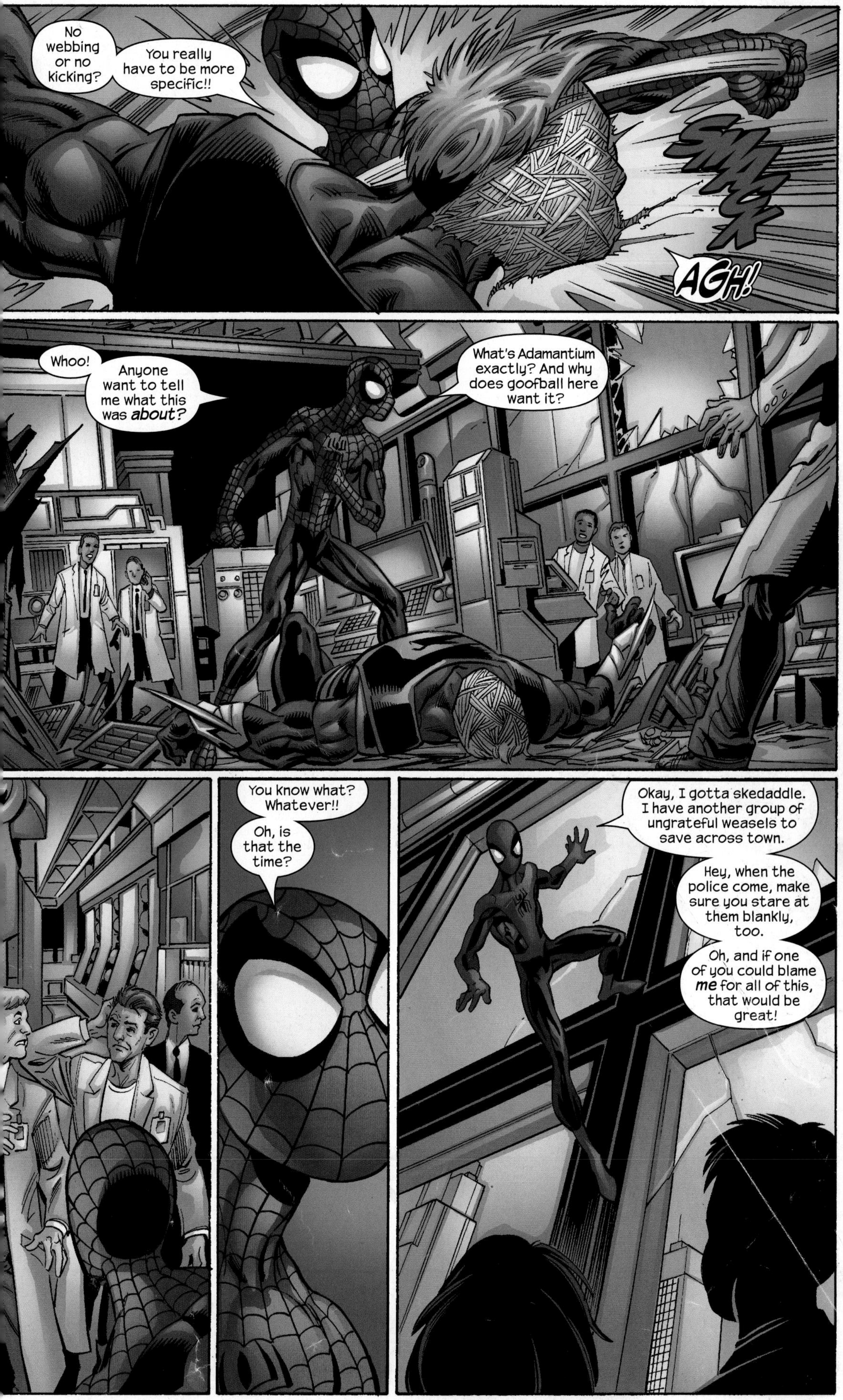

No webbing or no kicking?
You really have to be more specific!!
SMACK
AGH!
Whoo!
Anyone want to tell me what this was *about*?
What's Adamantium exactly? And why does goofball here want it?
You know what? Whatever!!
Oh, is that the time?
Okay, I gotta skedaddle. I have another group of ungrateful weasels to save across town.
Hey, when the police come, make sure you stare at them blankly, too.
Oh, and if one of you could blame *me* for all of this, that would be great!

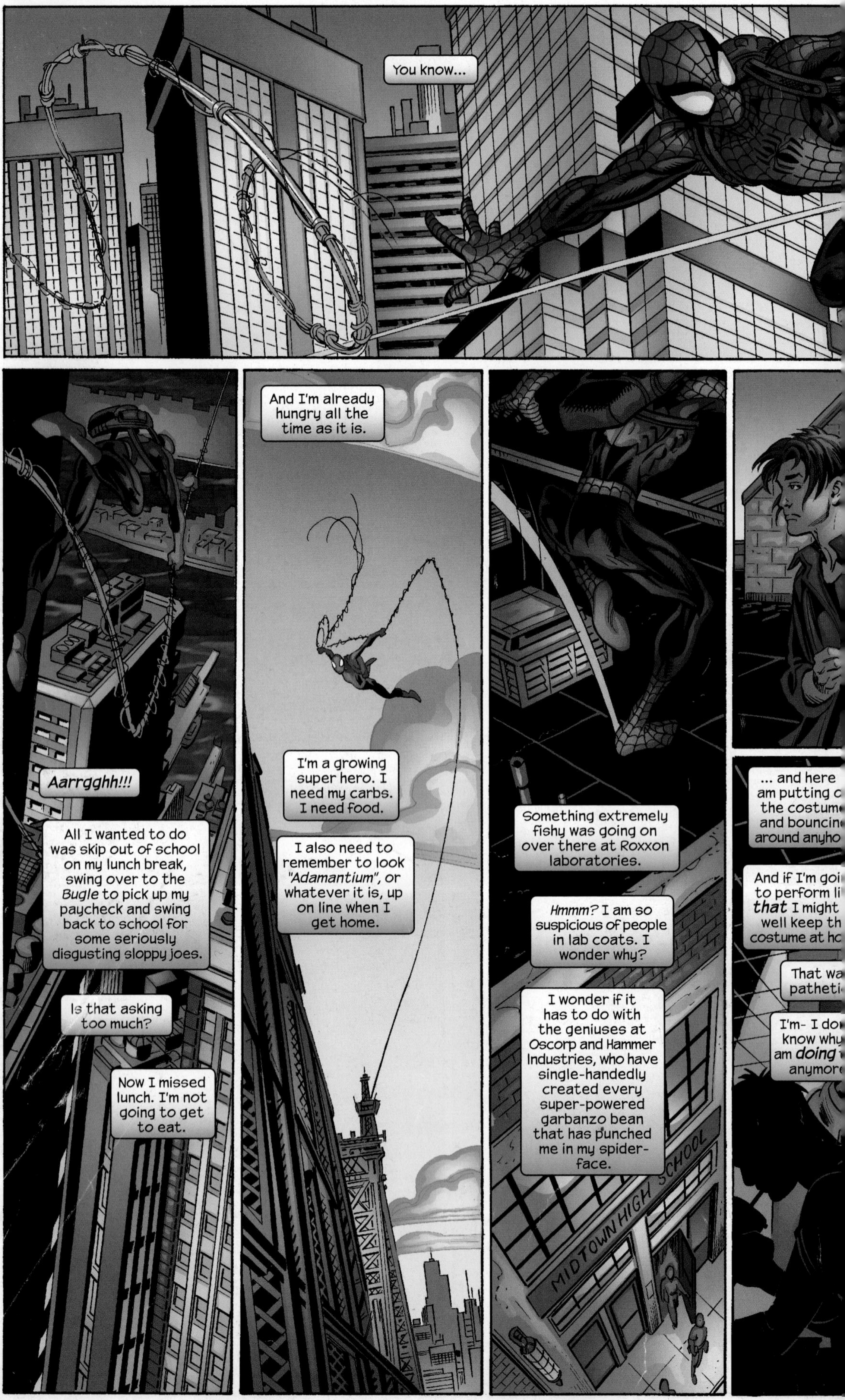
You know...
Aarrgghh!!!
All I wanted to do was skip out of school on my lunch break, swing over to the *Bugle* to pick up my paycheck and swing back to school for some seriously disgusting sloppy joes.
Is that asking too much?
Now I missed lunch. I'm not going to get to eat.
And I'm already hungry all the time as it is.
I'm a growing super hero. I need my carbs. I need food.
I also need to remember to look "*Adamantium*", or whatever it is, up on line when I get home.
Something extremely fishy was going on over there at Roxxon laboratories.
Hmmm? I am so suspicious of people in lab coats. I wonder why?
I wonder if it has to do with the geniuses at Oscorp and Hammer Industries, who have single-handedly created every super-powered garbanzo bean that has punched me in my spider-face.
MIDTOWN HIGH SCHOOL
... and here am putting the costum and bouncin around anyho
And if I'm goi to perform li *that* I might well keep th costume at ho
That wa patheti
I'm- I do know wh am *doing* anymore

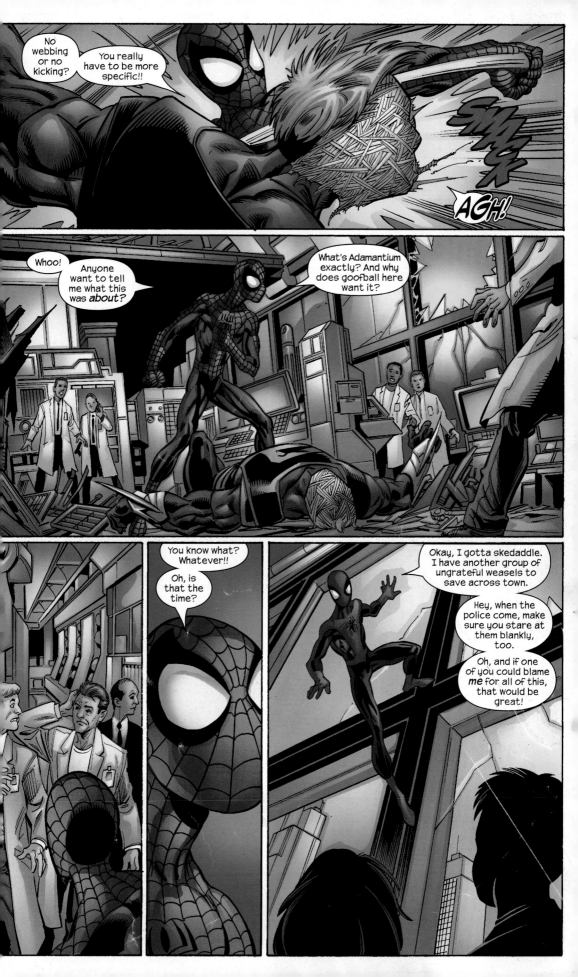

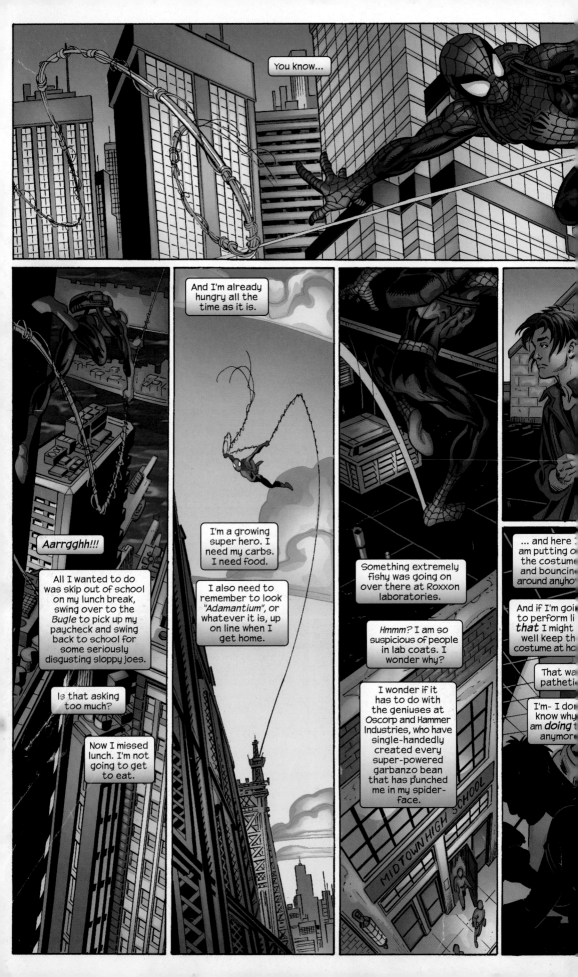

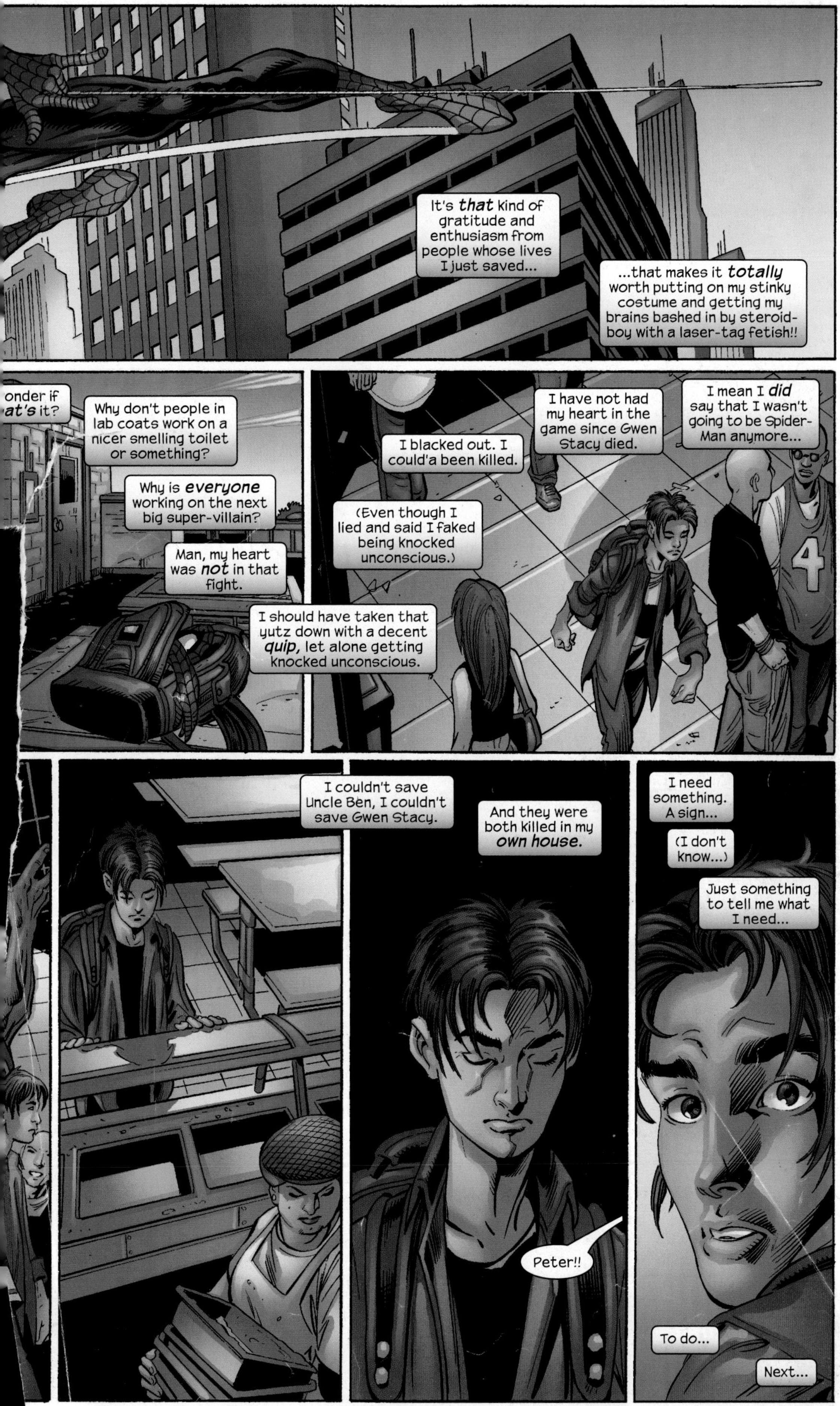
It's *that* kind of gratitude and enthusiasm from people whose lives I just saved...
...that makes it *totally* worth putting on my stinky costume and getting my brains bashed in by steroid-boy with a laser-tag fetish!!
onder if at's it?
Why don't people in lab coats work on a nicer smelling toilet or something?
Why is *everyone* working on the next big super-villain?
Man, my heart was *not* in that fight.
I should have taken that yutz down with a decent *quip,* let alone getting knocked unconscious.
I blacked out. I could'a been killed.
(Even though I lied and said I faked being knocked unconscious.)
I have not had my heart in the game since Gwen Stacy died.
I mean I *did* say that I wasn't going to be Spider-Man anymore...
I couldn't save Uncle Ben, I couldn't save Gwen Stacy.
And they were both killed in my *own house.*
Peter!!
I need something. A sign...
(I don't know...)
Just something to tell me what I need...
To do...
Next...

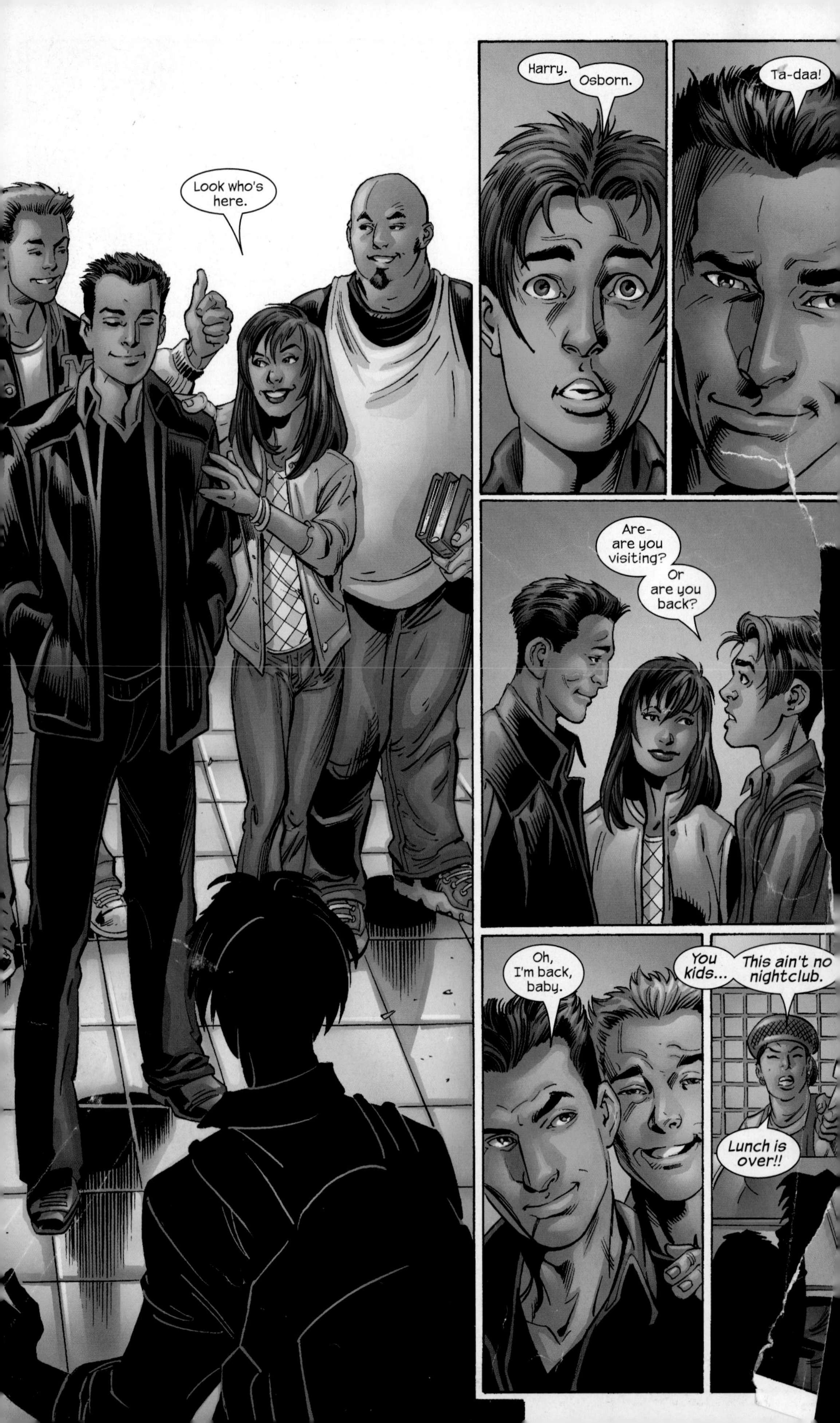
Look who's here.
Harry.
Osborn.
Ta-daa!
Are- are you visiting?
Or are you back?
Oh, I'm back, baby.
You kids...
This ain't no nightclub.
Lunch is over!!

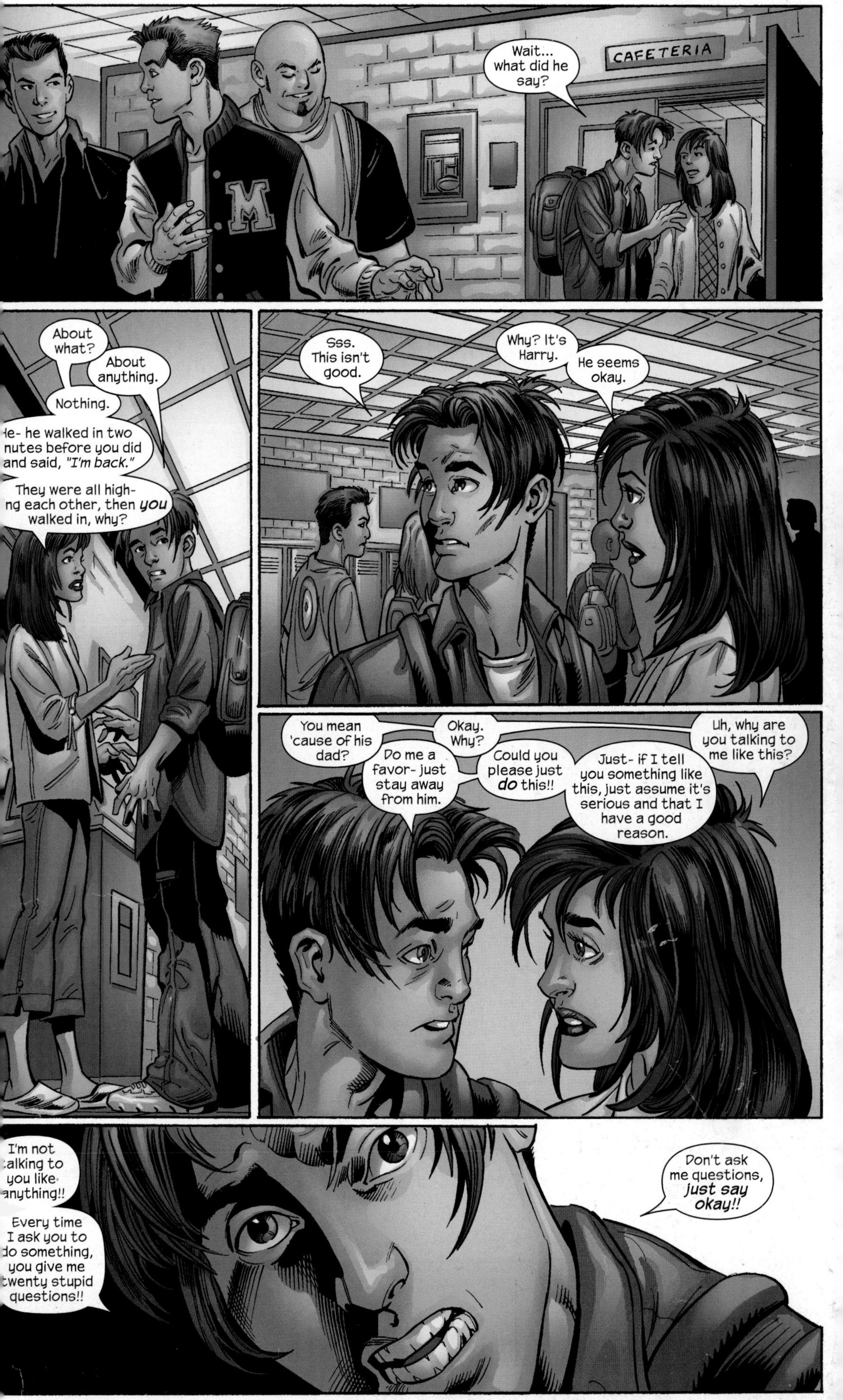
CAFETERIA
Wait... what did he say?
About what?
About anything.
Nothing.
He- he walked in two minutes before you did and said, "I'm back."
They were all high-ing each other, then you walked in, why?
Sss. This isn't good.
Why? It's Harry.
He seems okay.
You mean 'cause of his dad?
Okay. Why?
Do me a favor- just stay away from him.
Could you please just do this!!
Just- if I tell you something like this, just assume it's serious and that I have a good reason.
Uh, why are you talking to me like this?
I'm not talking to you like anything!!
Every time I ask you to do something, you give me twenty stupid questions!!
Don't ask me questions, just say okay!!

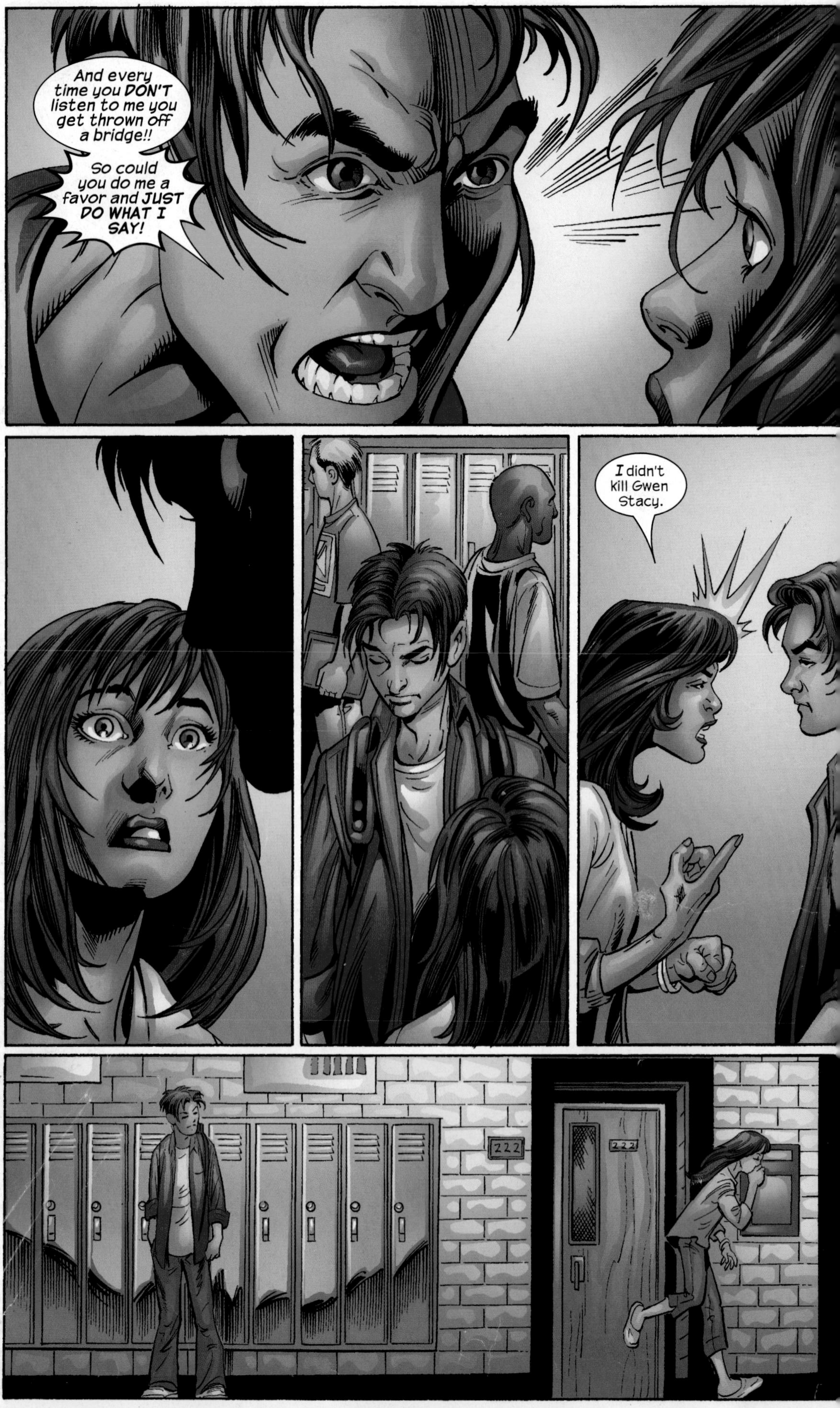
And every time you DON'T listen to me you get thrown off a bridge!!
So could you do me a favor and JUST DO WHAT I SAY!
I didn't kill Gwen Stacy.
222
222

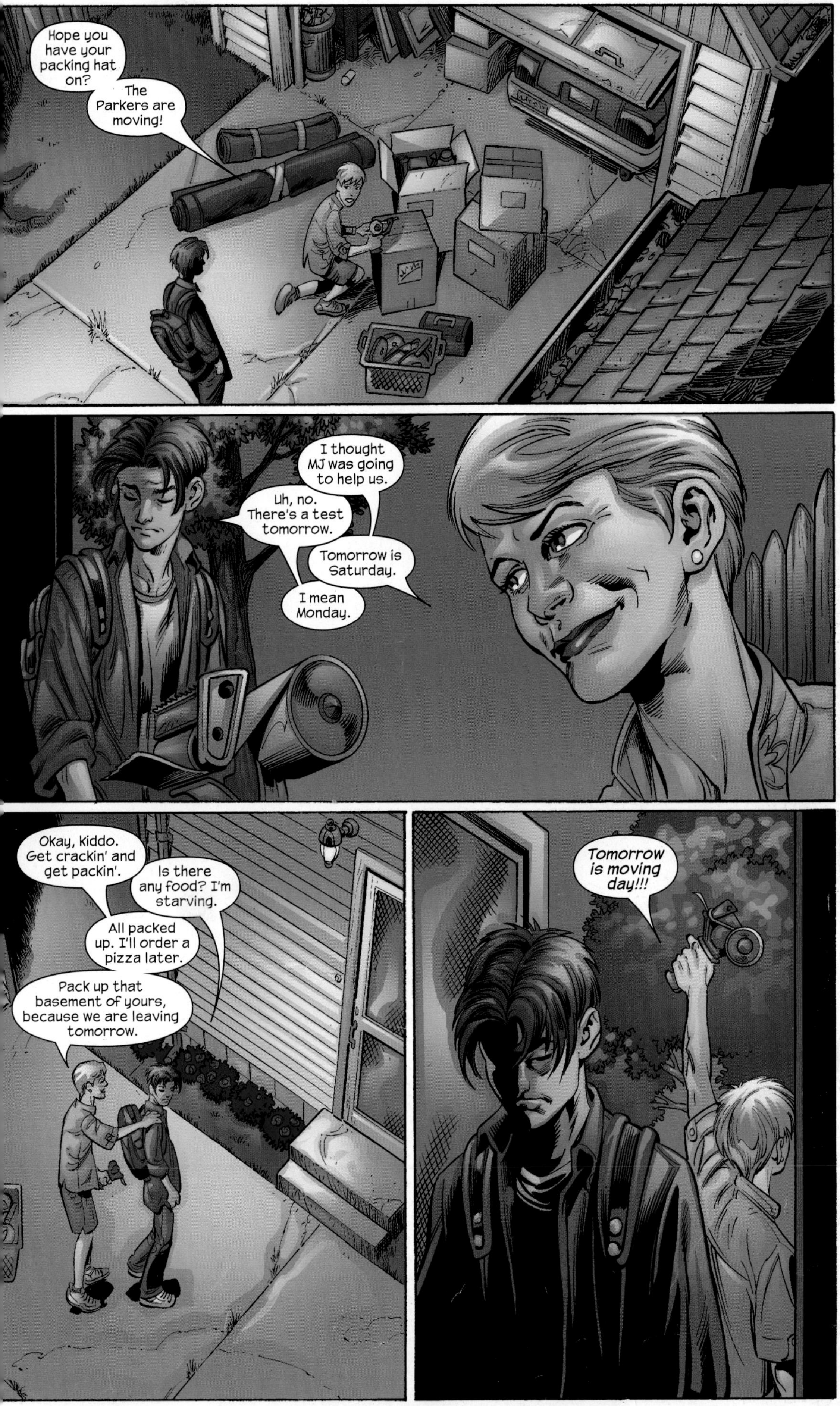
Hope you have your packing hat on?
The Parkers are moving!
I thought MJ was going to help us.
Uh, no. There's a test tomorrow.
Tomorrow is Saturday.
I mean Monday.
Okay, kiddo. Get crackin' and get packin'.
Is there any food? I'm starving.
All packed up. I'll order a pizza later.
Pack up that basement of yours, because we are leaving tomorrow.
Tomorrow is moving day!!!

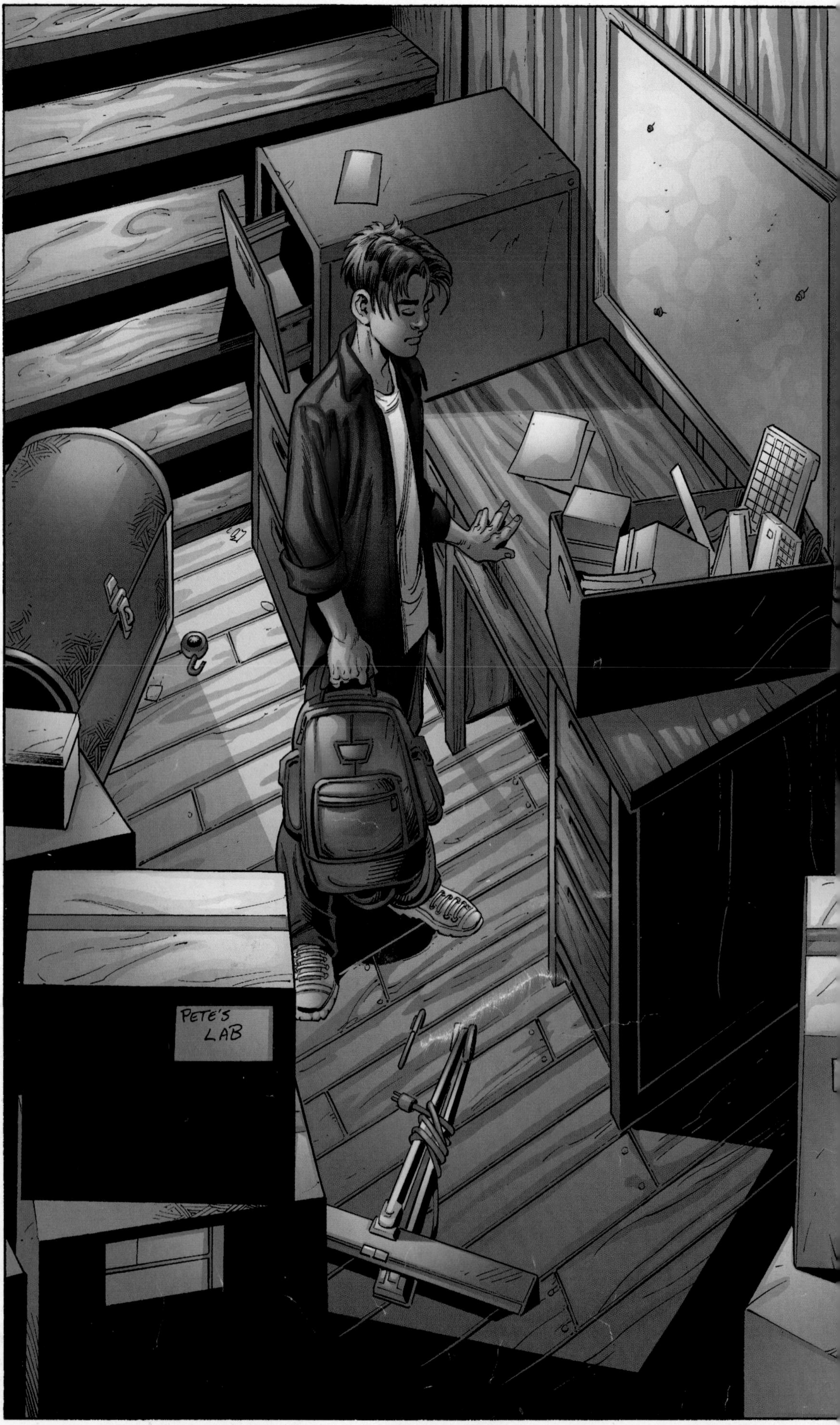
PETE'S LAB

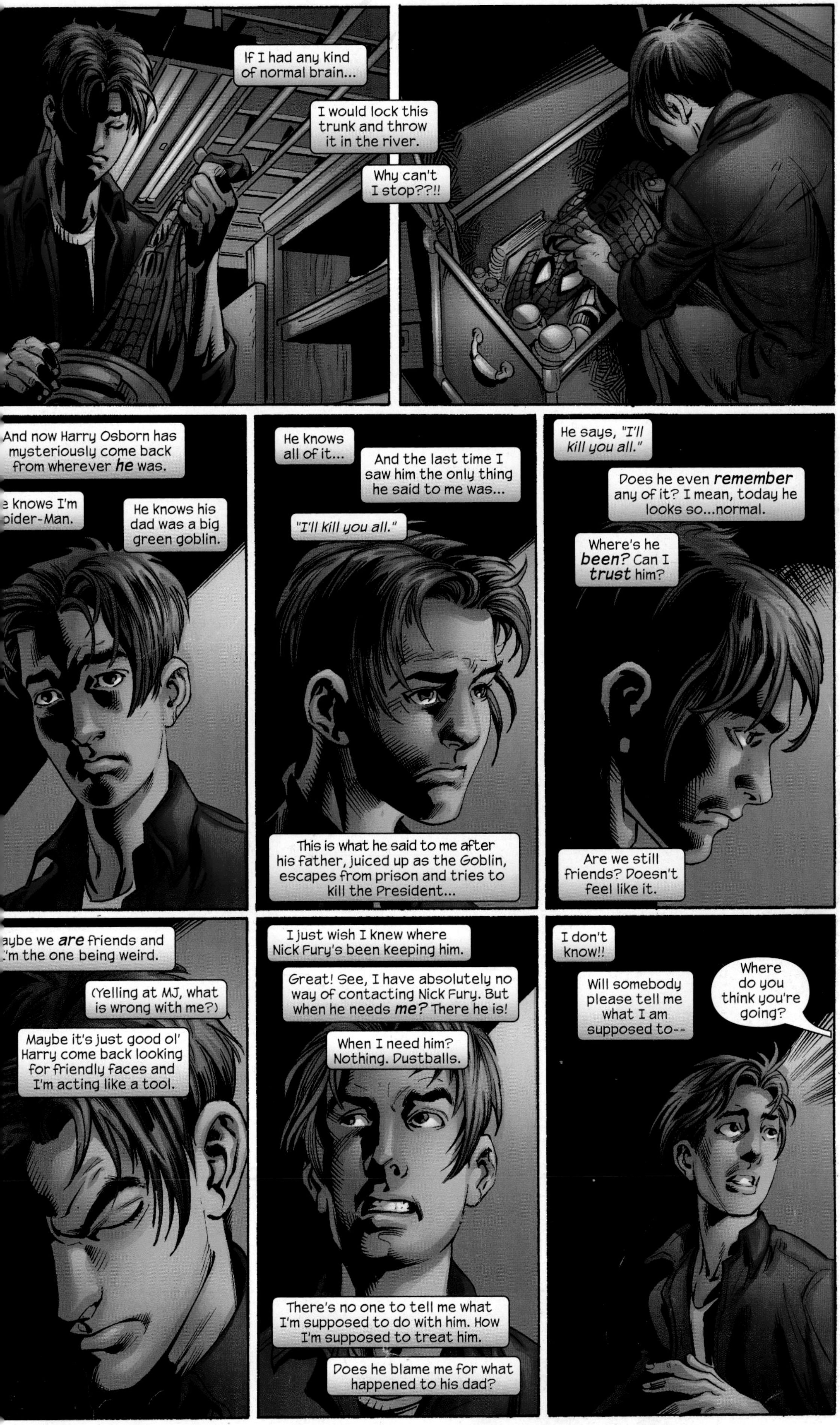
If I had any kind of normal brain...
I would lock this trunk and throw it in the river.
Why can't I stop??!!
And now Harry Osborn has mysteriously come back from wherever *he* was.
e knows I'm pider-Man.
He knows his dad was a big green goblin.
He knows all of it...
And the last time I saw him the only thing he said to me was...
"*I'll kill you all.*"
This is what he said to me after his father, juiced up as the Goblin, escapes from prison and tries to kill the President...
He says, "*I'll kill you all.*"
Does he even ***remember*** any of it? I mean, today he looks so...normal.
Where's he ***been?*** Can I ***trust*** him?
Are we still friends? Doesn't feel like it.
aybe we ***are*** friends and 'm the one being weird.
(Yelling at MJ, what is wrong with me?)
Maybe it's just good ol' Harry come back looking for friendly faces and I'm acting like a tool.
I just wish I knew where Nick Fury's been keeping him.
Great! See, I have absolutely no way of contacting Nick Fury. But when he needs ***me?*** There he is!
When I need him? Nothing. Dustballs.
There's no one to tell me what I'm supposed to do with him. How I'm supposed to treat him.
Does he blame me for what happened to his dad?
I don't know!!
Will somebody please tell me what I am supposed to--
Where do you think you're going?

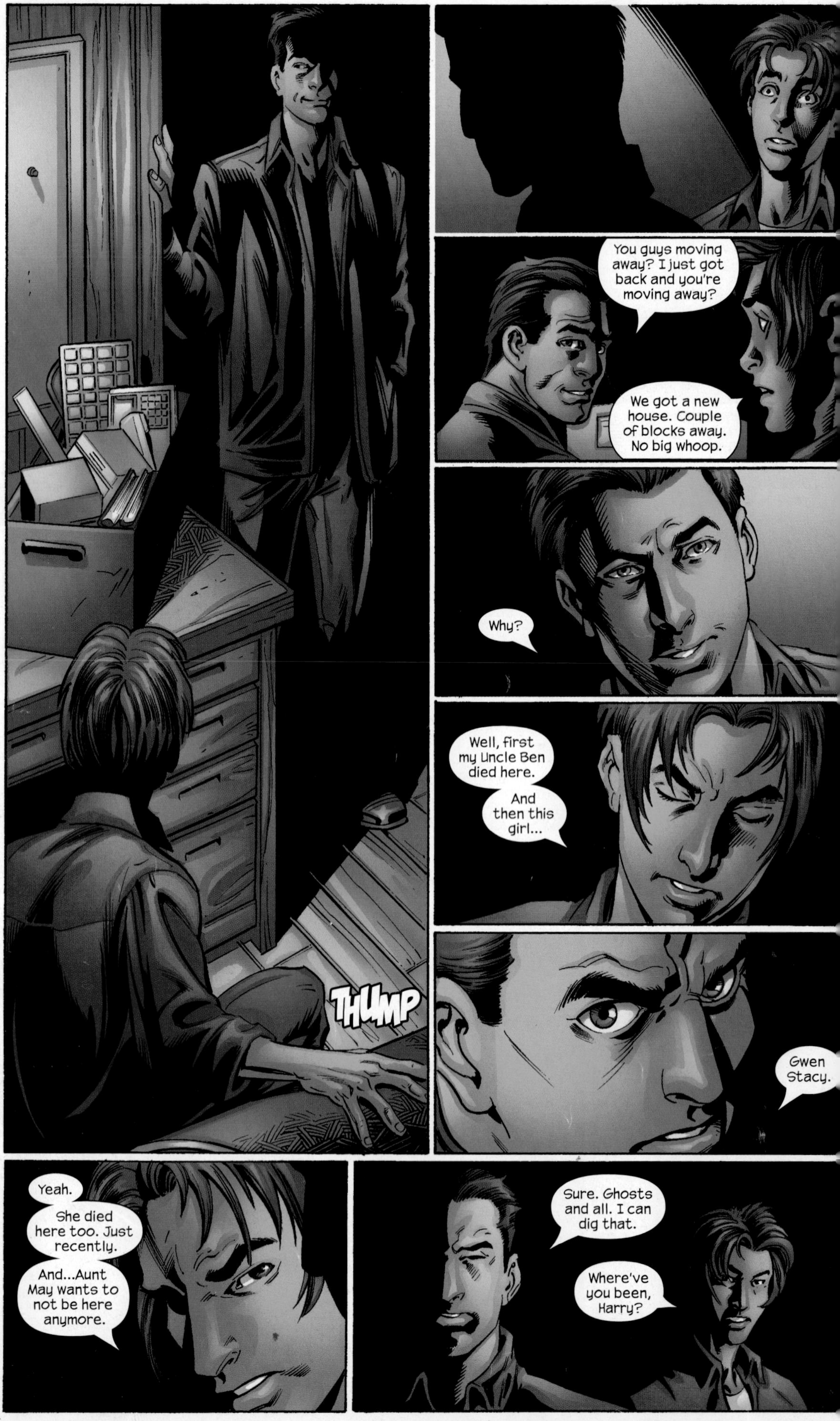
You guys moving away? I just got back and you're moving away?
We got a new house. Couple of blocks away. No big whoop.
Why?
Well, first my Uncle Ben died here.
And then this girl...
THUMP
Gwen Stacy.
Yeah.
She died here too. Just recently.
And...Aunt May wants to not be here anymore.
Sure. Ghosts and all. I can dig that.
Where've you been, Harry?

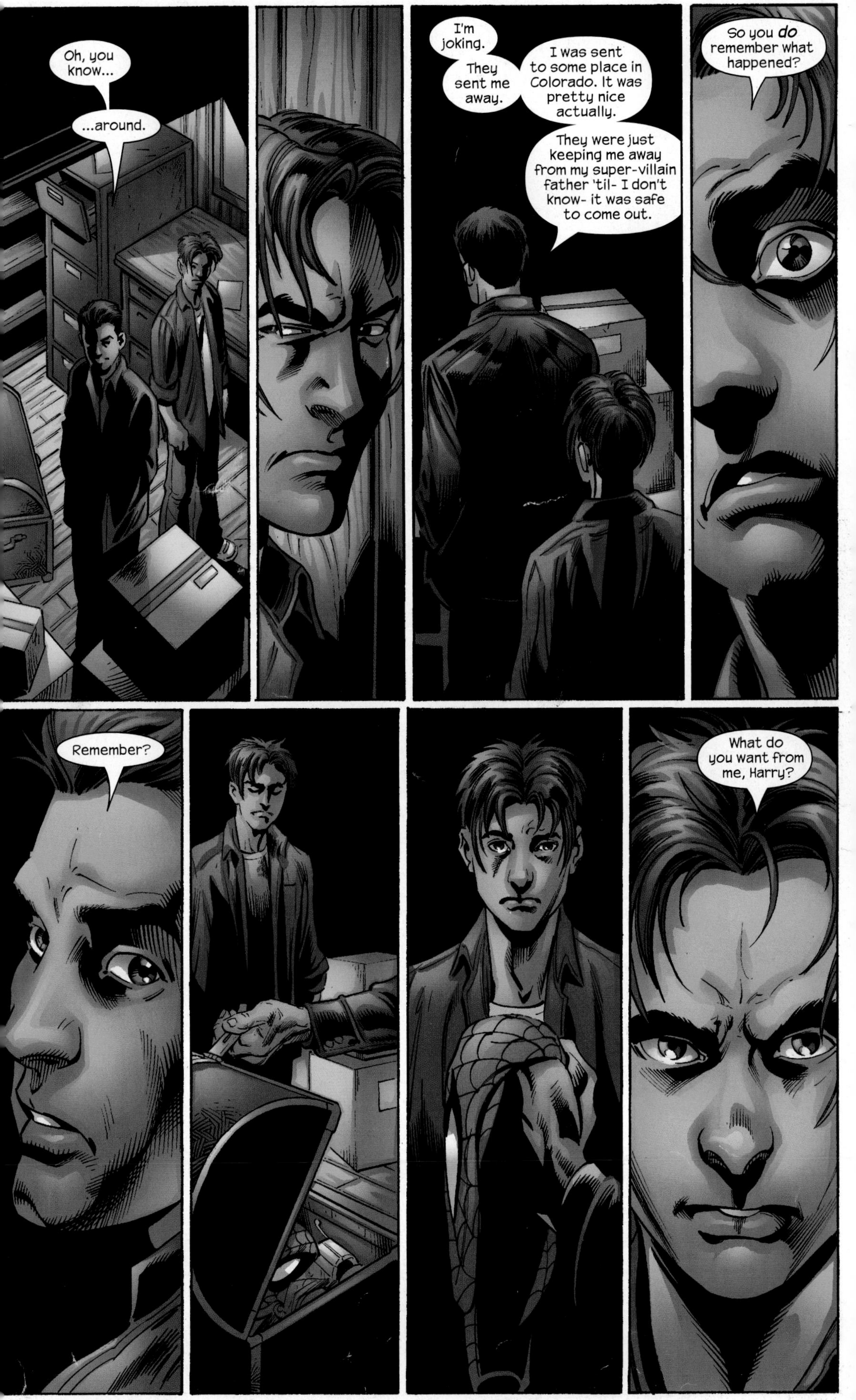
Oh, you know...
...around.
I'm joking.
They sent me away.
I was sent to some place in Colorado. It was pretty nice actually.
They were just keeping me away from my super-villain father 'til- I don't know- it was safe to come out.
So you *do* remember what happened?
Remember?
What do you want from me, Harry?

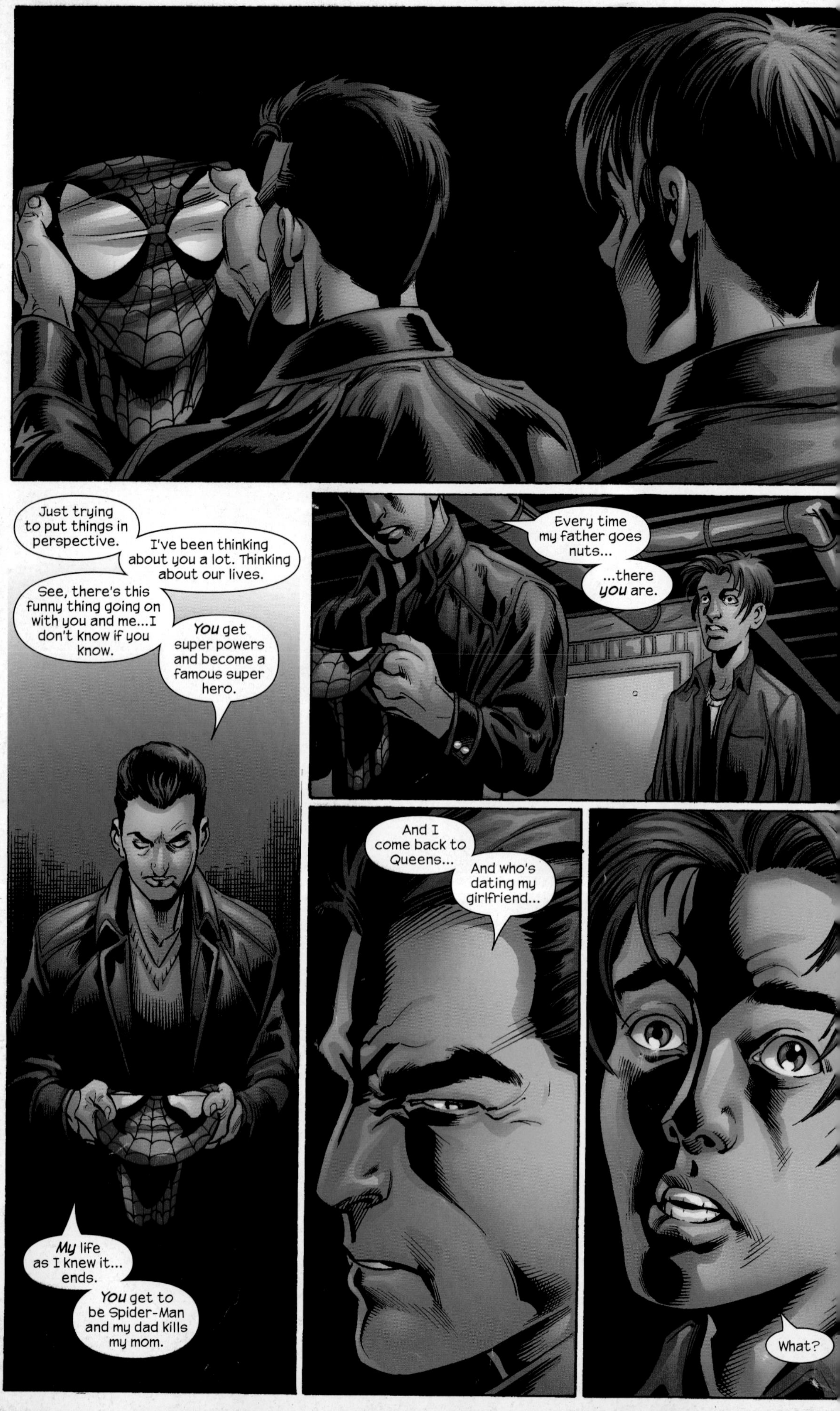
Just trying to put things in perspective.
I've been thinking about you a lot. Thinking about our lives.
See, there's this funny thing going on with you and me...I don't know if you know.
You get super powers and become a famous super hero.
Every time my father goes nuts...
...there *you* are.
My life as I knew it... ends.
You get to be Spider-Man and my dad kills my mom.
And I come back to Queens...
And who's dating my girlfriend...
What?

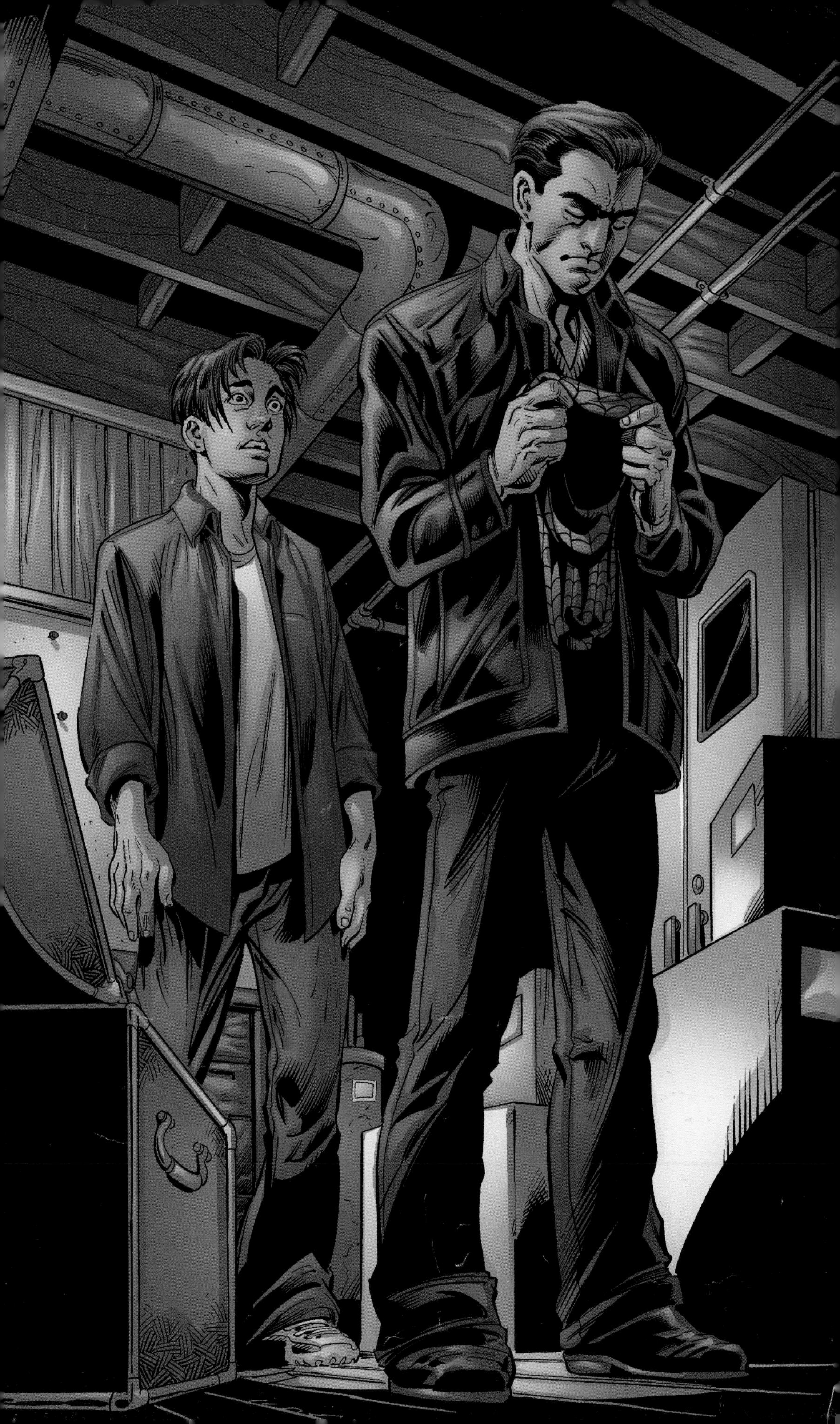

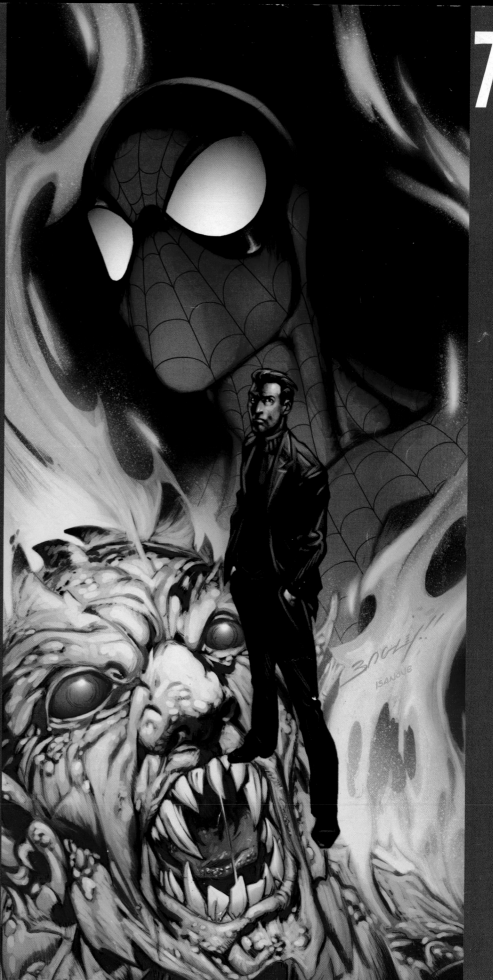

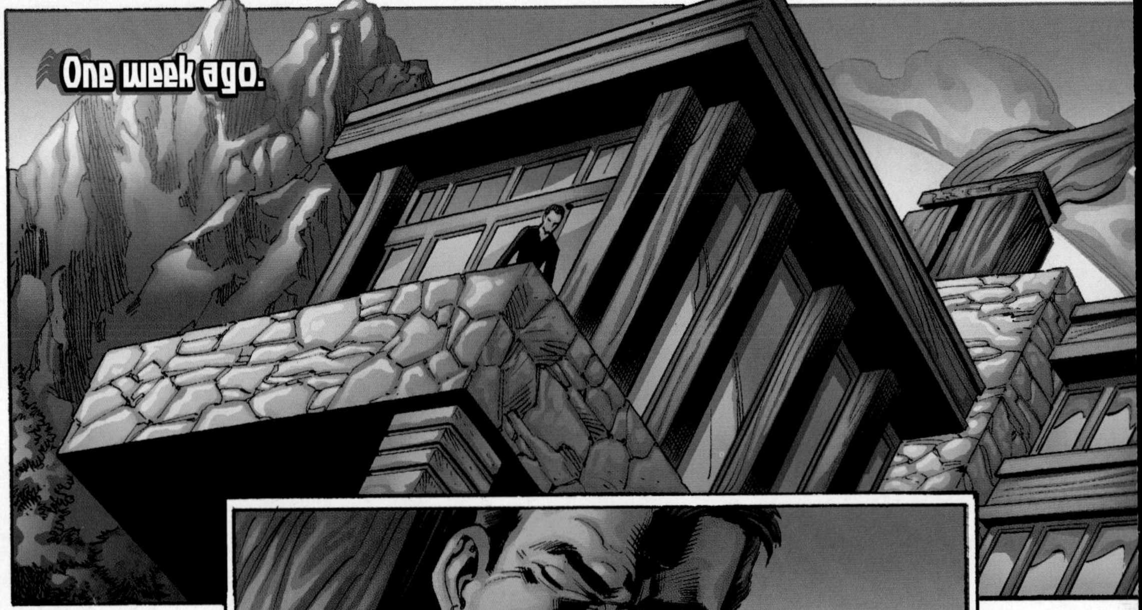
One week ago.

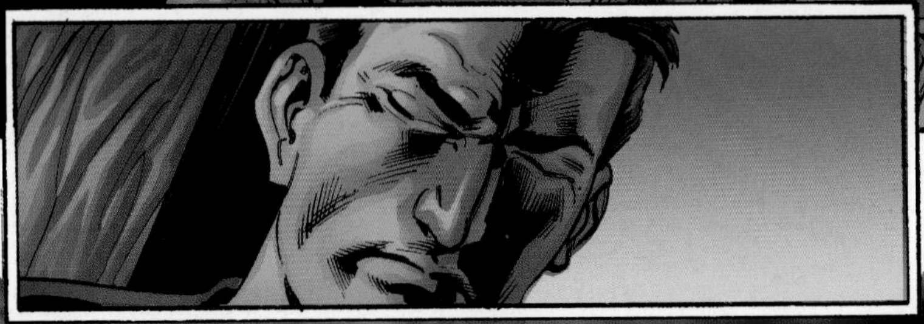

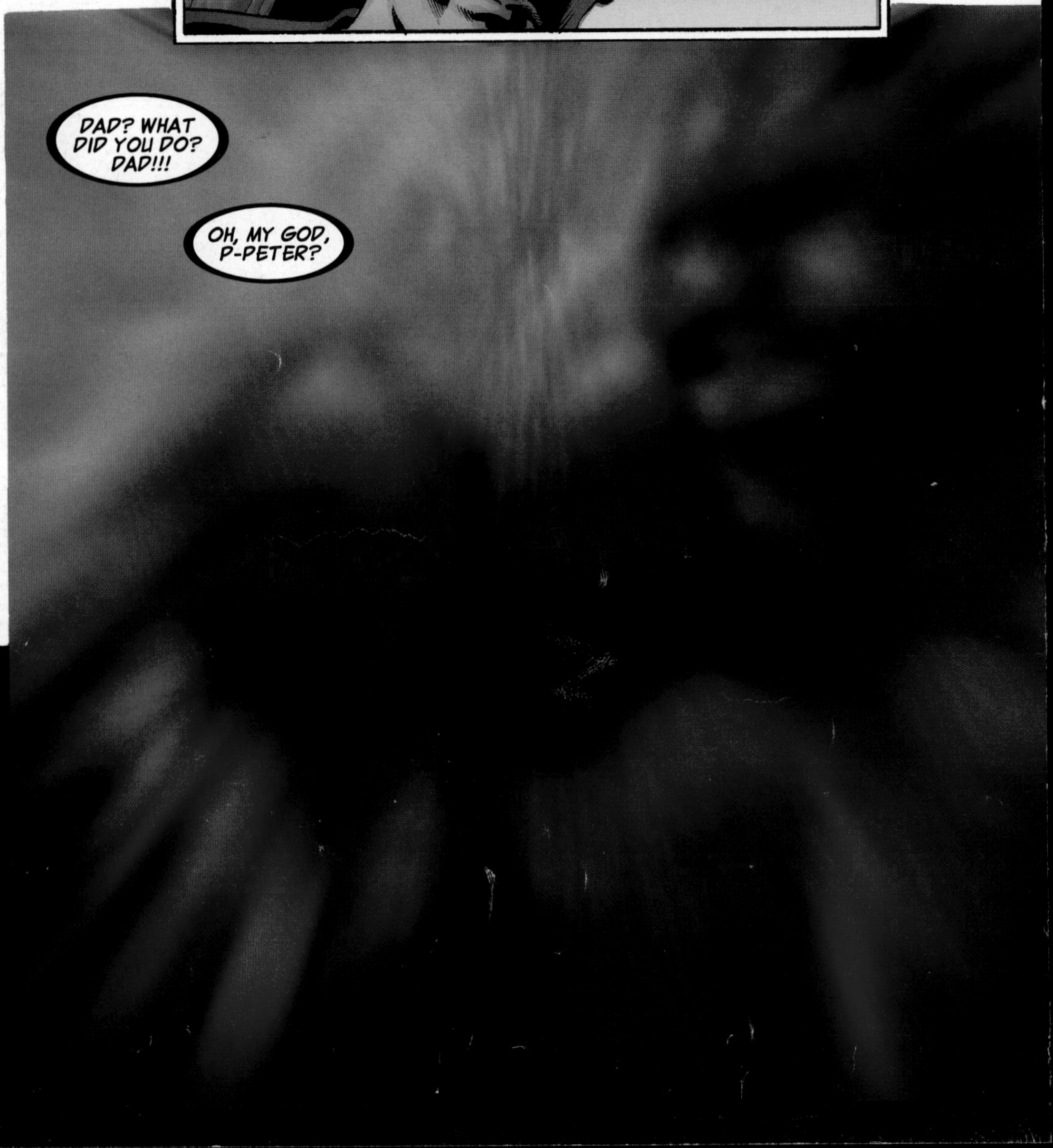
DAD? WHAT DID YOU DO? DAD!!!
OH, MY GOD, P-PETER?

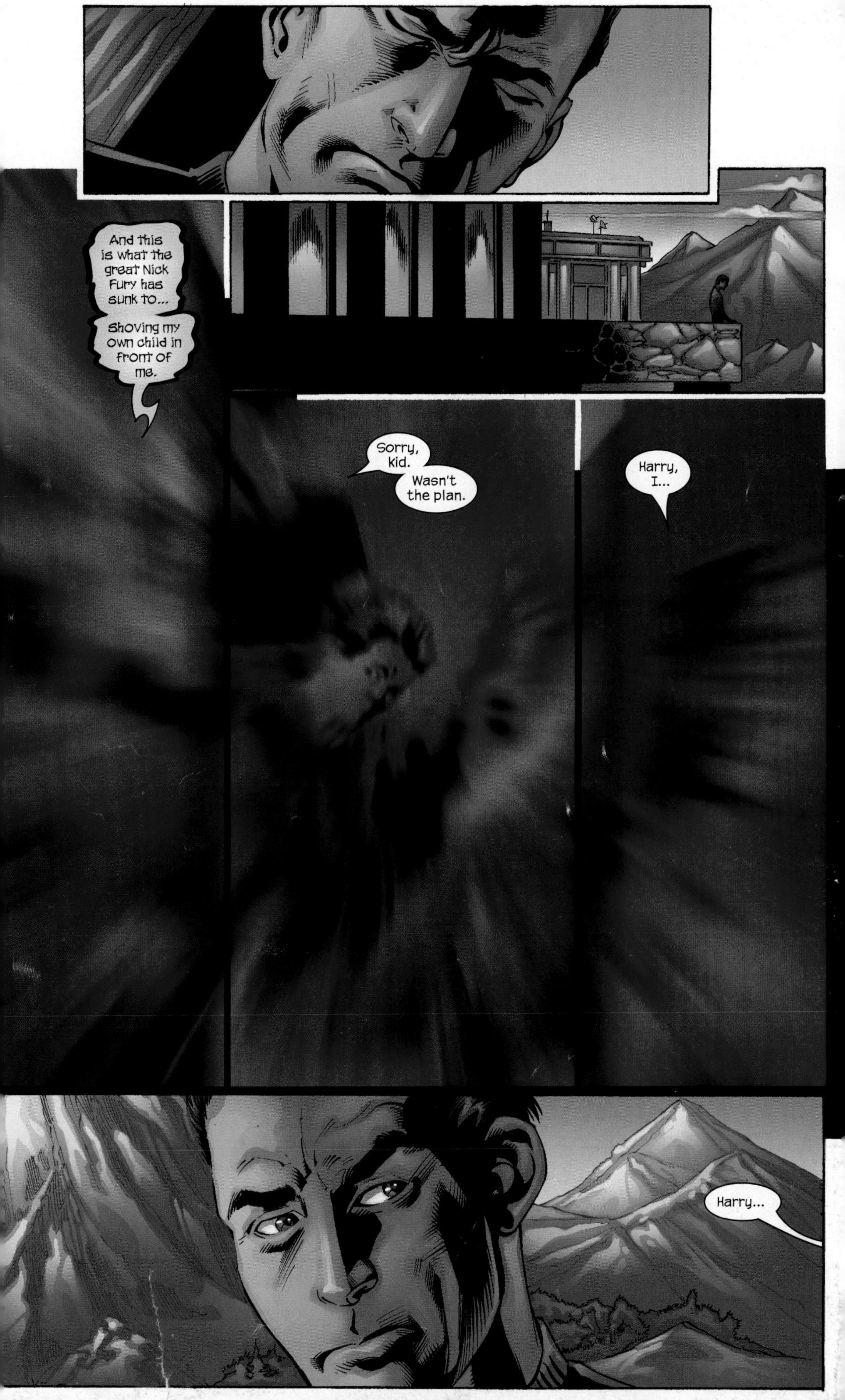

And this is what the great Nick Fury has sunk to...
Shoving my own child in front of me.
Sorry, kid.
Wasn't the plan.
Harry, I...
Harry...

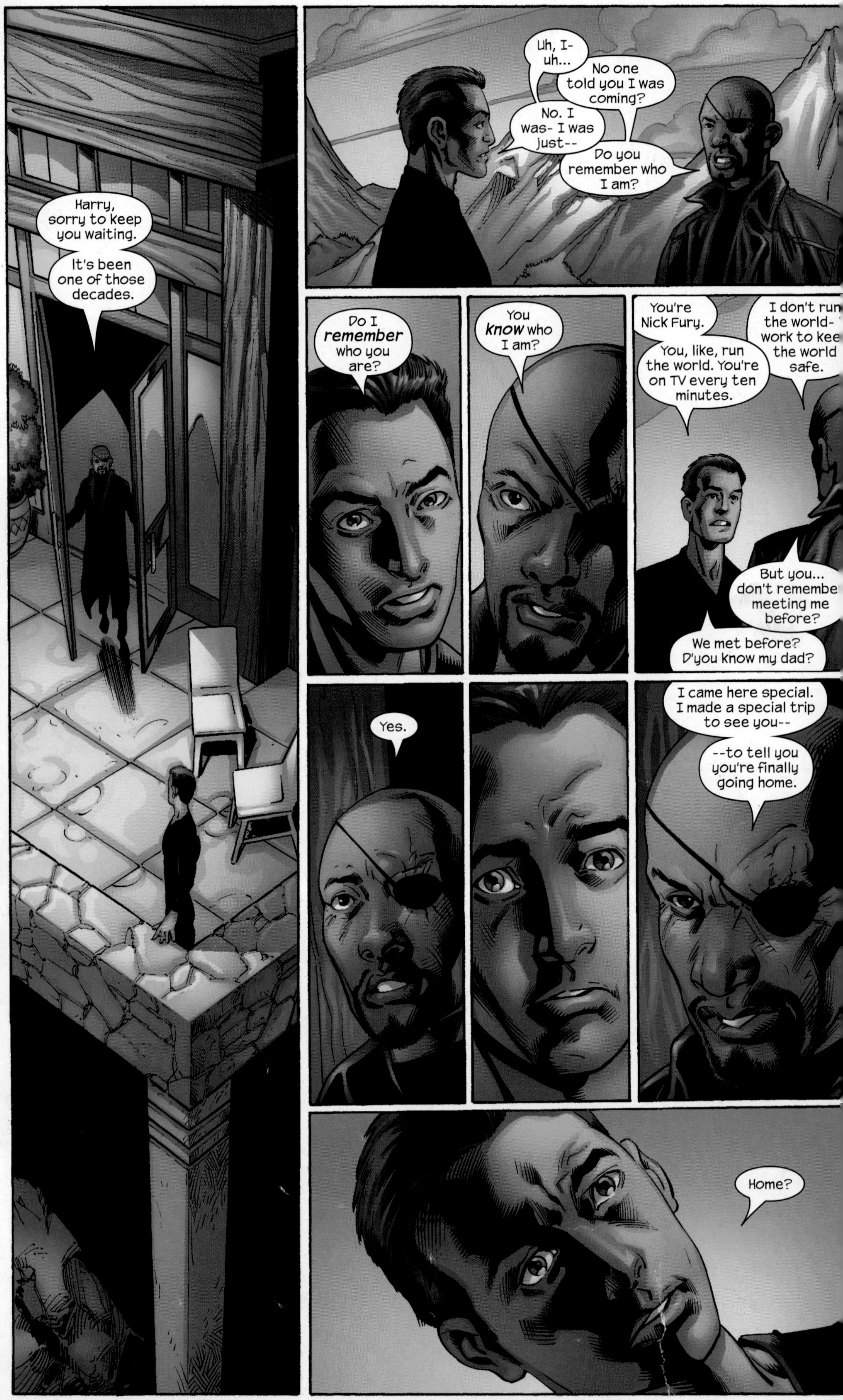
Harry, sorry to keep you waiting.
It's been one of those decades.
Uh, I- uh...
No one told you I was coming?
No. I was- I was just--
Do you remember who I am?
Do I *remember* who you are?
You *know* who I am?
You're Nick Fury.
You, like, run the world. You're on TV every ten minutes.
I don't run the world- work to kee the world safe.
But you... don't remembe meeting me before?
We met before? D'you know my dad?
Yes.
I came here special. I made a special trip to see you--
--to tell you you're finally going home.
Home?

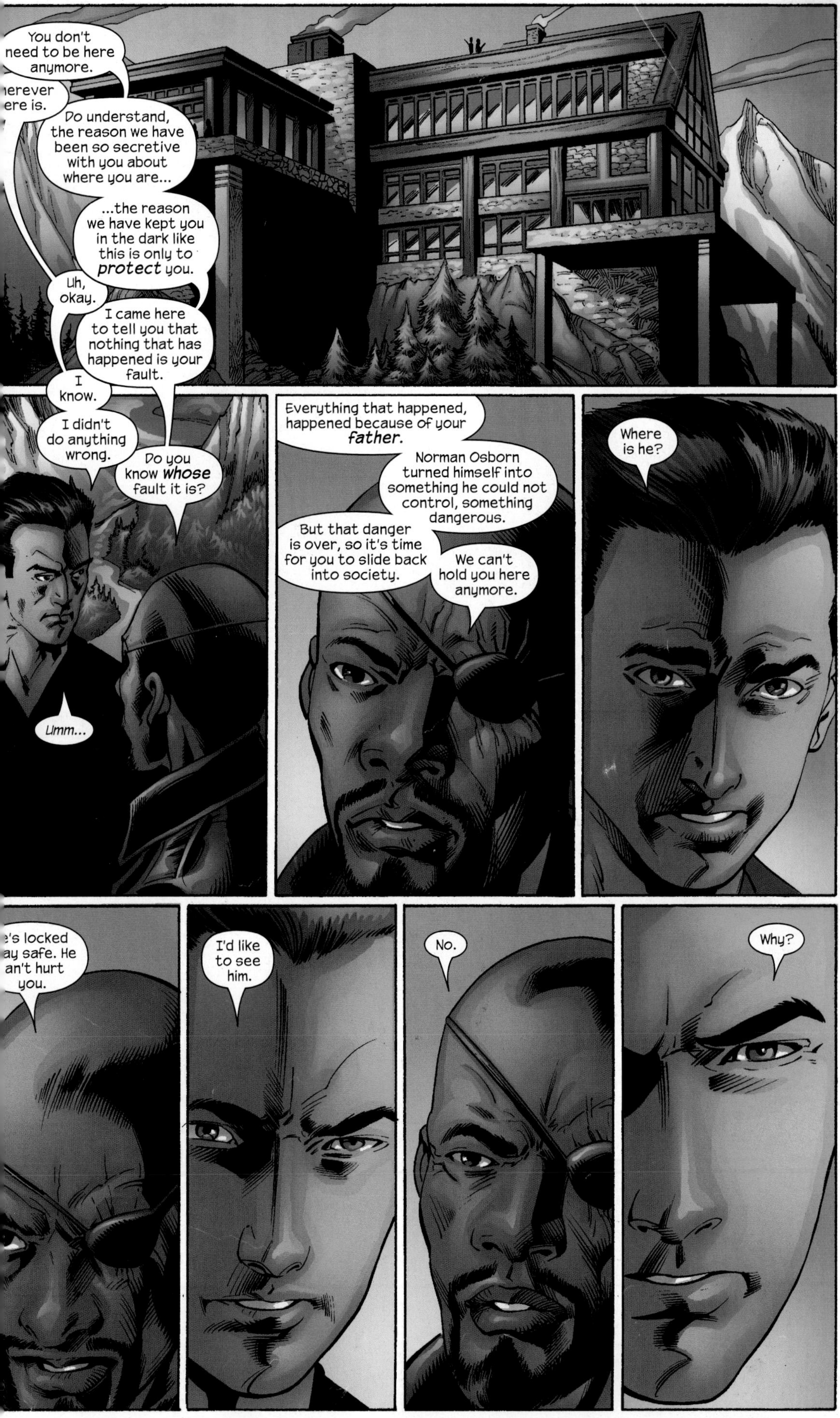

You don't need to be here anymore.
herever ere is.
Do understand, the reason we have been so secretive with you about where you are...
...the reason we have kept you in the dark like this is only to *protect* you.
Uh, okay.
I came here to tell you that nothing that has happened is your fault.
I know.
I didn't do anything wrong.
Do you know *whose* fault it is?
Umm...
Everything that happened, happened because of your *father*.
Norman Osborn turned himself into something he could not control, something dangerous.
But that danger is over, so it's time for you to slide back into society.
We can't hold you here anymore.
Where is he?
's locked ay safe. He an't hurt you.
I'd like to see him.
No.
Why?

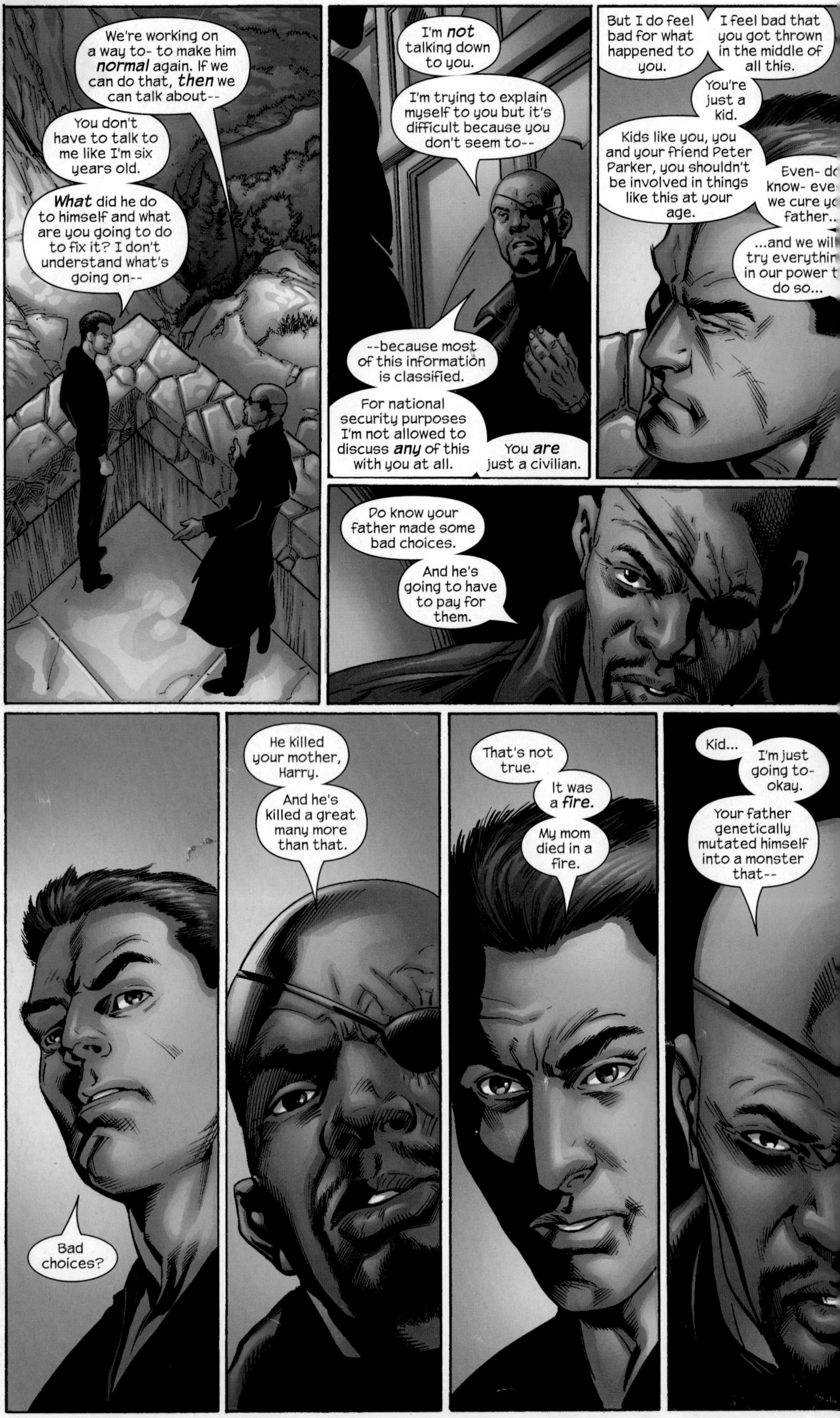

We're working on a way to- to make him normal again. If we can do that, then we can talk about--
You don't have to talk to me like I'm six years old.
What did he do to himself and what are you going to do to fix it? I don't understand what's going on--
I'm not talking down to you.
I'm trying to explain myself to you but it's difficult because you don't seem to--
--because most of this information is classified.
For national security purposes I'm not allowed to discuss any of this with you at all.
You are just a civilian.
But I do feel bad for what happened to you.
I feel bad that you got thrown in the middle of all this.
You're just a kid.
Kids like you, you and your friend Peter Parker, you shouldn't be involved in things like this at your age.
Do know your father made some bad choices.
And he's going to have to pay for them.
Bad choices?
He killed your mother, Harry.
And he's killed a great many more than that.
That's not true.
It was a fire.
My mom died in a fire.
Kid...
I'm just going to- okay.
Your father genetically mutated himself into a monster that--

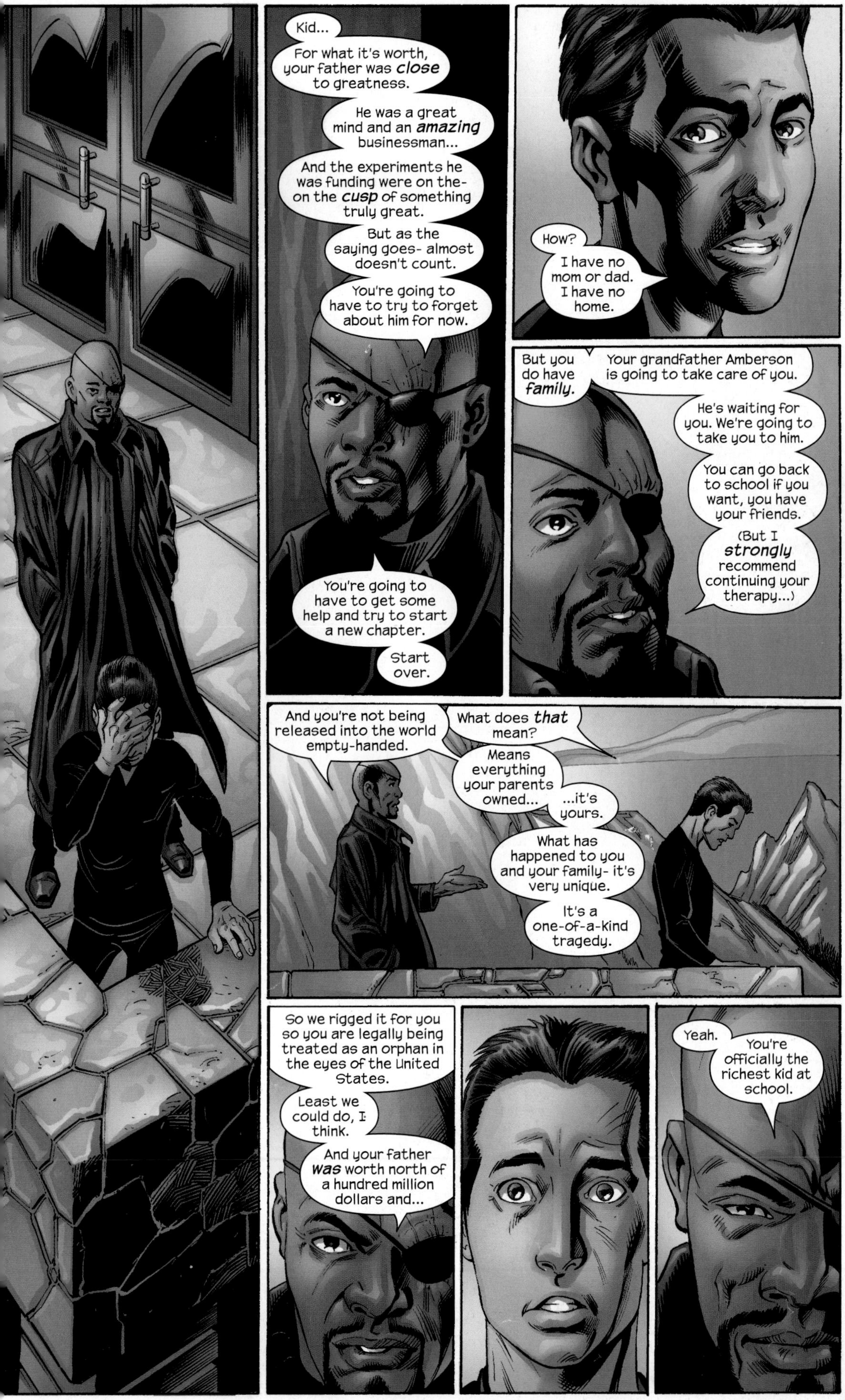

Kid...
For what it's worth, your father was *close* to greatness.
He was a great mind and an *amazing* businessman...
And the experiments he was funding were on the- on the *cusp* of something truly great.
But as the saying goes- almost doesn't count.
You're going to have to try to forget about him for now.
You're going to have to get some help and try to start a new chapter.
Start over.
How?
I have no mom or dad. I have no home.
But you do have *family.*
Your grandfather Amberson is going to take care of you.
He's waiting for you. We're going to take you to him.
You can go back to school if you want, you have your friends.
(But I *strongly* recommend continuing your therapy...)
And you're not being released into the world empty-handed.
What does *that* mean?
Means everything your parents owned...
...it's yours.
What has happened to you and your family- it's very unique.
It's a one-of-a-kind tragedy.
So we rigged it for you so you are legally being treated as an orphan in the eyes of the United States.
Least we could do, I think.
And your father *was* worth north of a hundred million dollars and...
Yeah.
You're officially the richest kid at school.

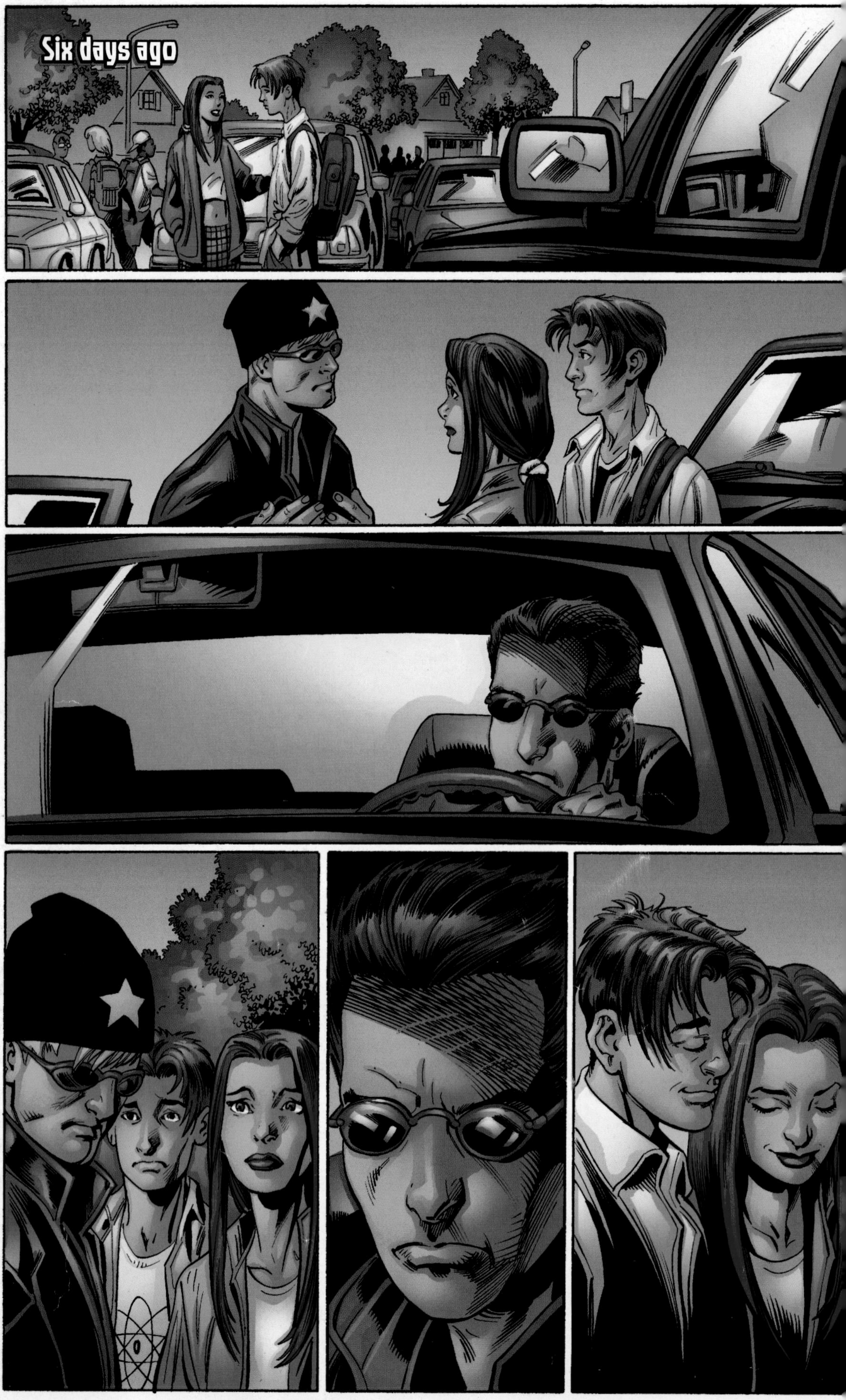
Six days ago

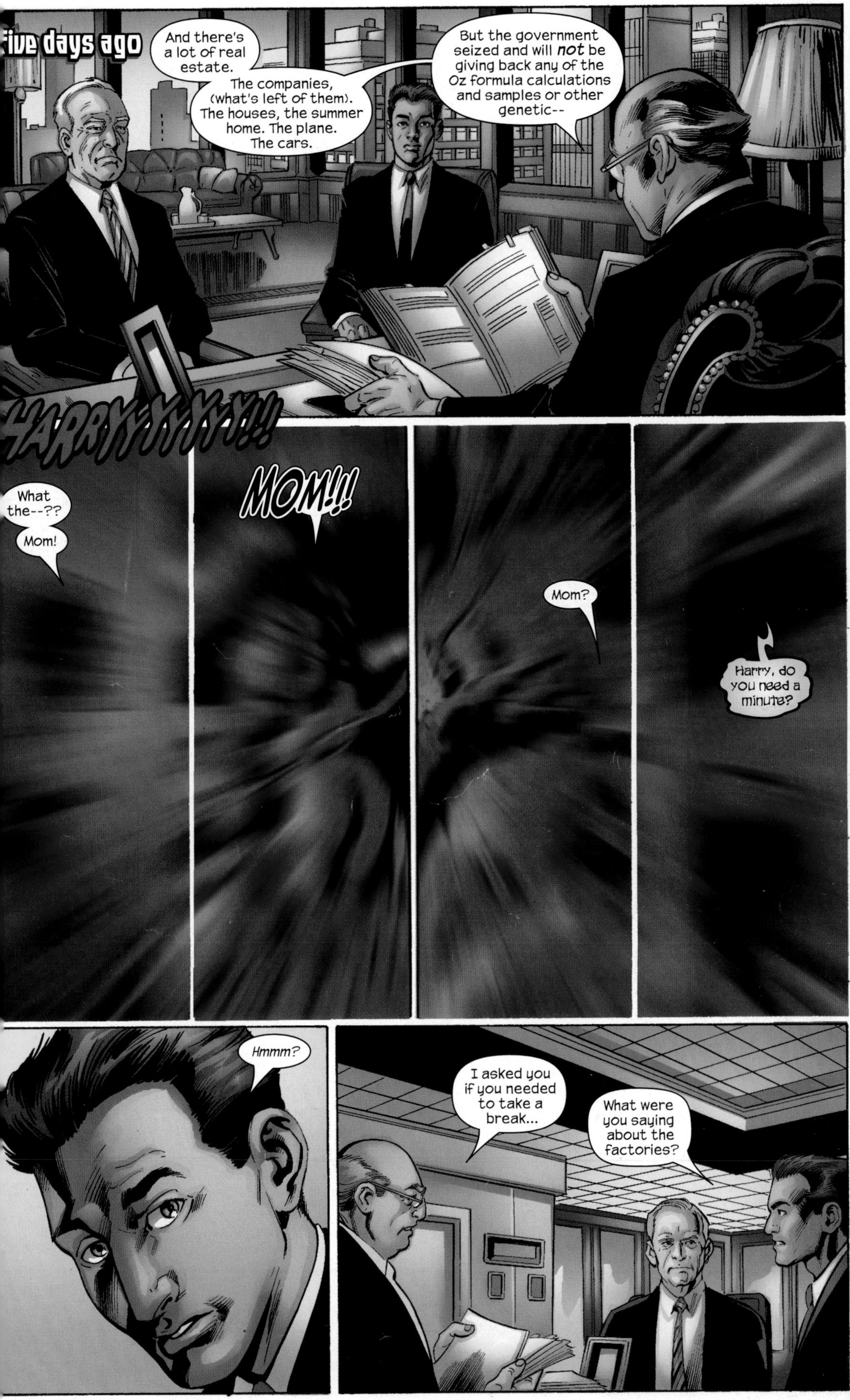

five days ago
And there's a lot of real estate.
The companies, (what's left of them). The houses, the summer home. The plane. The cars.
But the government seized and will *not* be giving back any of the Oz formula calculations and samples or other genetic--
HARRYYYYYY!!
What the--??
Mom!
MOM!!!
Mom?
Harry, do you need a minute?
Hmmm?
I asked you if you needed to take a break...
What were you saying about the factories?

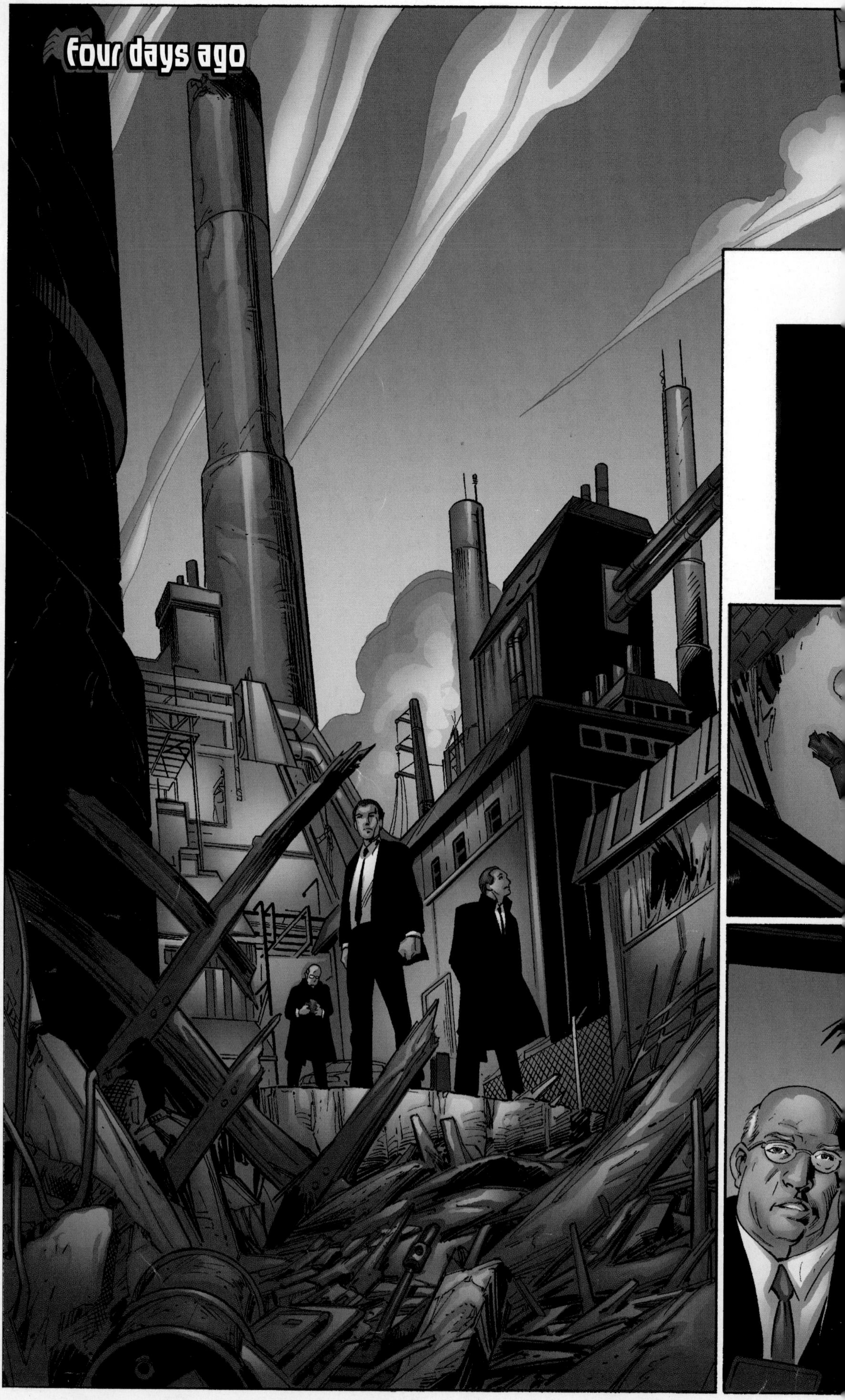
four days ago

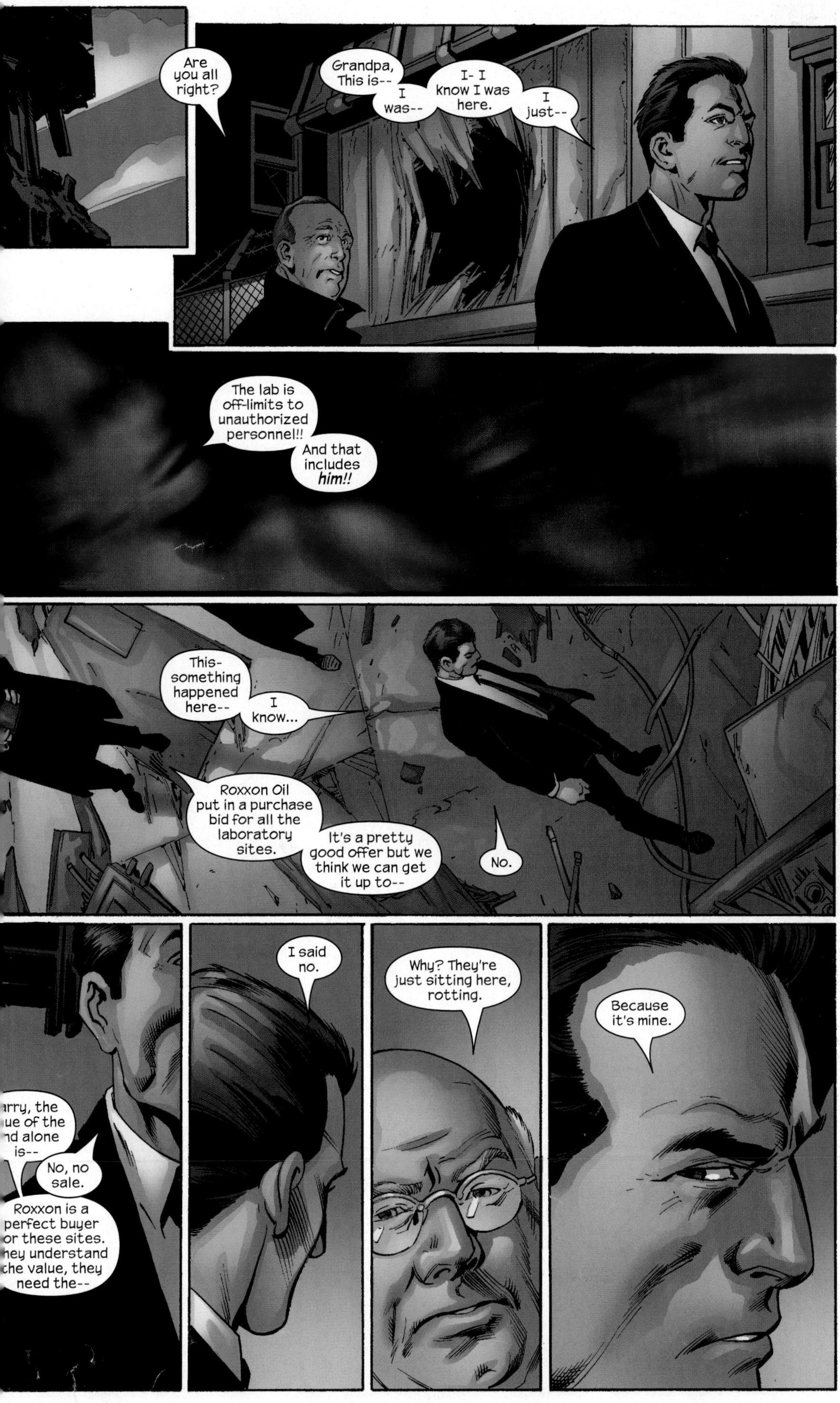

Are you all right?
Grandpa, This is--
I was--
I- I know I was here.
I just--
The lab is off-limits to unauthorized personnel!!
And that includes *him!!*
This- something happened here--
I know...
Roxxon Oil put in a purchase bid for all the laboratory sites.
It's a pretty good offer but we think we can get it up to--
No.
arry, the ue of the nd alone is--
No, no sale.
Roxxon is a perfect buyer or these sites. hey understand che value, they need the--
I said no.
Why? They're just sitting here, rotting.
Because it's mine.

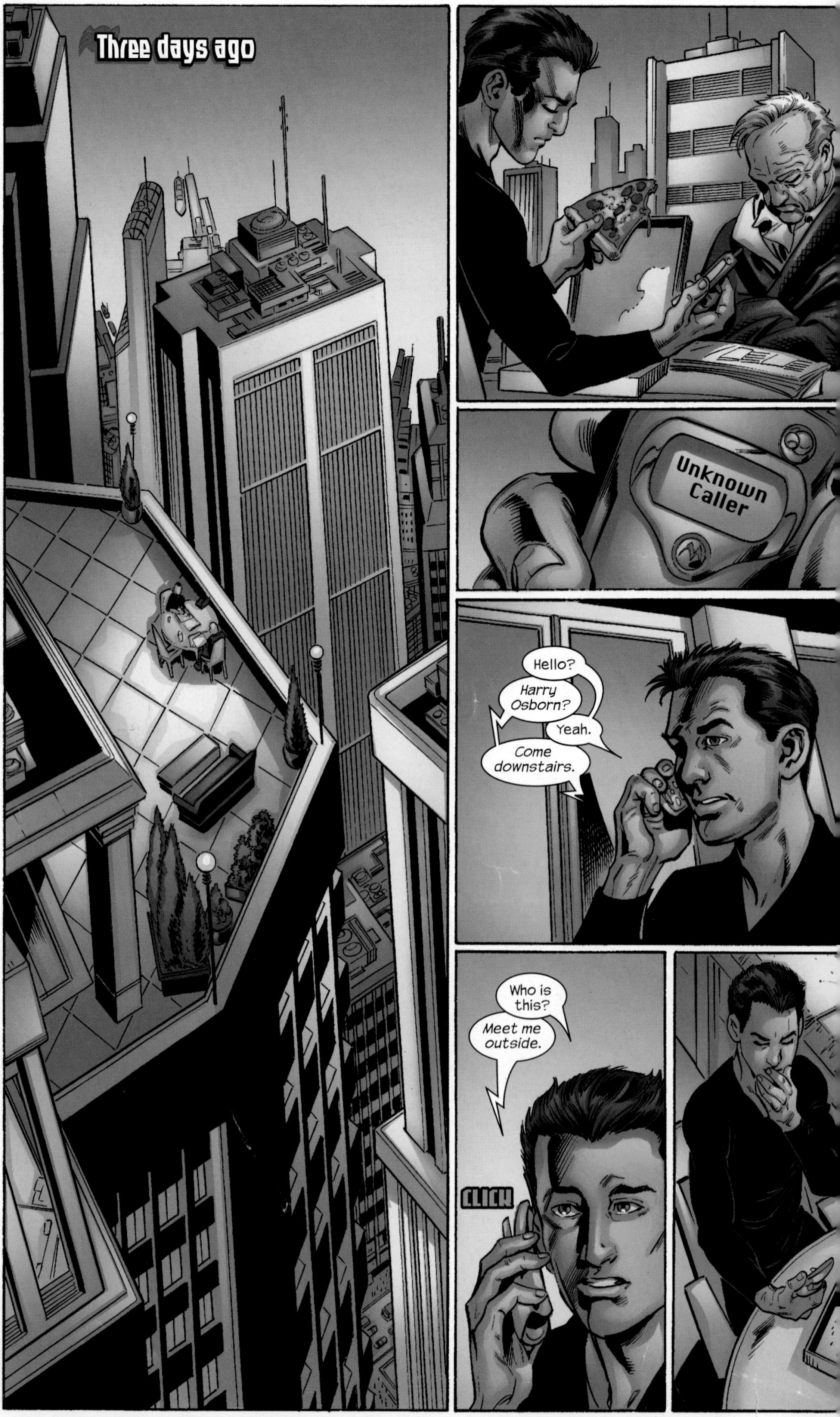

Three days ago
Unknown Caller
Hello?
Harry Osborn?
Yeah.
Come downstairs.
Who is this?
Meet me outside.
CLICK

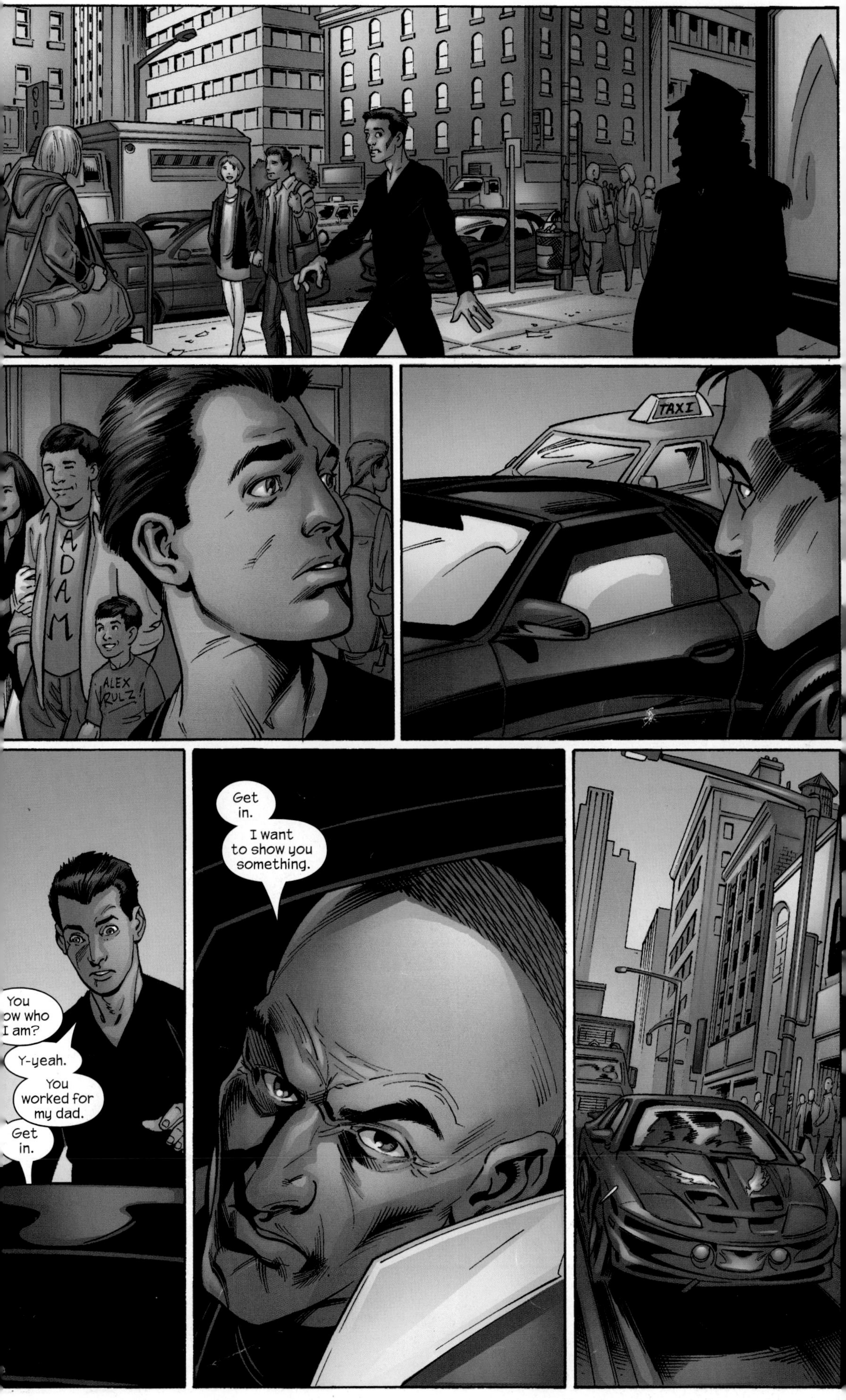
ADAM
ALEX RULZ
TAXI
Get in.
I want to show you something.
You ow who I am?
Y-yeah.
You worked for my dad.
Get in.

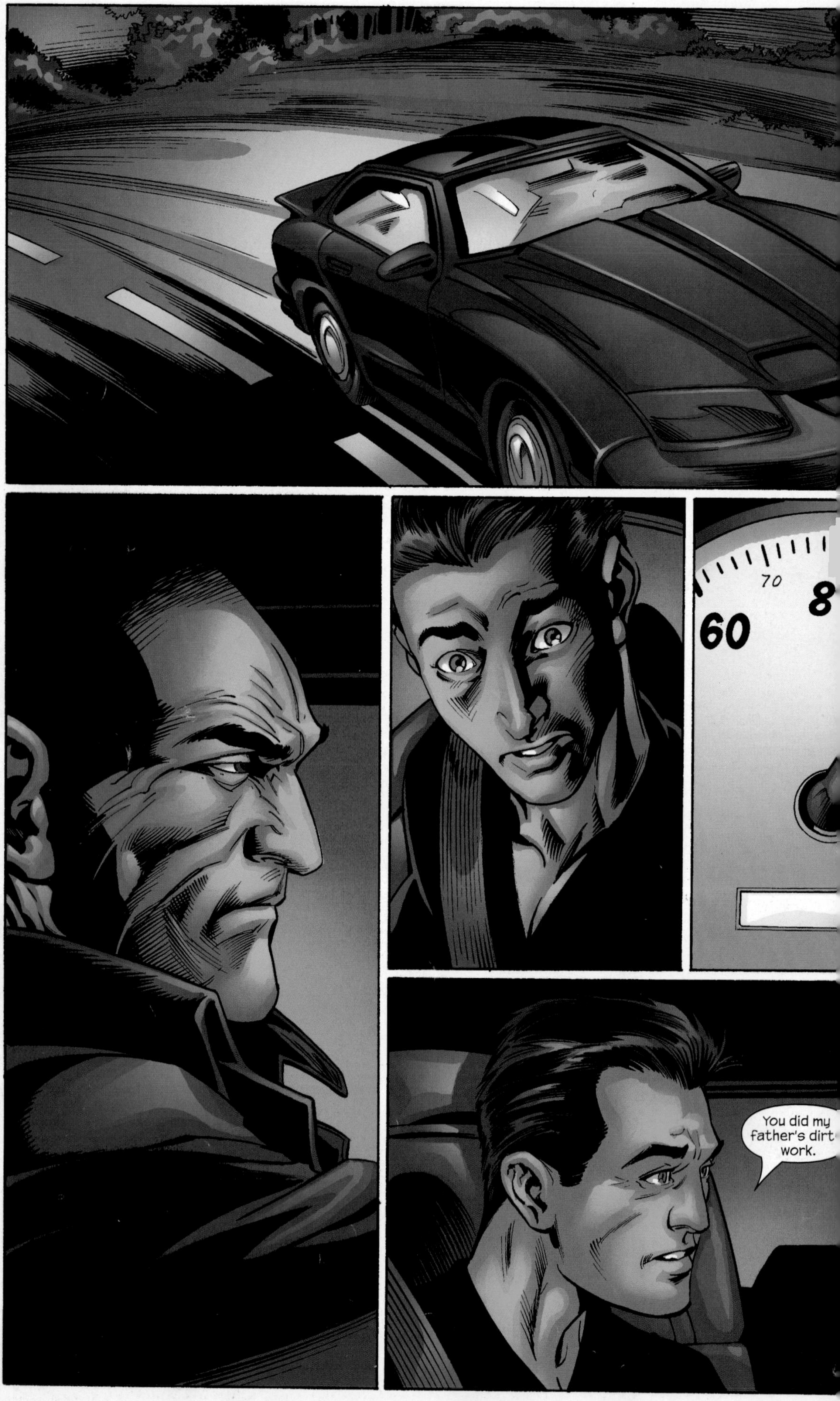
60
70
8
You did my father's dirt work.

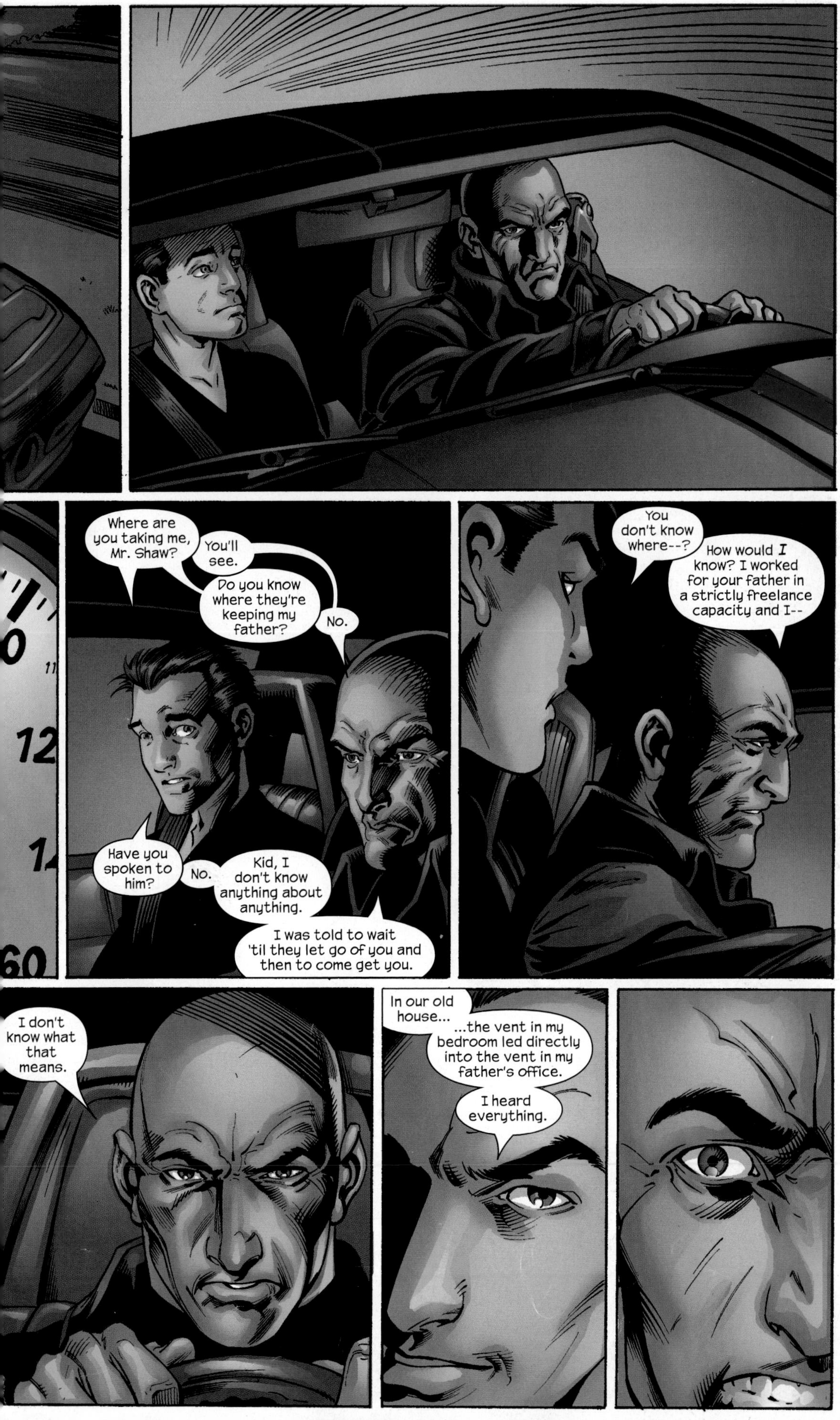
Where are you taking me, Mr. Shaw?
You'll see.
Do you know where they're keeping my father?
No.
Have you spoken to him?
No.
Kid, I don't know anything about anything.
I was told to wait 'til they let go of you and then to come get you.
You don't know where--?
How would *I* know? I worked for your father in a strictly freelance capacity and I--
I don't know what that means.
In our old house...
...the vent in my bedroom led directly into the vent in my father's office.
I heard everything.

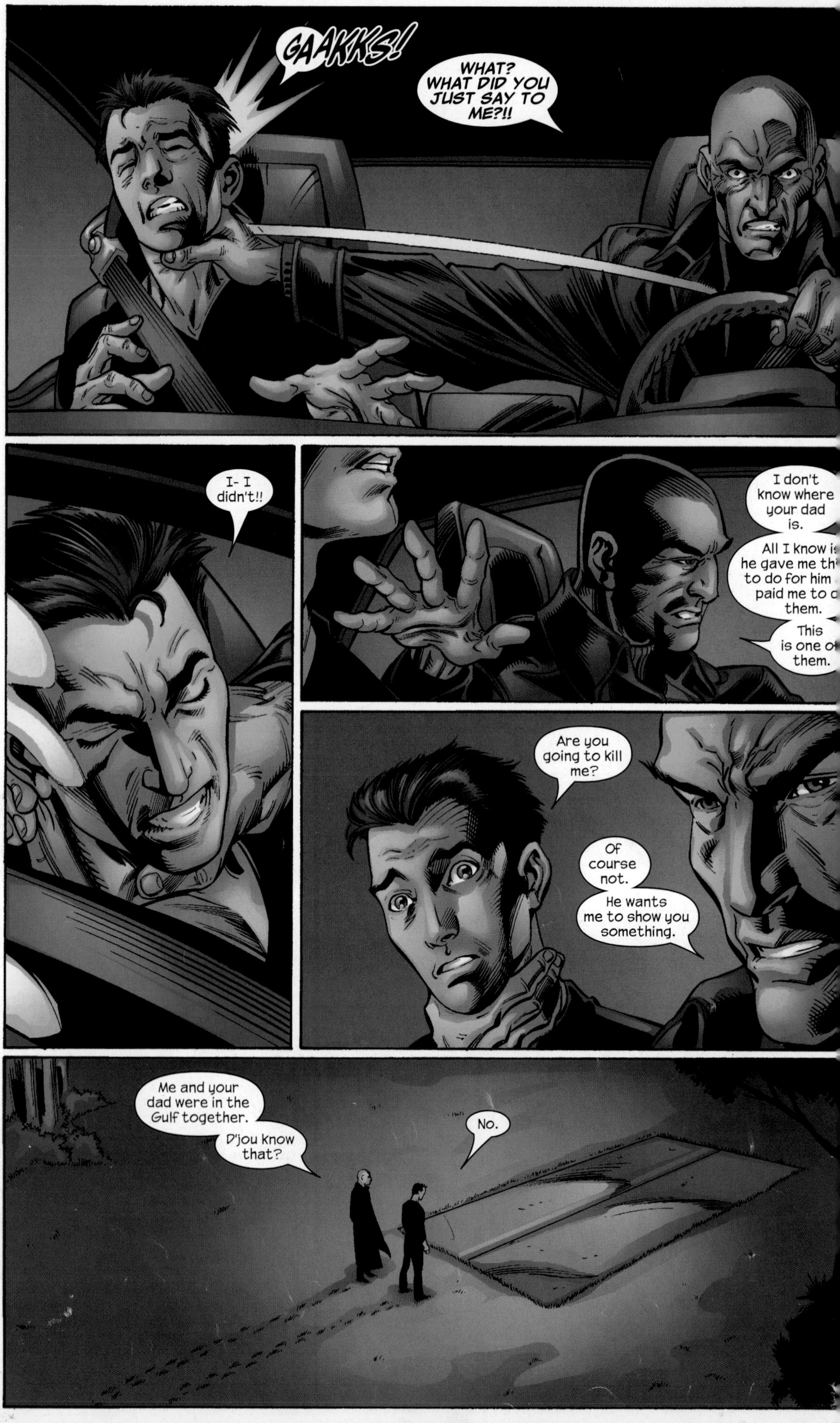
GAAKKS!
WHAT? WHAT DID YOU JUST SAY TO ME?!!
I- I didn't!!
I don't know where your dad is.
All I know i he gave me th to do for him paid me to d them.
This is one o them.
Are you going to kill me?
Of course not.
He wants me to show you something.
Me and your dad were in the Gulf together.
D'jou know that?
No.

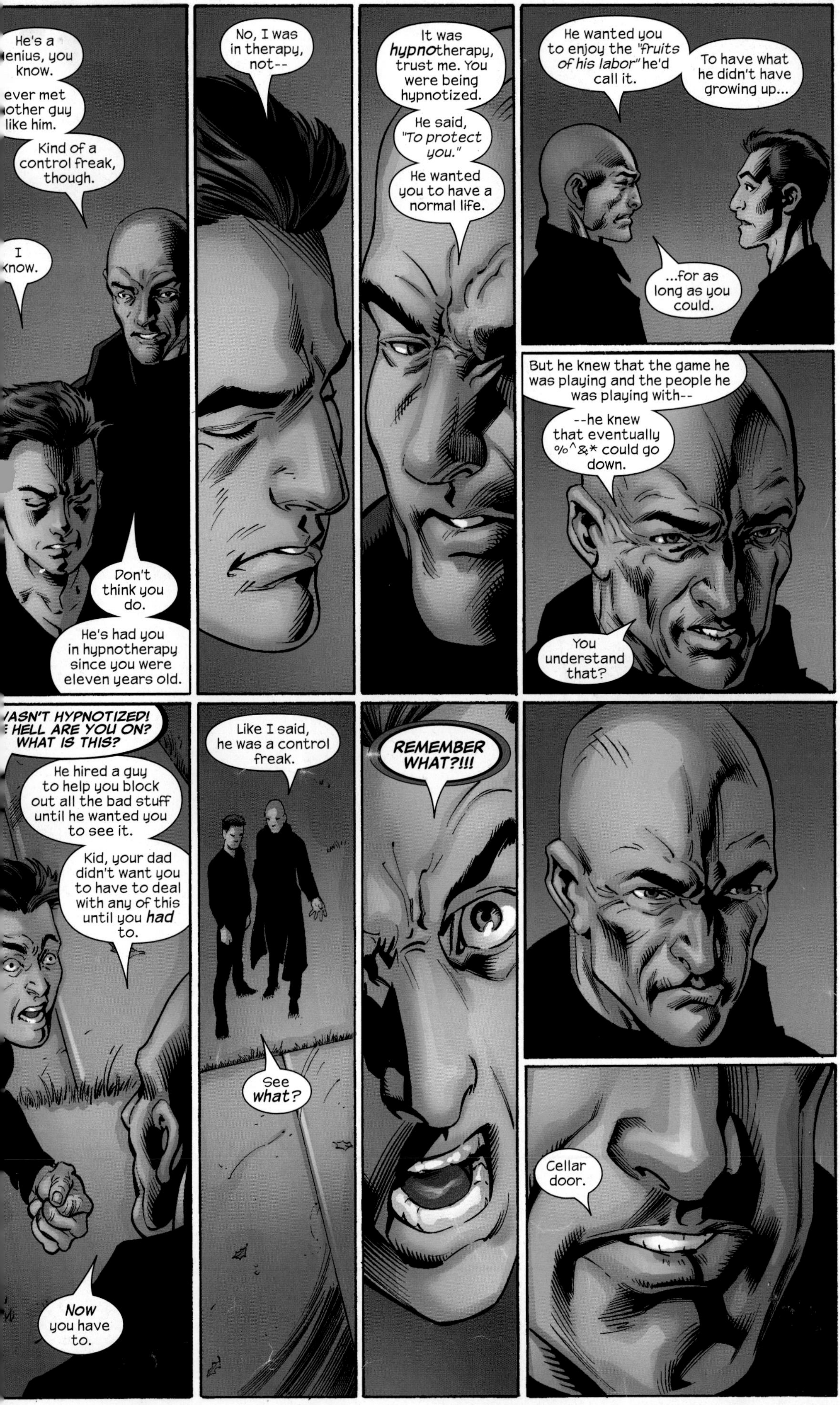
He's a
enius, you know.
ever met
other guy
like him.
Kind of a control freak, though.
I
know.
Don't think you do.
He's had you in hypnotherapy since you were eleven years old.
No, I was in therapy, not--
It was *hypno*therapy, trust me. You were being hypnotized.
He said, *"To protect you."*
He wanted you to have a normal life.
He wanted you to enjoy the *"fruits of his labor"* he'd call it.
To have what he didn't have growing up...
...for as long as you could.
But he knew that the game he was playing and the people he was playing with--
--he knew that eventually %^&* could go down.
You understand that?
/ASN'T HYPNOTIZED!
E HELL ARE YOU ON?
WHAT IS THIS?
He hired a guy to help you block out all the bad stuff until he wanted you to see it.
Kid, your dad didn't want you to have to deal with any of this until you *had* to.
Now you have to.
Like I said, he was a control freak.
See *what?*
REMEMBER WHAT?!!!
Cellar door.

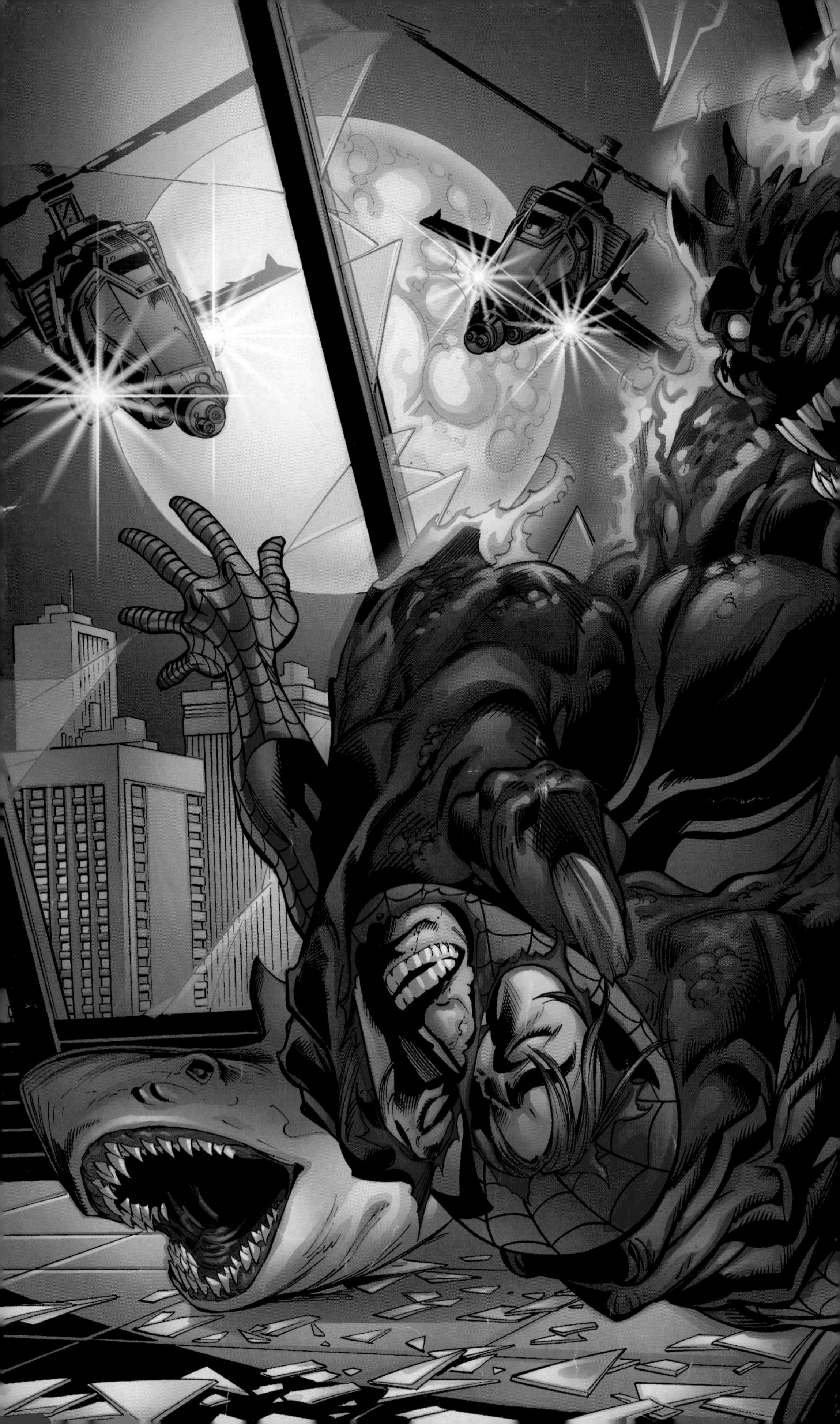

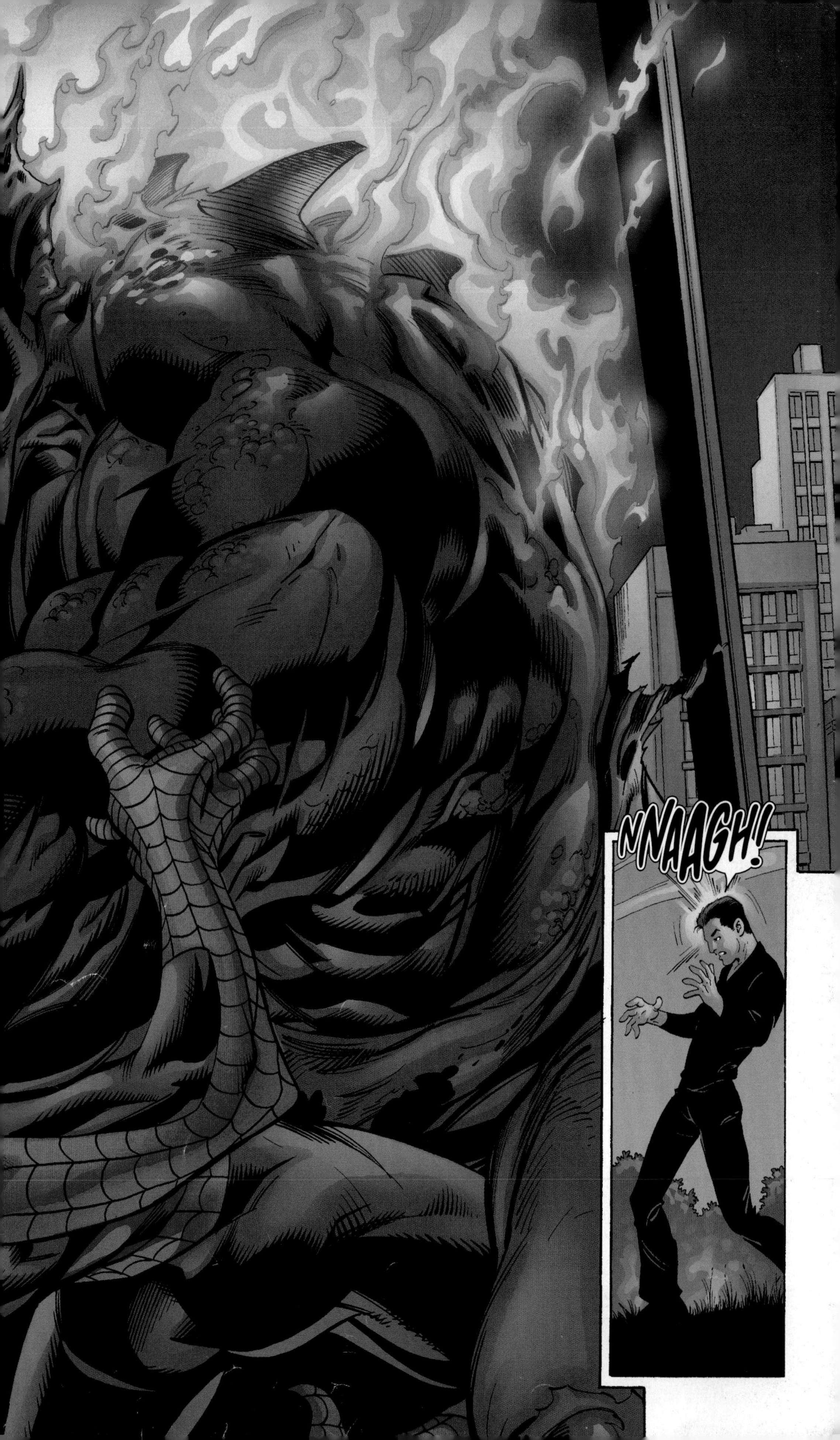
NNAAGH!

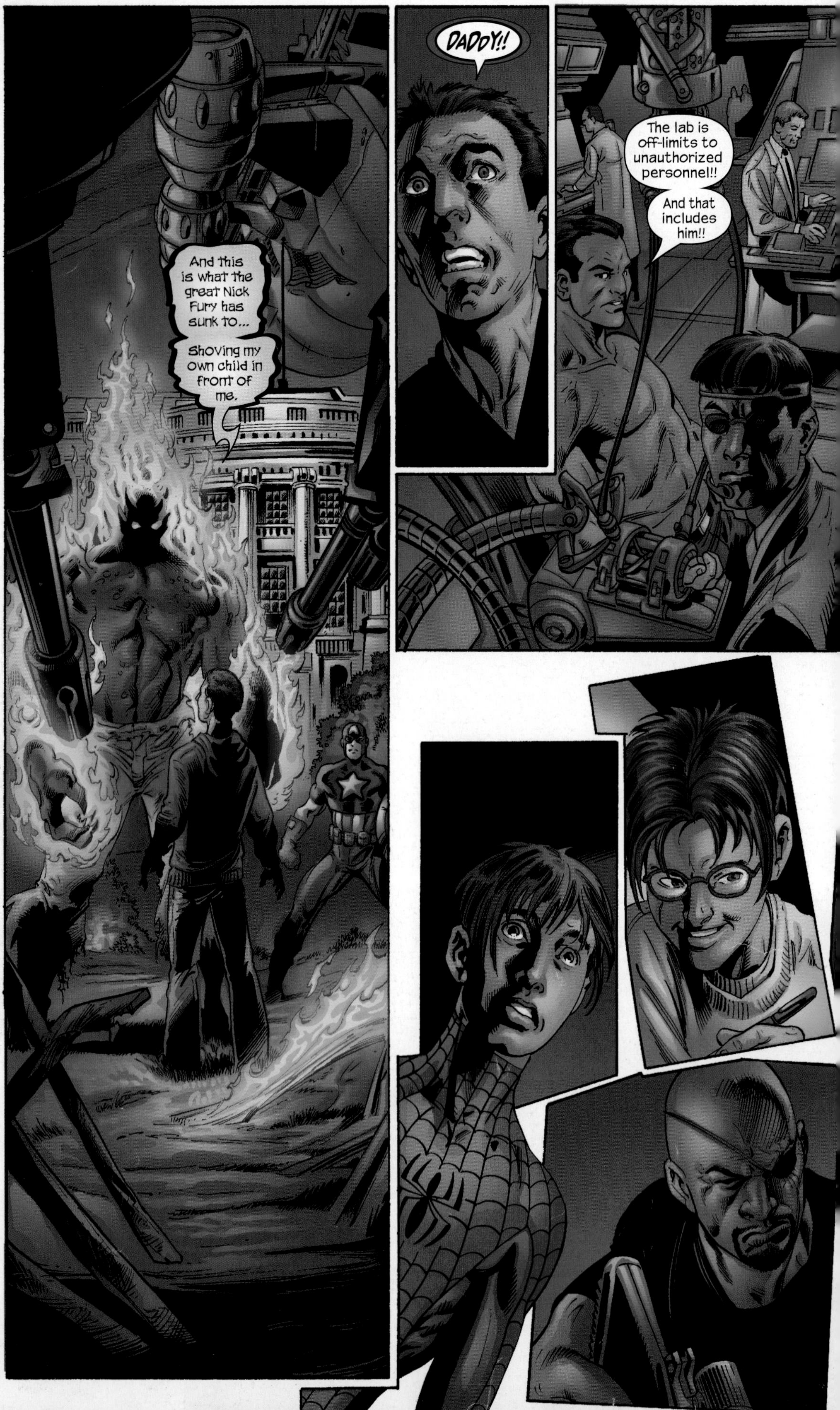
And this is what the great Nick Fury has sunk to...
Shoving my own child in front of me.
DADDY!!
The lab is off-limits to unauthorized personnel!!
And that includes him!!

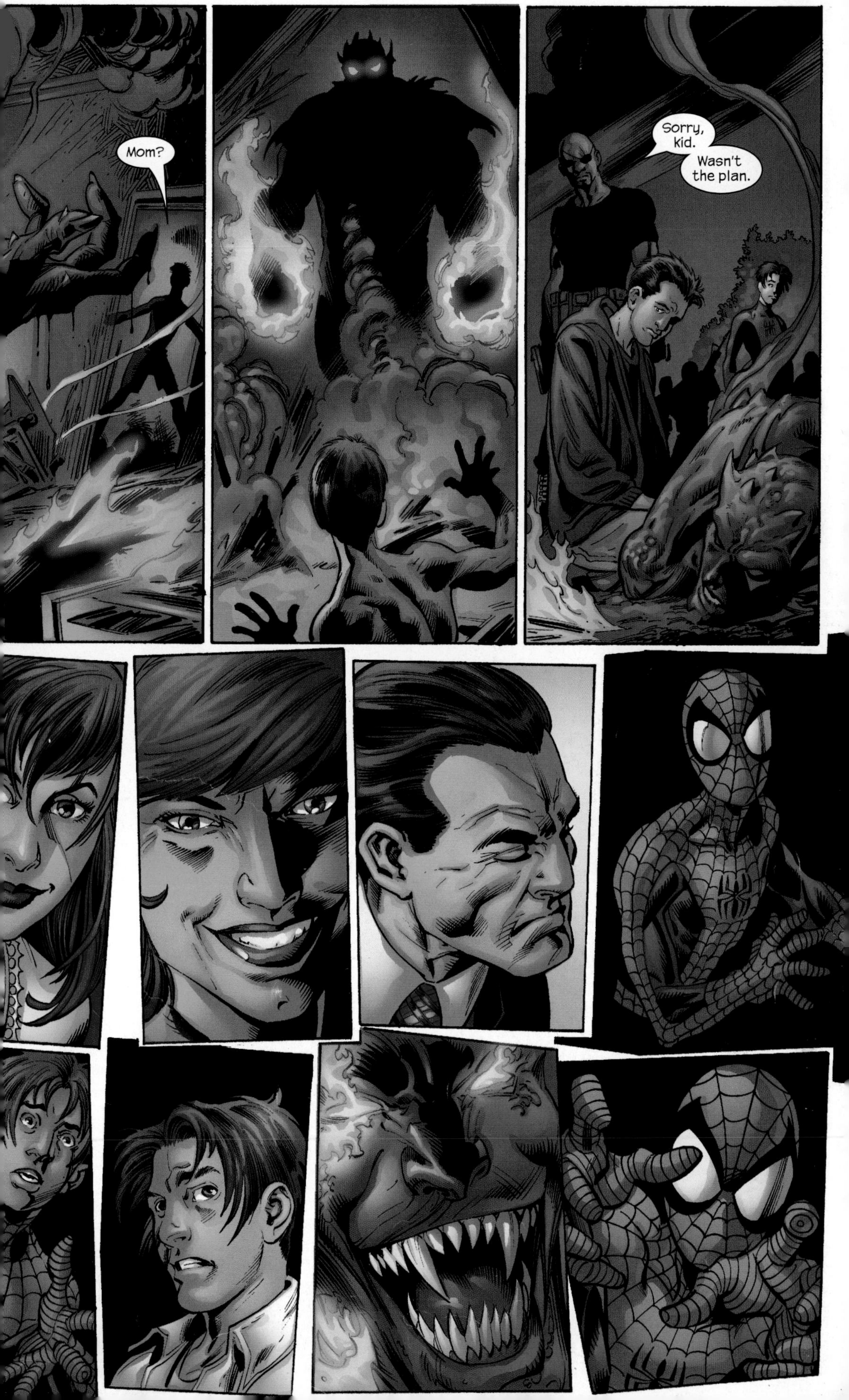
Mom?
Sorry, kid.
Wasn't the plan.

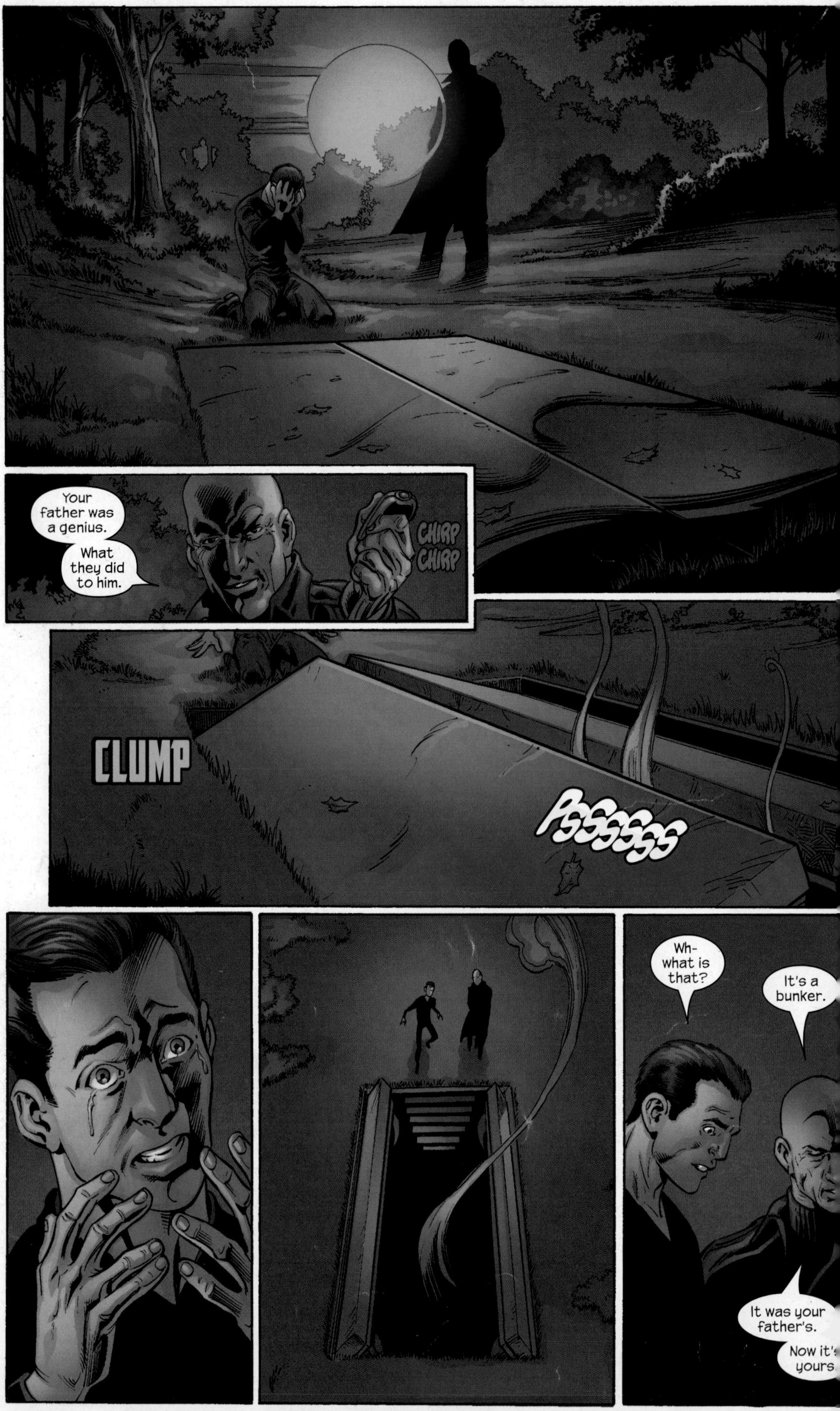

Your father was a genius.
What they did to him.
CHIRP CHIRP
CLUMP
PSSSSSS
Wh- what is that?
It's a bunker.
It was your father's.
Now it's yours

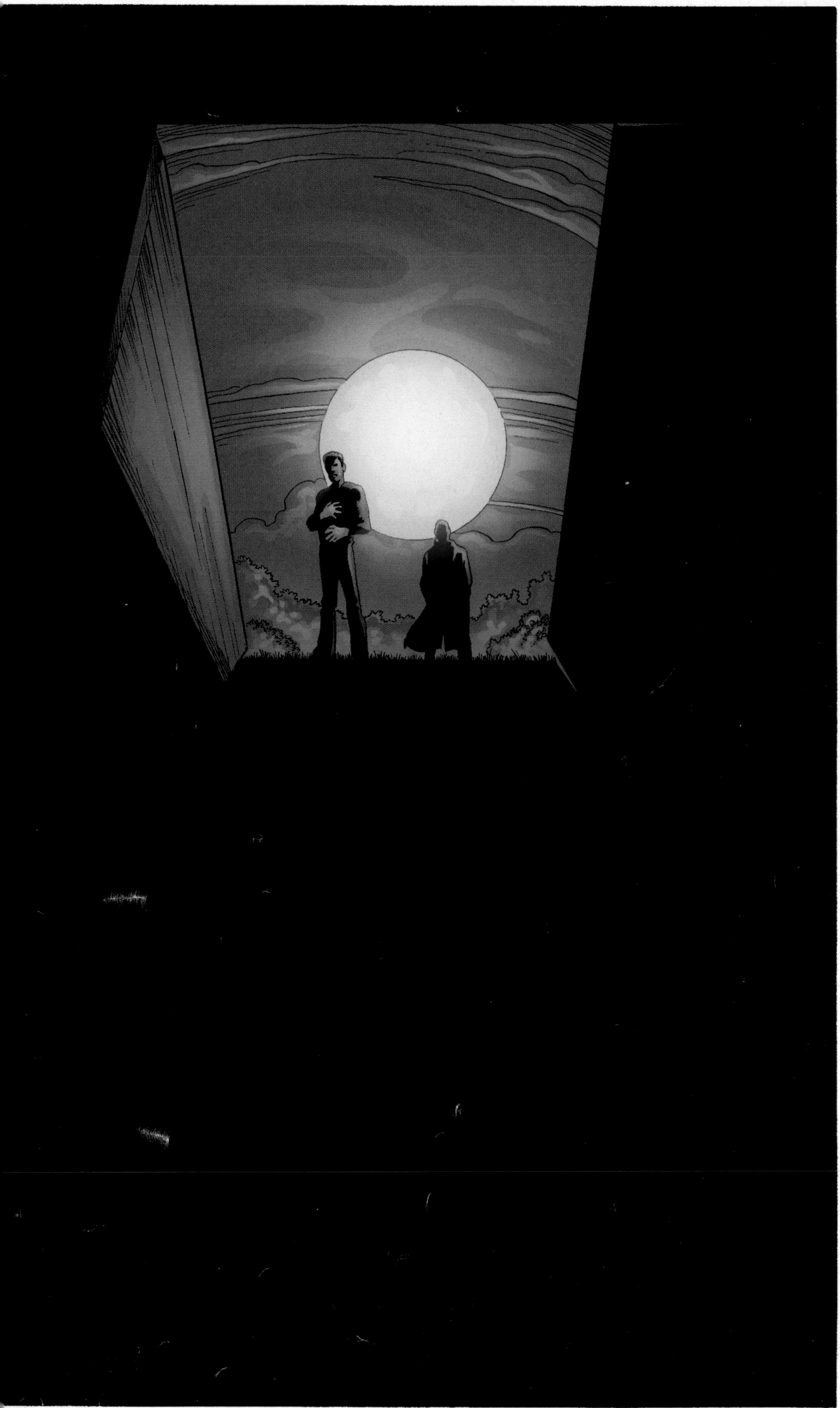

74

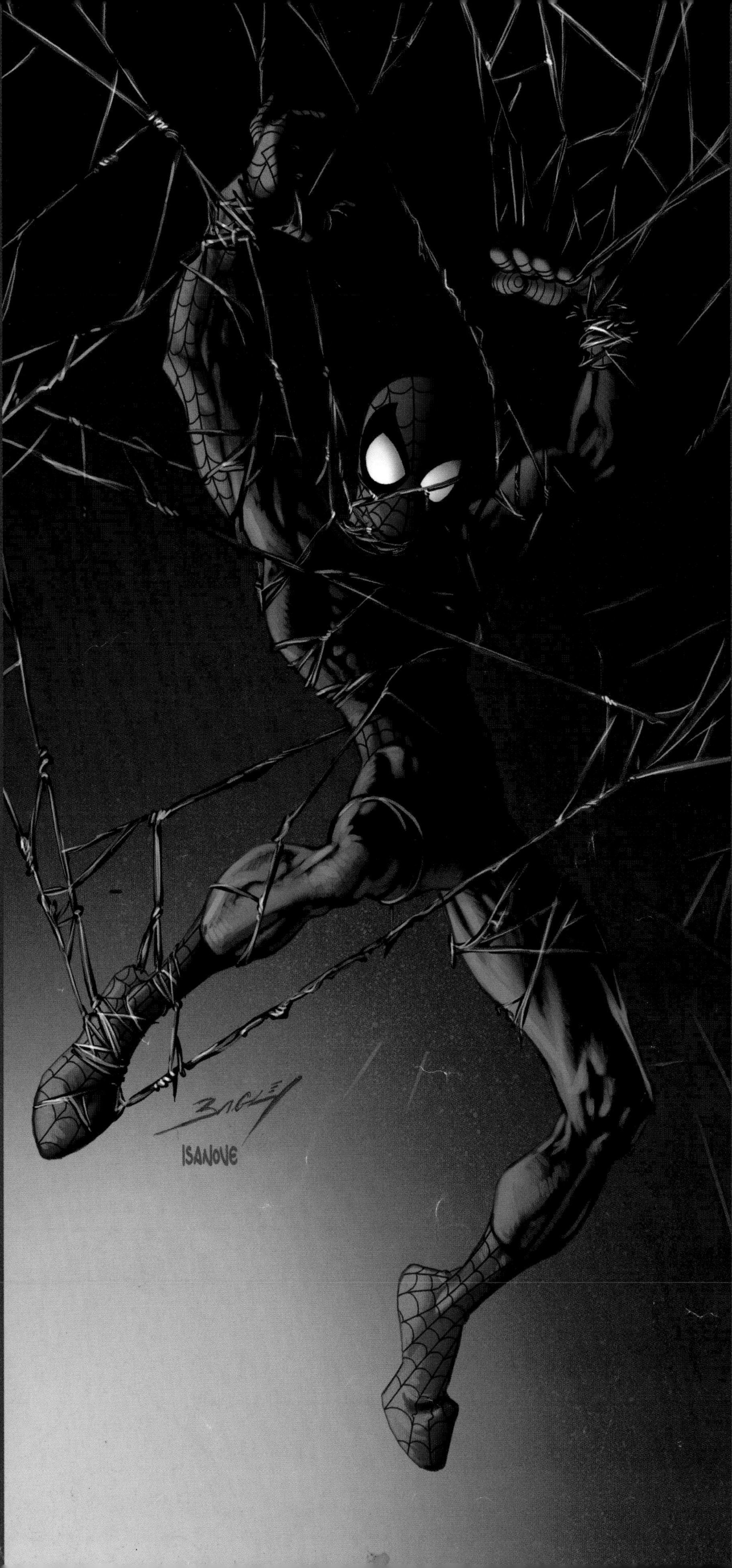
ISANOVE

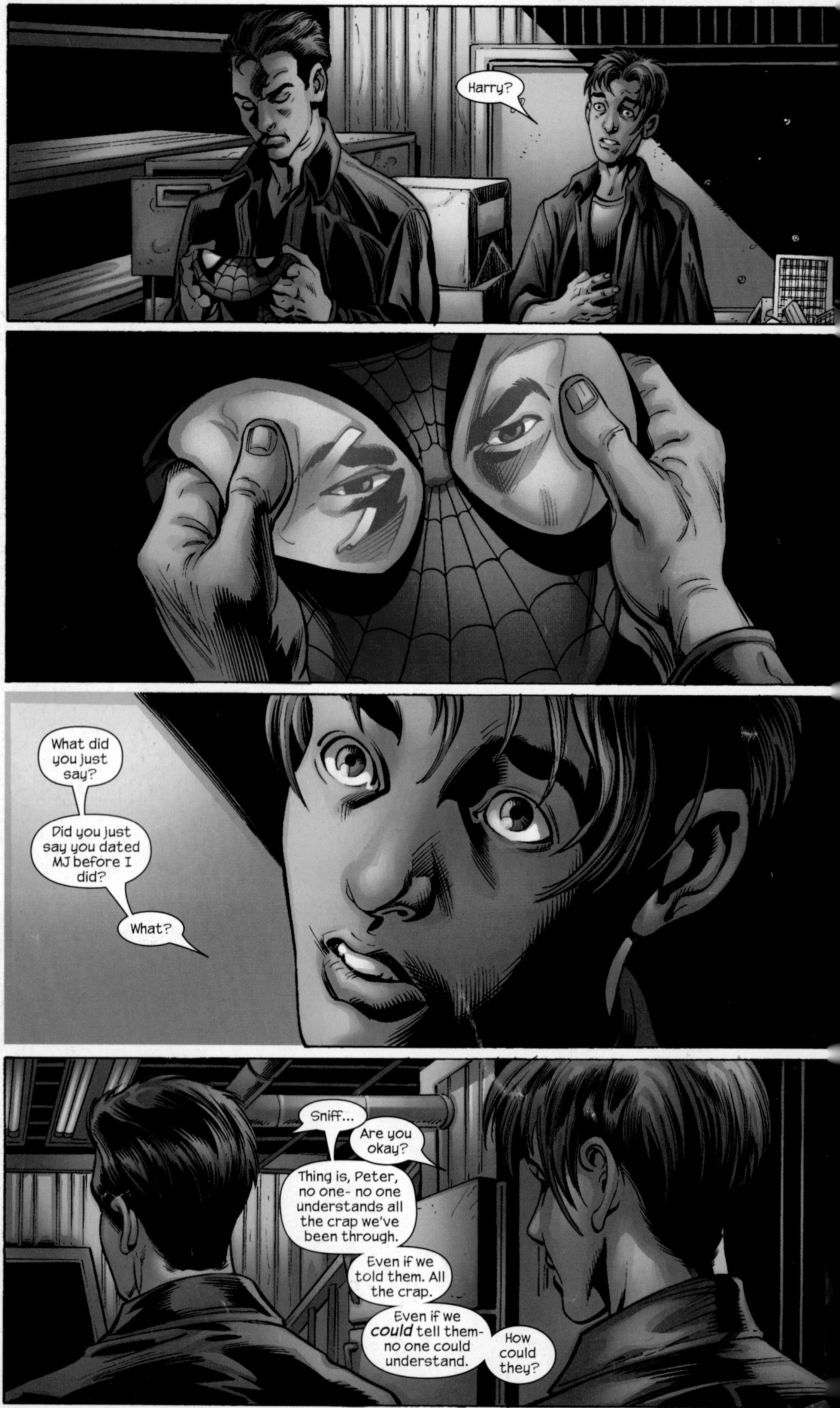

Harry?
What did you just say?
Did you just say you dated MJ before I did?
What?
Sniff...
Are you okay?
Thing is, Peter, no one- no one understands all the crap we've been through.
Even if we told them. All the crap.
Even if we *could* tell them- no one could understand.
How could they?

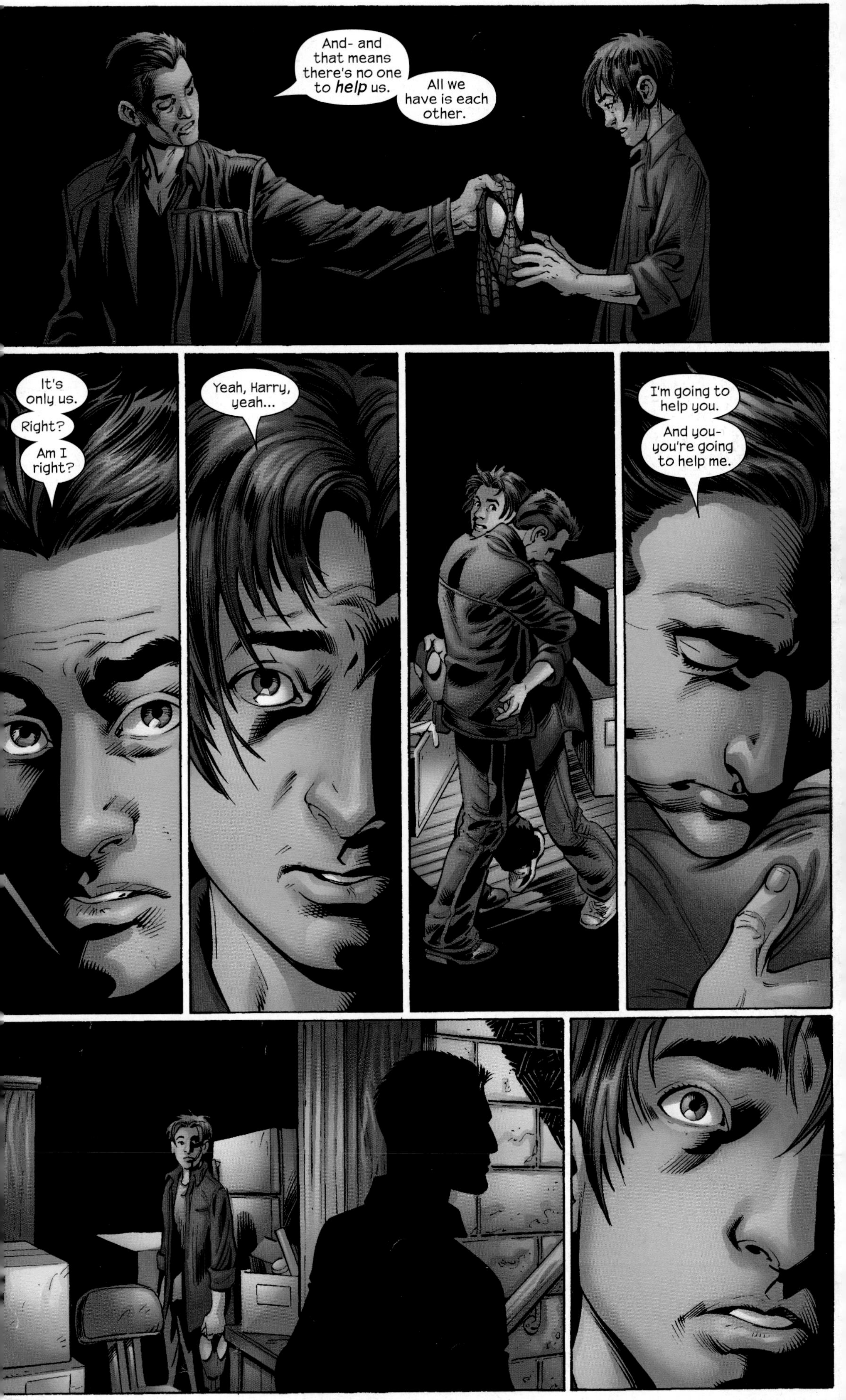
And- and that means there's no one to *help* us.
All we have is each other.
It's only us.
Right?
Am I right?
Yeah, Harry, yeah...
I'm going to help you.
And you- you're going to help me.

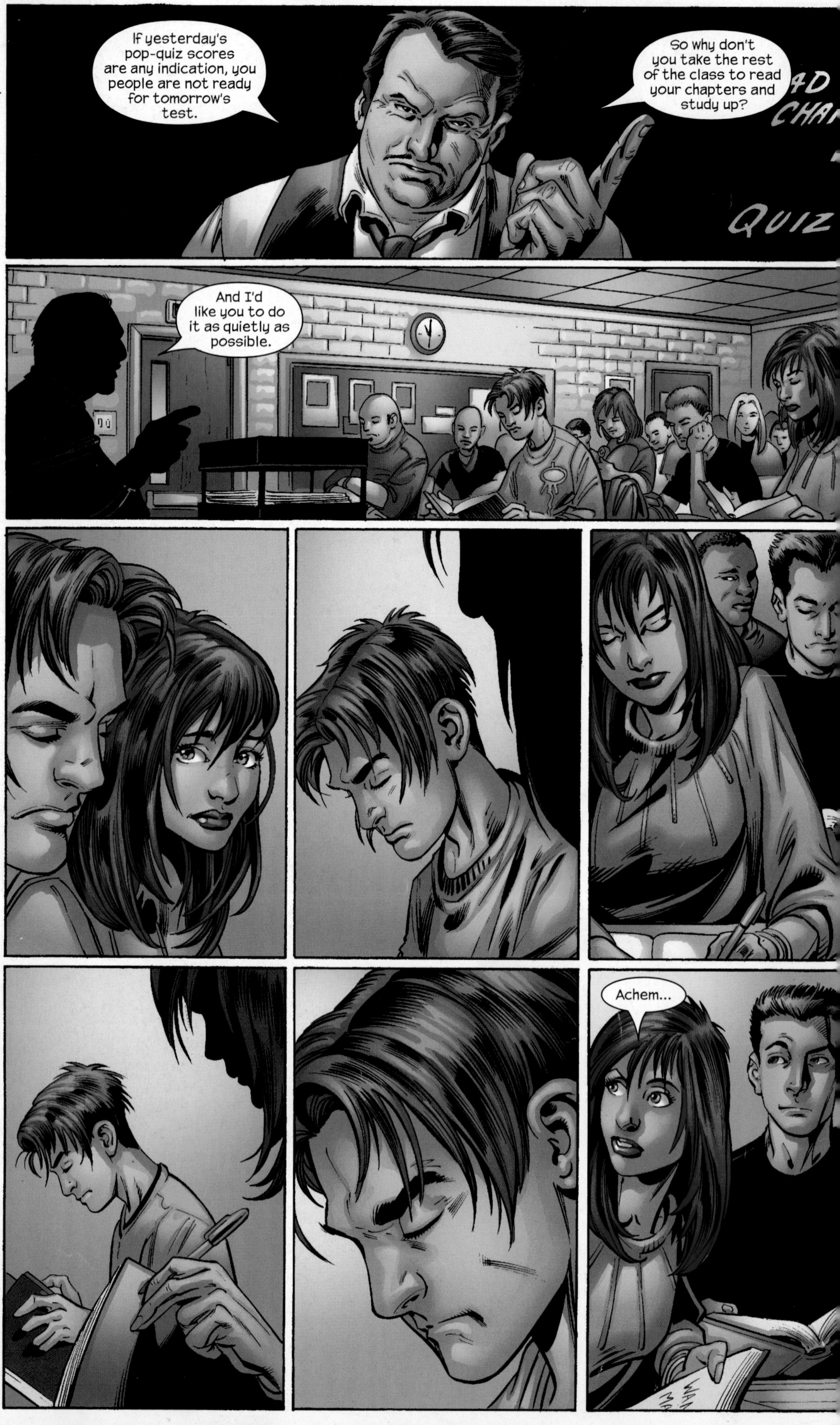
If yesterday's pop-quiz scores are any indication, you people are not ready for tomorrow's test.
So why don't you take the rest of the class to read your chapters and study up?
QUIZ
And I'd like you to do it as quietly as possible.
Achem...

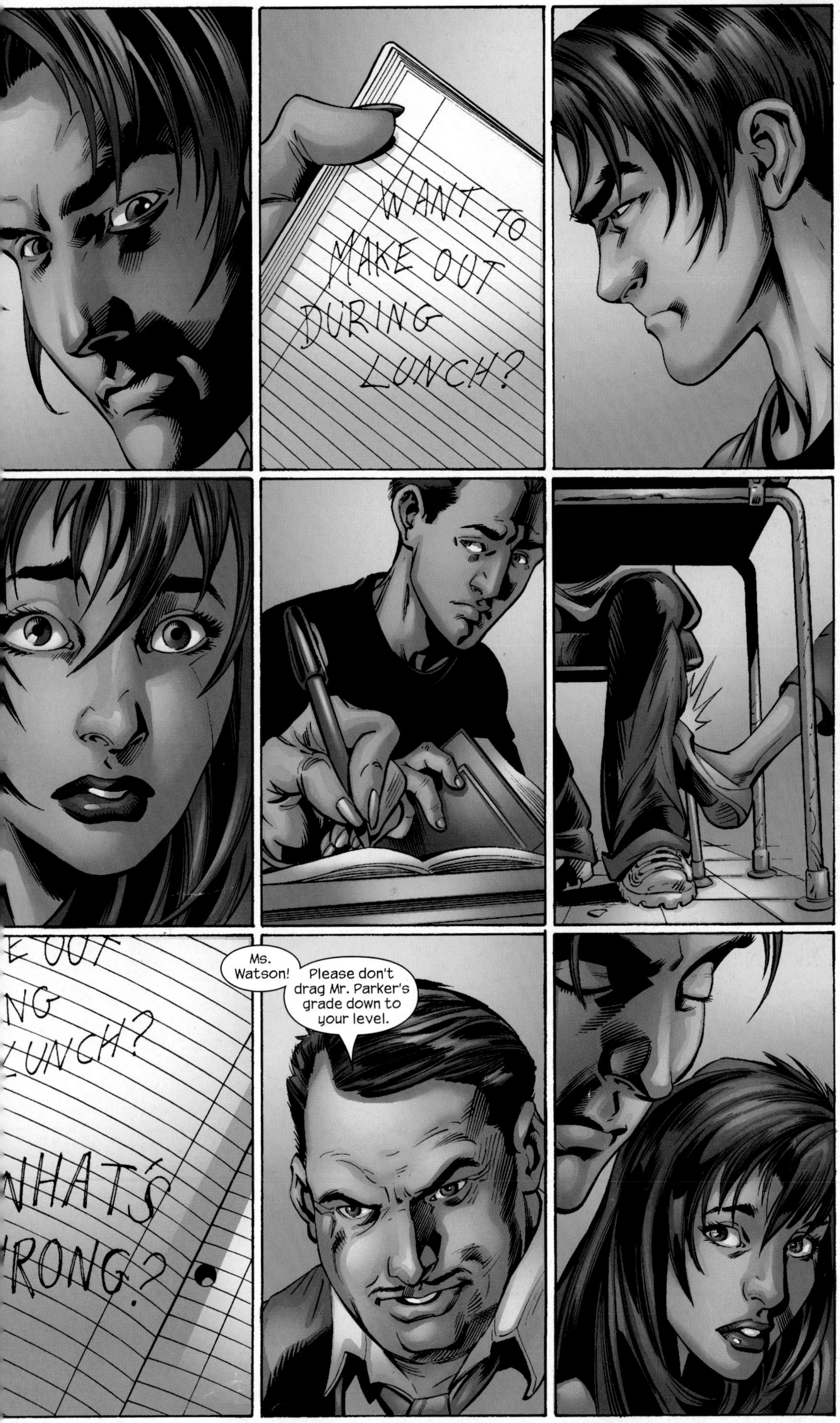
WANT TO MAKE OUT DURING LUNCH?
E OUT
NG
LUNCH?
WHAT'S
WRONG?
Ms. Watson!
Please don't drag Mr. Parker's grade down to your level.

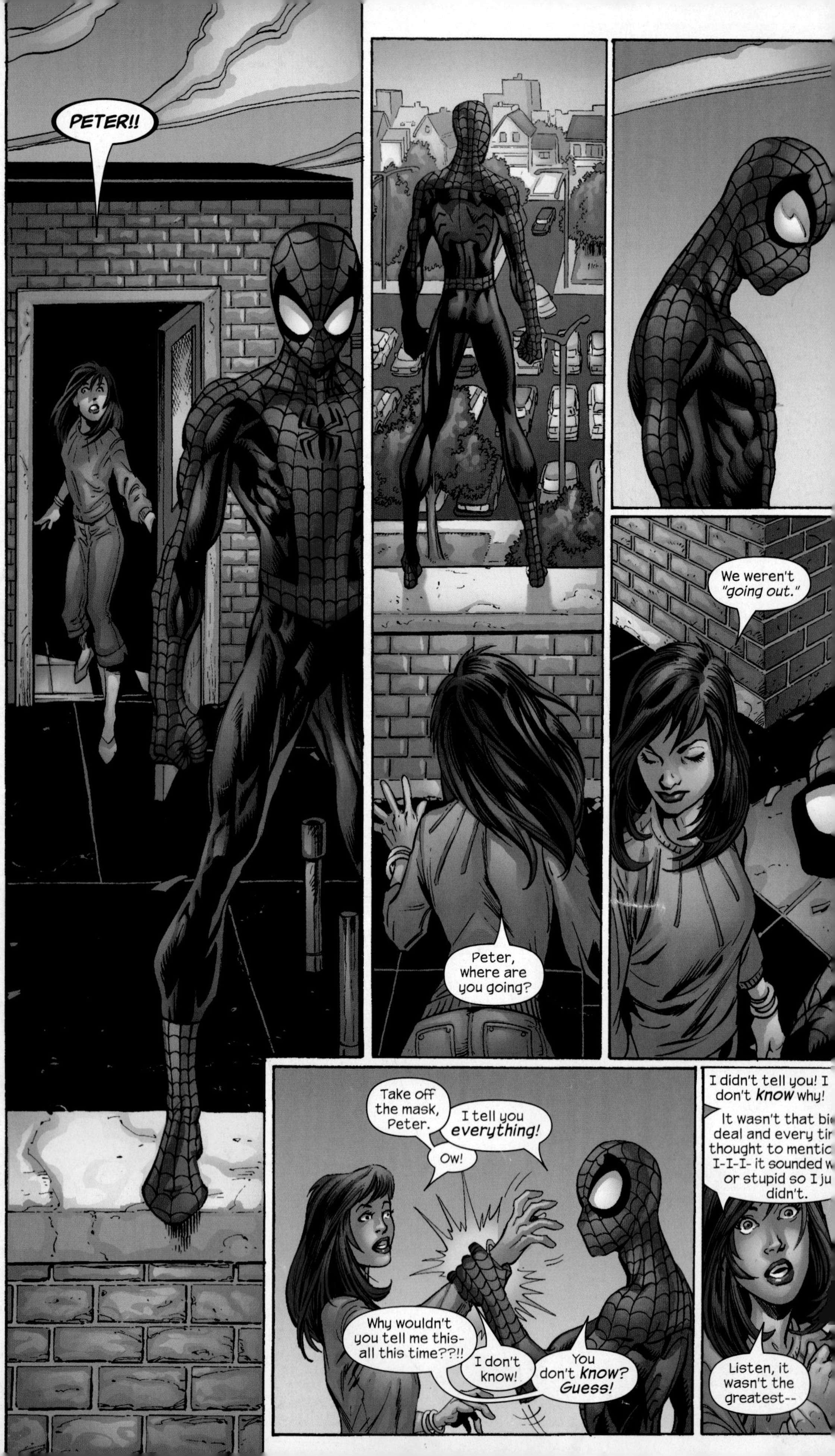
PETER!!
Peter, where are you going?
We weren't "going out."
Take off the mask, Peter.
Ow!
I tell you *everything*!
Why wouldn't you tell me this- all this time??!!
I don't know!
You don't *know*? Guess!
I didn't tell you! I don't *know* why!
Listen, it wasn't the greatest--

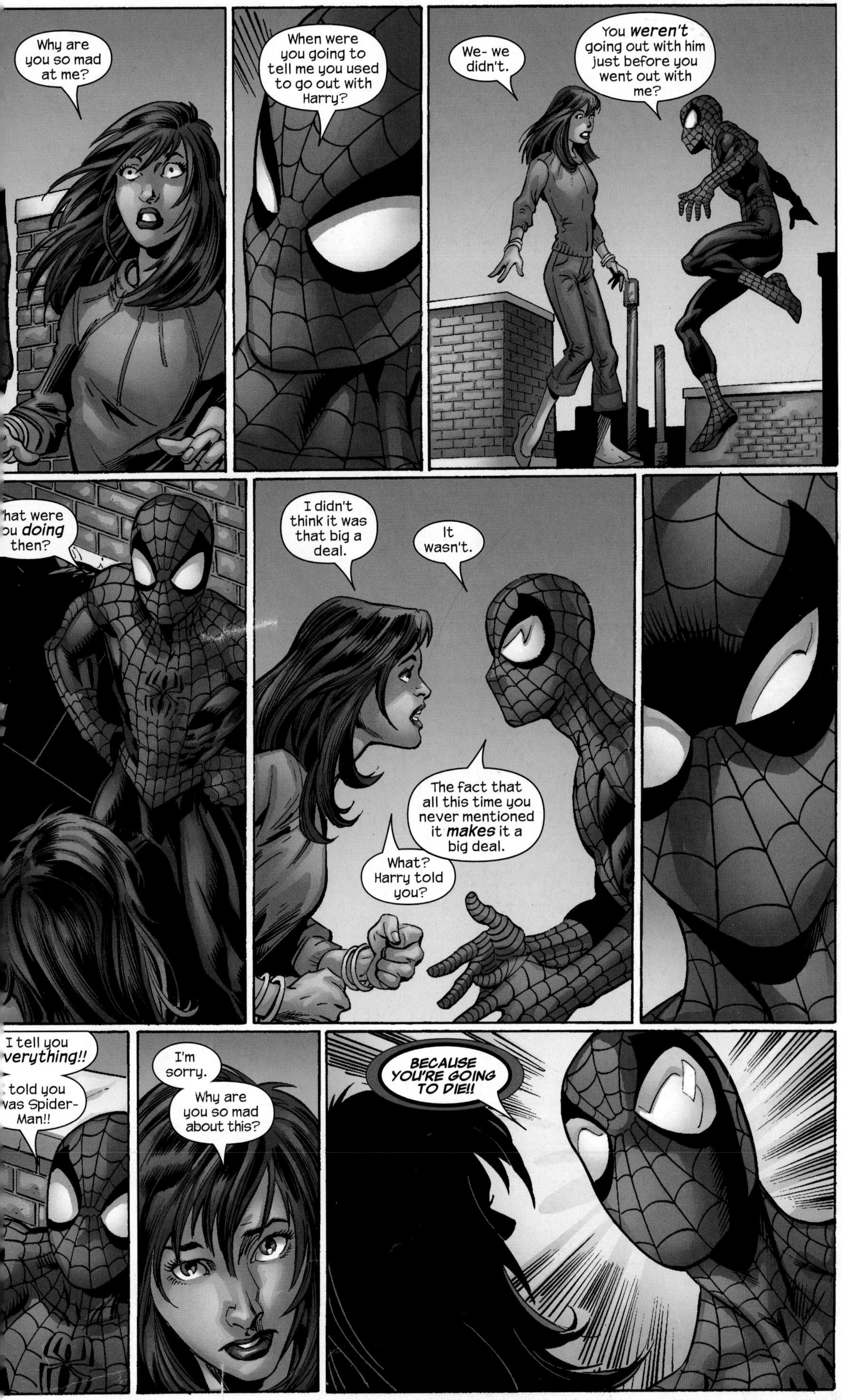

Why are you so mad at me?
When were you going to tell me you used to go out with Harry?
We- we didn't.
You *weren't* going out with him just before you went out with me?
hat were ou *doing* then?
I didn't think it was that big a deal.
It wasn't.
The fact that all this time you never mentioned it *makes* it a big deal.
What? Harry told you?
I tell you verything!!
told you vas Spider-Man!!
I'm sorry.
Why are you so mad about this?
BECAUSE YOU'RE GOING TO DIE!!

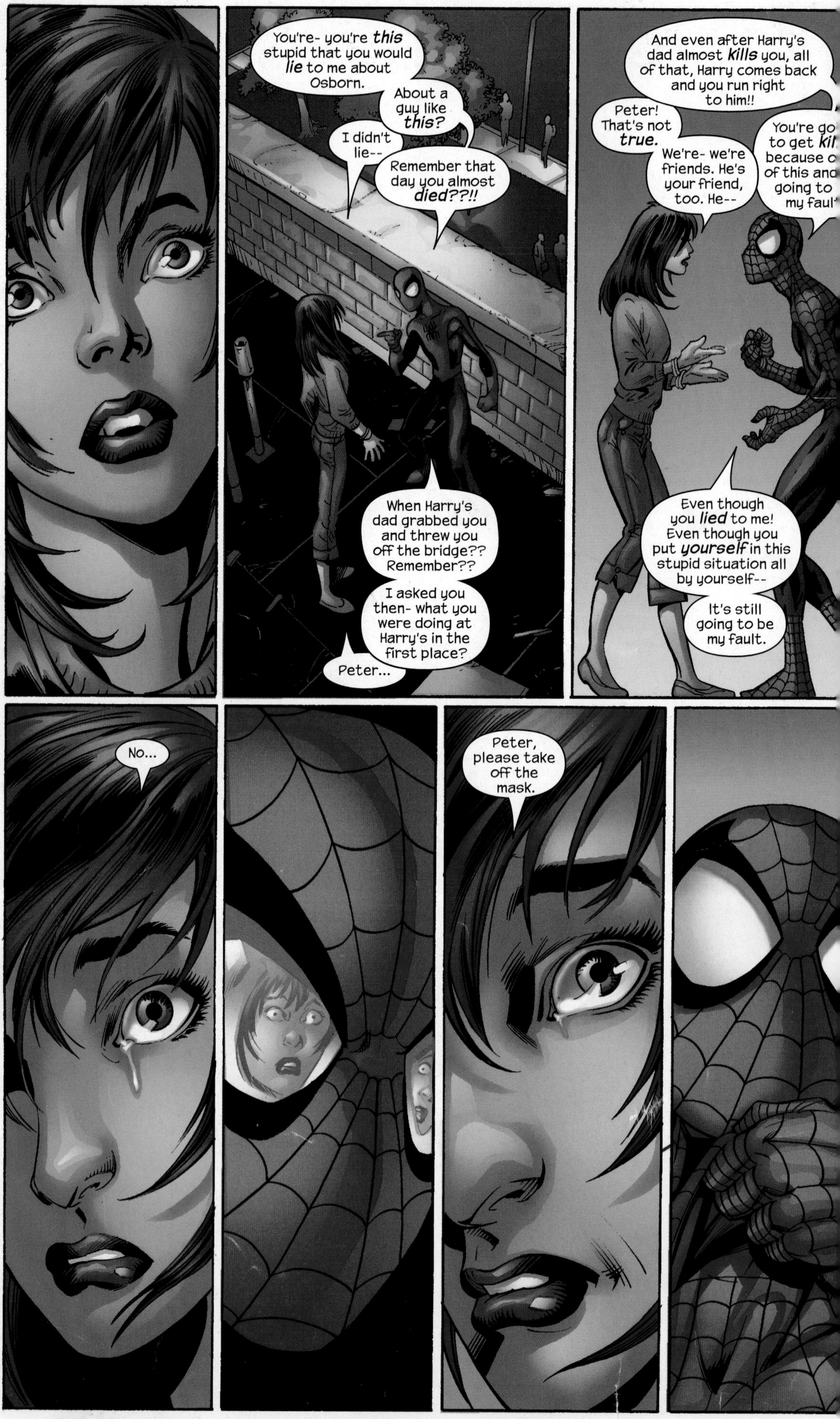

You're- you're *this* stupid that you would *lie* to me about Osborn.
About a guy like *this?*
I didn't lie--
Remember that day you almost *died??!!*
When Harry's dad grabbed you and threw you off the bridge?? Remember??
I asked you then- what you were doing at Harry's in the first place?
Peter...
And even after Harry's dad almost *kills* you, all of that, Harry comes back and you run right to him!!
Peter! That's not *true.*
We're- we're friends. He's your friend, too. He--
Even though you *lied* to me! Even though you put *yourself* in this stupid situation all by yourself--
It's still going to be my fault.
No...
Peter, please take off the mask.

Peter,
please...

Listen very
carefully!

The
Osborns are
nuts!!

You hear
what I am saying?
Stay away from
them. Harry is
dangerous.

ow is he
ngerous?

Because
he--

(I should
never have
told you who
I was.)

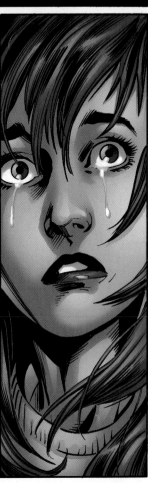

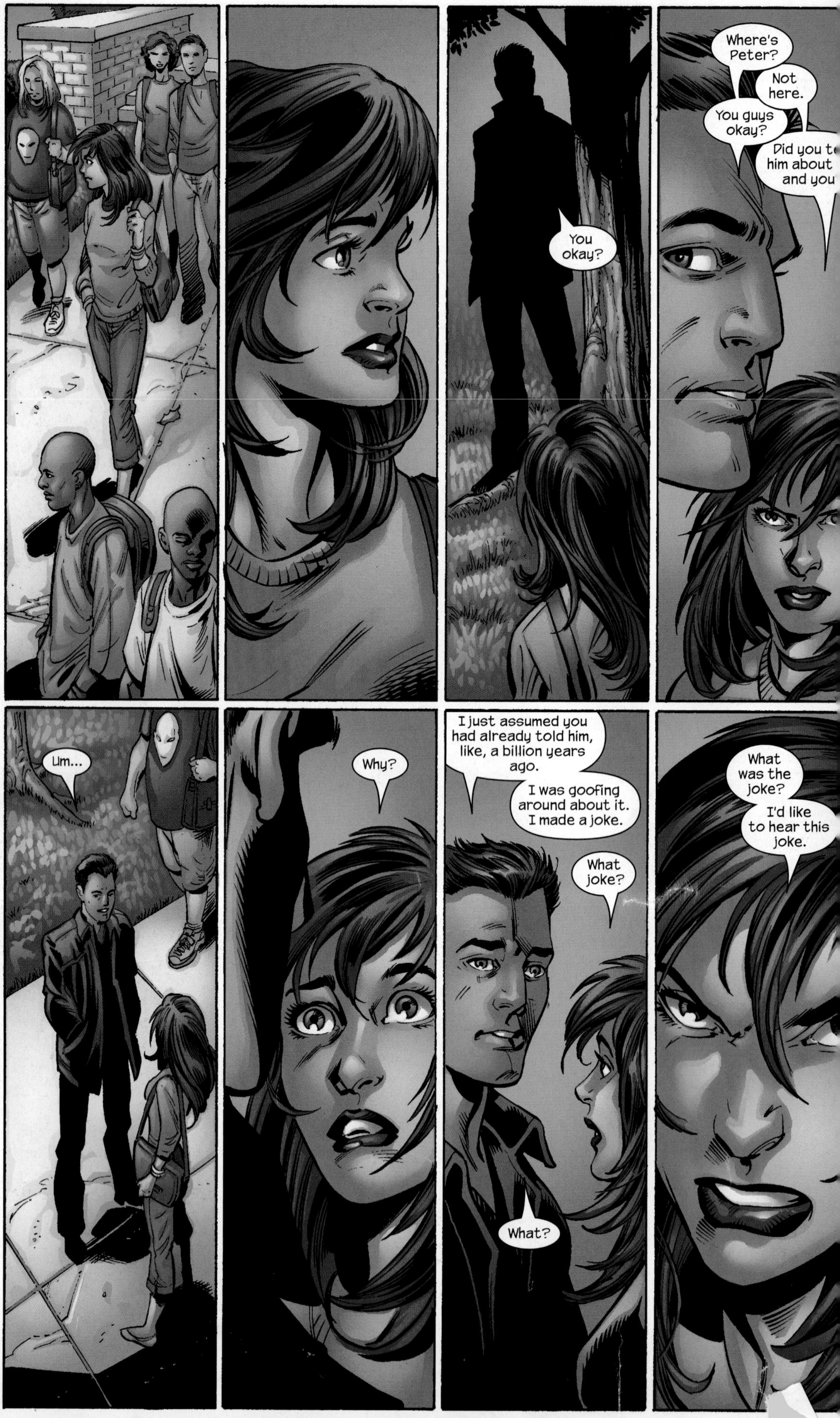
You okay?
Where's Peter?
Not here.
You guys okay?
Did you t
him about
and you
Um...
Why?
I just assumed you had already told him, like, a billion years ago.
I was goofing around about it. I made a joke.
What joke?
What?
What was the joke?
I'd like to hear this joke.

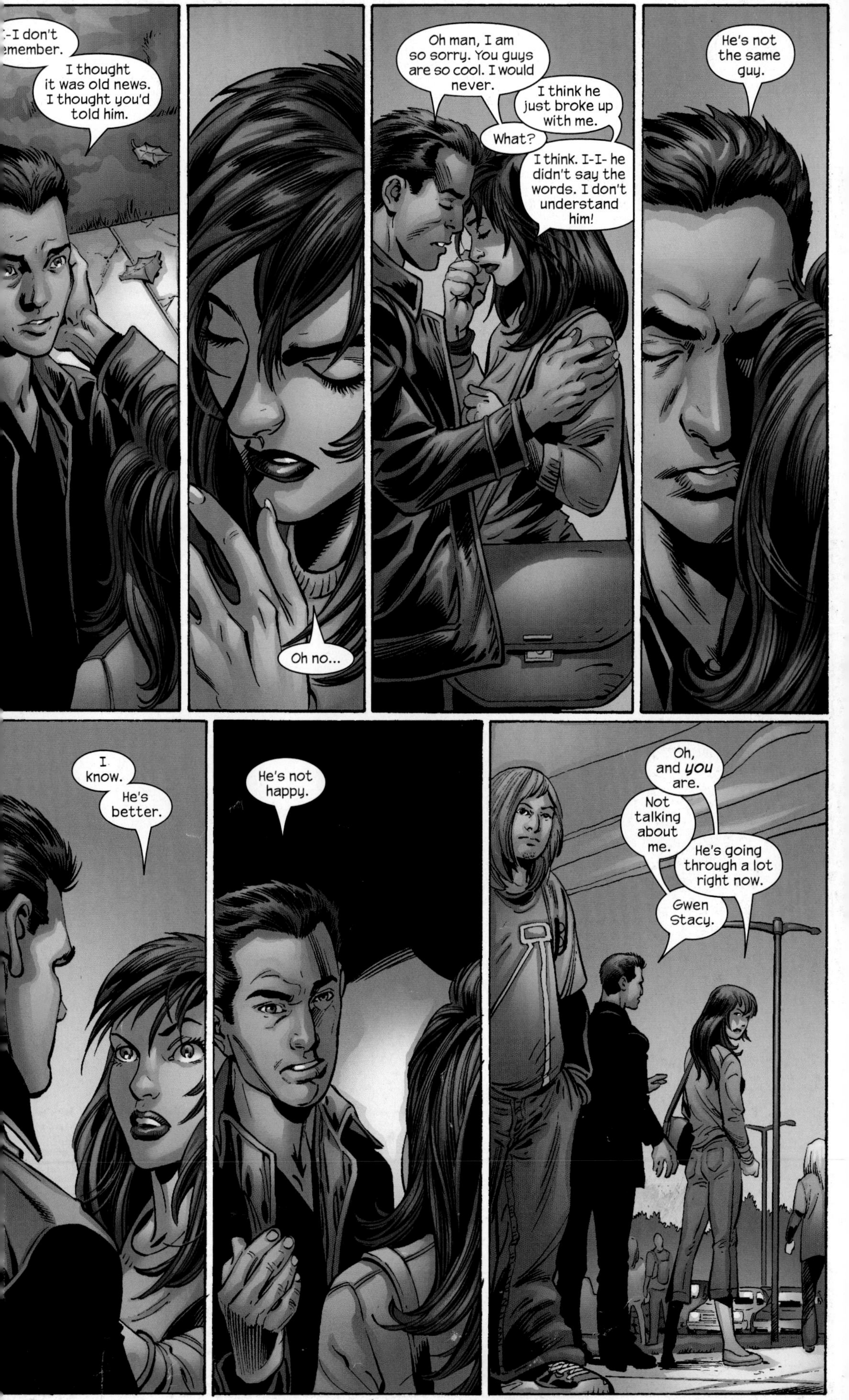

I-I don't remember.
I thought it was old news. I thought you'd told him.
Oh no...
Oh man, I am so sorry. You guys are so cool. I would never.
What?
I think he just broke up with me.
I think. I-I- he didn't say the words. I don't understand him!
He's not the same guy.
I know.
He's better.
He's not happy.
Oh, and *you* are.
Not talking about me.
He's going through a lot right now.
Gwen Stacy.

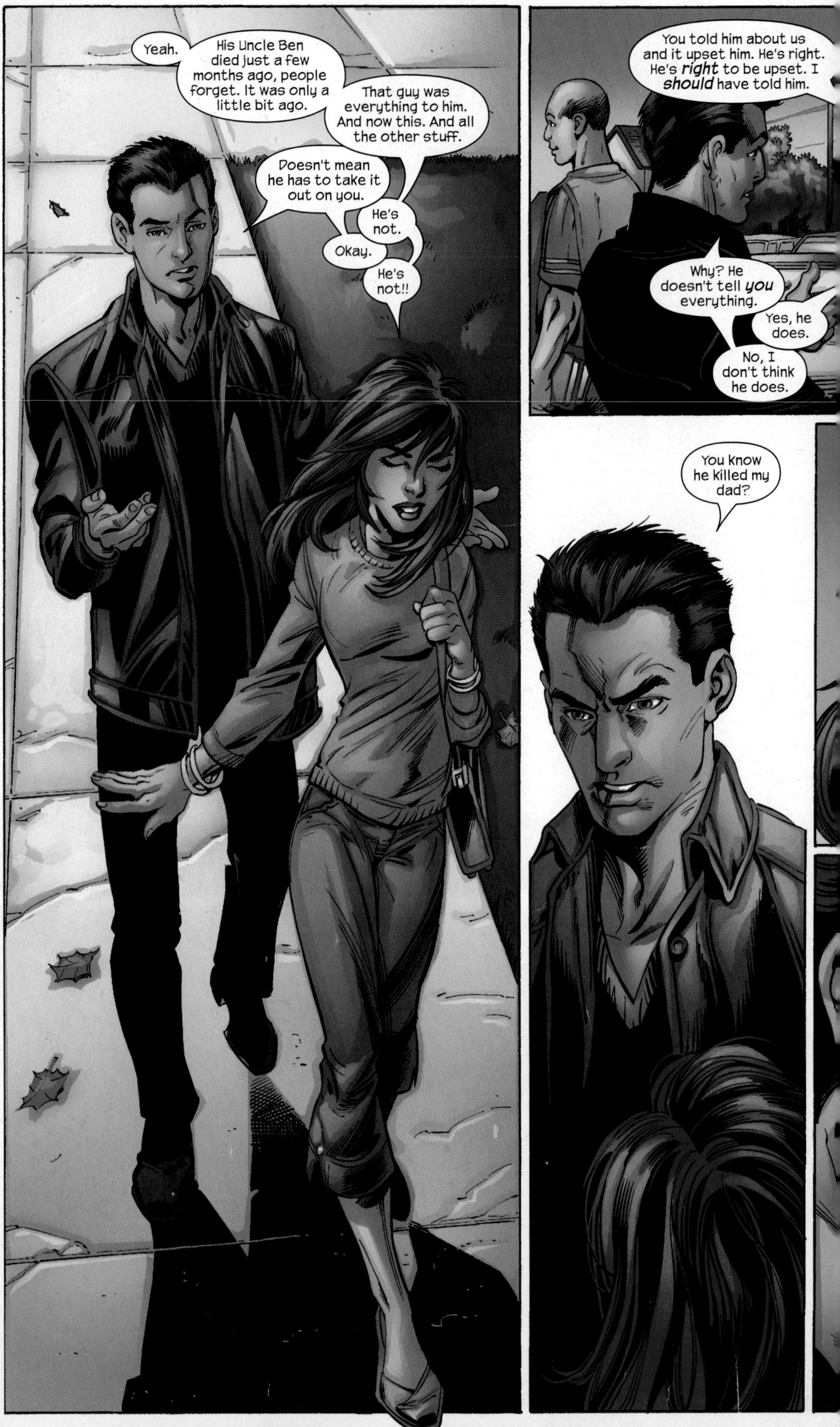
Yeah.
His Uncle Ben died just a few months ago, people forget. It was only a little bit ago.
That guy was everything to him. And now this. And all the other stuff.
Doesn't mean he has to take it out on you.
He's not.
Okay.
He's not!!
You told him about us and it upset him. He's right. He's *right* to be upset. I *should* have told him.
Why? He doesn't tell *you* everything.
Yes, he does.
No, I don't think he does.
You know he killed my dad?

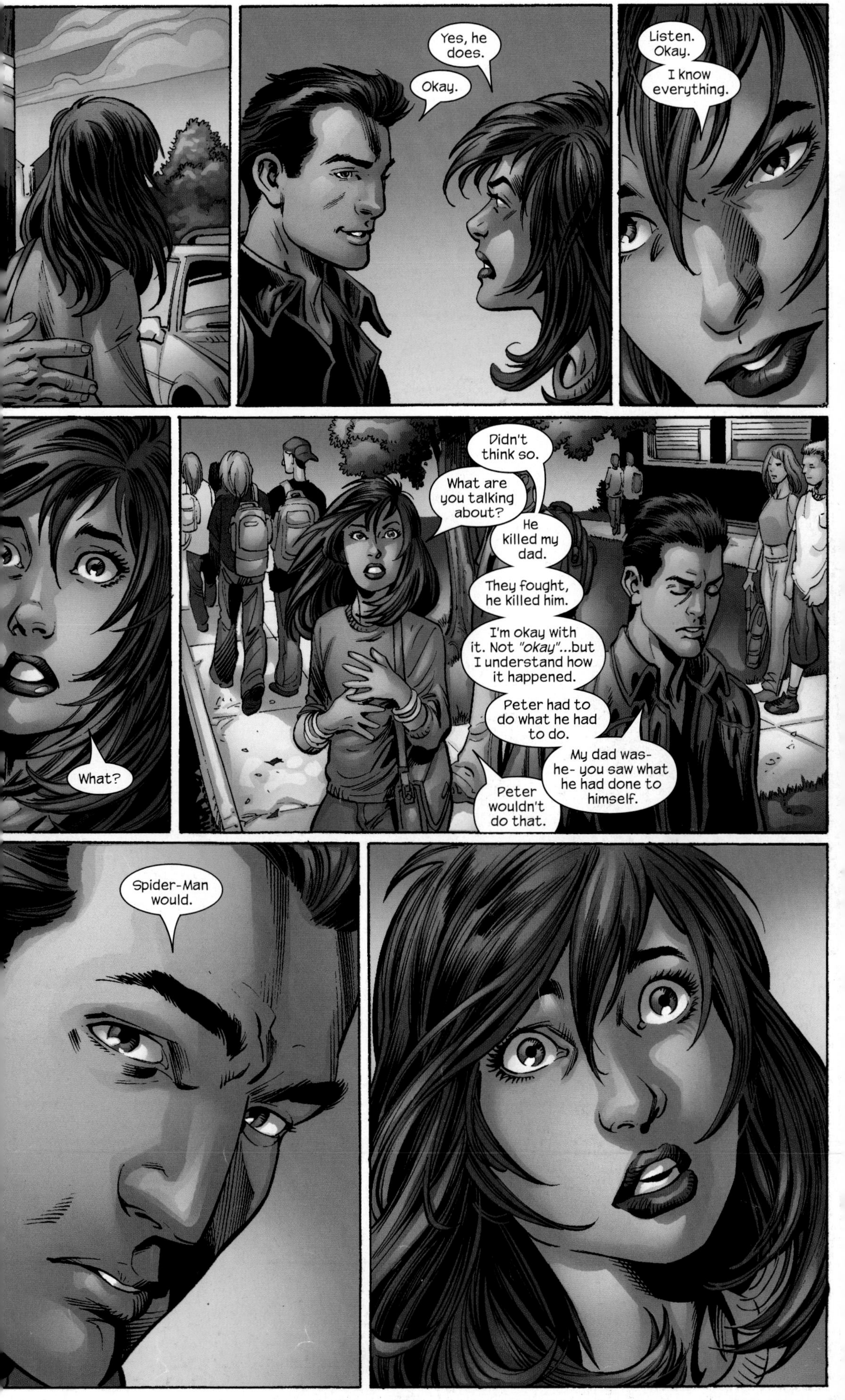

Yes, he does.
Okay.
Listen. Okay.
I know everything.
What?
Didn't think so.
What are you talking about?
He killed my dad.
They fought, he killed him.
I'm okay with it. Not "okay"...but I understand how it happened.
Peter had to do what he had to do.
My dad was- he- you saw what he had done to himself.
Peter wouldn't do that.
Spider-Man would.

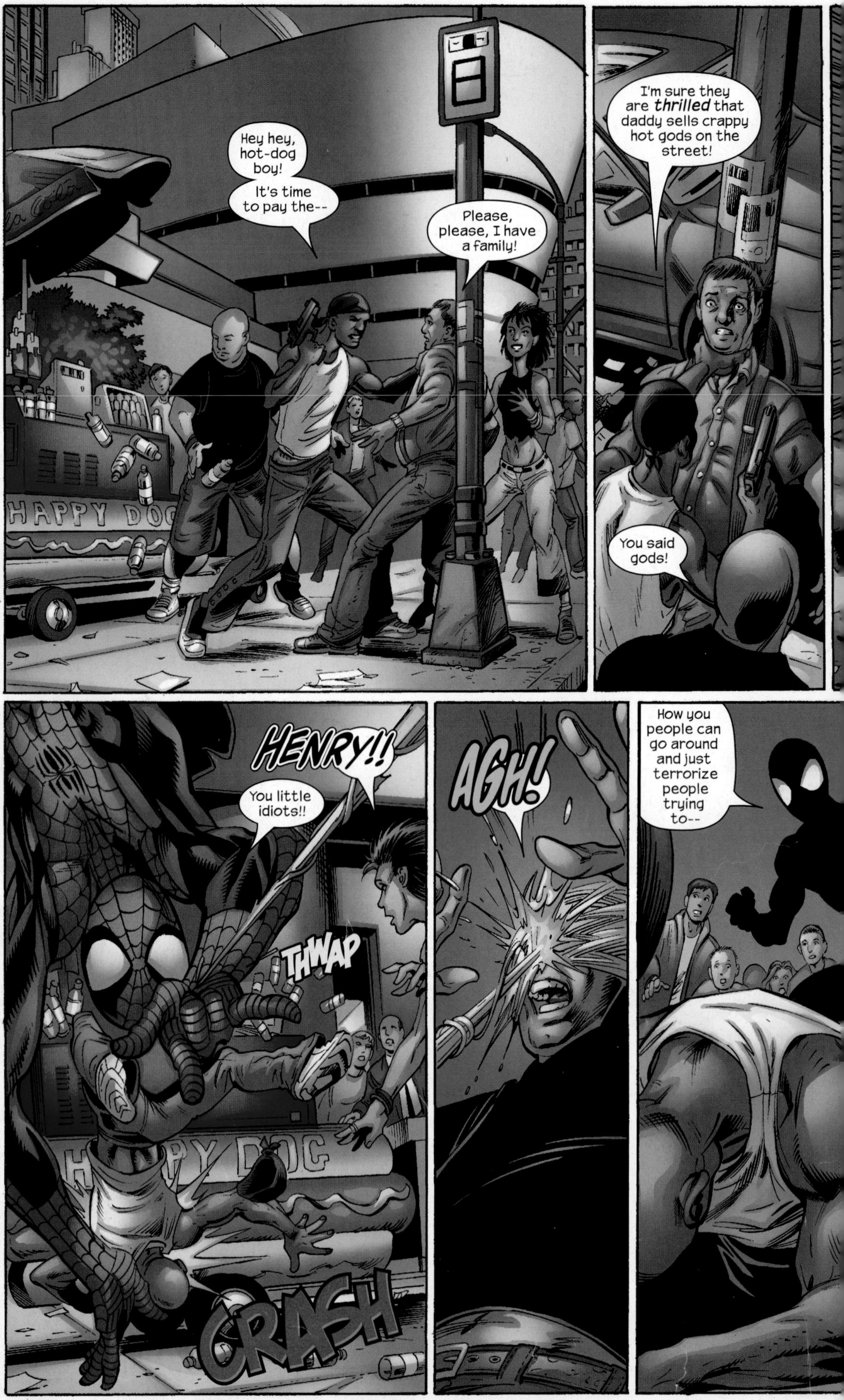

Hey hey, hot-dog boy!
It's time to pay the--
Please, please, I have a family!
HAPPY DOG
I'm sure they are *thrilled* that daddy sells crappy hot gods on the street!
You said gods!
HENRY!!
You little idiots!!
THWAP
CRASH
AGH!
How you people can go around and just terrorize people trying to--

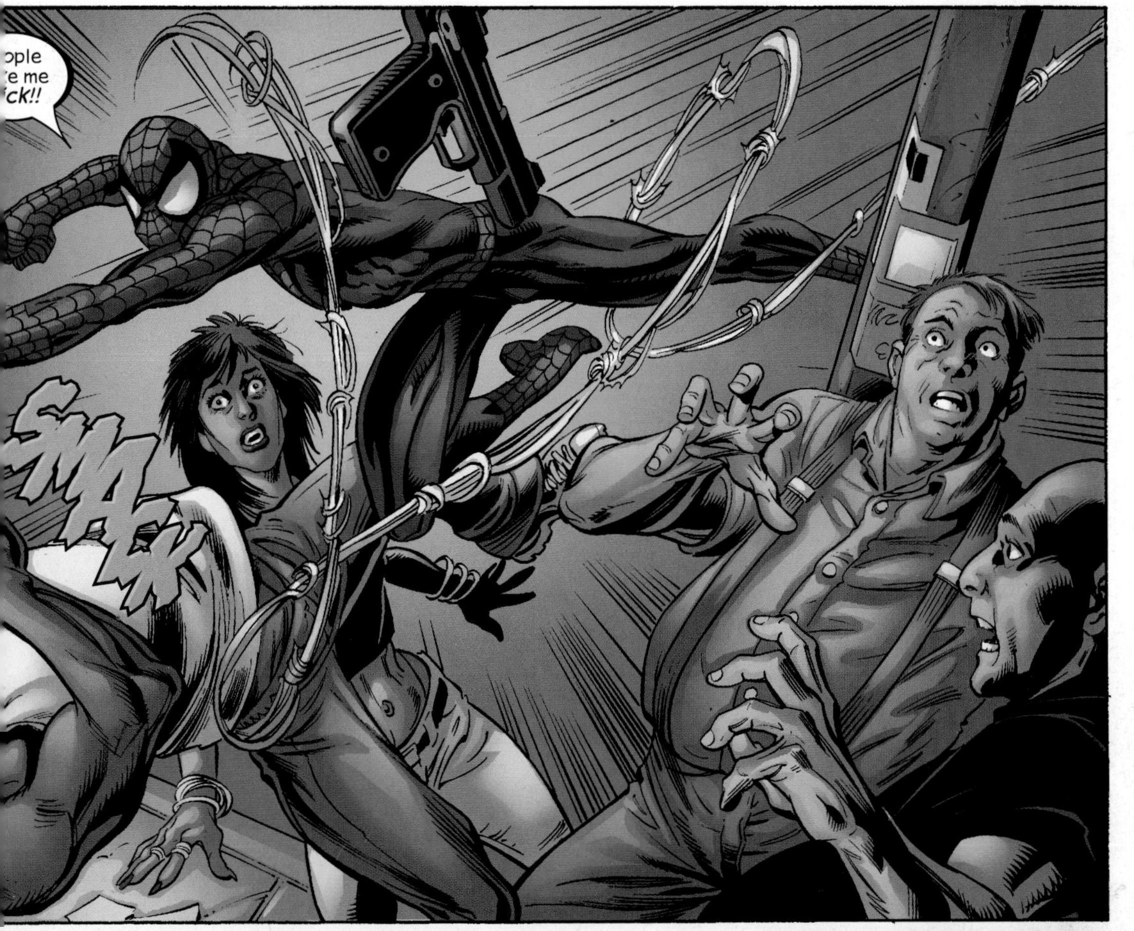
ople
re me
ck!!
SMACK

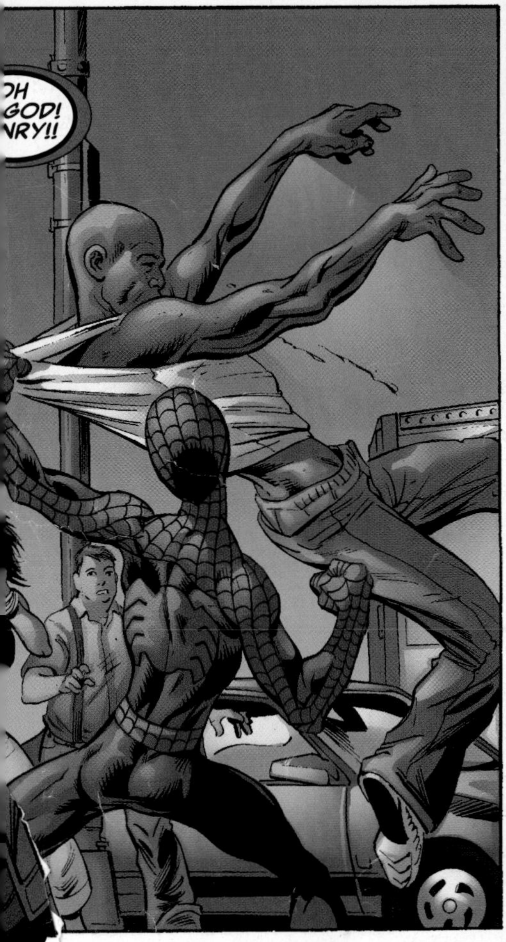
OH
GOD!
NRY!!

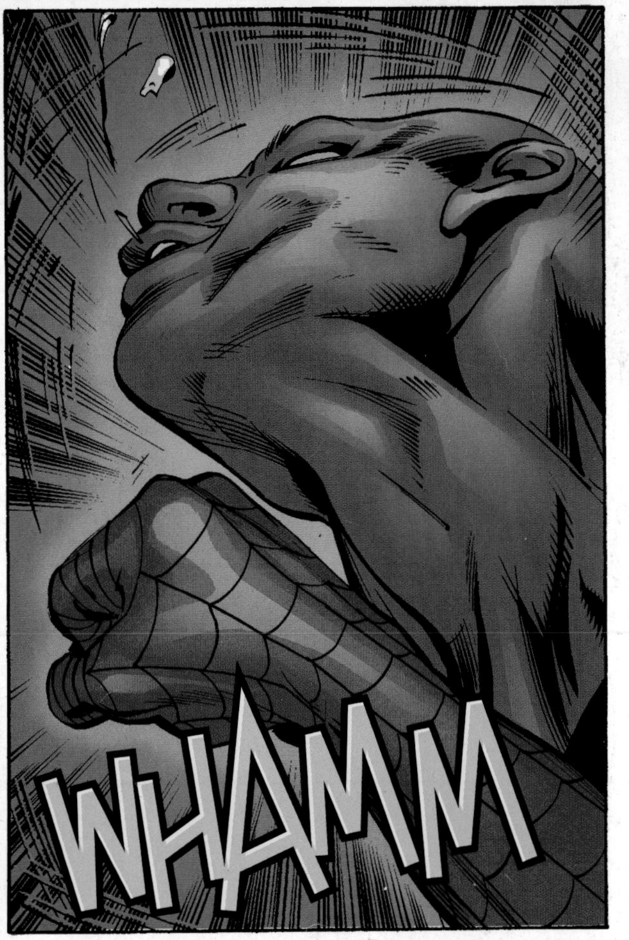
WHAMM

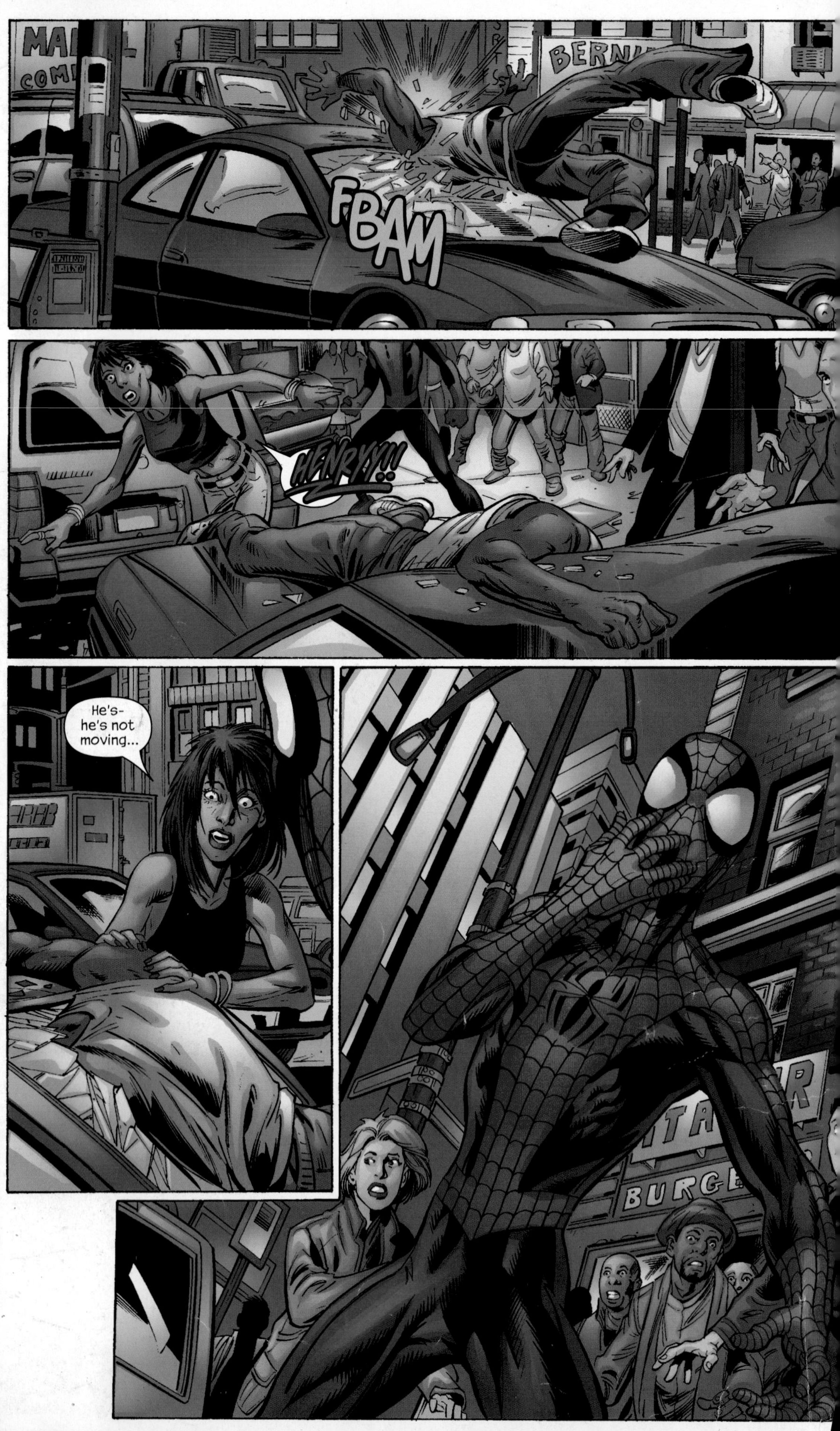
FBAM
HENRYY!!
He's- he's not moving...

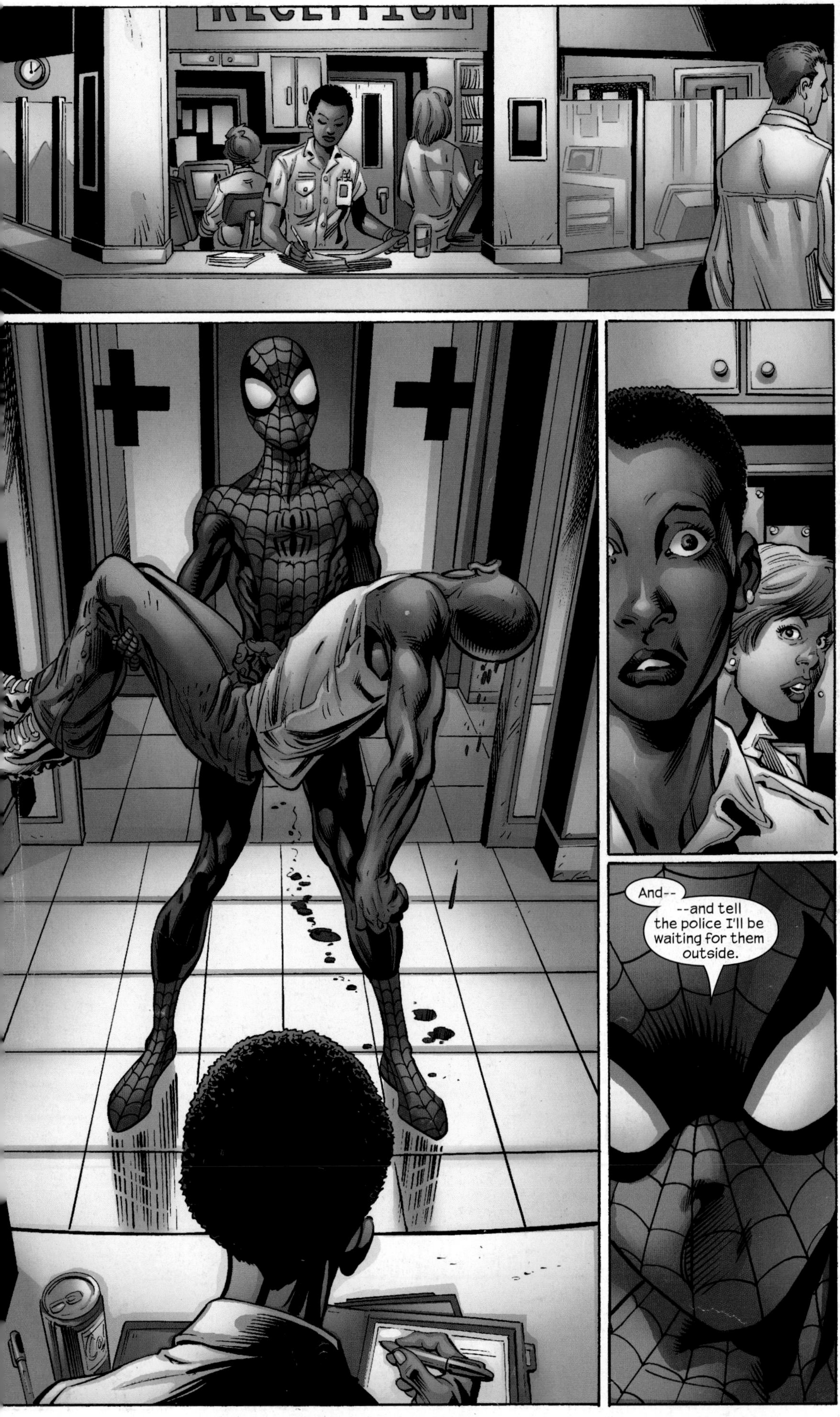
And--
--and tell the police I'll be waiting for them outside.

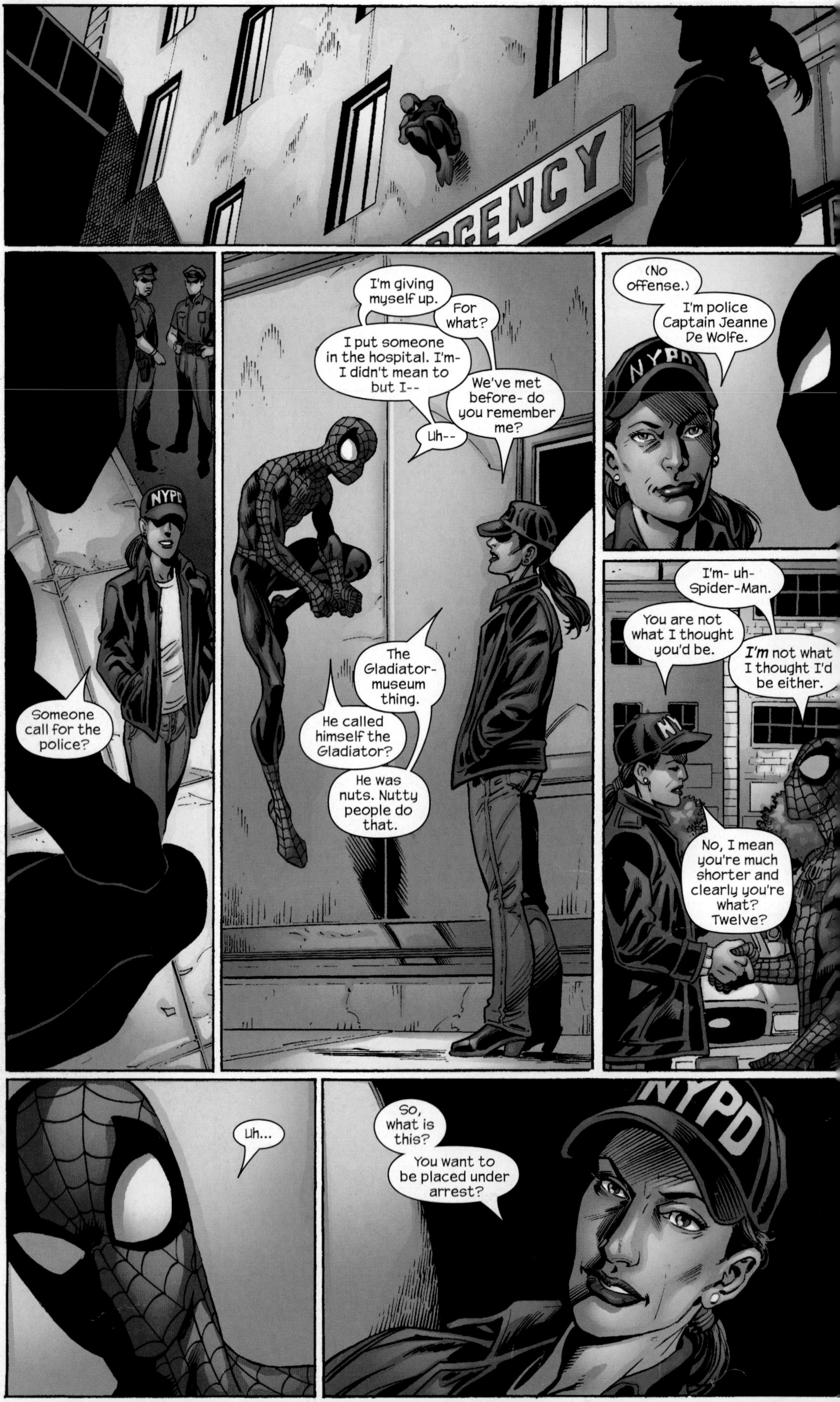

RGENCY
Someone call for the police?
I'm giving myself up.
For what?
I put someone in the hospital. I'm- I didn't mean to but I--
Uh--
We've met before- do you remember me?
The Gladiator-museum thing.
He called himself the Gladiator?
He was nuts. Nutty people do that.
(No offense.)
I'm police Captain Jeanne De Wolfe.
I'm- uh- Spider-Man.
You are not what I thought you'd be.
I'm not what I thought I'd be either.
No, I mean you're much shorter and clearly you're what? Twelve?
Uh...
So, what is this?
You want to be placed under arrest?

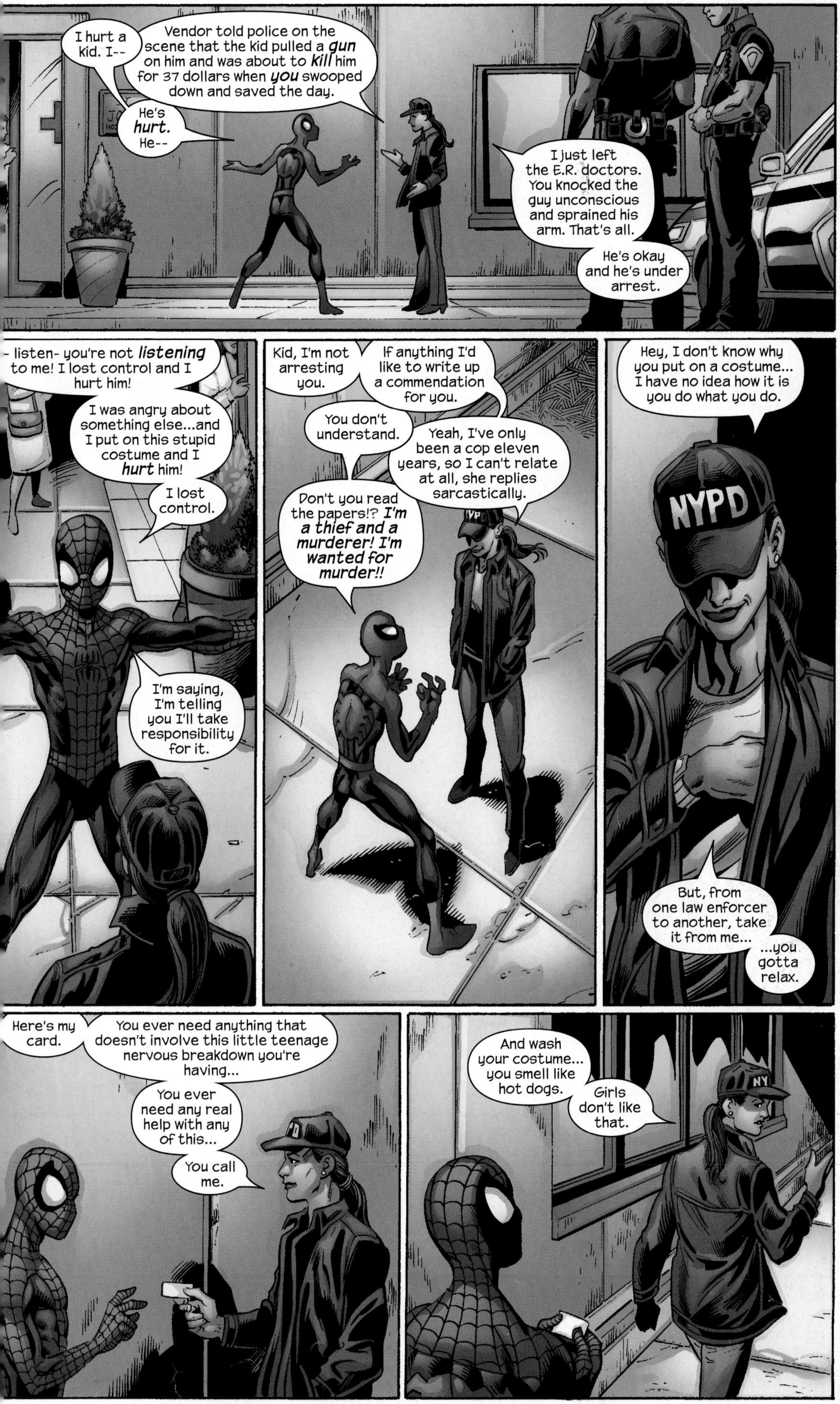
I hurt a kid. I--
Vendor told police on the scene that the kid pulled a *gun* on him and was about to *kill* him for 37 dollars when *you* swooped down and saved the day.
He's *hurt.* He--
I just left the E.R. doctors. You knocked the guy unconscious and sprained his arm. That's all.
He's okay and he's under arrest.
- listen- you're not *listening* to me! I lost control and I hurt him!
I was angry about something else...and I put on this stupid costume and I *hurt* him!
I lost control.
I'm saying, I'm telling you I'll take responsibility for it.
Kid, I'm not arresting you.
If anything I'd like to write up a commendation for you.
You don't understand.
Yeah, I've only been a cop eleven years, so I can't relate at all, she replies sarcastically.
Don't you read the papers!? *I'm a thief and a murderer! I'm wanted for murder!!*
Hey, I don't know why you put on a costume... I have no idea how it is you do what you do.
NYPD
But, from one law enforcer to another, take it from me...
...you gotta relax.
Here's my card.
You ever need anything that doesn't involve this little teenage nervous breakdown you're having...
You ever need any real help with any of this...
You call me.
And wash your costume... you smell like hot dogs.
Girls don't like that.

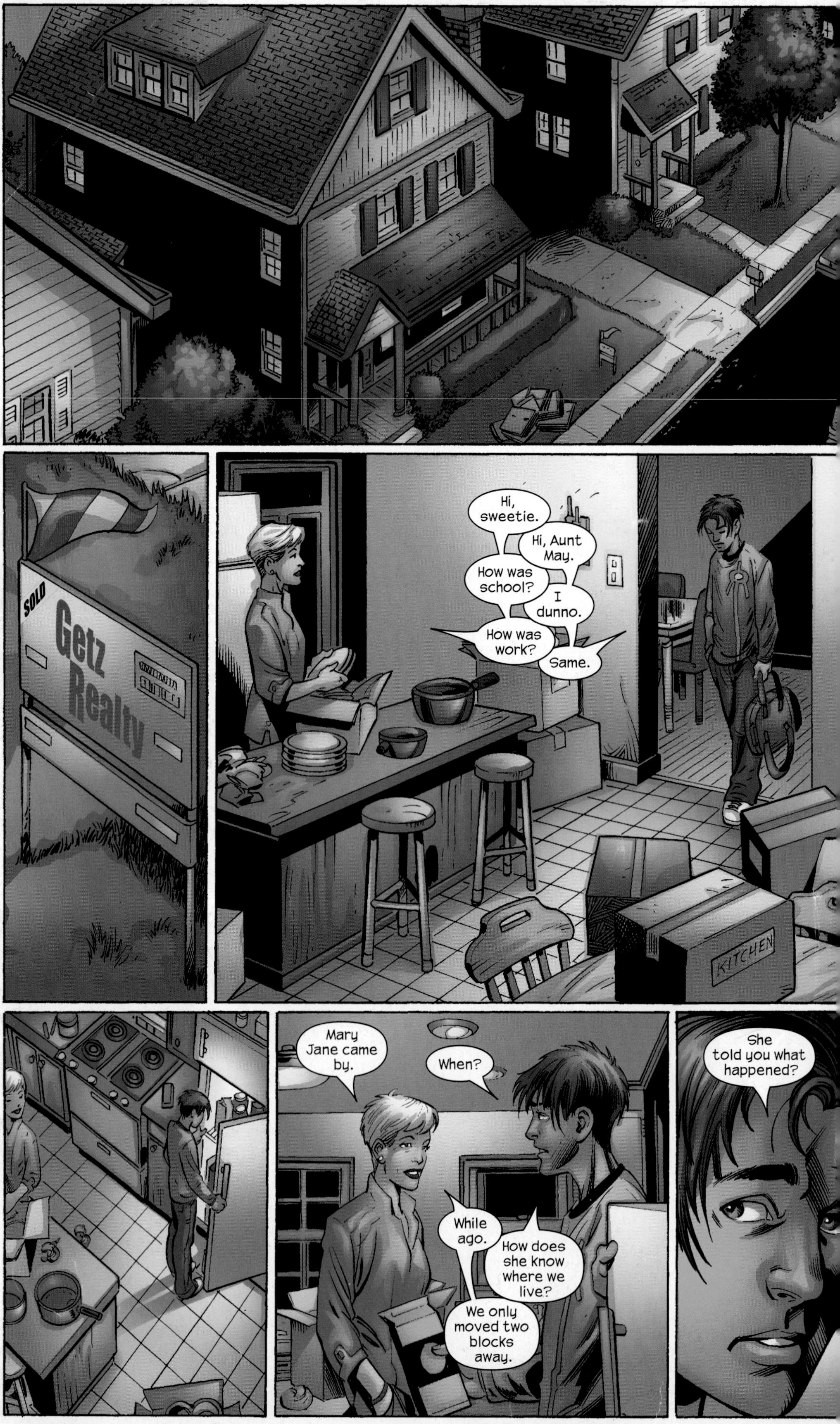
SOLD
Getz Realty
Hi, sweetie.
Hi, Aunt May.
How was school?
I dunno.
How was work?
Same.
KITCHEN
Mary Jane came by.
When?
While ago.
How does she know where we live?
We only moved two blocks away.
She told you what happened?

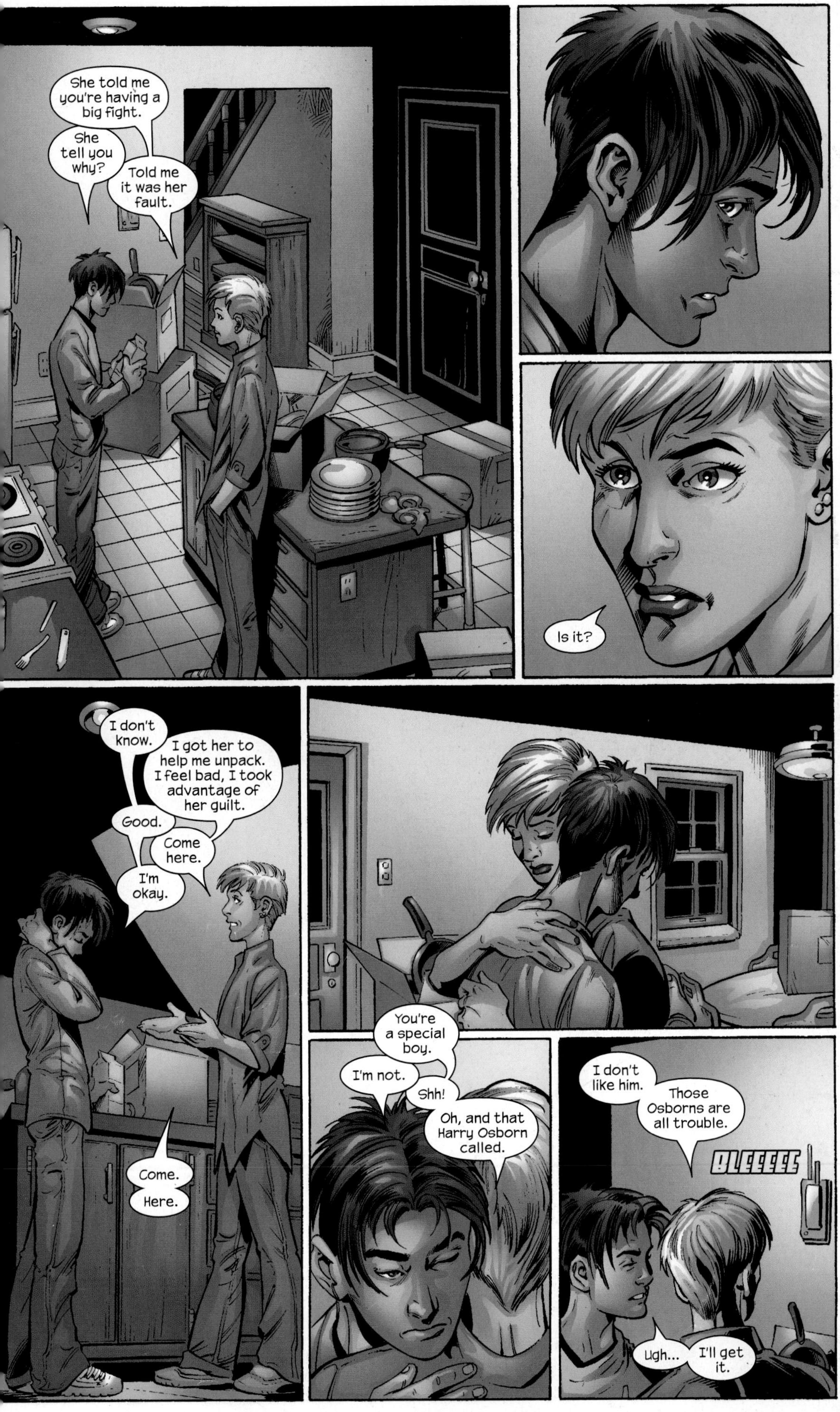

She told me you're having a big fight.
She tell you why?
Told me it was her fault.
Is it?
I don't know.
I got her to help me unpack. I feel bad, I took advantage of her guilt.
Good.
Come here.
I'm okay.
Come.
Here.
You're a special boy.
I'm not.
Shh!
Oh, and that Harry Osborn called.
I don't like him.
Those Osborns are all trouble.
BLEEEEE
Ugh...
I'll get it.

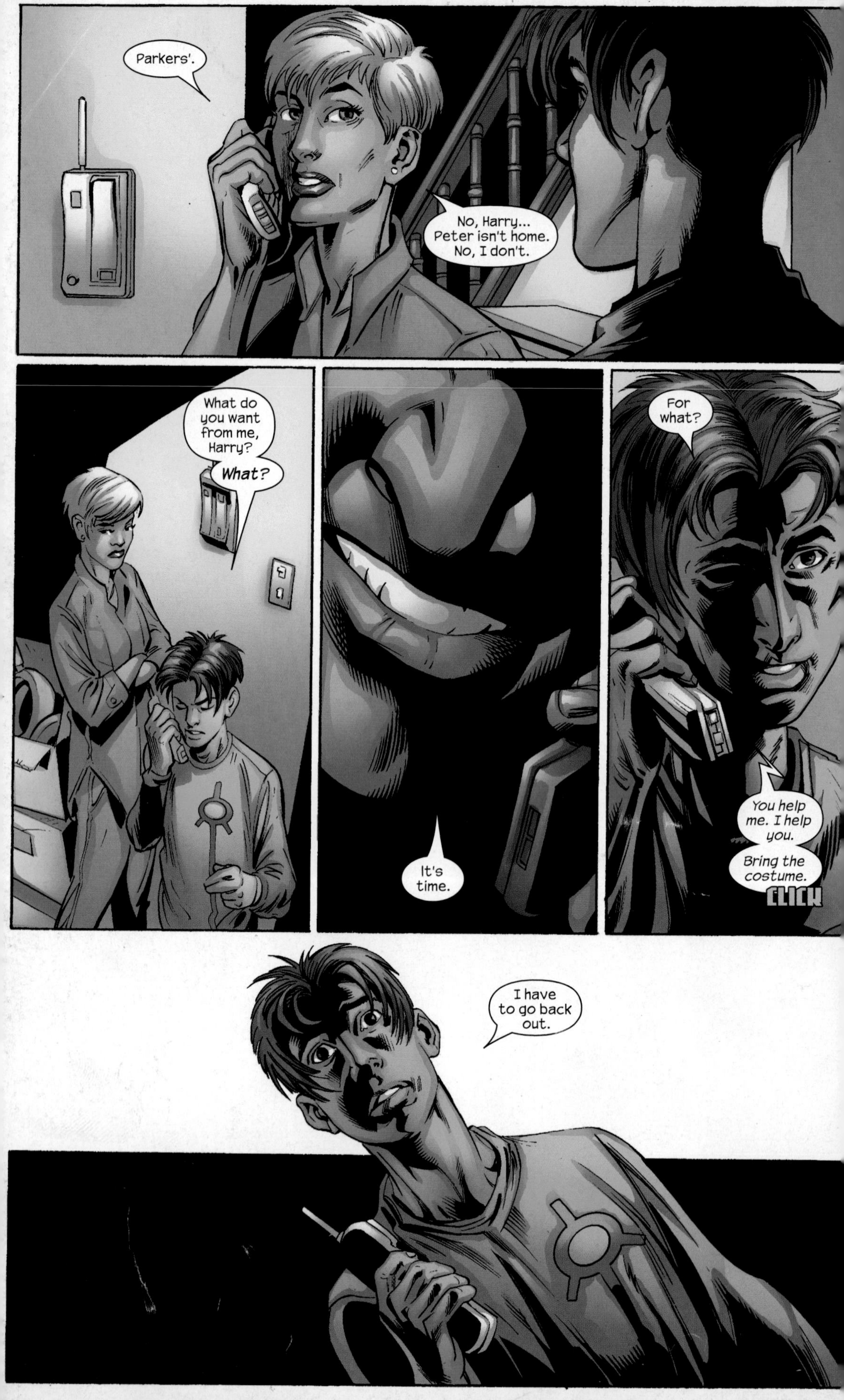
Parkers'.
No, Harry... Peter isn't home. No, I don't.
What do you want from me, Harry?
What?
It's time.
For what?
You help me. I help you.
Bring the costume.
CLICK
I have to go back out.

75

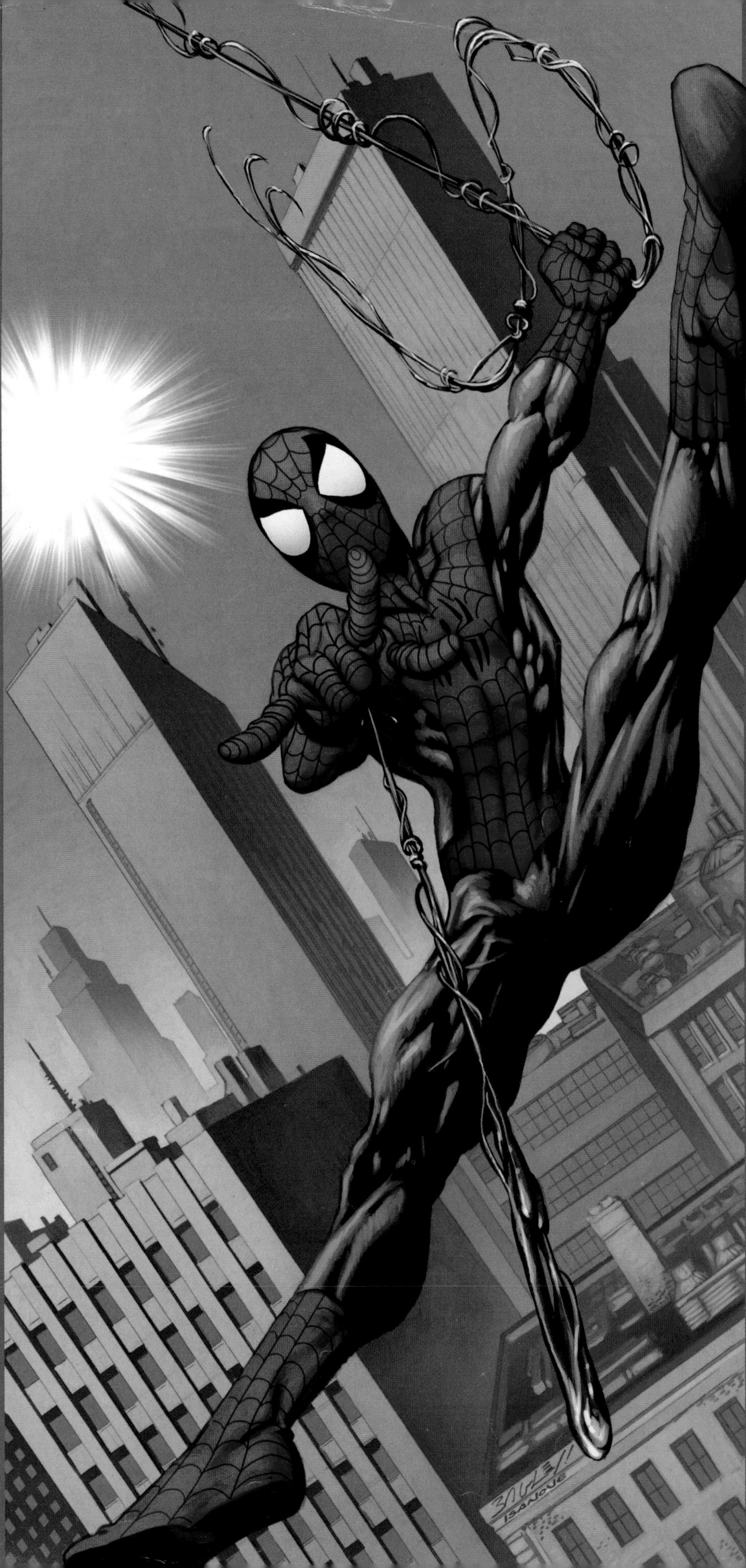

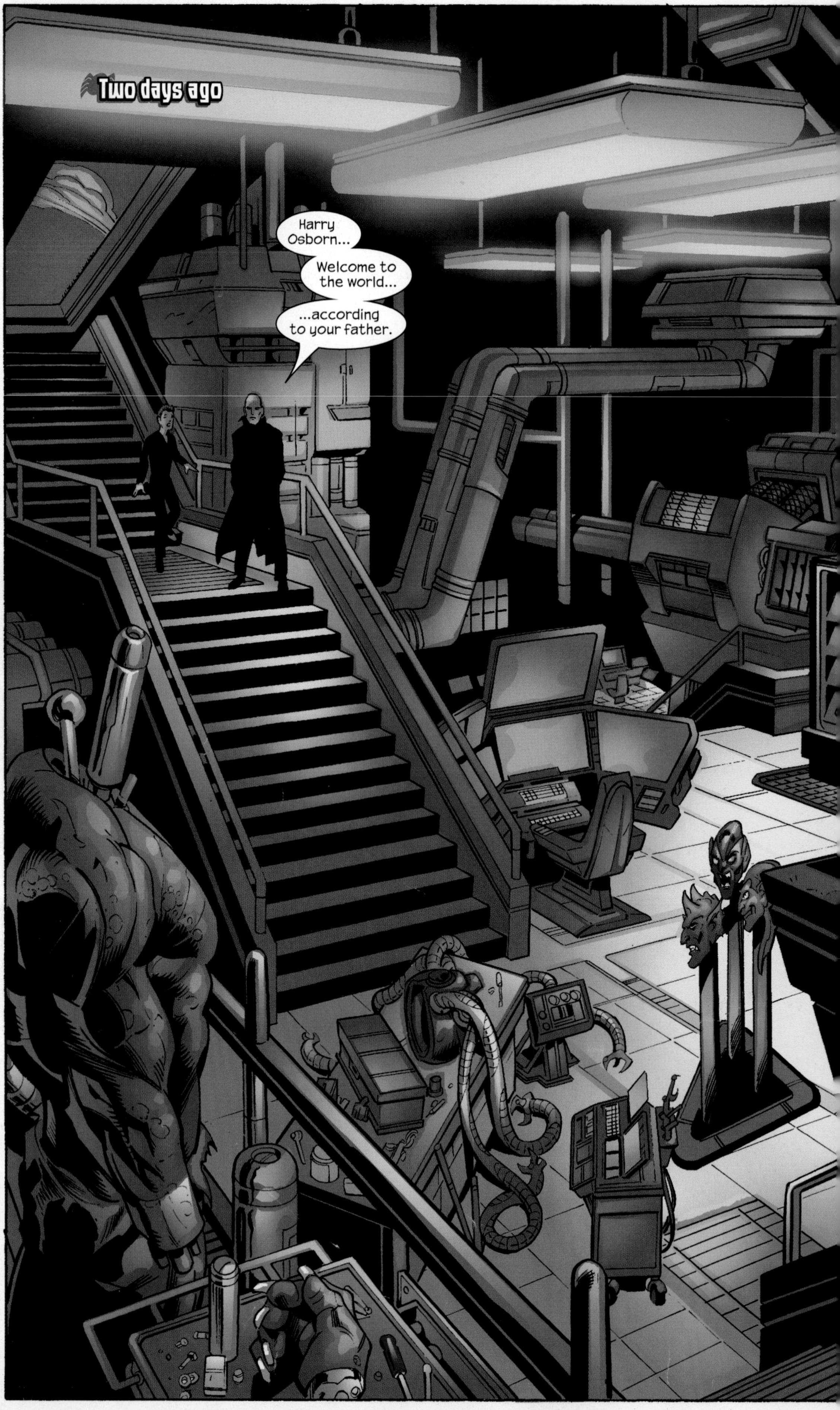

Two days ago
Harry Osborn...
Welcome to the world...
...according to your father.

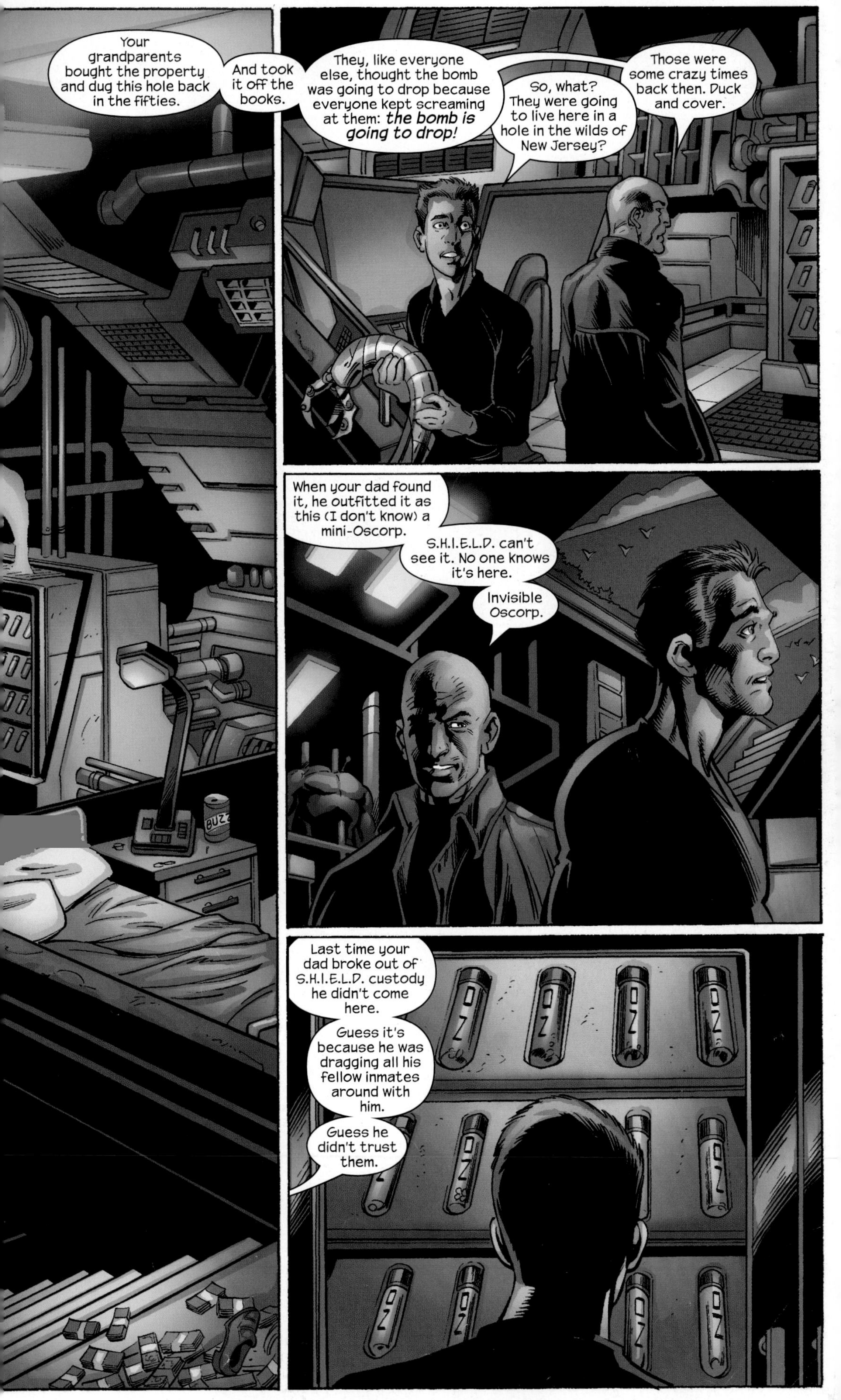
Your grandparents bought the property and dug this hole back in the fifties.
And took it off the books.
They, like everyone else, thought the bomb was going to drop because everyone kept screaming at them: *the bomb is going to drop!*
So, what? They were going to live here in a hole in the wilds of New Jersey?
Those were some crazy times back then. Duck and cover.
When your dad found it, he outfitted it as this (I don't know) a mini-Oscorp.
S.H.I.E.L.D. can't see it. No one knows it's here.
Invisible Oscorp.
Last time your dad broke out of S.H.I.E.L.D. custody he didn't come here.
Guess it's because he was dragging all his fellow inmates around with him.
Guess he didn't trust them.

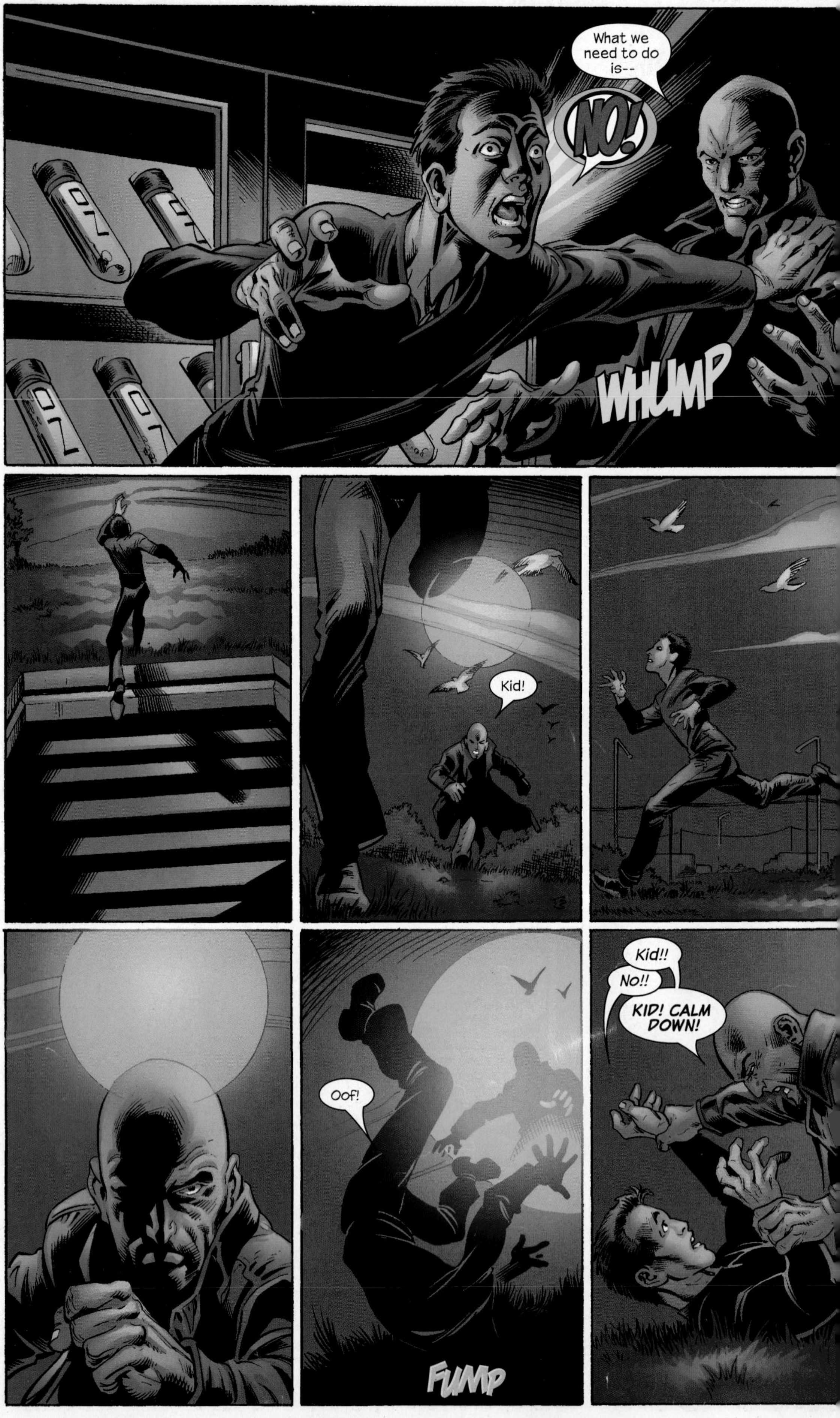
What we need to do is--
NO!
WHUMP
Kid!
Oof!
FUMP
Kid!!
No!!
KID! CALM DOWN!

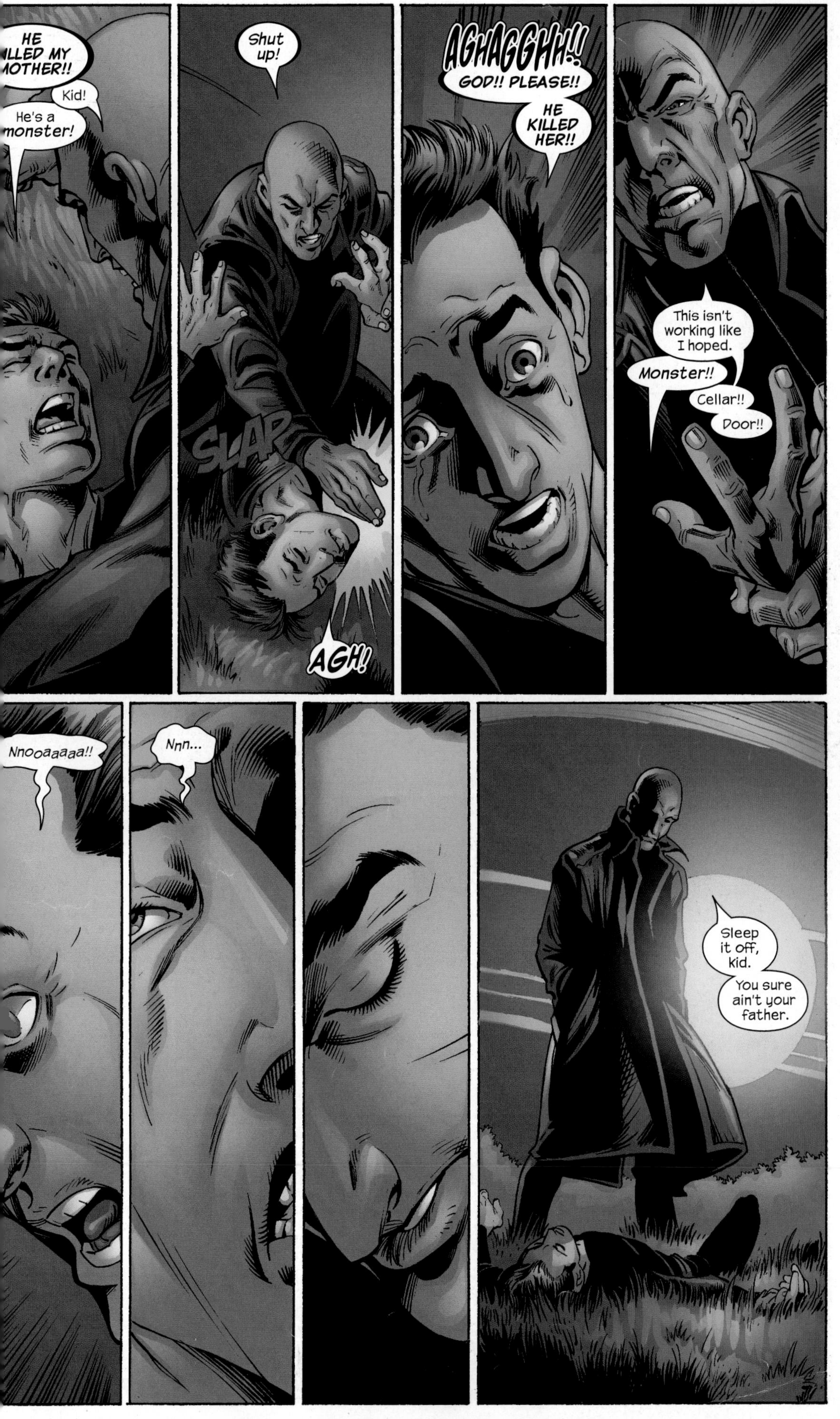
HE ILLED MY OTHER!!
Kid!
He's a monster!
Shut up!
SLAP
AGH!
AGHAGGHH!!
GOD!! PLEASE!!
HE KILLED HER!!
This isn't working like I hoped.
Monster!!
Cellar!!
Door!!
Nnooaaaaa!!
Nnn...
Sleep it off, kid.
You sure ain't your father.

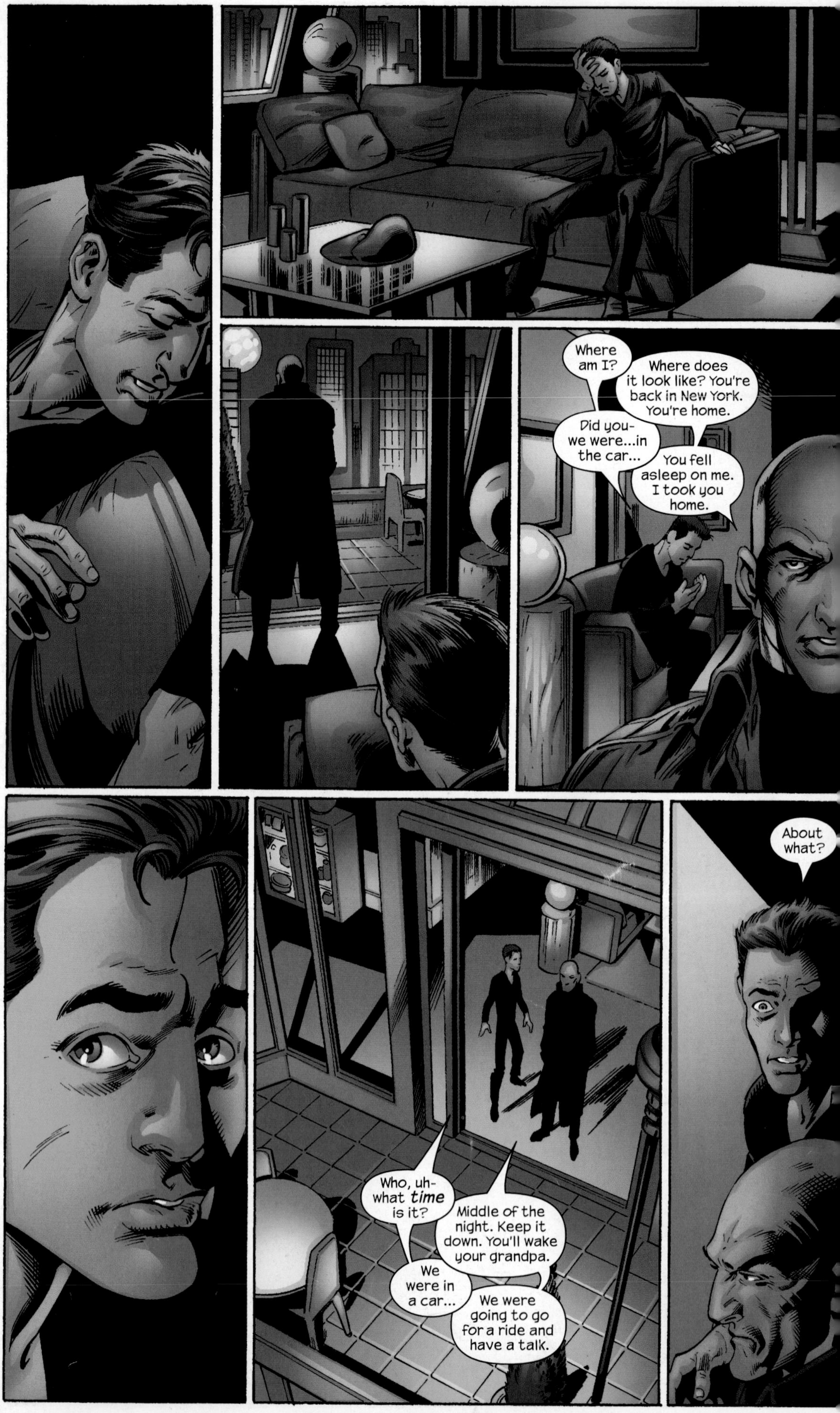

Where am I?
Where does it look like? You're back in New York. You're home.
Did you- we were...in the car...
You fell asleep on me. I took you home.
Who, uh- what *time* is it?
Middle of the night. Keep it down. You'll wake your grandpa.
We were in a car...
We were going to go for a ride and have a talk.
About what?

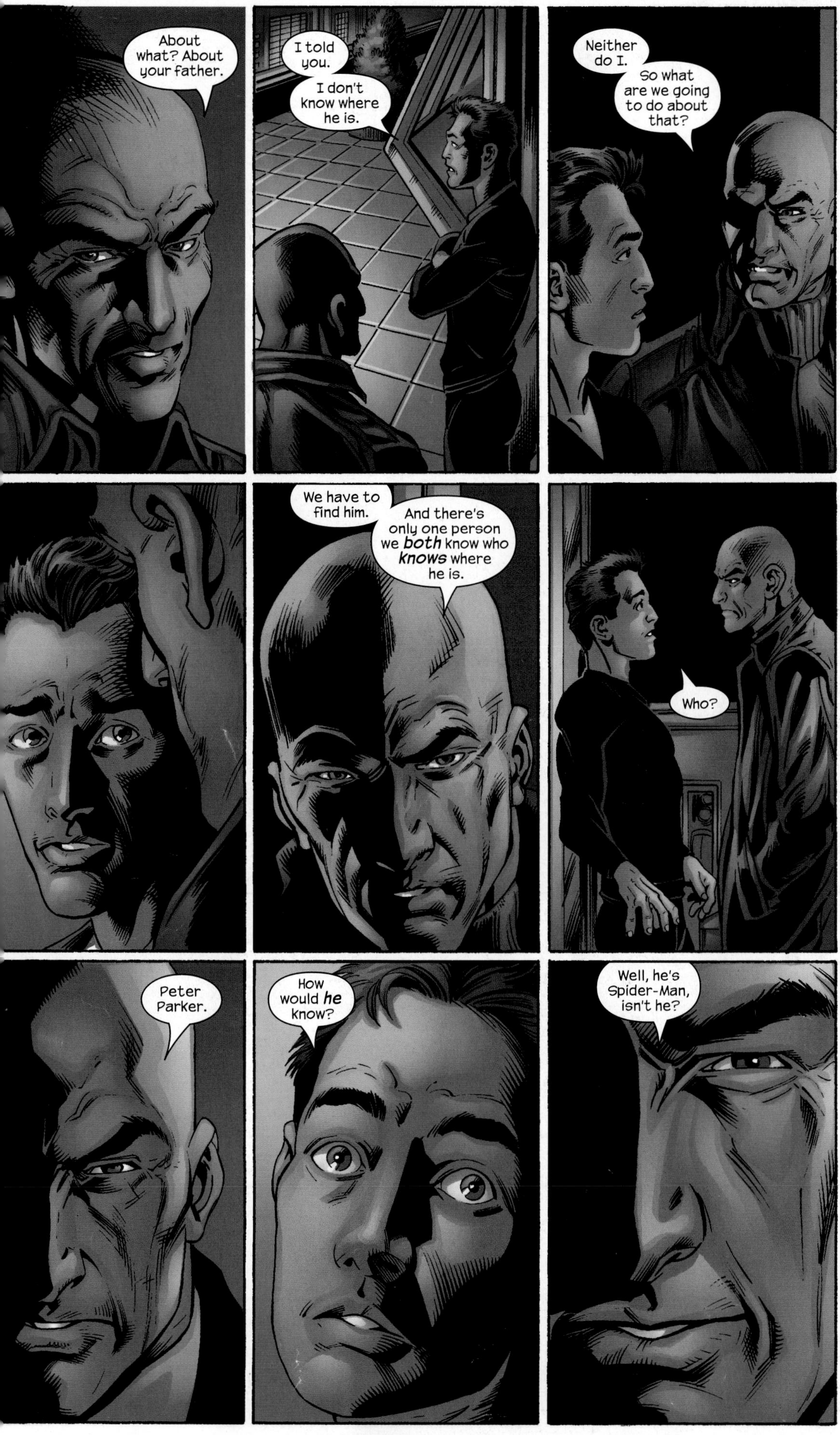
About what? About your father.
I told you.
I don't know where he is.
Neither do I.
So what are we going to do about that?
We have to find him.
And there's only one person we *both* know who *knows* where he is.
Who?
Peter Parker.
How would *he* know?
Well, he's Spider-Man, isn't he?

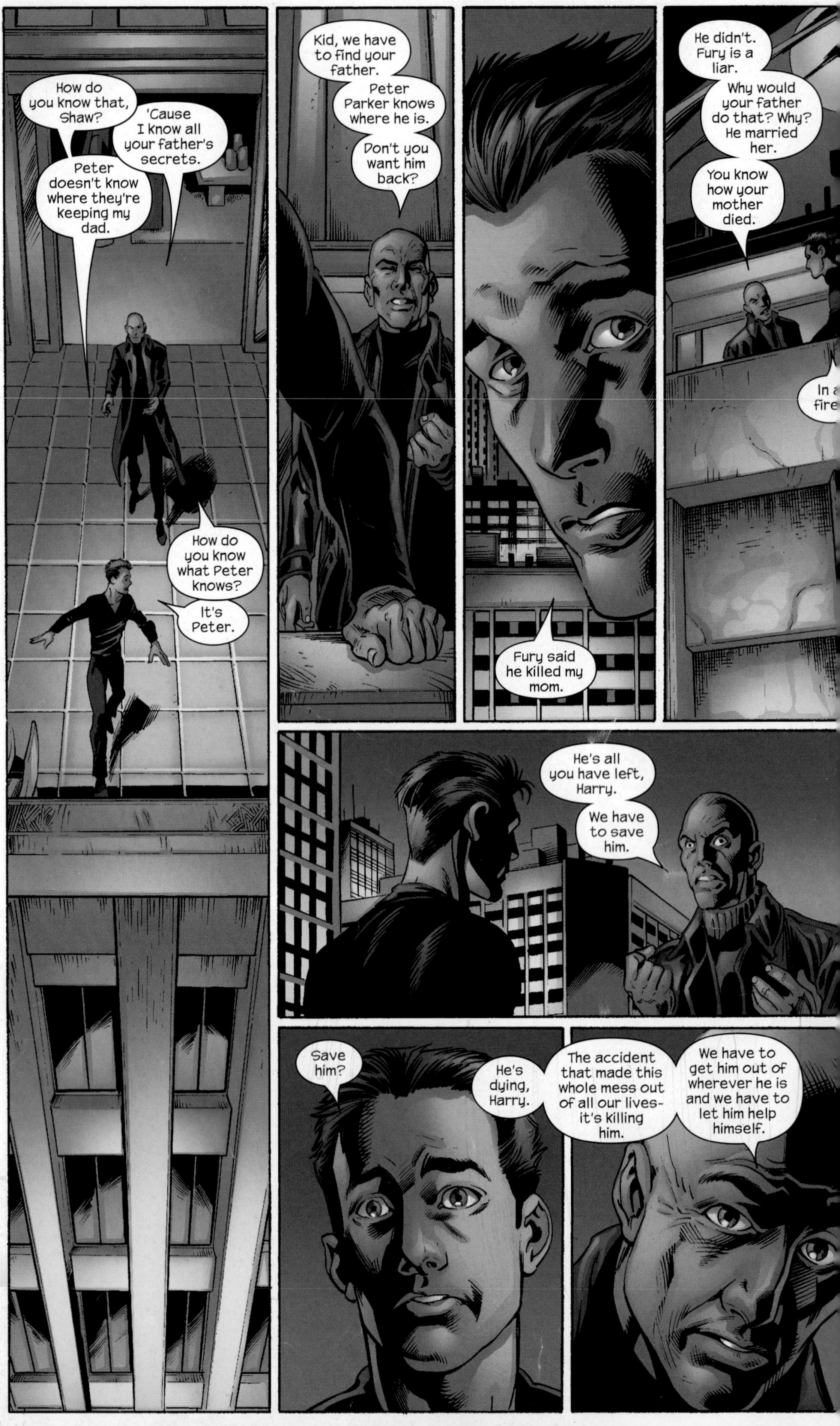
How do you know that, Shaw?
'Cause I know all your father's secrets.
Peter doesn't know where they're keeping my dad.
How do you know what Peter knows?
It's Peter.
Kid, we have to find your father.
Peter Parker knows where he is.
Don't you want him back?
Fury said he killed my mom.
He didn't. Fury is a liar.
Why would your father do that? Why? He married her.
You know how your mother died.
In a fire
He's all you have left, Harry.
We have to save him.
Save him?
He's dying, Harry.
The accident that made this whole mess out of all our lives- it's killing him.
We have to get him out of wherever he is and we have to let him help himself.

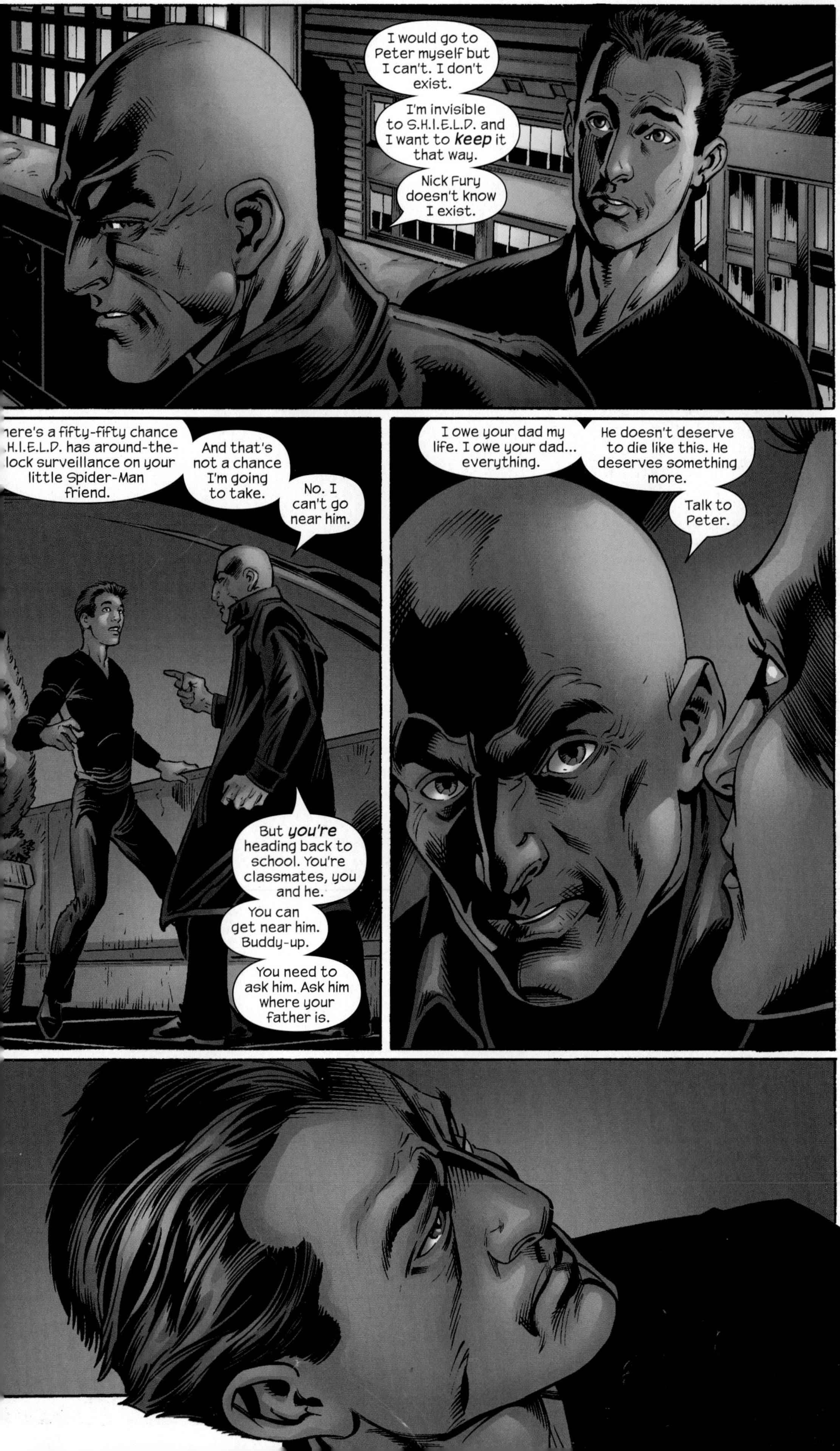

I would go to Peter myself but I can't. I don't exist.
I'm invisible to S.H.I.E.L.D. and I want to keep it that way.
Nick Fury doesn't know I exist.
here's a fifty-fifty chance .H.I.E.L.D. has around-the-lock surveillance on your little Spider-Man friend.
And that's not a chance I'm going to take.
No. I can't go near him.
But you're heading back to school. You're classmates, you and he.
You can get near him. Buddy-up.
You need to ask him. Ask him where your father is.
I owe your dad my life. I owe your dad... everything.
He doesn't deserve to die like this. He deserves something more.
Talk to Peter.

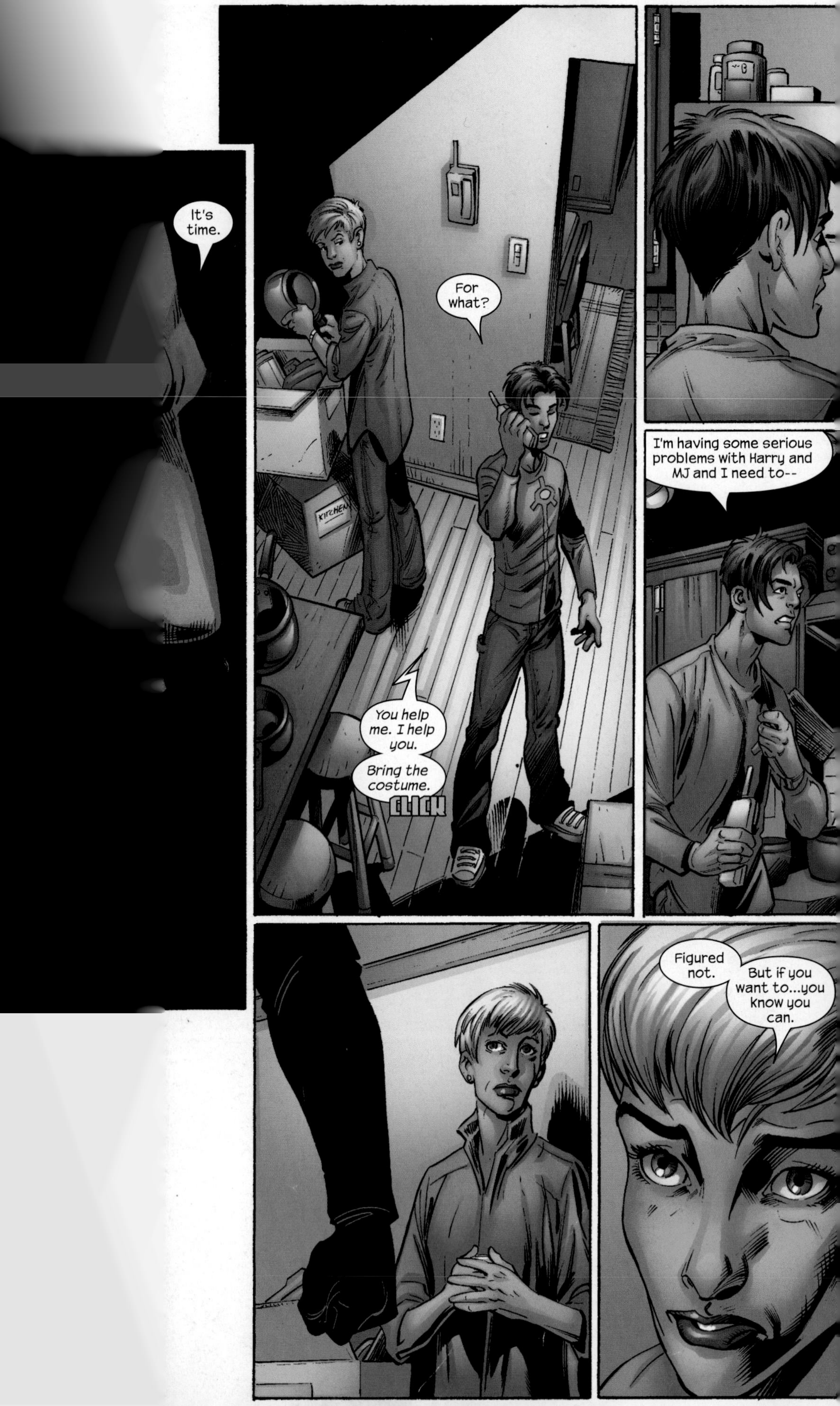
It's time.
For what?
You help me. I help you.
Bring the costume.
CLICK
KITCHEN
I'm having some serious problems with Harry and MJ and I need to--
Figured not.
But if you want to...you know you can.

ave
o back
ut.

Now?

st for
ittle--

No.

Just
for a little
bit!

No. It's eight
o'clock at night
and you're **not** going
into Manhattan in
the middle of the
night.

But--

Absolutely
not!

And you're fifteen
years old and you're
not going into the
city in the middle of
the night.

WHAT THE
HELL?!!

Peter, I'm **sorry**
for whatever is
going on.

Ugh!

If you want
to **talk** about
it--

No.

Just- you're
better off cooling
down and- just go
do your homework
and relax.

You know, sweety,
those Osborns are
nothing but trouble.
They have brought
nothing good to
the world.

Harry's a
troubled boy.
And trouble always
goes looking for
more trouble.

Don't get
sucked into
it.

You're fifty
times better
than them.

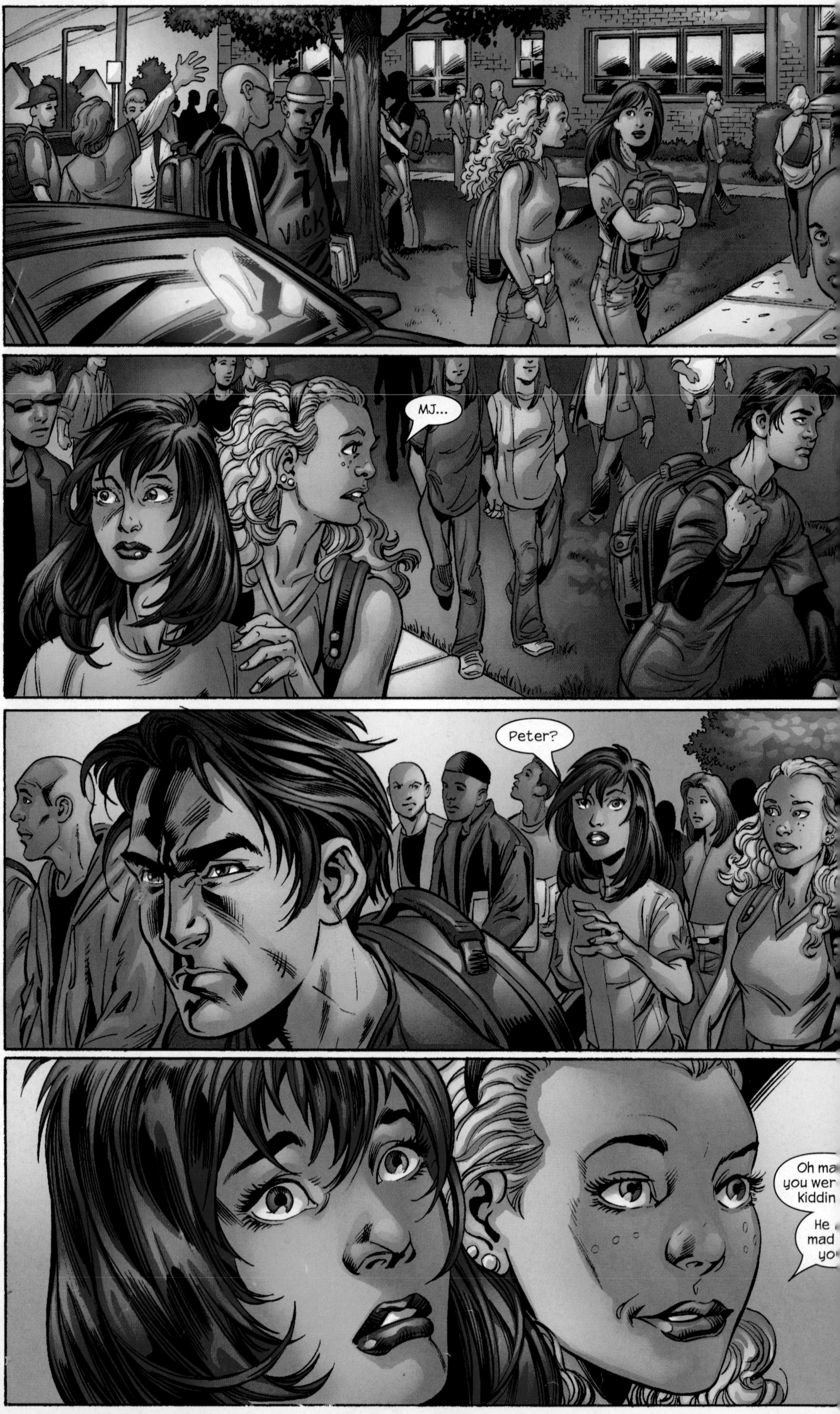
MJ...
Peter?
Oh ma you wer kiddin
He mad yo

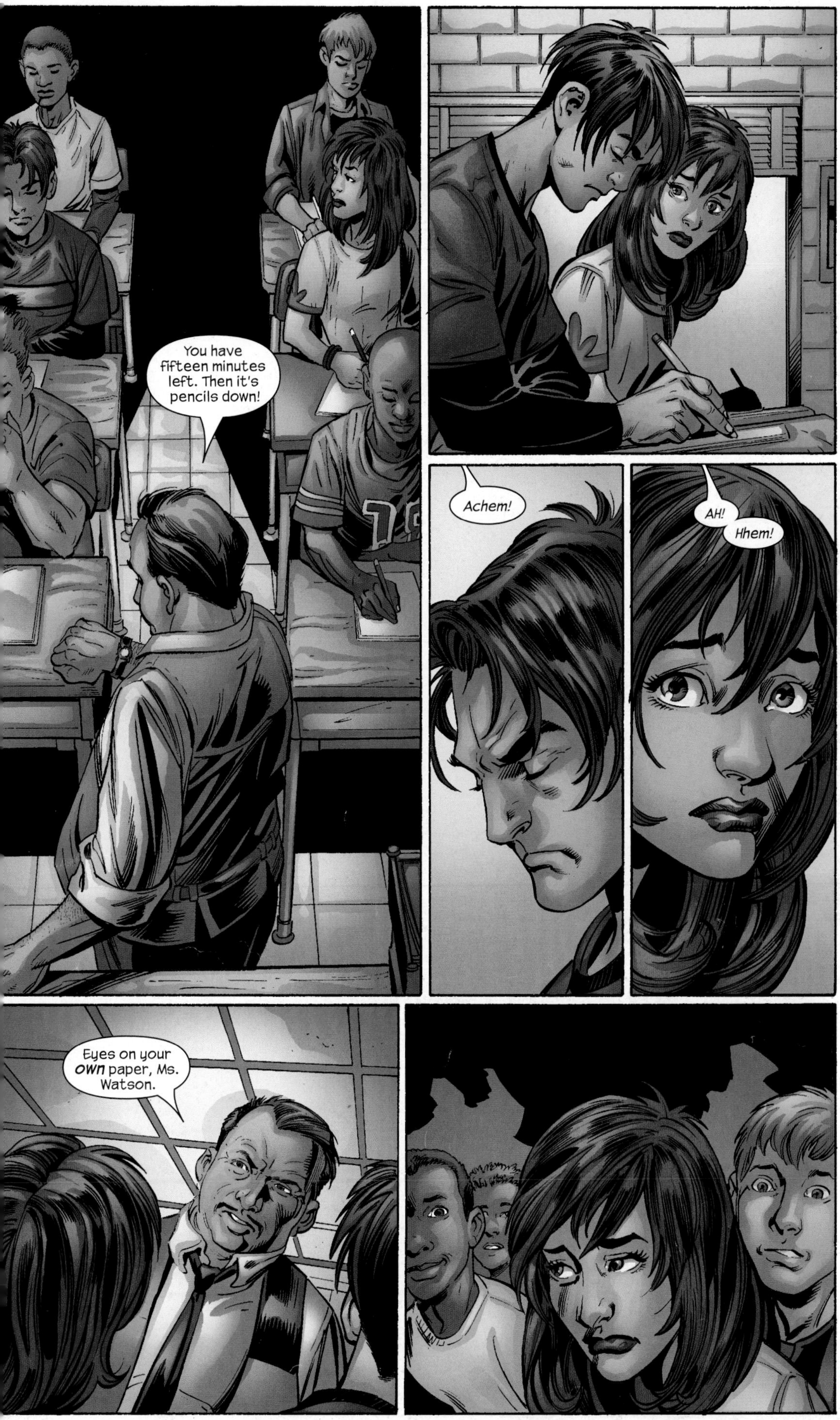
You have fifteen minutes left. Then it's pencils down!
Achem!
AH!
Hhem!
Eyes on your OWN paper, Ms. Watson.

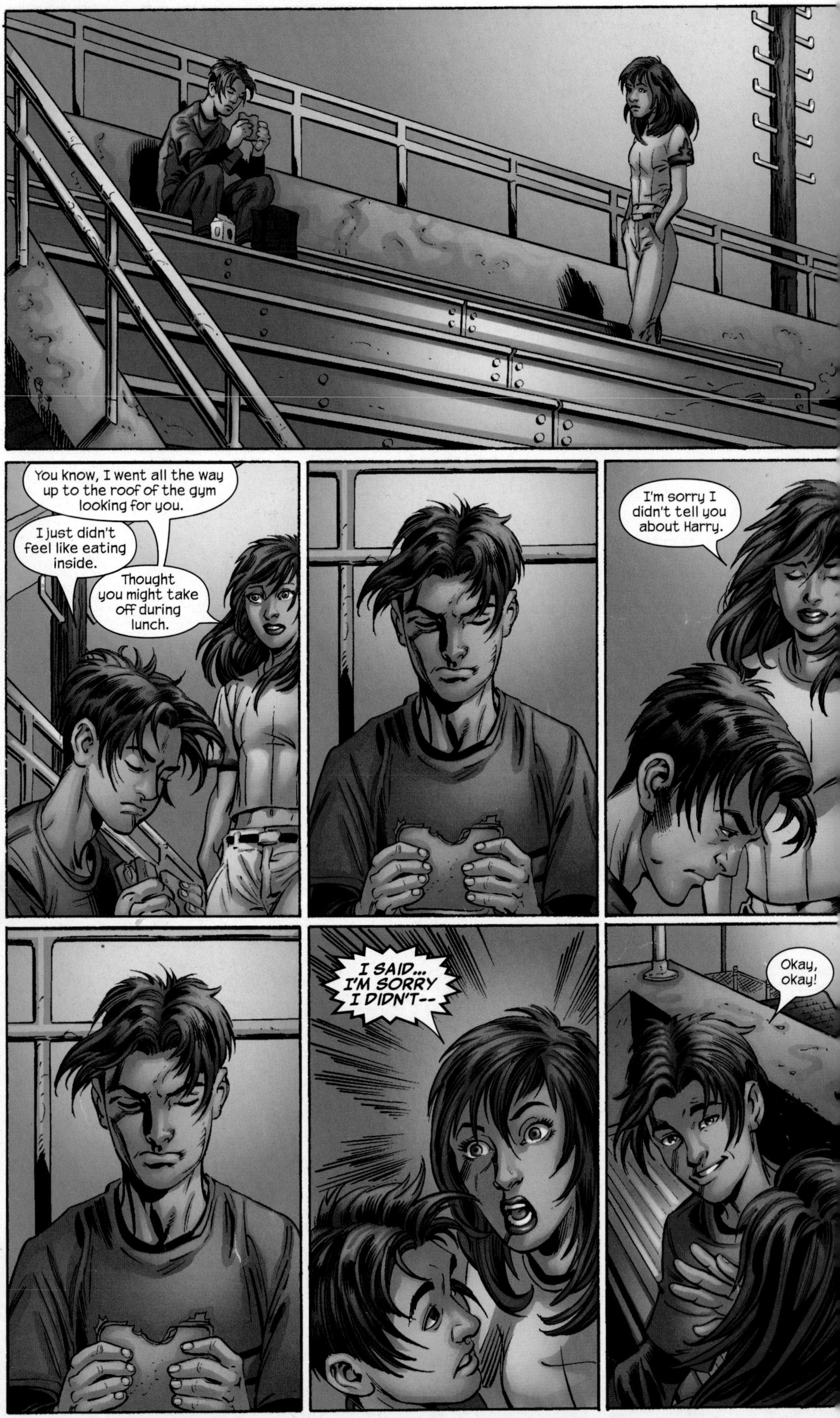
You know, I went all the way up to the roof of the gym looking for you.
I just didn't feel like eating inside.
Thought you might take off during lunch.
I'm sorry I didn't tell you about Harry.
I SAID... I'M SORRY I DIDN'T--
Okay, okay!

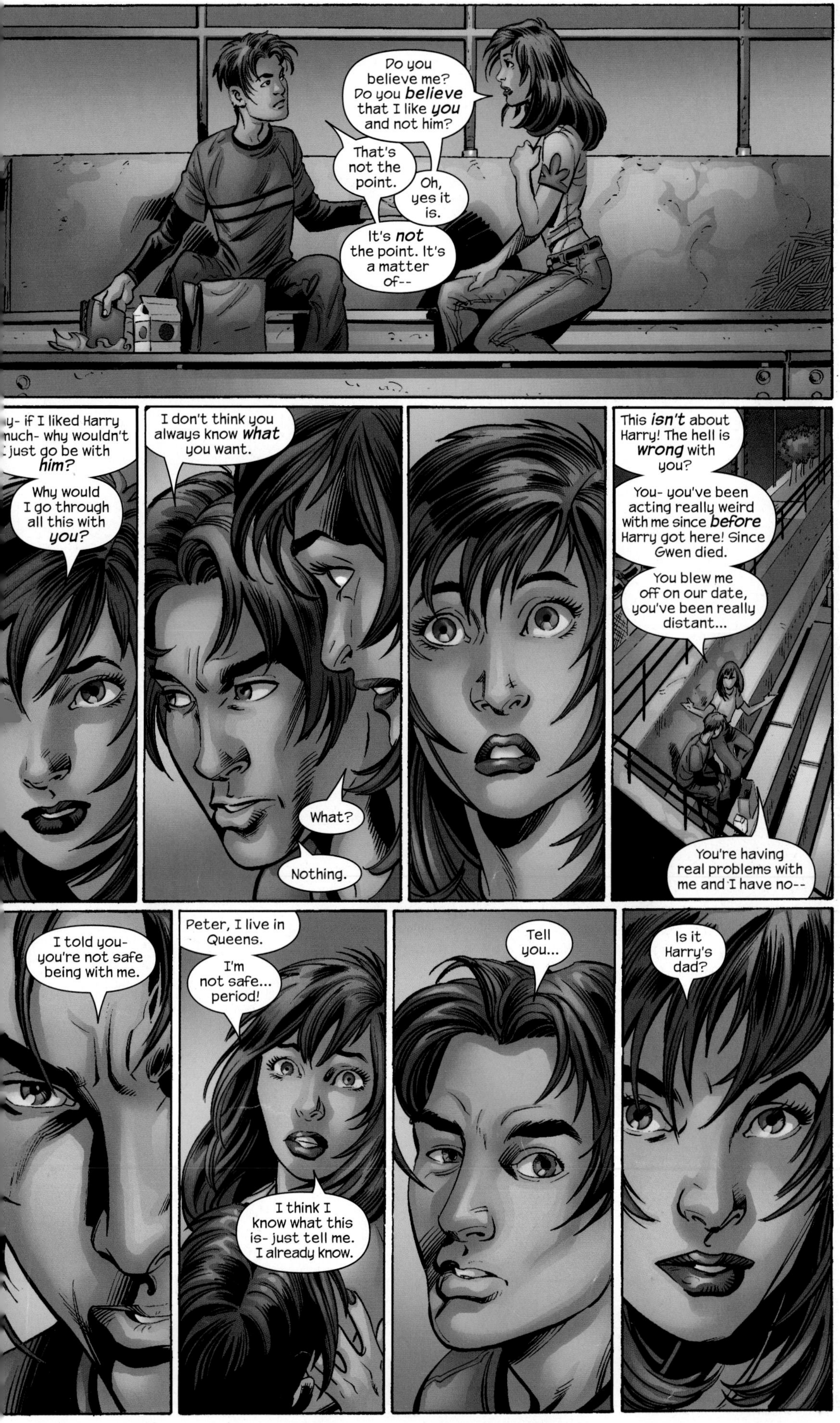

Do you believe me? Do you *believe* that I like *you* and not him?
That's not the point.
Oh, yes it is.
It's *not* the point. It's a matter of--
y- if I liked Harry much- why wouldn't I just go be with *him?*
Why would I go through all this with *you?*
I don't think you always know *what* you want.
What?
Nothing.
This *isn't* about Harry! The hell is *wrong* with you?
You- you've been acting really weird with me since *before* Harry got here! Since Gwen died.
You blew me off on our date, you've been really distant...
You're having real problems with me and I have no--
I told you- you're not safe being with me.
Peter, I live in Queens.
I'm not safe... period!
I think I know what this is- just tell me. I already know.
Tell you...
Is it Harry's dad?

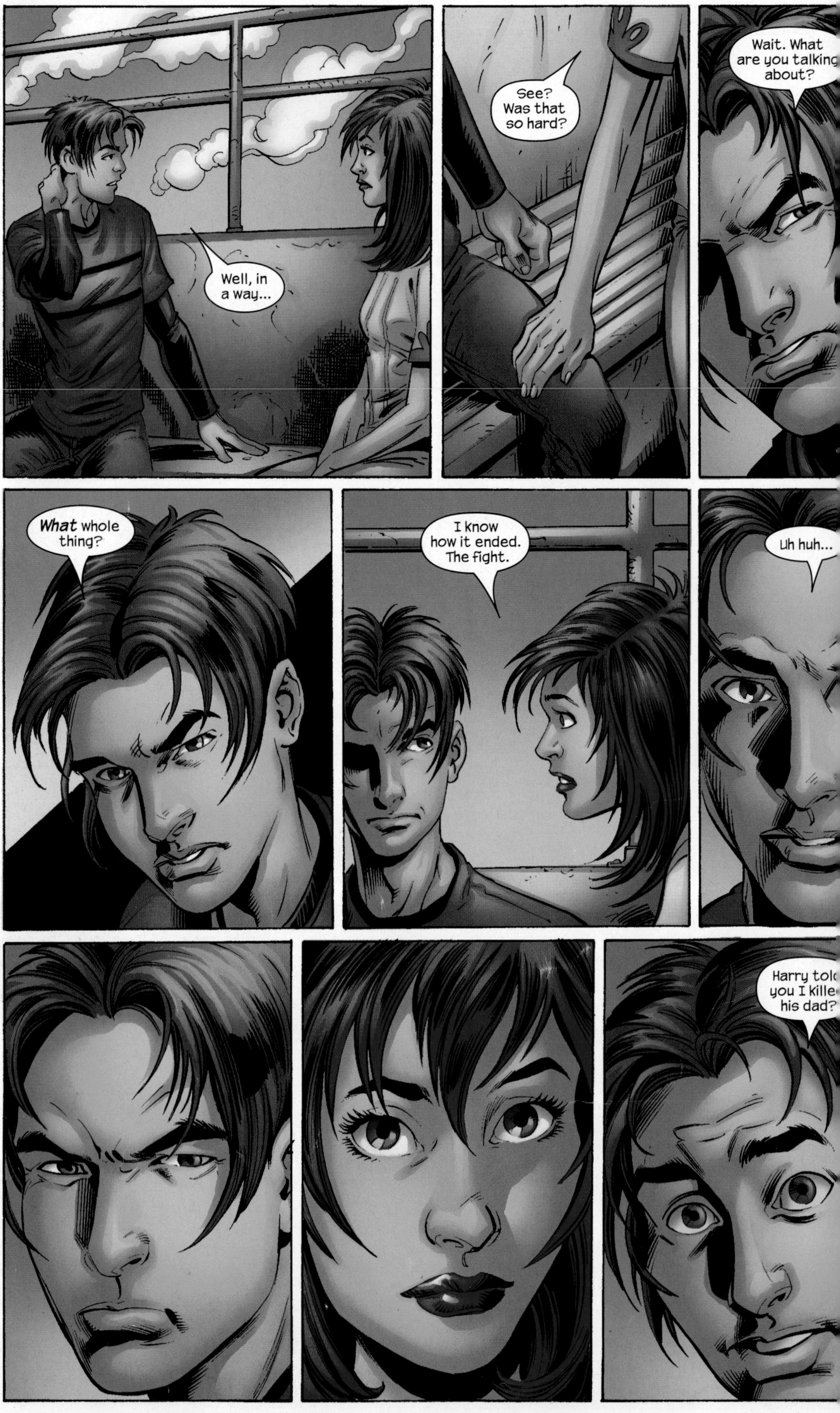
Well, in a way...
See? Was that so hard?
Wait. What are you talking about?
What whole thing?
I know how it ended. The fight.
Uh huh...
Harry tol
you I kille
his dad?

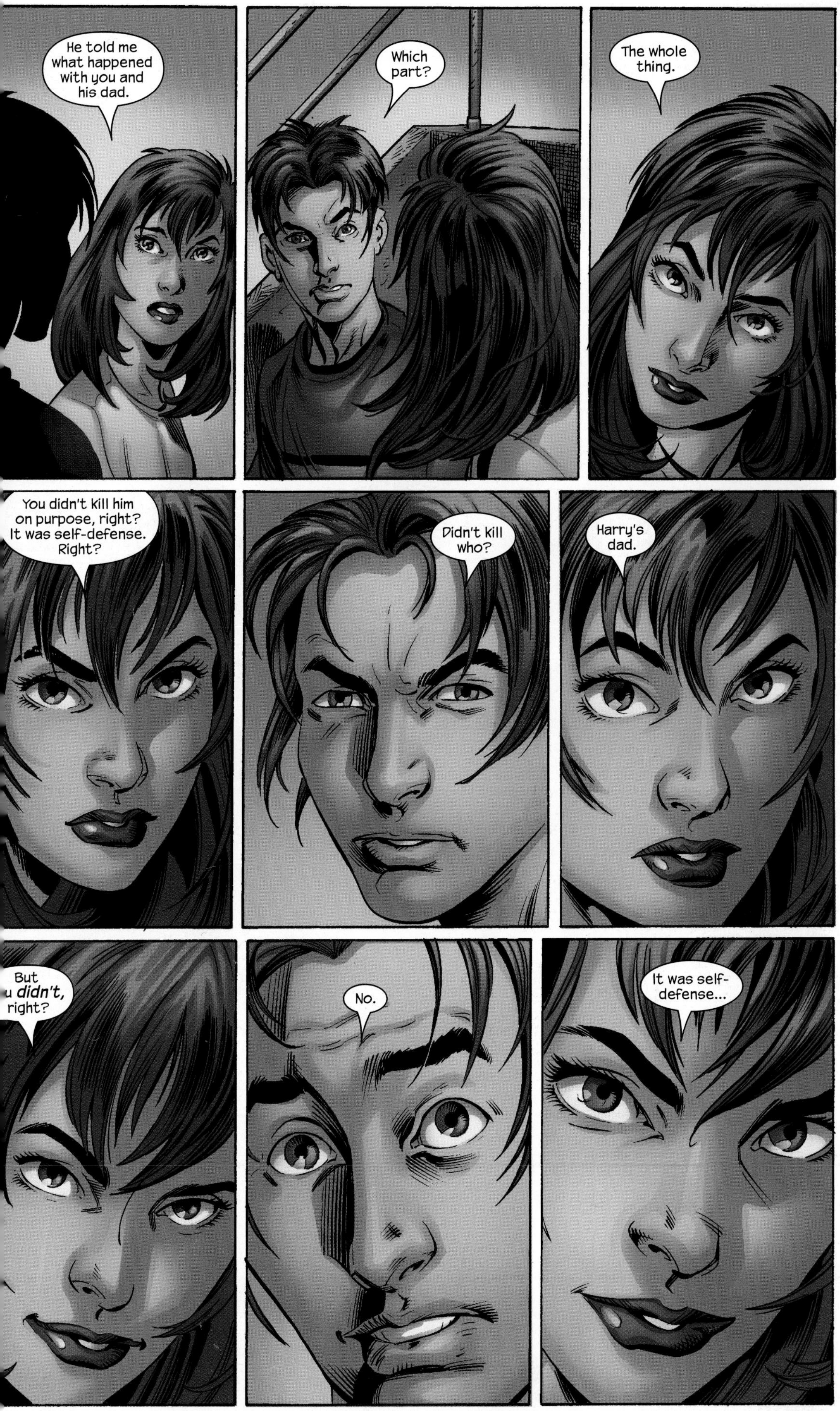
He told me what happened with you and his dad.
Which part?
The whole thing.
You didn't kill him on purpose, right? It was self-defense. Right?
Didn't kill who?
Harry's dad.
But u *didn't,* right?
No.
It was self-defense...

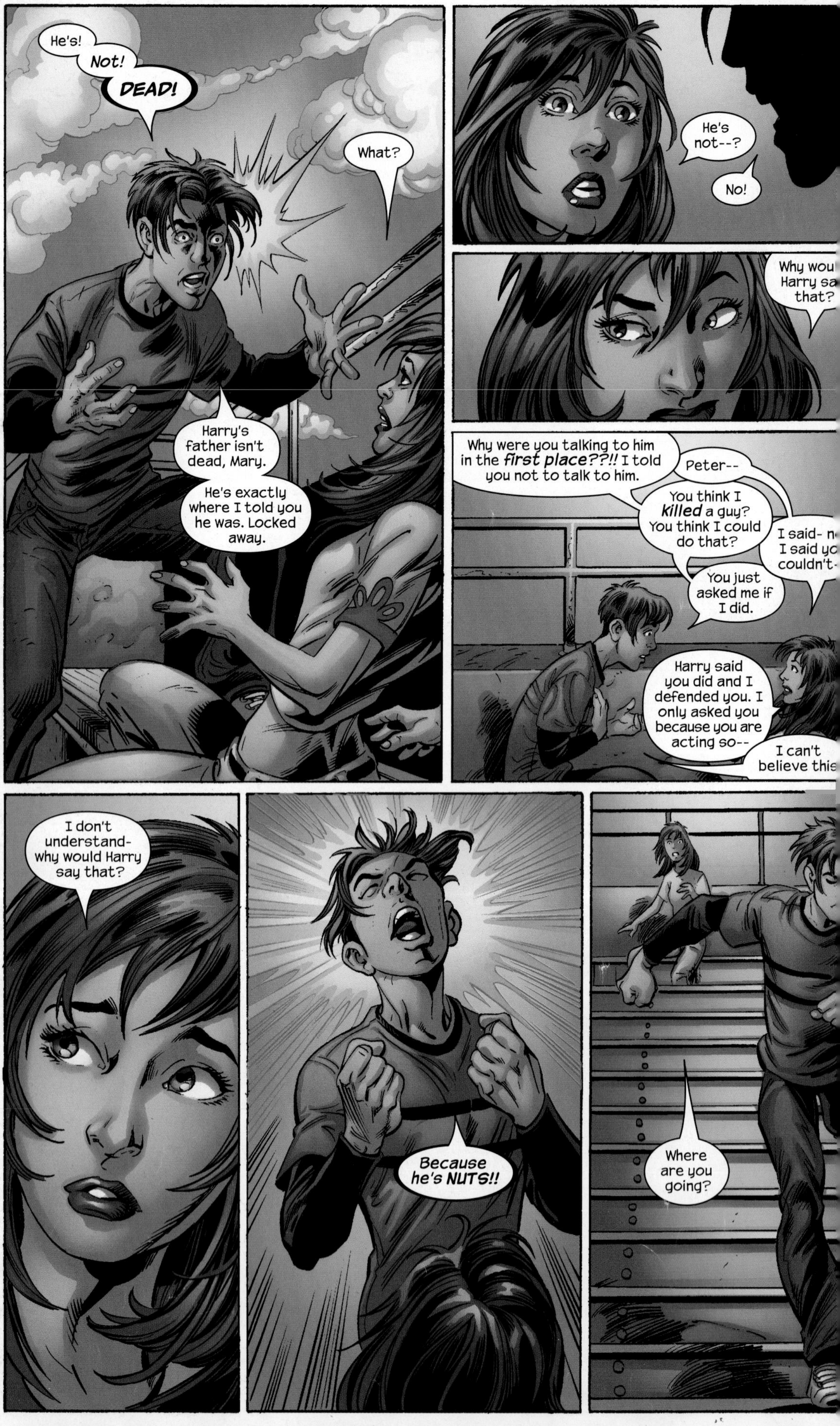
He's!
Not!
DEAD!
What?
Harry's father isn't dead, Mary.
He's exactly where I told you he was. Locked away.
He's not--?
No!
Why wou
Harry sa
that?
Why were you talking to him in the first place??!! I told you not to talk to him.
Peter--
You think I killed a guy? You think I could do that?
I said- n
I said yo
couldn't-
You just asked me if I did.
Harry said you did and I defended you. I only asked you because you are acting so--
I can't believe this
I don't understand- why would Harry say that?
Because he's NUTS!!
Where are you going?

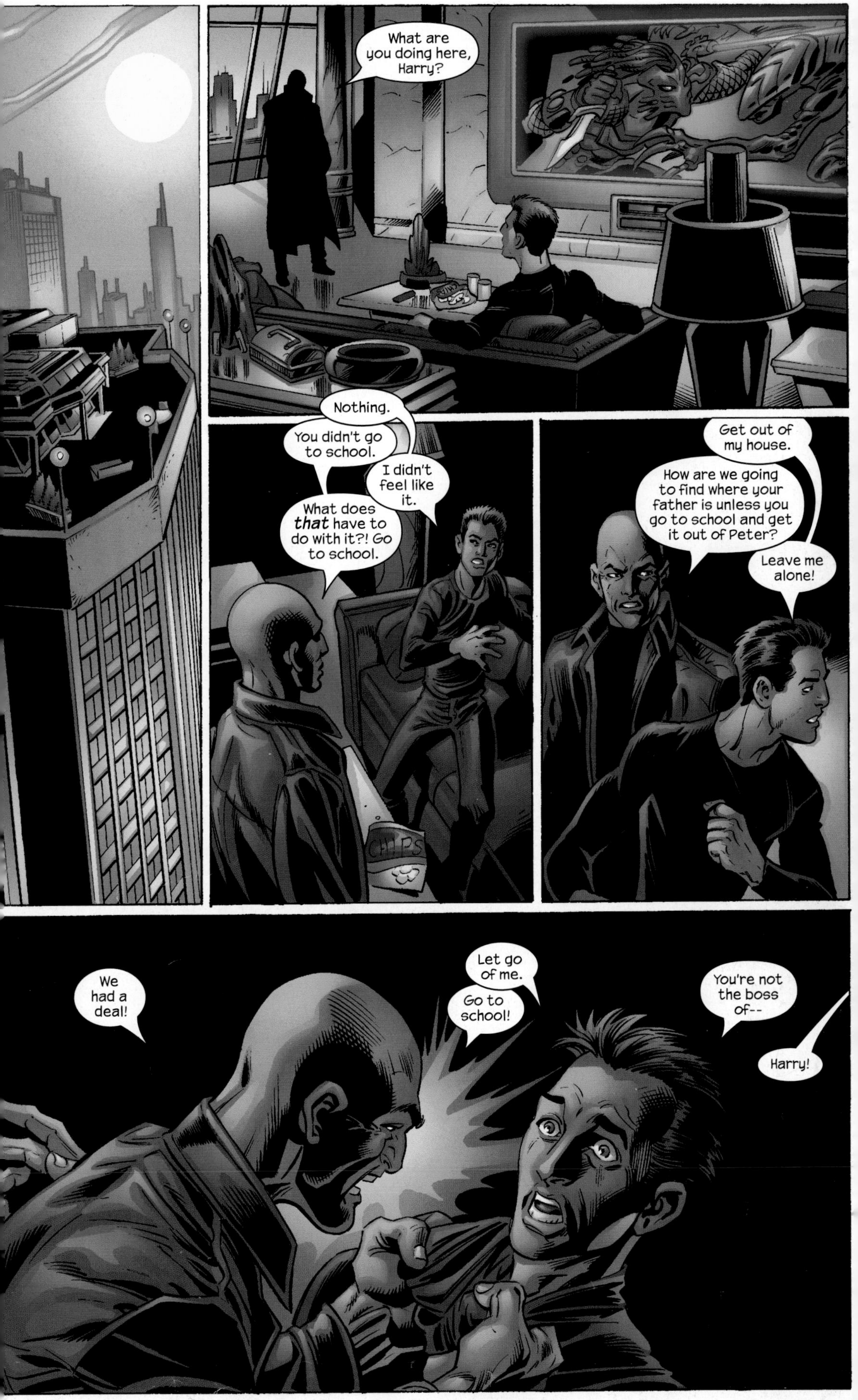
What are you doing here, Harry?
Nothing.
You didn't go to school.
I didn't feel like it.
What does *that* have to do with it?! Go to school.
CHIPS
Get out of my house.
How are we going to find where your father is unless you go to school and get it out of Peter?
Leave me alone!
We had a deal!
Let go of me.
Go to school!
You're not the boss of--
Harry!

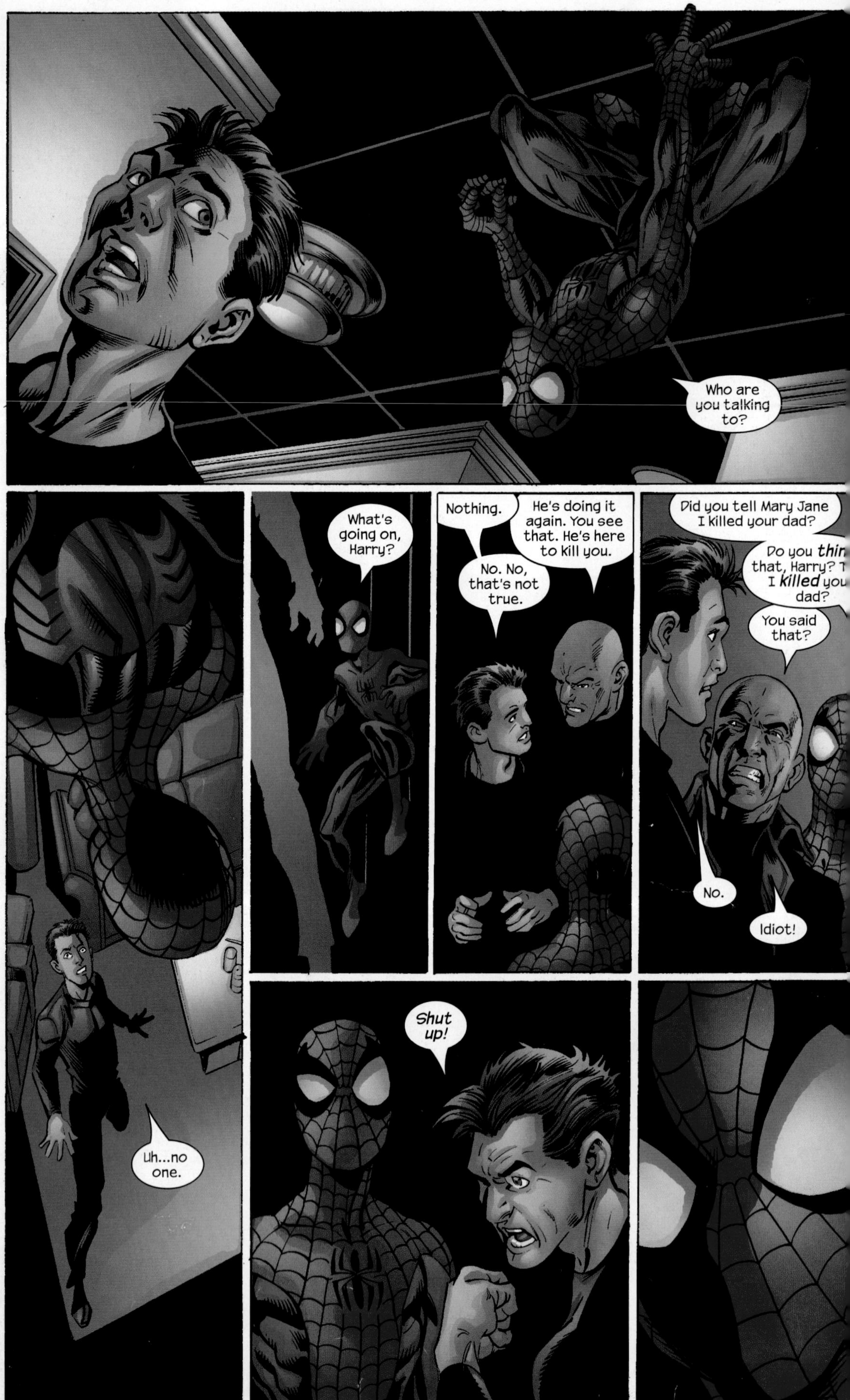

Who are you talking to?
Uh...no one.
What's going on, Harry?
Nothing.
He's doing it again. You see that. He's here to kill you.
No. No, that's not true.
Did you tell Mary Jane I killed your dad?
Do you thin that, Harry? T I killed you dad?
You said that?
No.
Idiot!
Shut up!

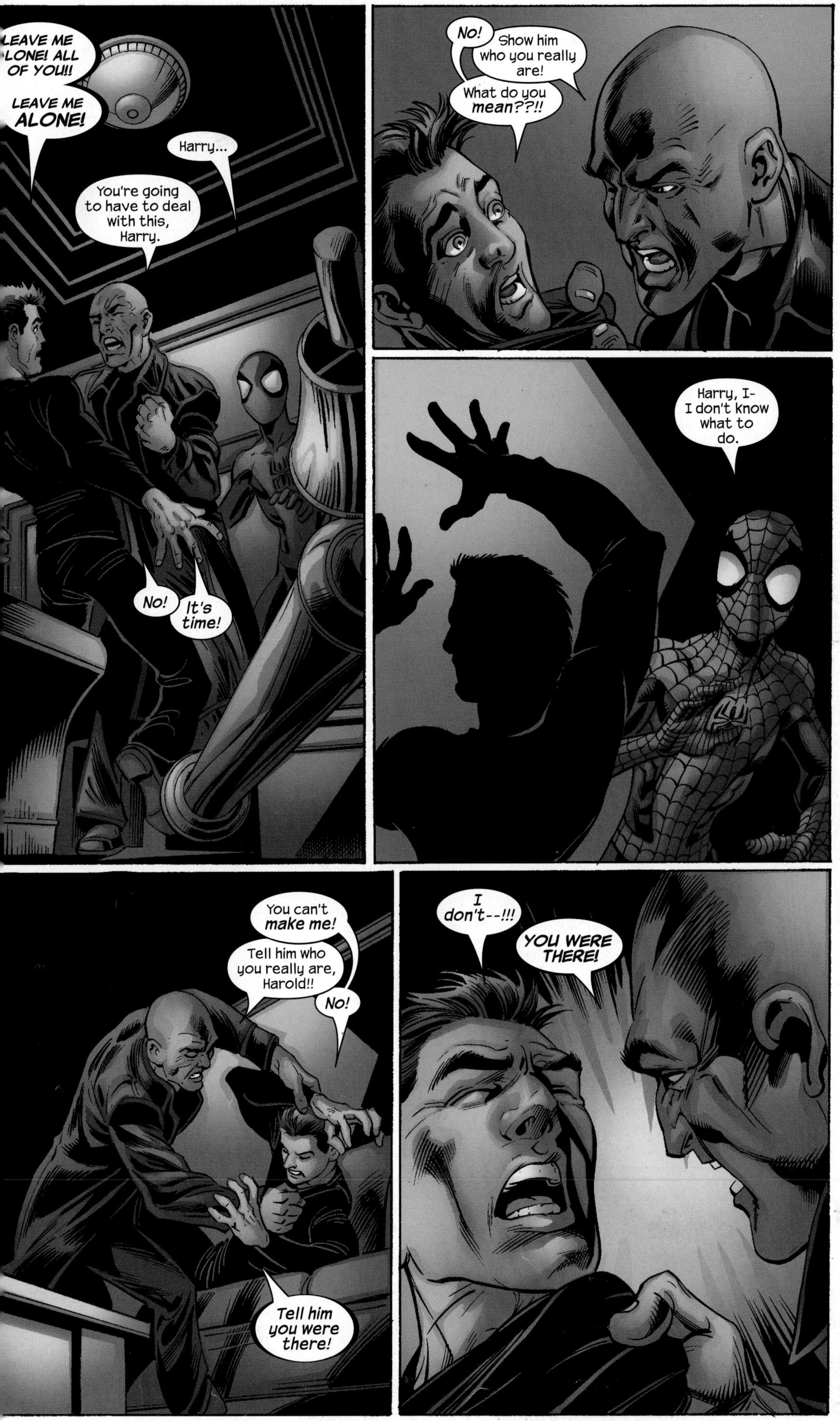
LEAVE ME LONE! ALL OF YOU!!
LEAVE ME ALONE!
Harry...
You're going to have to deal with this, Harry.
No!
It's time!
No!
Show him who you really are!
What do you mean??!!
Harry, I- I don't know what to do.
You can't make me!
Tell him who you really are, Harold!!
No!
Tell him you were there!
I don't--!!!
YOU WERE THERE!

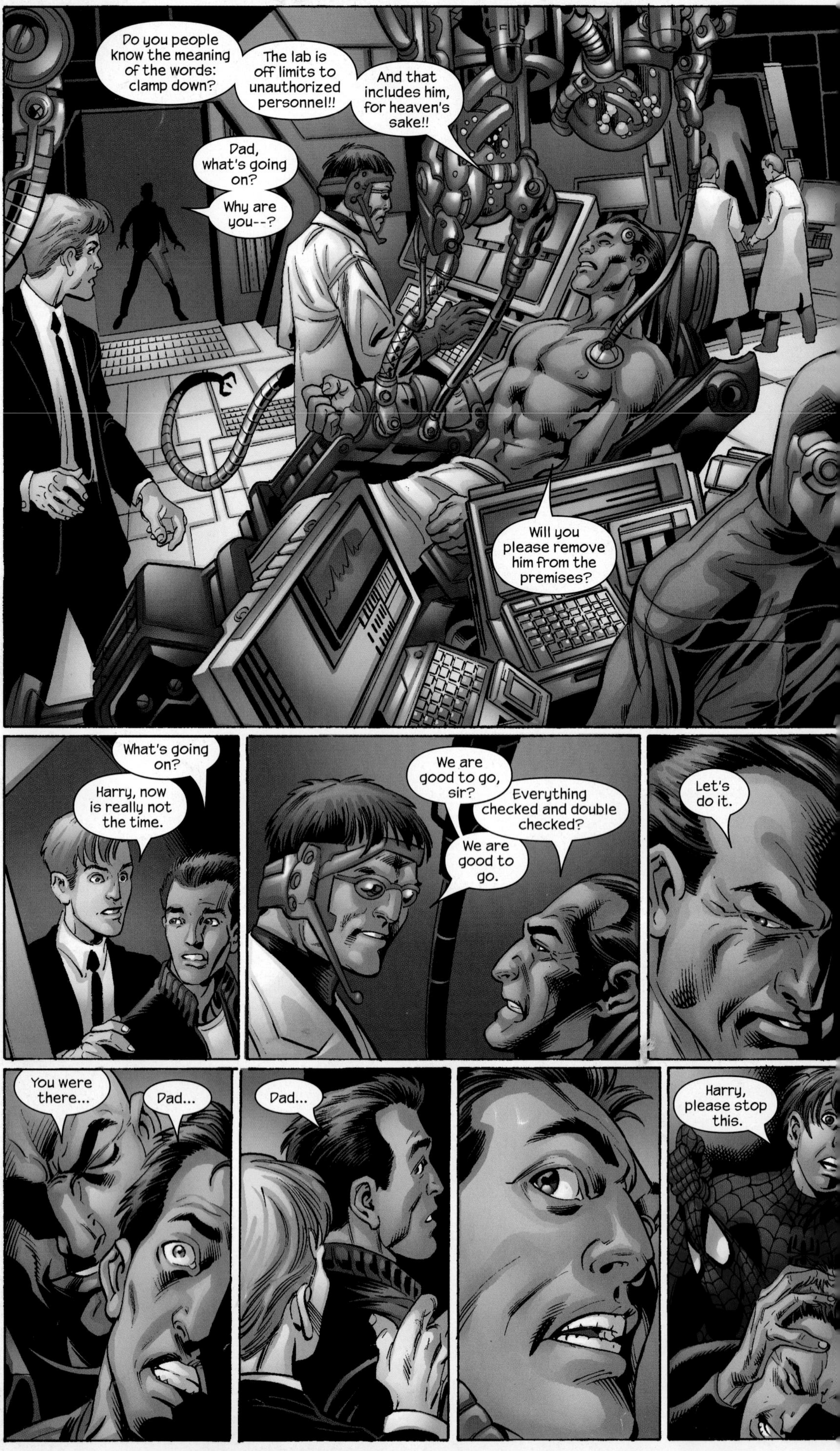

Do you people know the meaning of the words: clamp down?
The lab is off limits to unauthorized personnel!!
And that includes him, for heaven's sake!!
Dad, what's going on?
Why are you--?
Will you please remove him from the premises?
What's going on?
Harry, now is really not the time.
We are good to go, sir?
Everything checked and double checked?
We are good to go.
Let's do it.
You were there...
Dad...
Dad...
Harry, please stop this.

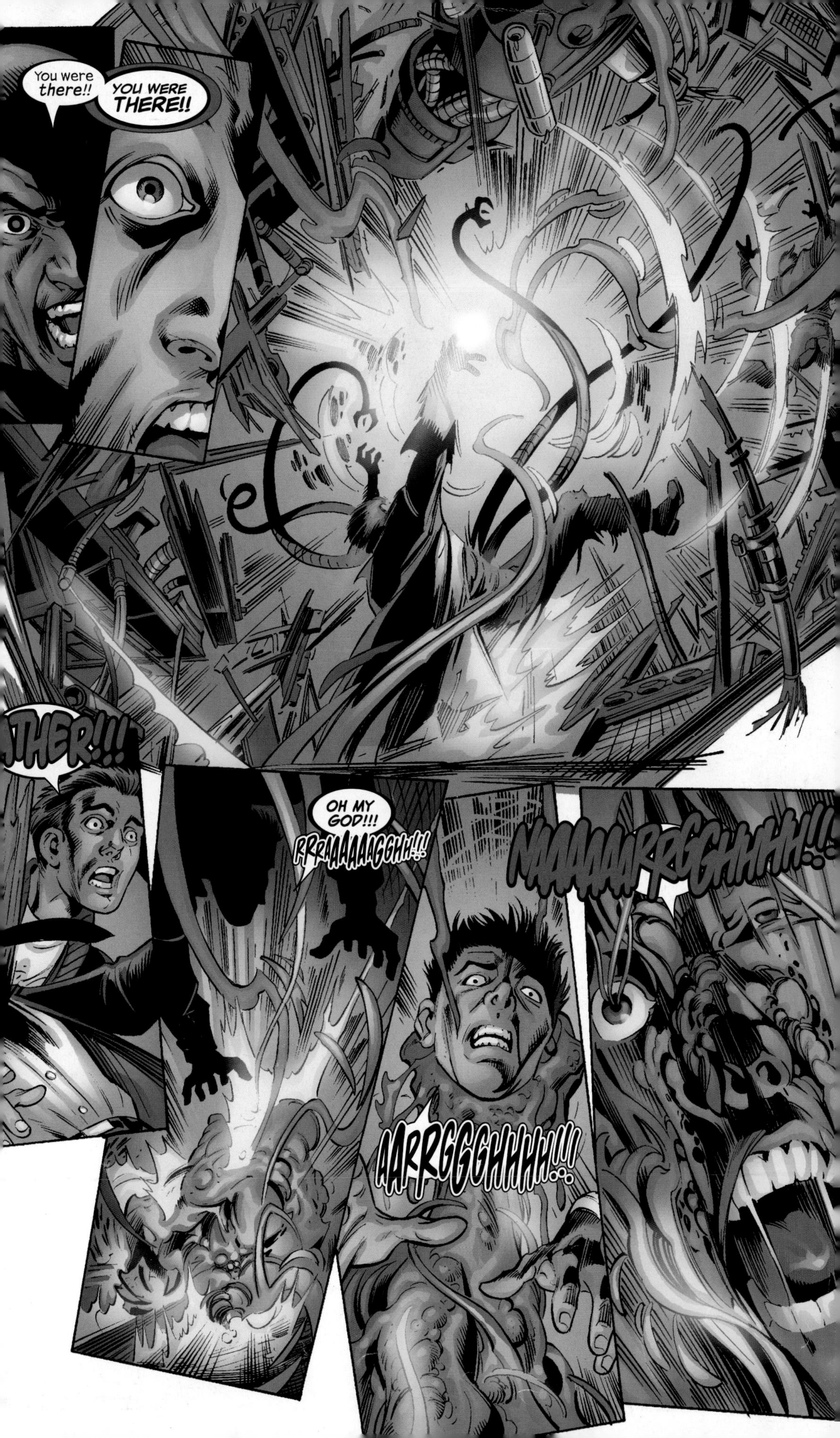
You were there!!
YOU WERE THERE!!
THER!!!
OH MY GOD!!!
RRRAAAAAAGGHH!!!
NAAAAARRGHHHH!!!
AARRGGGHHHH!!!

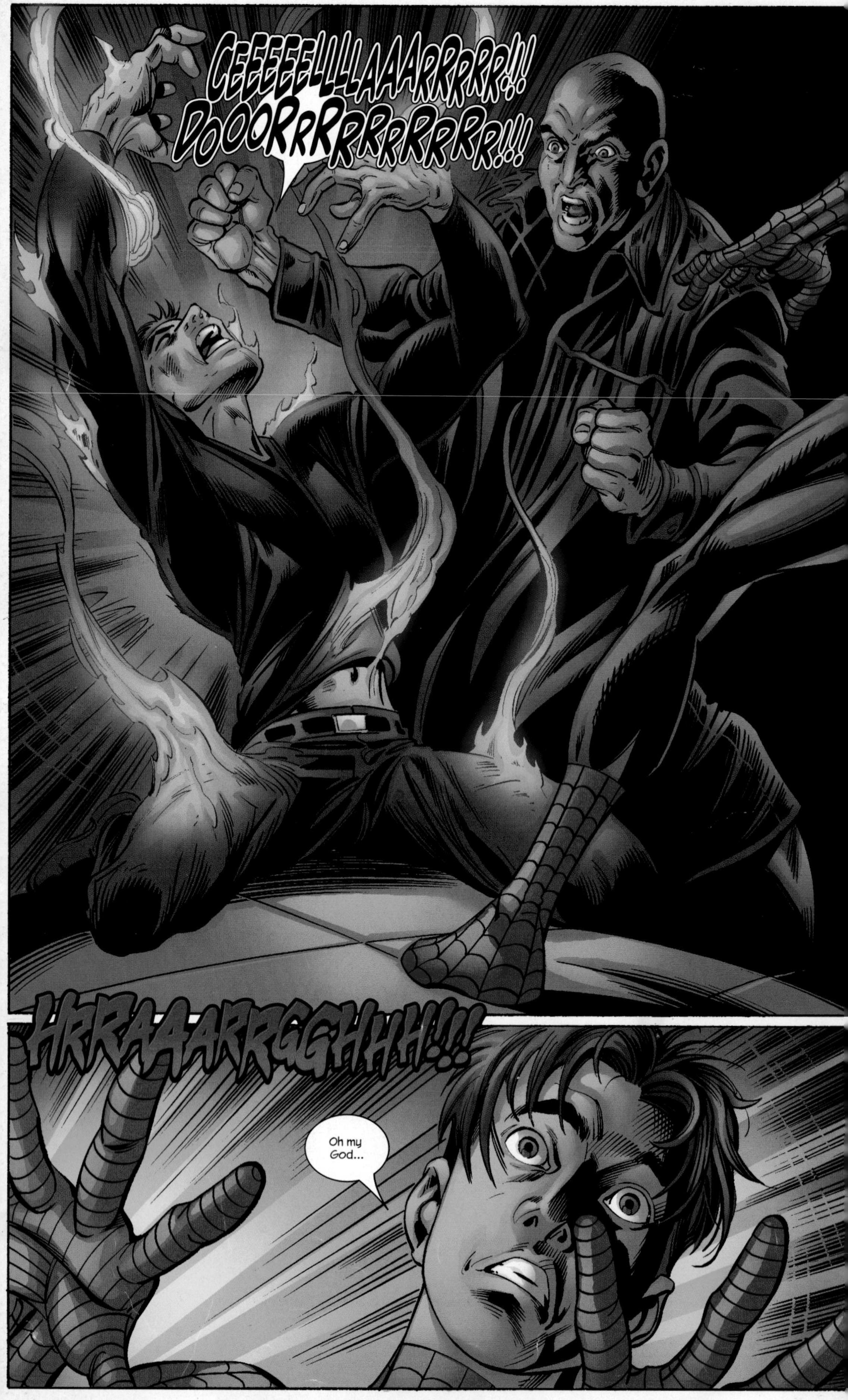
CEEEEELLLLAAARRRRR!!! DOOORRRRRRRRRR!!!
HRRAAARRGGHHH!!!
Oh my God...

76

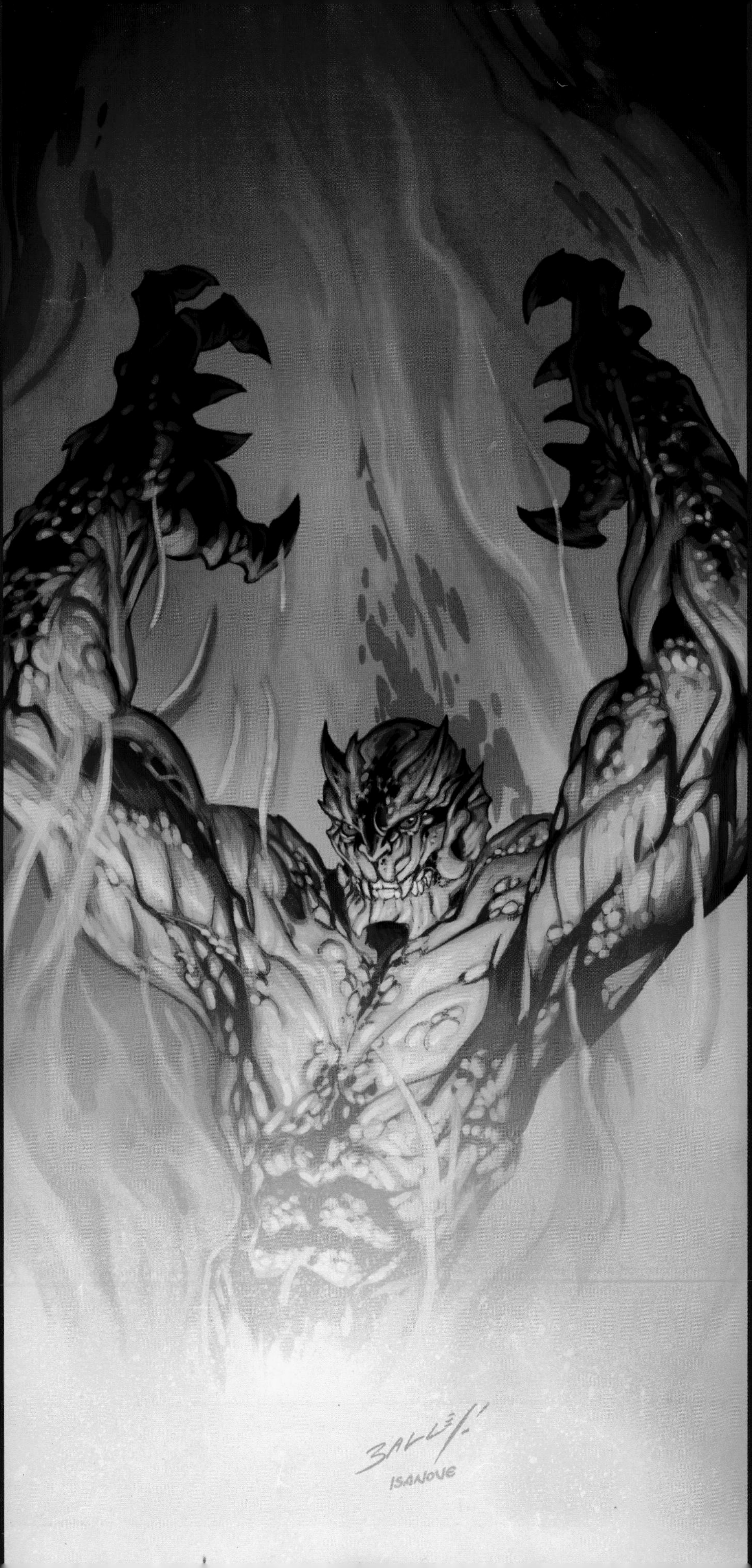
ISANOVE

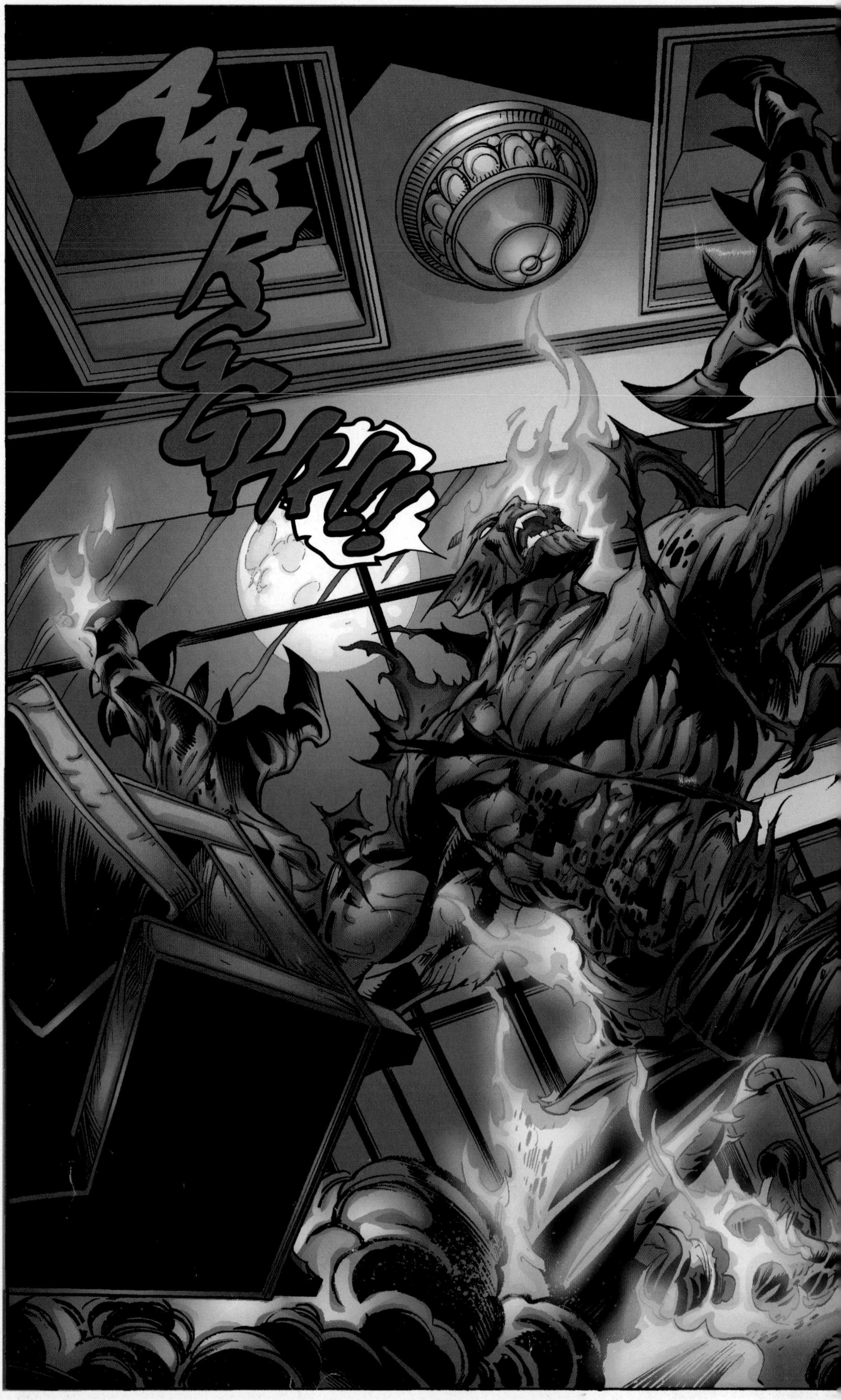
AARRGGHH!!

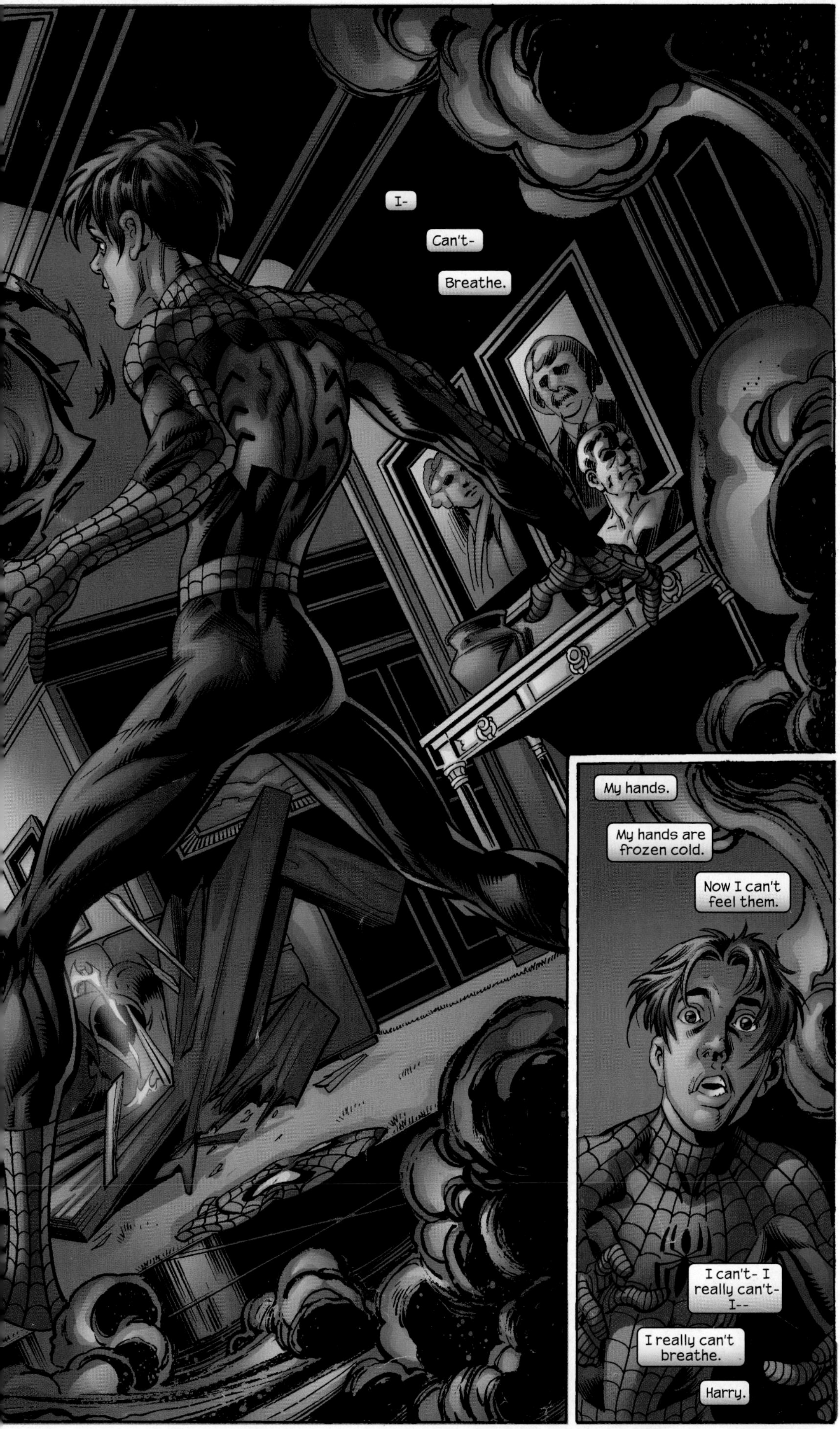
I-
Can't-
Breathe.
My hands.
My hands are frozen cold.
Now I can't feel them.
I can't- I really can't- I--
I really can't breathe.
Harry.

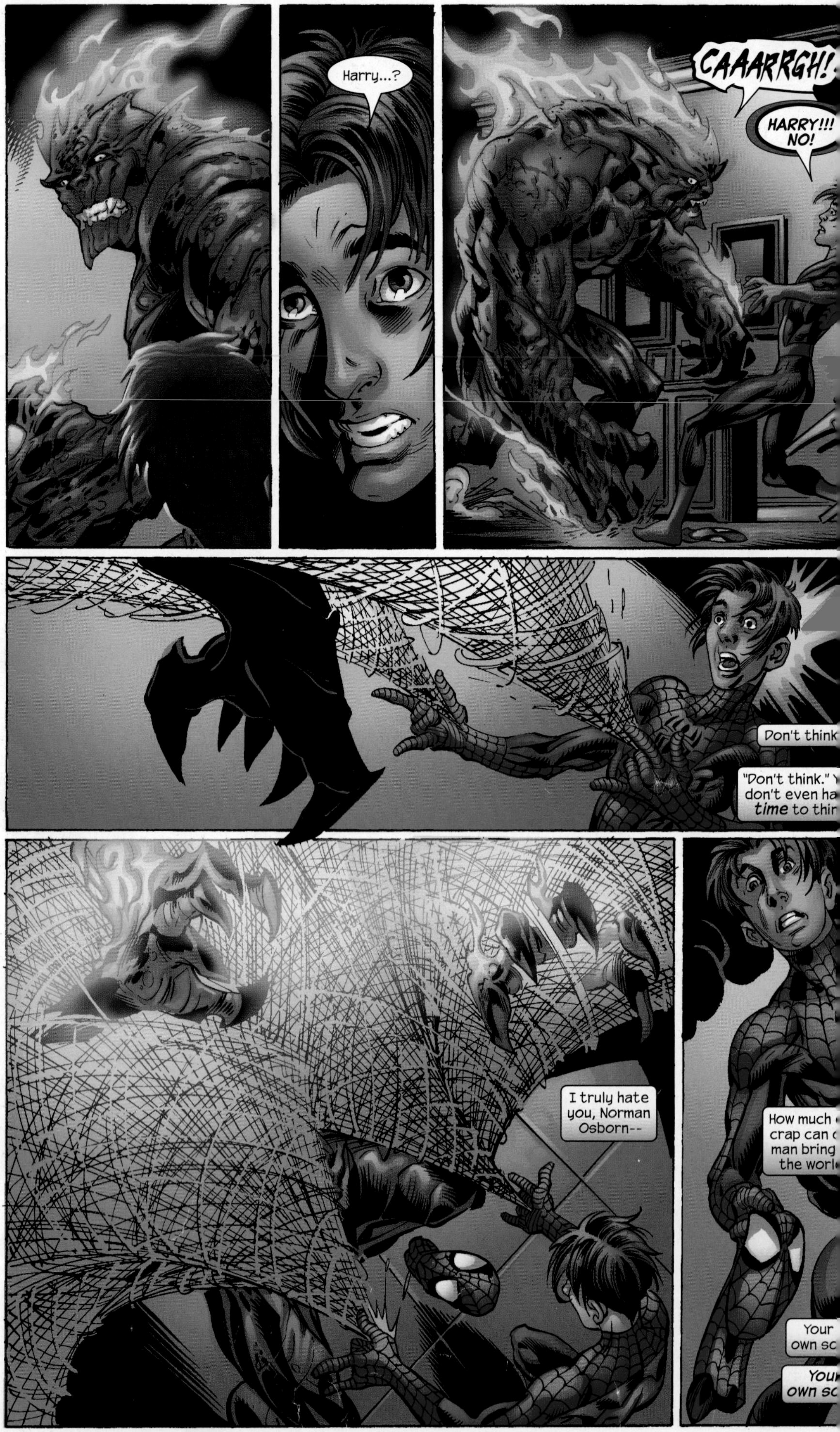

Harry...?
CAAARRGH!
HARRY!!! NO!
Don't think
"Don't think." Y don't even ha time to thir
I truly hate you, Norman Osborn--
How much crap can man bring the worl
Your own sc
Your own sc

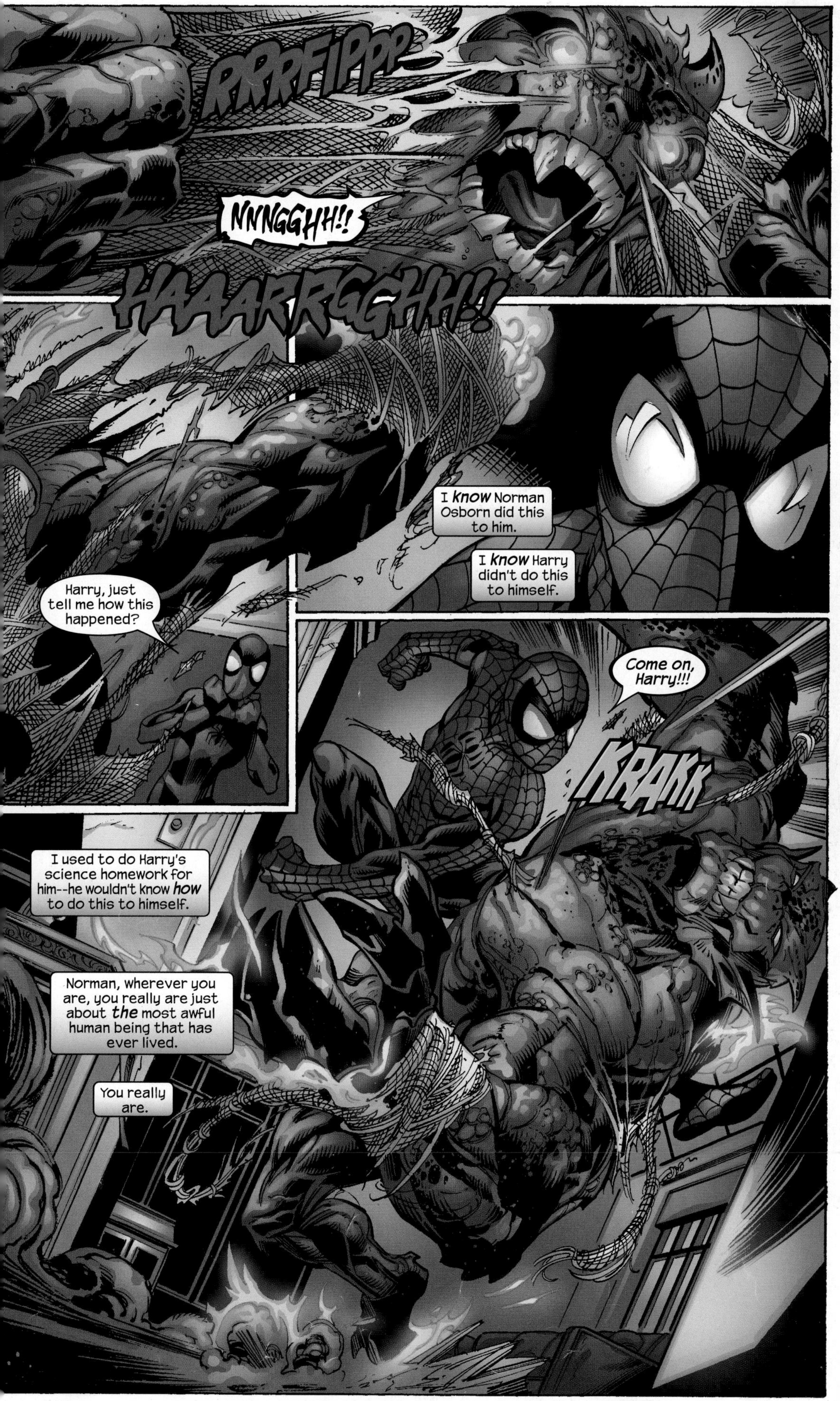
RRRFIPPP
NNNGGHH!!
HAAARRGGHH!!
Harry, just tell me how this happened?
I know Norman Osborn did this to him.
I know Harry didn't do this to himself.
Come on, Harry!!!
KRAKK
I used to do Harry's science homework for him--he wouldn't know how to do this to himself.
Norman, wherever you are, you really are just about the most awful human being that has ever lived.
You really are.

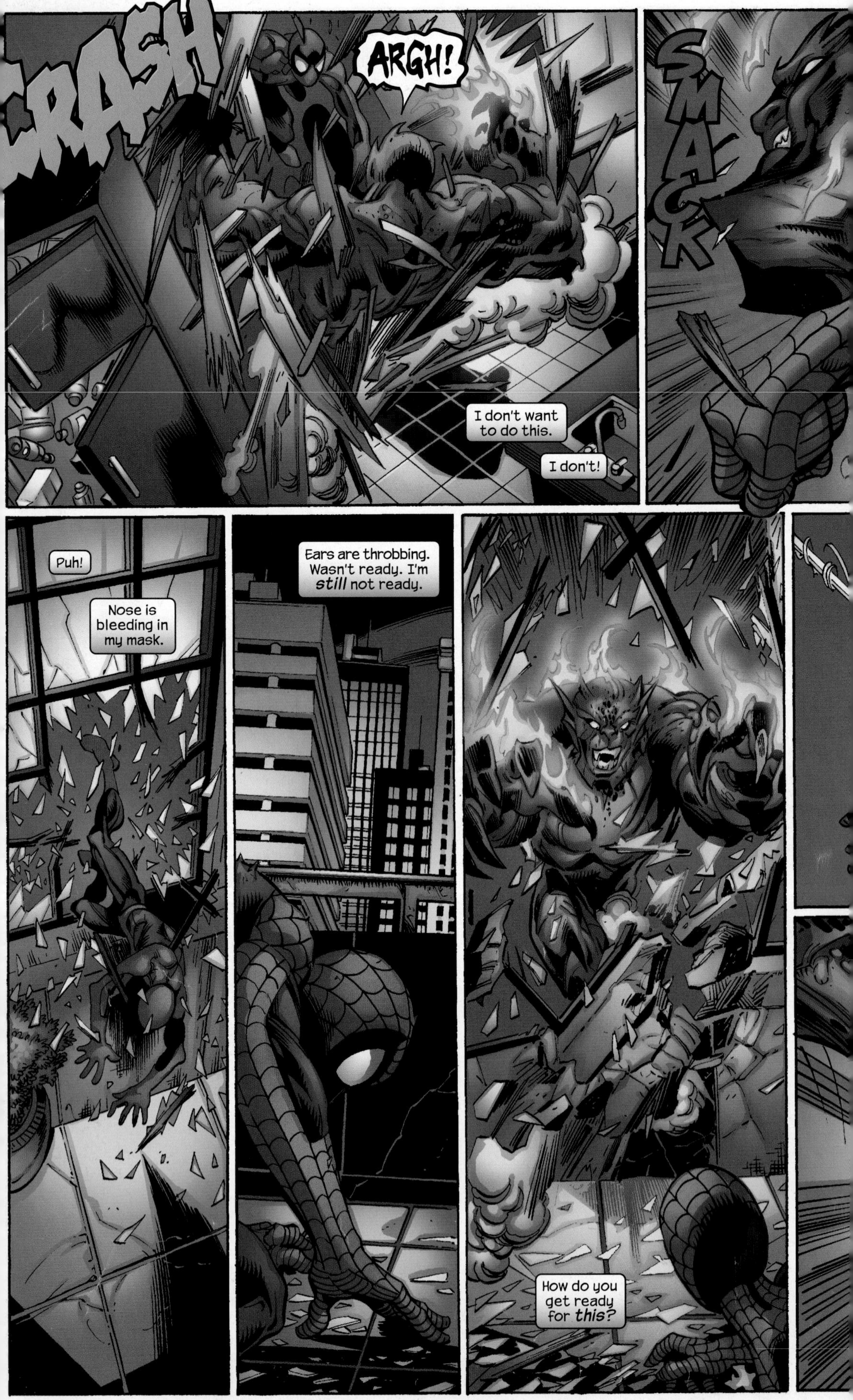
CRASH
ARGH!
I don't want to do this.
I don't!
SMACK
Puh!
Nose is bleeding in my mask.
Ears are throbbing. Wasn't ready. I'm *still* not ready.
How do you get ready for *this*?

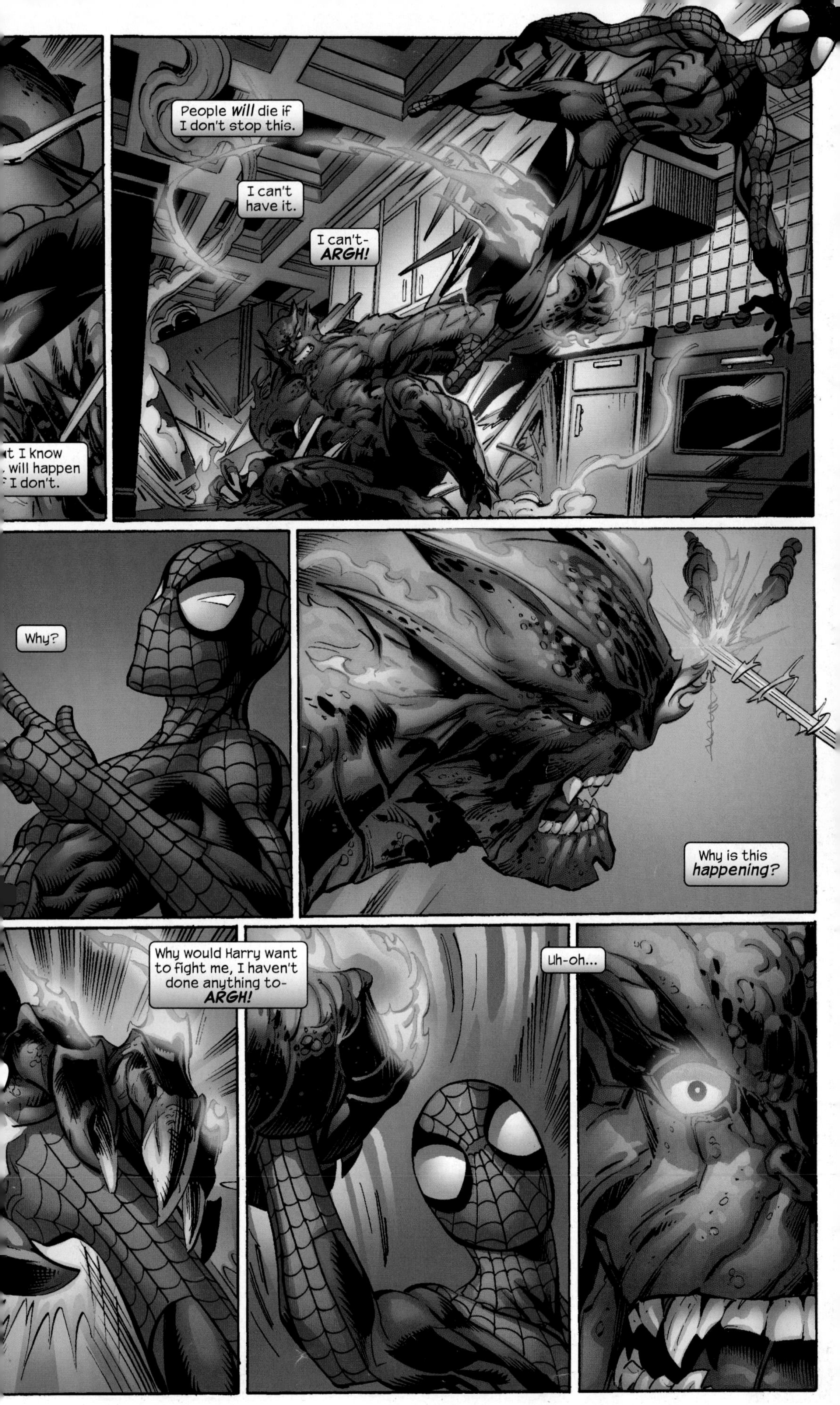
t I know
. will happen
f I don't.
People *will* die if
I don't stop this.
I can't
have it.
I can't-
ARGH!
Why?
Why is this
happening?
Why would Harry want
to fight me, I haven't
done anything to-
ARGH!
Uh-oh...

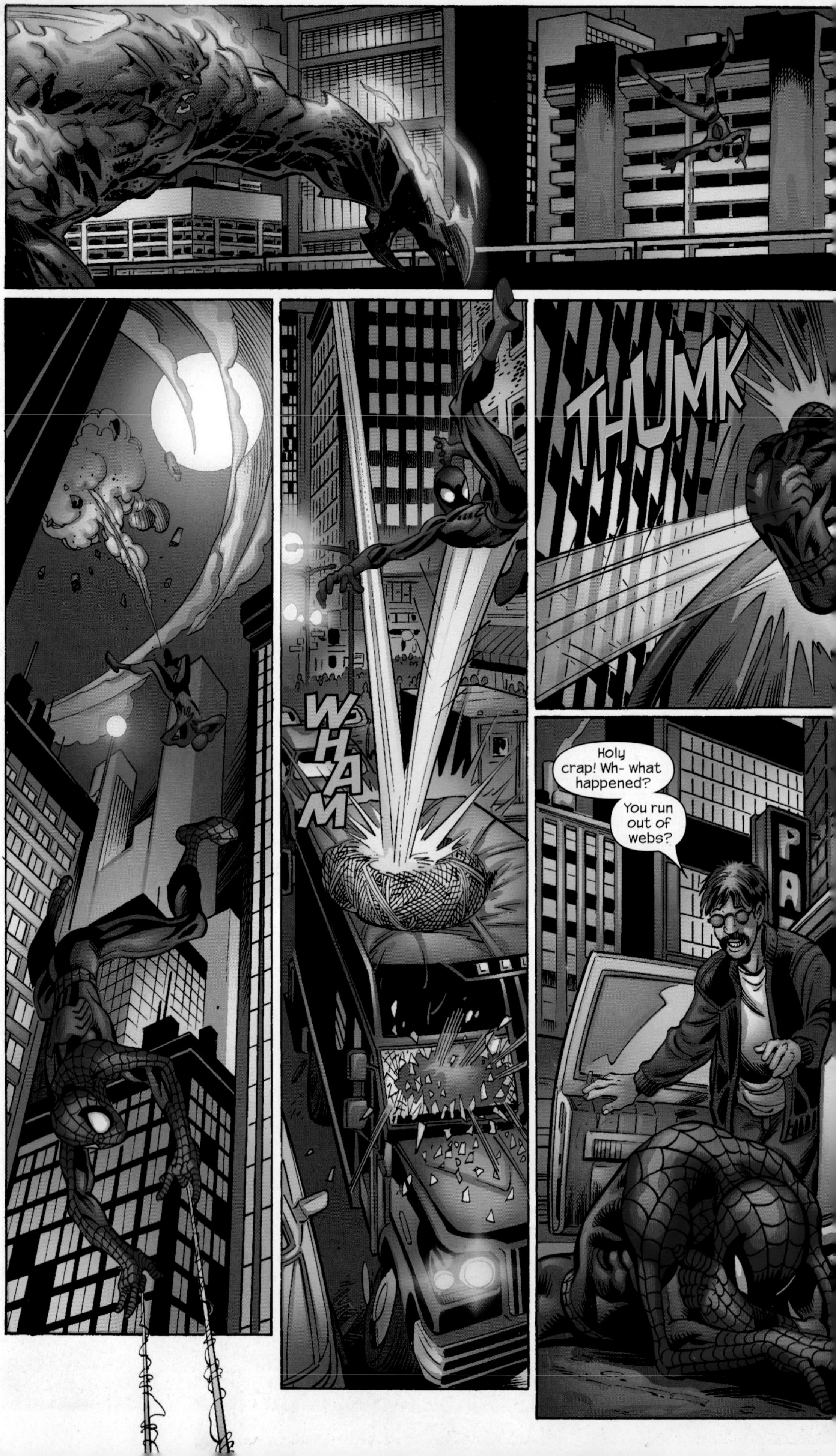

WHAM
THUMK
Holy crap! Wh- what happened?
You run out of webs?

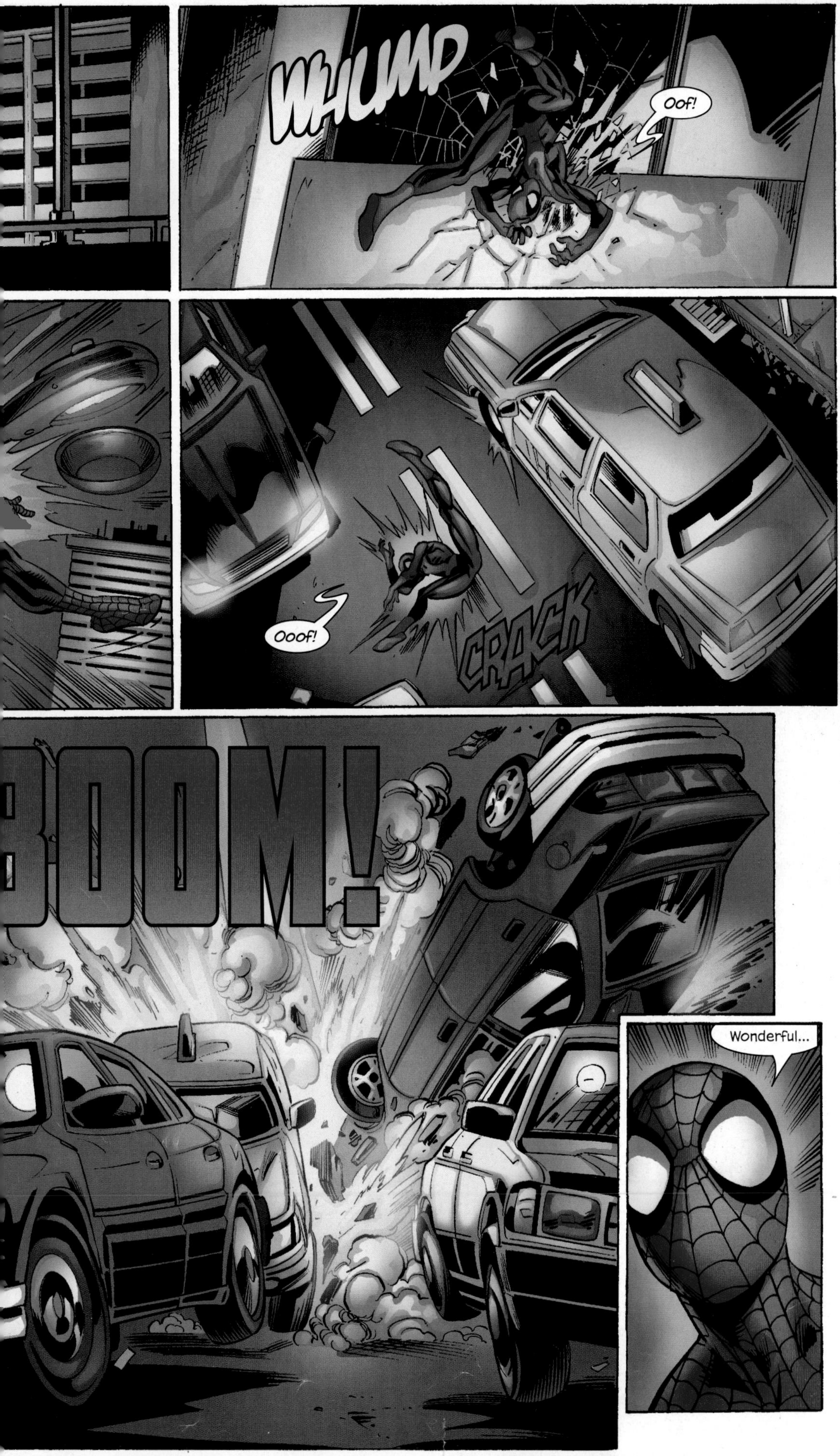
WHUMP
Oof!
Ooof!
CRACK
BOOM!
Wonderful...

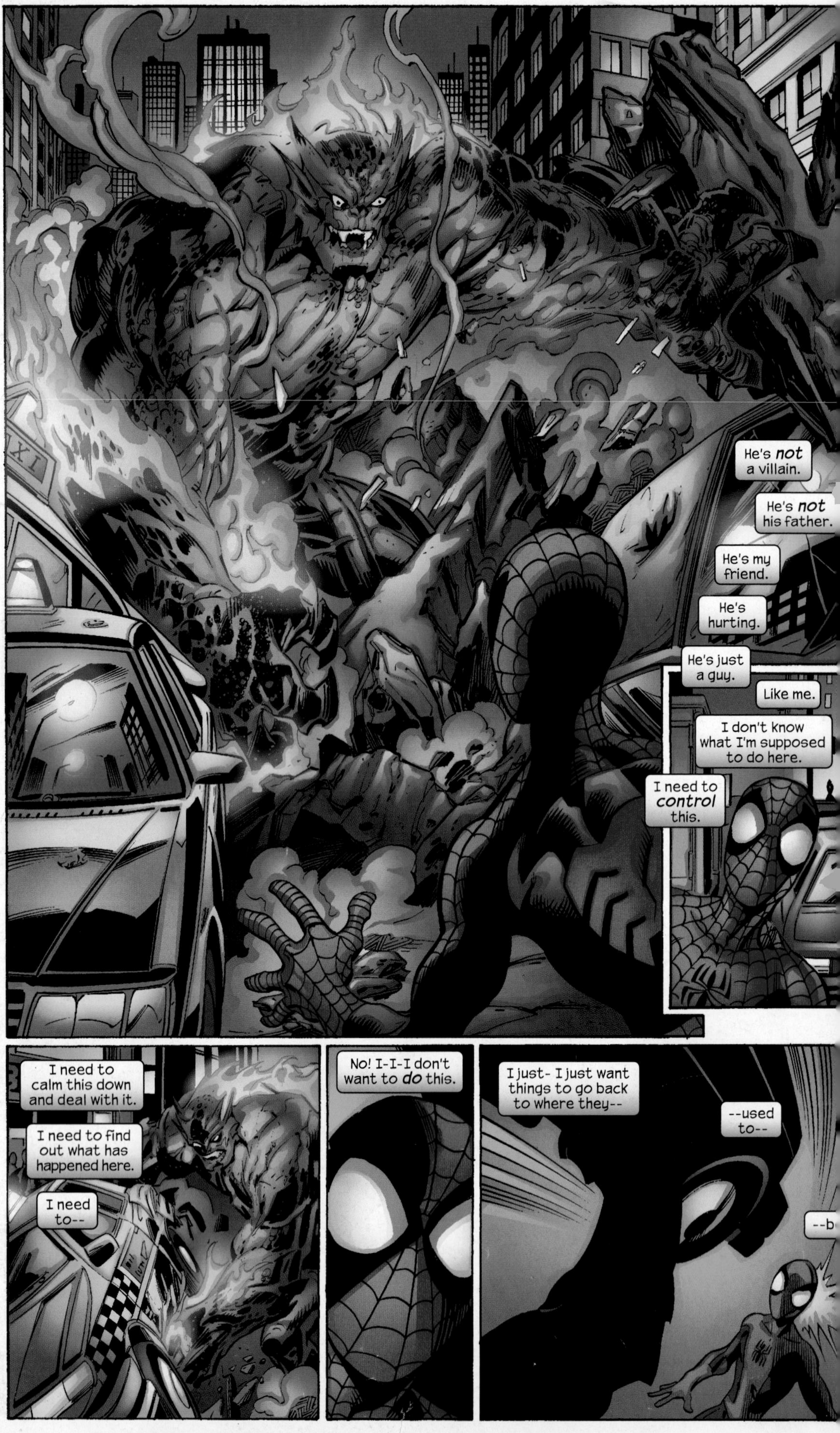
He's not a villain.
He's not his father.
He's my friend.
He's hurting.
He's just a guy.
Like me.
I don't know what I'm supposed to do here.
I need to control this.
I need to calm this down and deal with it.
I need to find out what has happened here.
I need to--
No! I-I-I don't want to do this.
I just- I just want things to go back to where they--
--used to--
--b

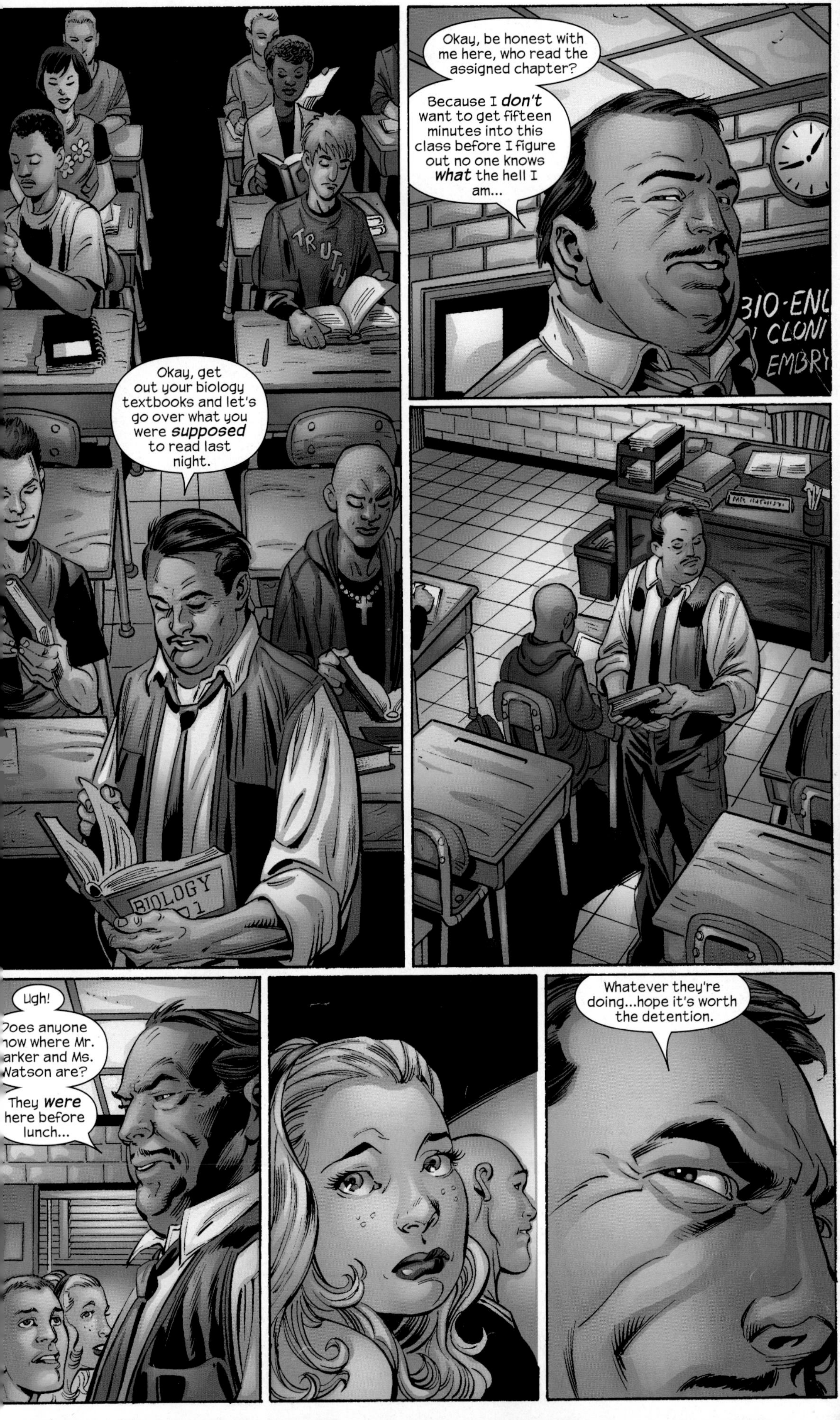

Okay, get out your biology textbooks and let's go over what you were *supposed* to read last night.
BIOLOGY 101
Okay, be honest with me here, who read the assigned chapter?
Because I *don't* want to get fifteen minutes into this class before I figure out no one knows *what* the hell I am...
Ugh!
Does anyone know where Mr. Parker and Ms. Watson are?
They *were* here before lunch...
Whatever they're doing...hope it's worth the detention.

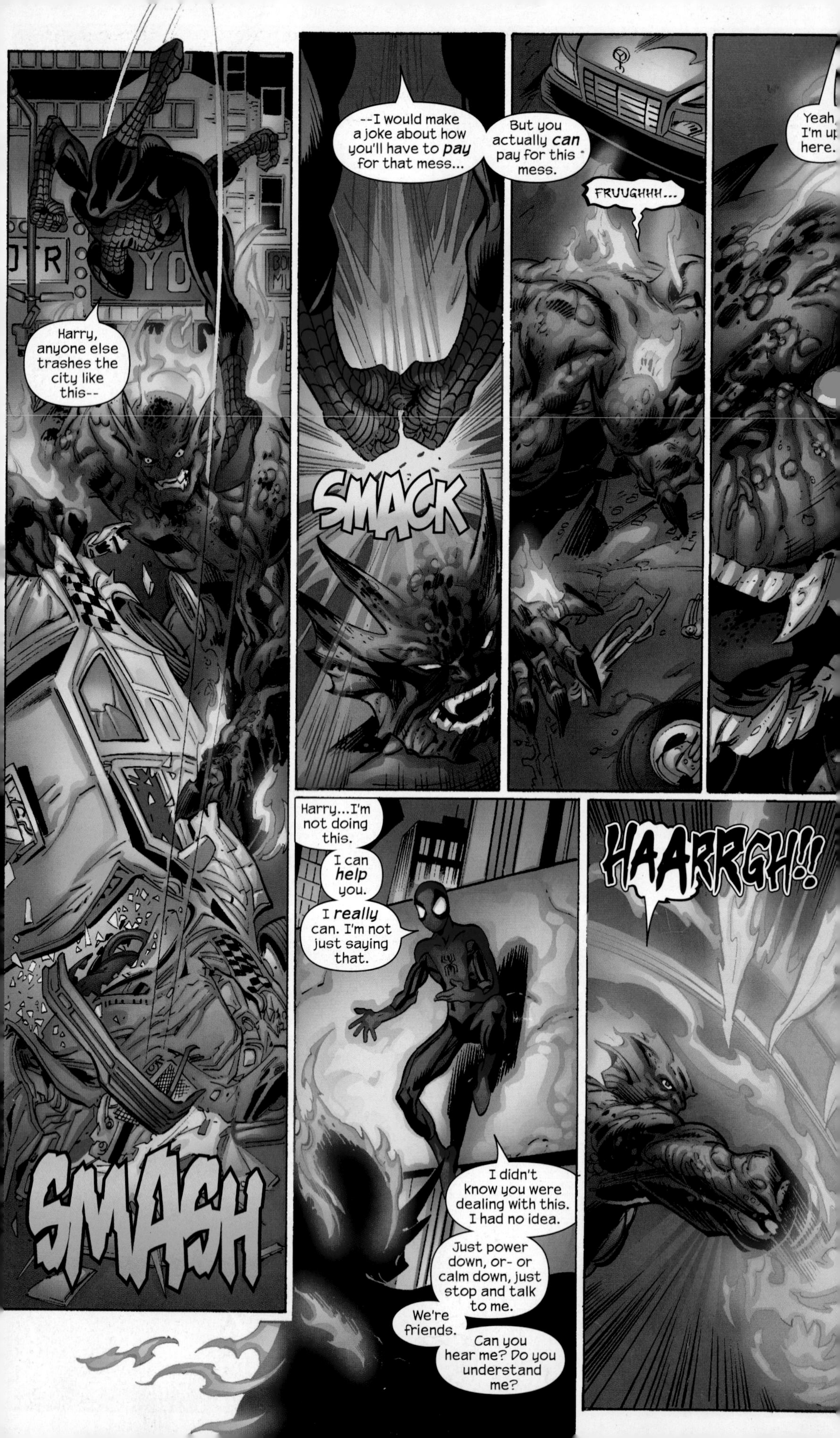
Harry, anyone else trashes the city like this--
SMASH
--I would make a joke about how you'll have to *pay* for that mess...
SMACK
But you actually *can* pay for this mess.
FRUUGHHH...
Harry...I'm not doing this.
I can *help* you.
I *really* can. I'm not just saying that.
I didn't know you were dealing with this. I had no idea.
Just power down, or- or calm down, just stop and talk to me.
We're friends.
Can you hear me? Do you understand me?
HAARRGH!!

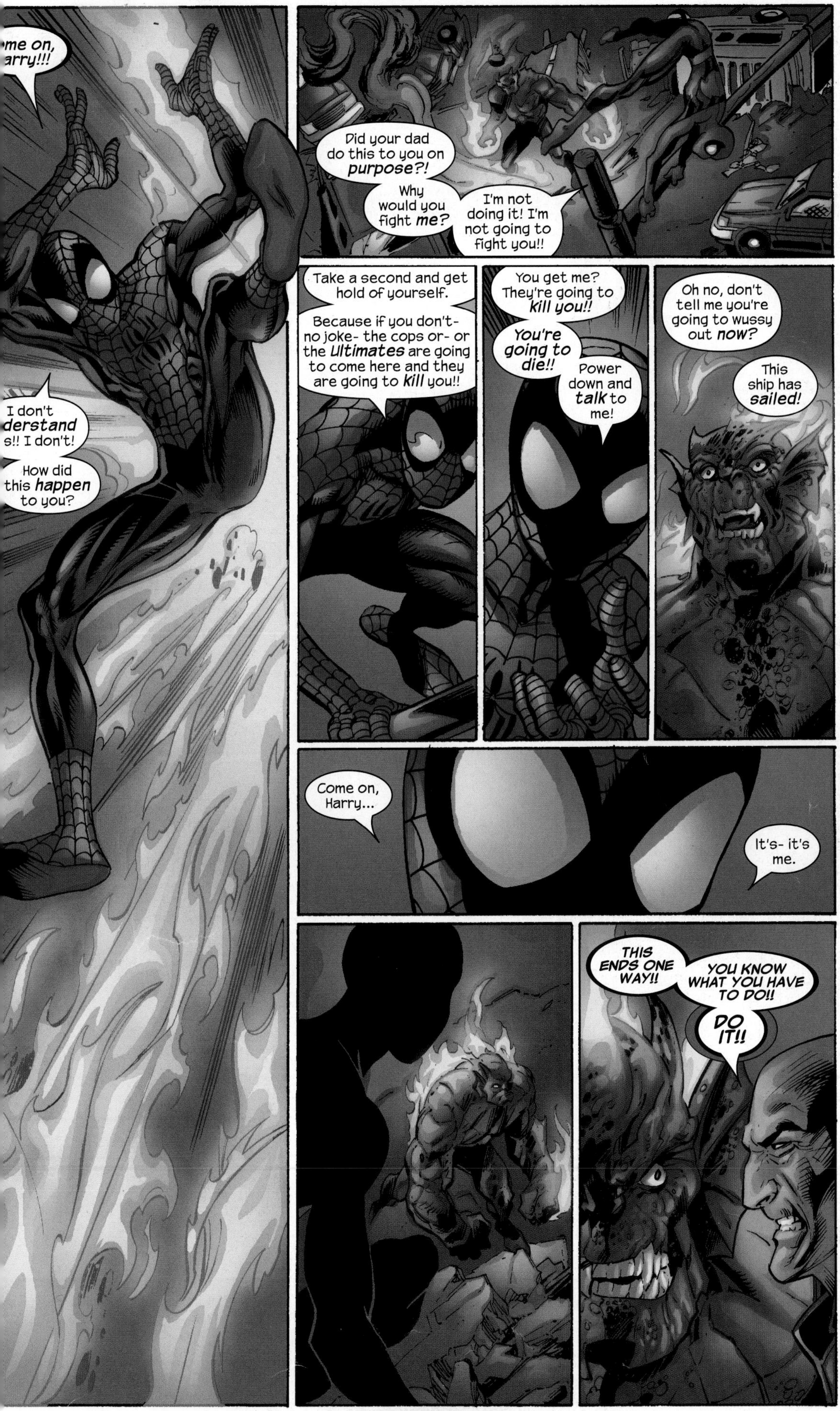

me on,
arry!!!
I don't
derstand
s!! I don't!
How did this *happen* to you?
Did your dad do this to you on *purpose?!*
Why would you fight *me?*
I'm not doing it! I'm not going to fight you!!
Take a second and get hold of yourself.
Because if you don't- no joke- the cops or- or the *Ultimates* are going to come here and they are going to *kill* you!!
You get me? They're going to *kill you!!*
You're going to die!!
Power down and *talk* to me!
Oh no, don't tell me you're going to wussy out *now?*
This ship has *sailed!*
Come on, Harry...
It's- it's me.
THIS ENDS ONE WAY!!
YOU KNOW WHAT YOU HAVE TO DO!!
DO IT!!

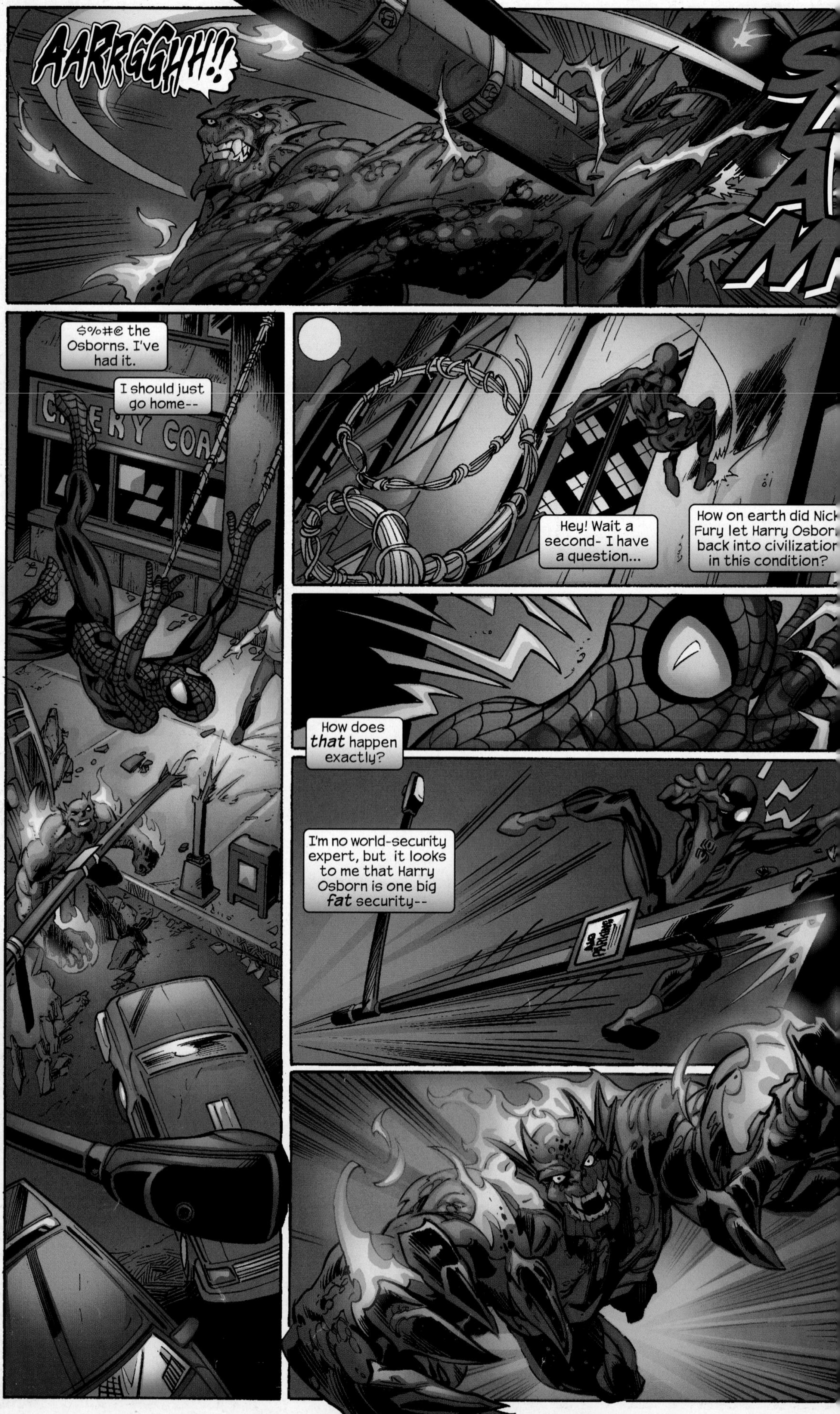
AARRGGHH!!
$%#@ the Osborns. I've had it.
I should just go home--
Hey! Wait a second- I have a question...
How on earth did Nick Fury let Harry Osborn back into civilization in this condition?
How does *that* happen exactly?
I'm no world-security expert, but it looks to me that Harry Osborn is one big *fat* security--

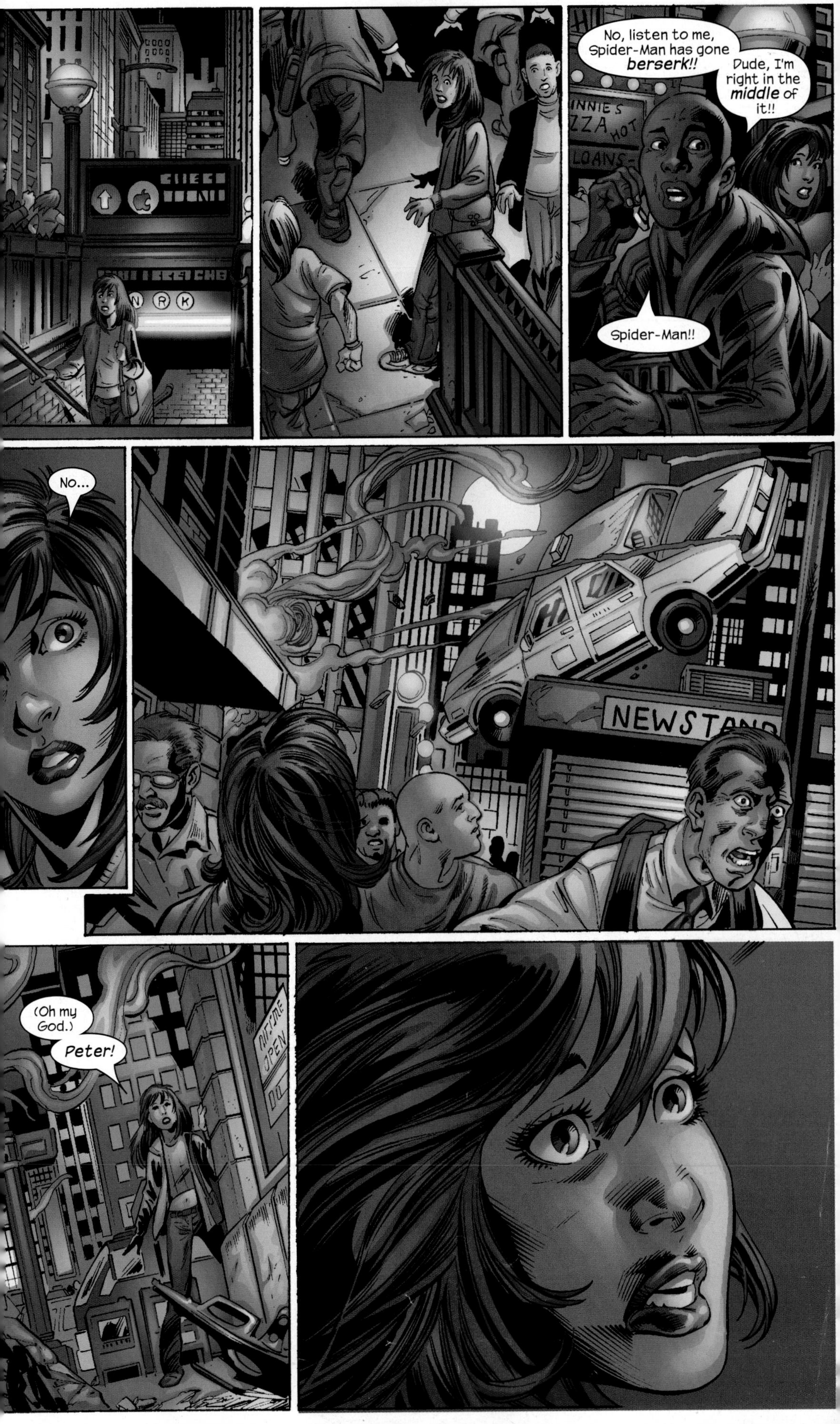
No, listen to me, Spider-Man has gone berserk!!
Dude, I'm right in the middle of it!!
Spider-Man!!
No...
NEWSTAND
(Oh my God.)
Peter!

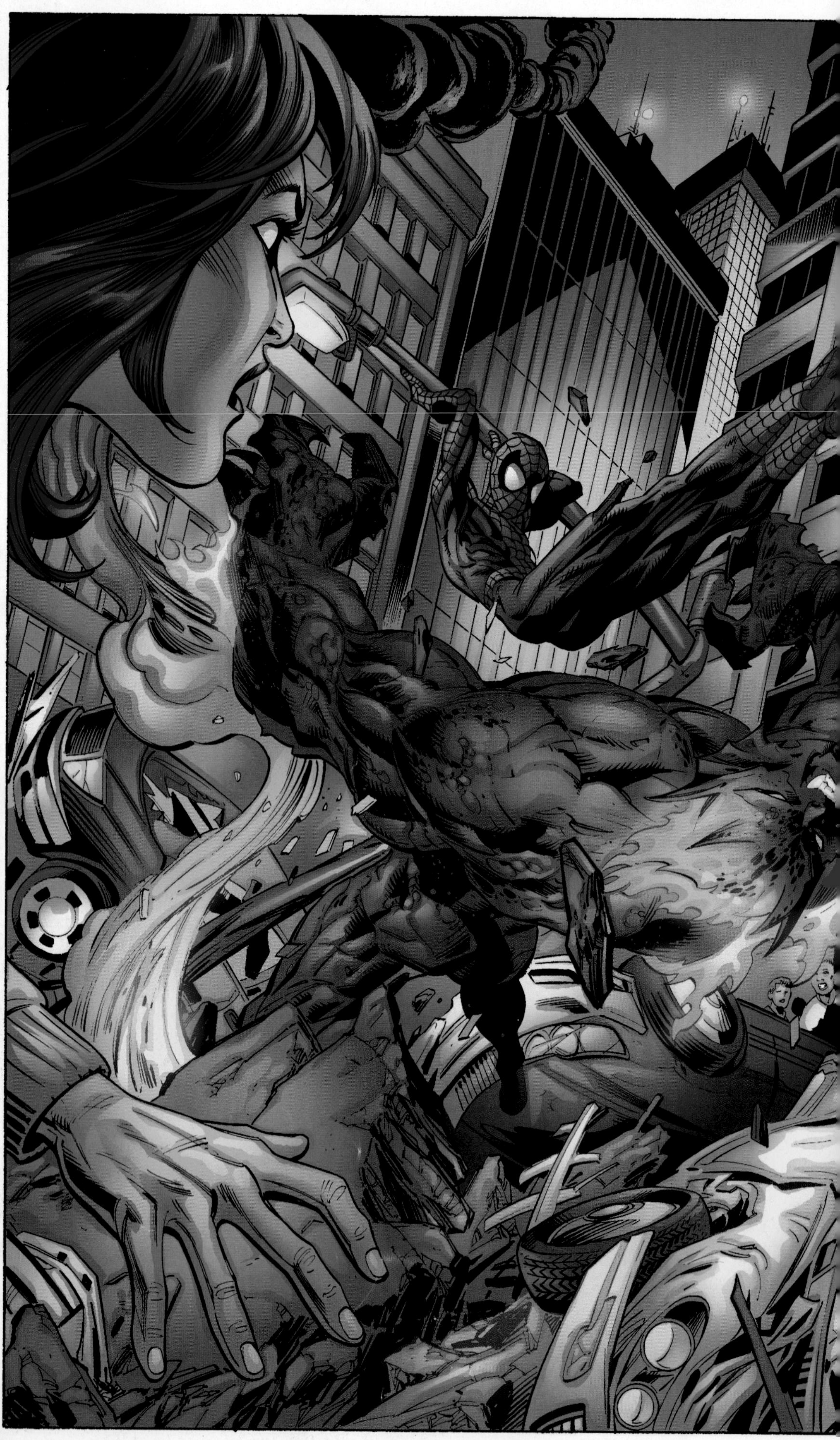

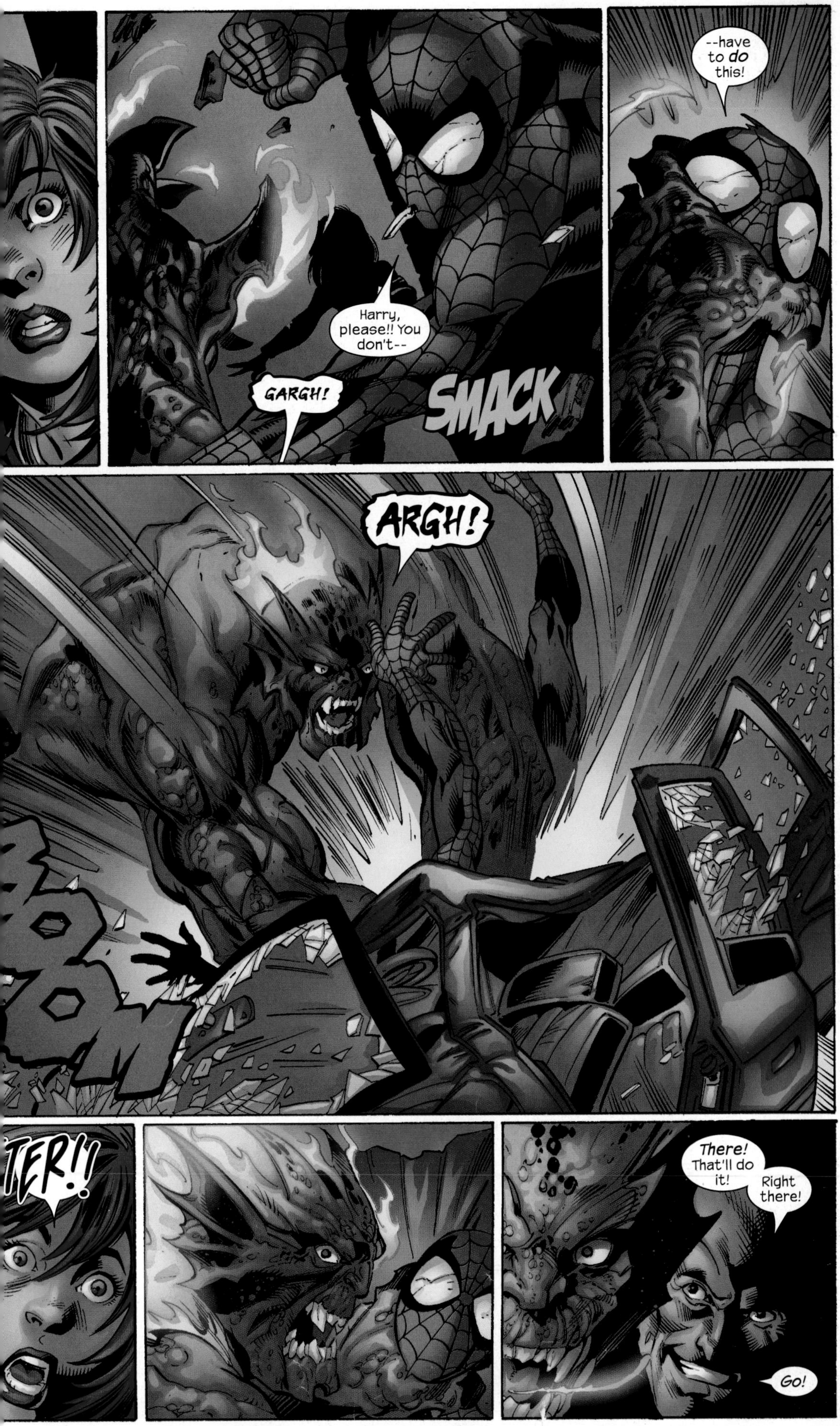
Harry, please!! You don't--
GARGH!
SMACK
--have to do this!
ARGH!
TER!!
There! That'll do it!
Right there!
Go!

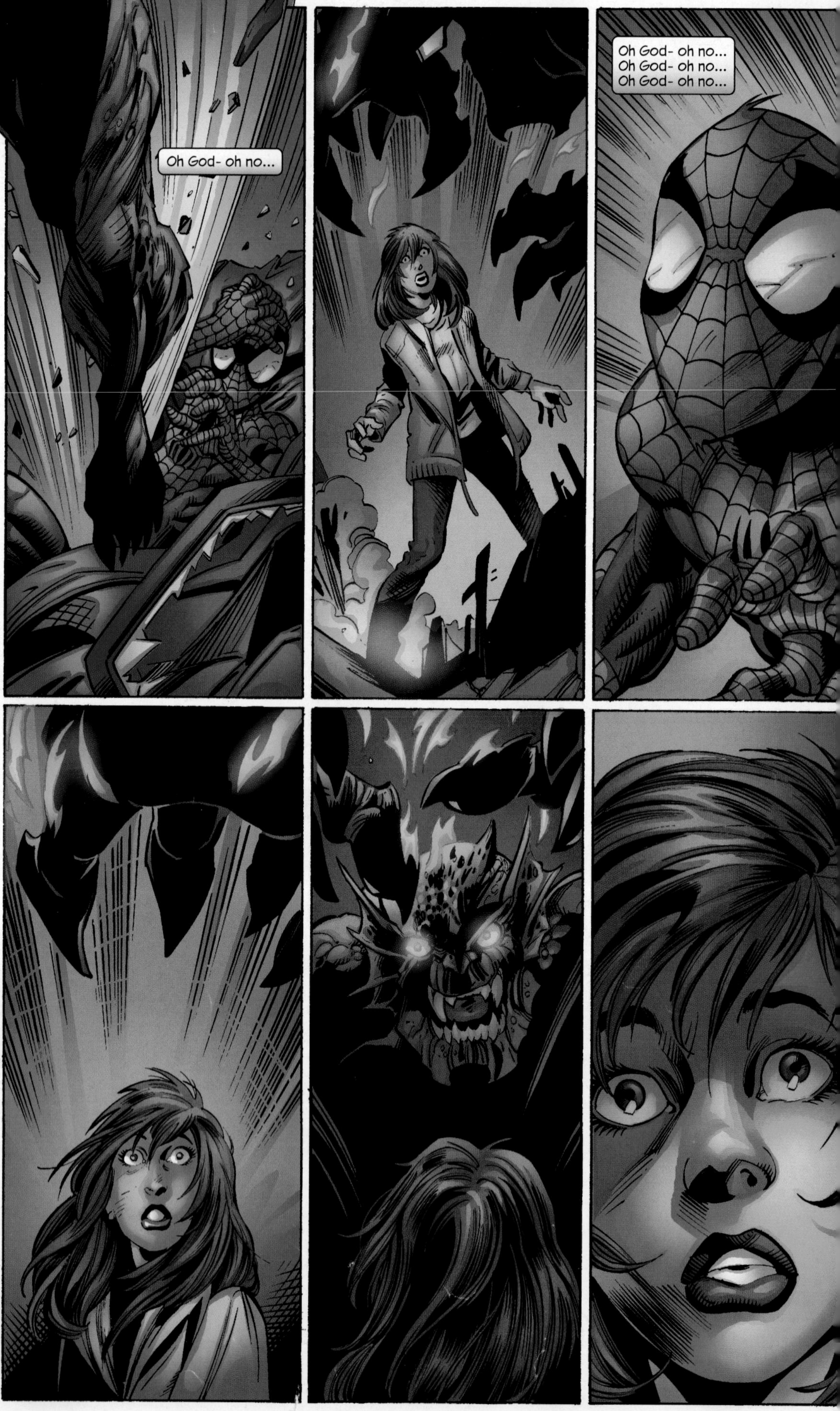
Oh God- oh no...
Oh God- oh no...
Oh God- oh no...
Oh God- oh no...

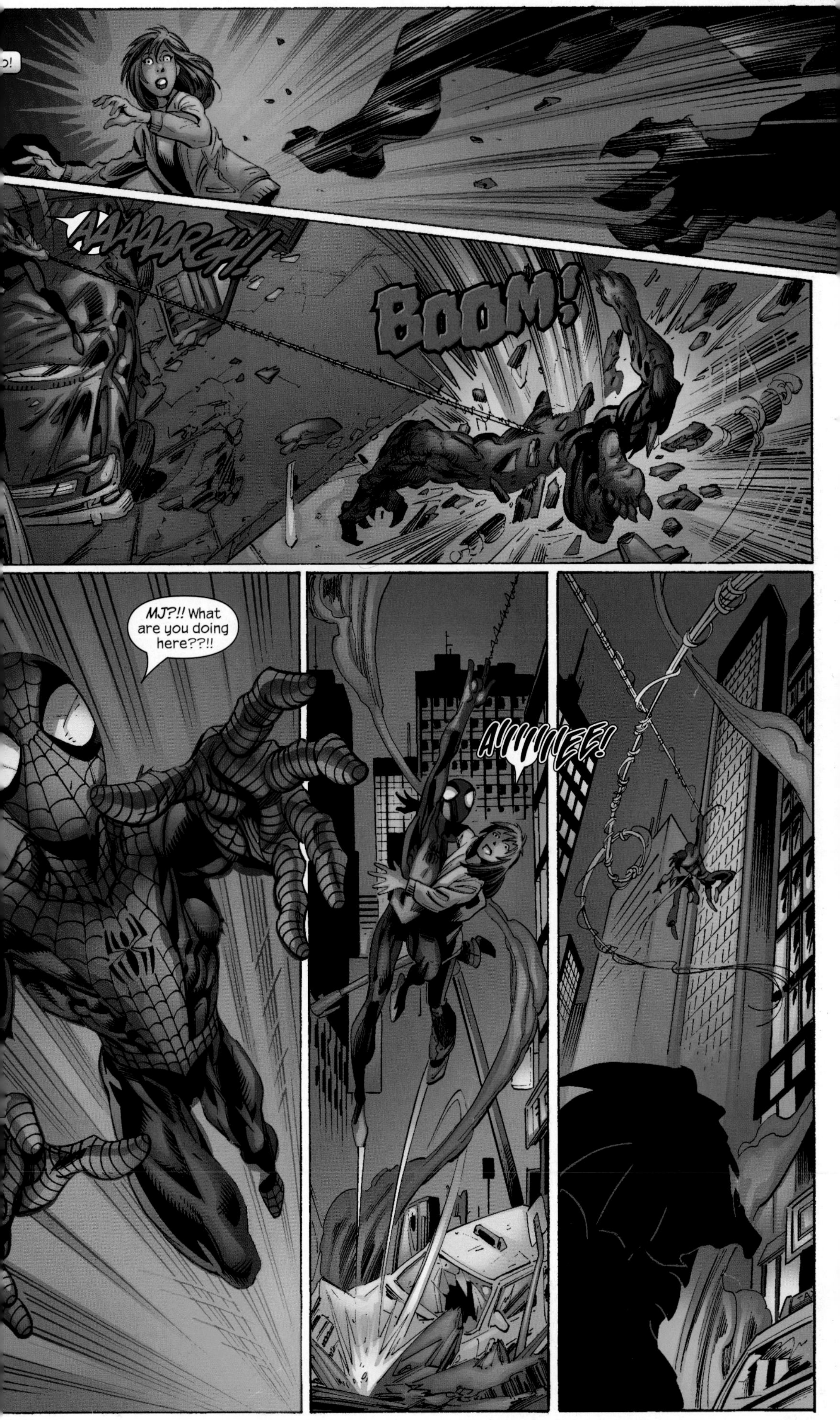

AAAAARGH!!
BOOM!
MJ?!! What are you doing here??!!
AIIIIIEE!

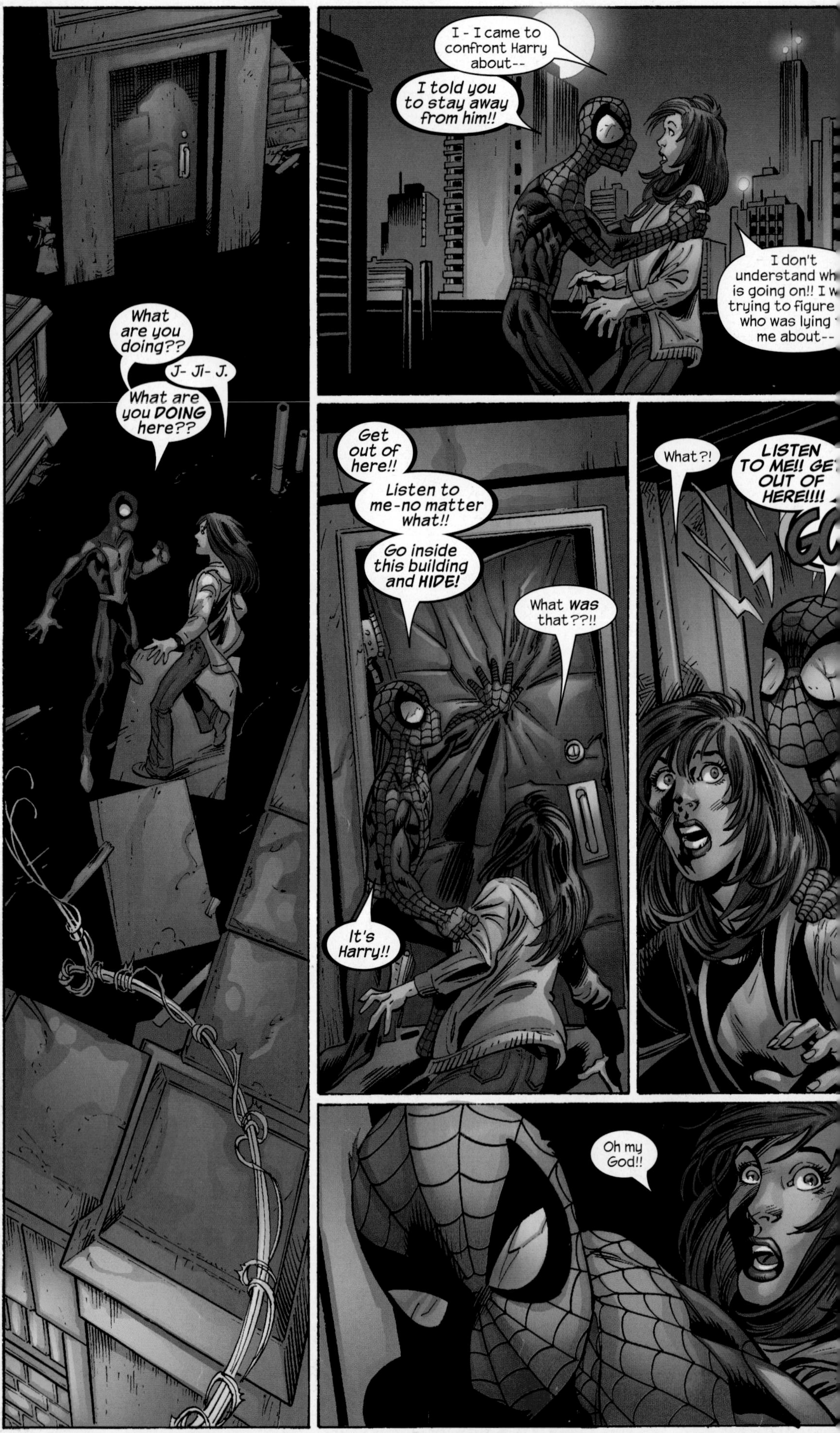

What are you doing??
J- Ji- J.
What are you DOING here??
I - I came to confront Harry about--
I told you to stay away from him!!
I don't understand wh
is going on!! I w
trying to figure
who was lying
me about--
Get out of here!!
Listen to me-no matter what!!
Go inside this building and HIDE!
It's Harry!!
What was that??!!
What?!
LISTEN TO ME!! GE
OUT OF HERE!!!!
Oh my God!!

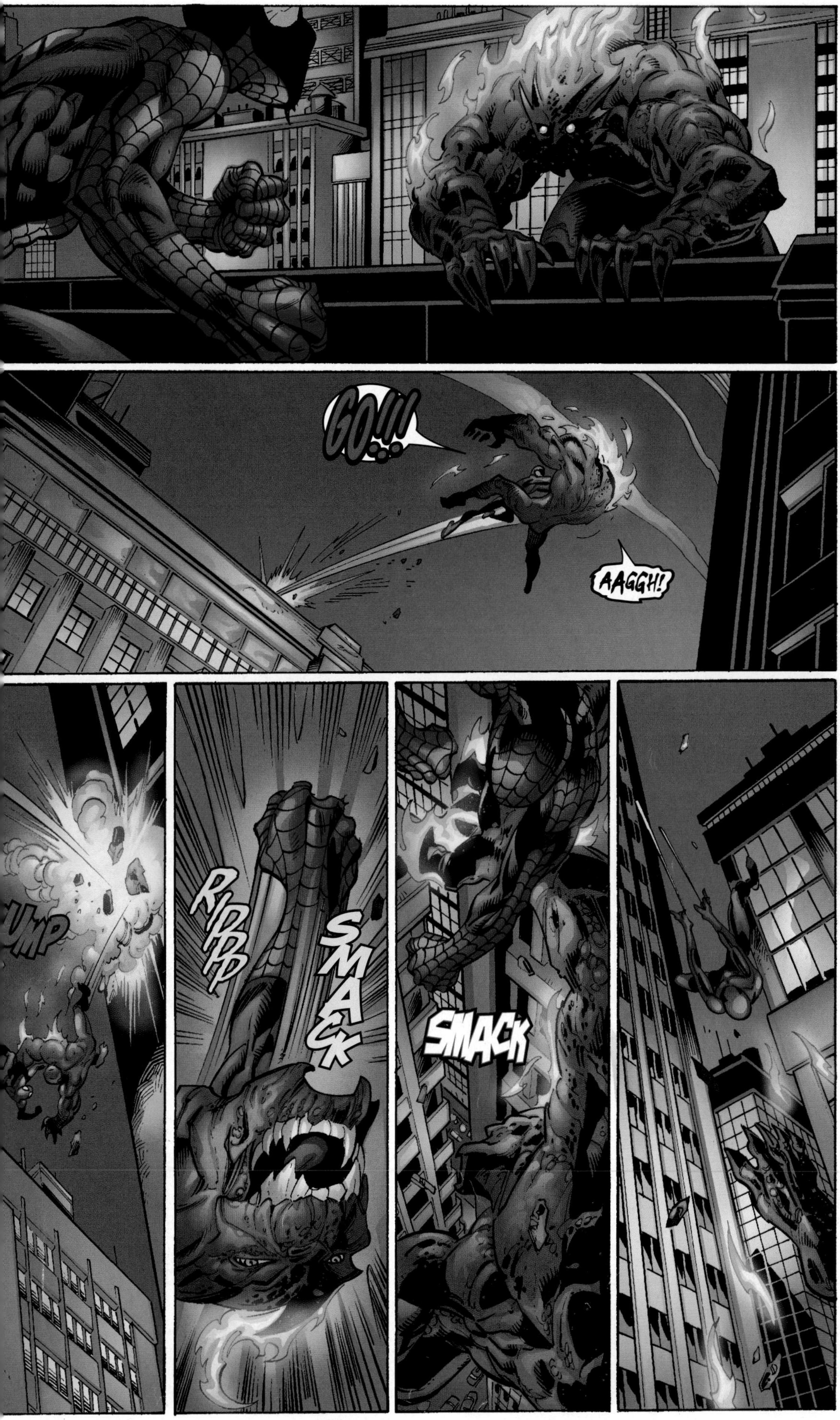
GO...!!!
AAGGH!
UMP
RIPPP
SMACK
SMACK

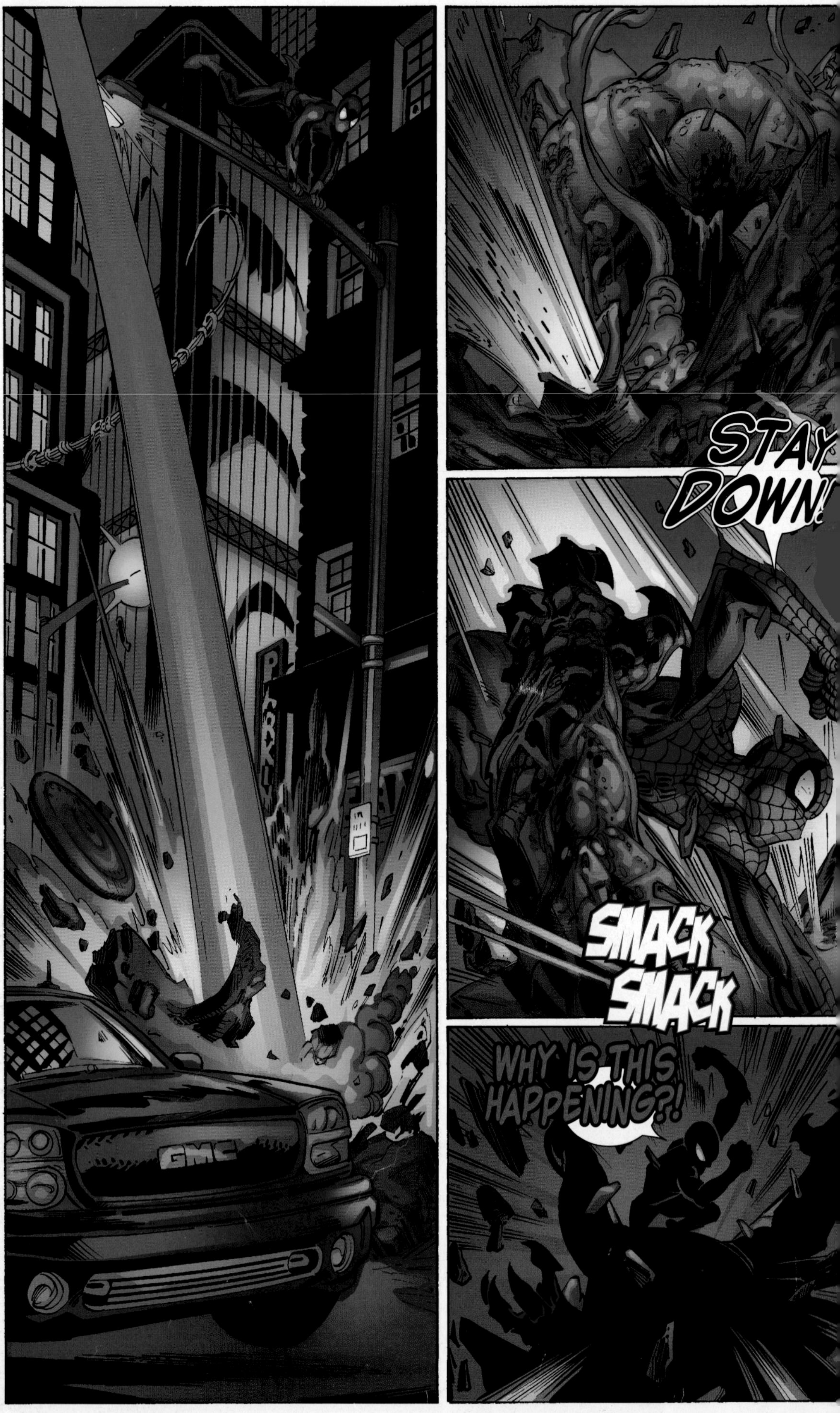
STAY DOWN!
SMACK
SMACK
WHY IS THIS HAPPENING?!

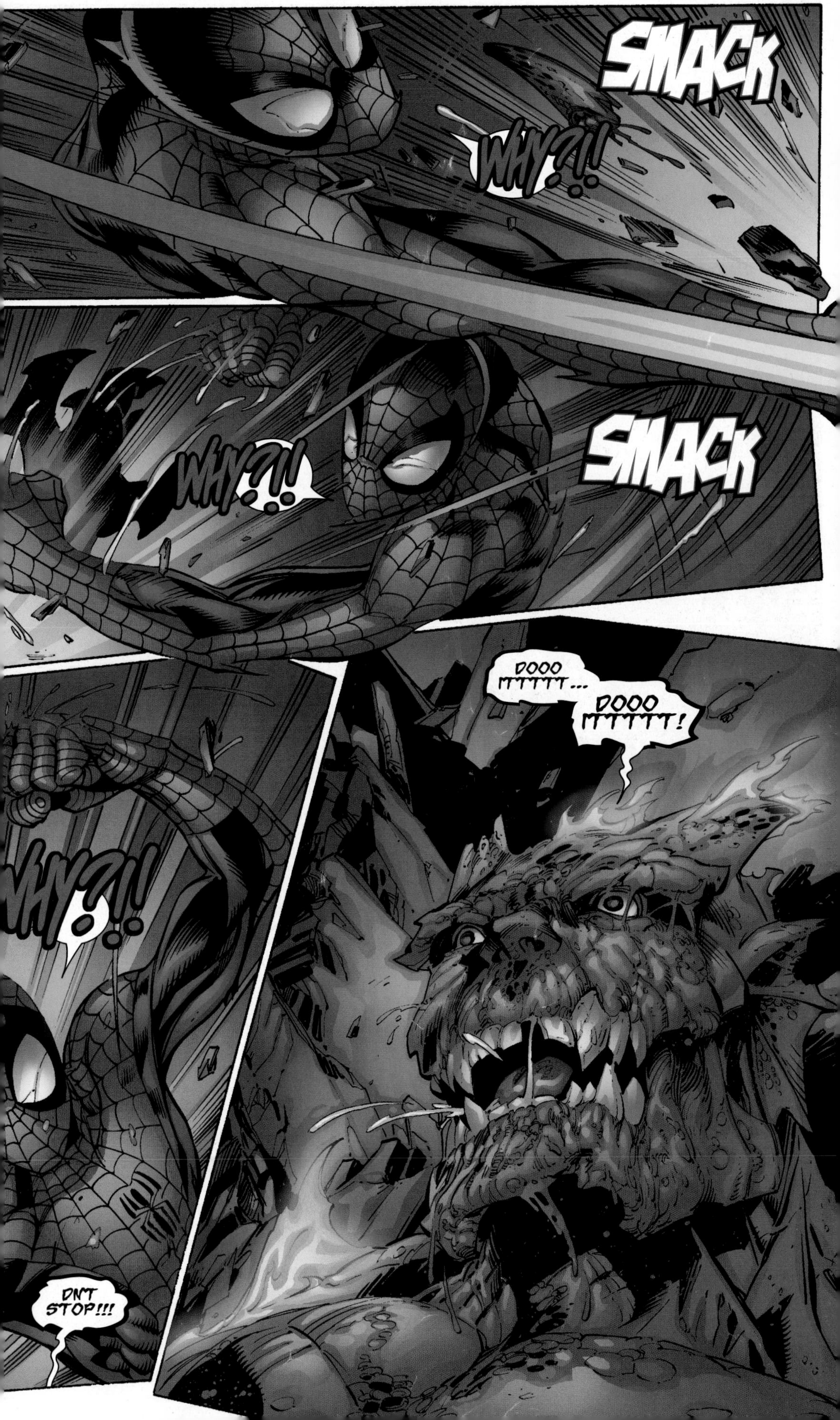

SMACK
WHY?!!
WHY?!!
SMACK
WHY?!!
DOOO
N'T T T T T...
DOOO
N'T T T T T!
DN'T STOP!!!

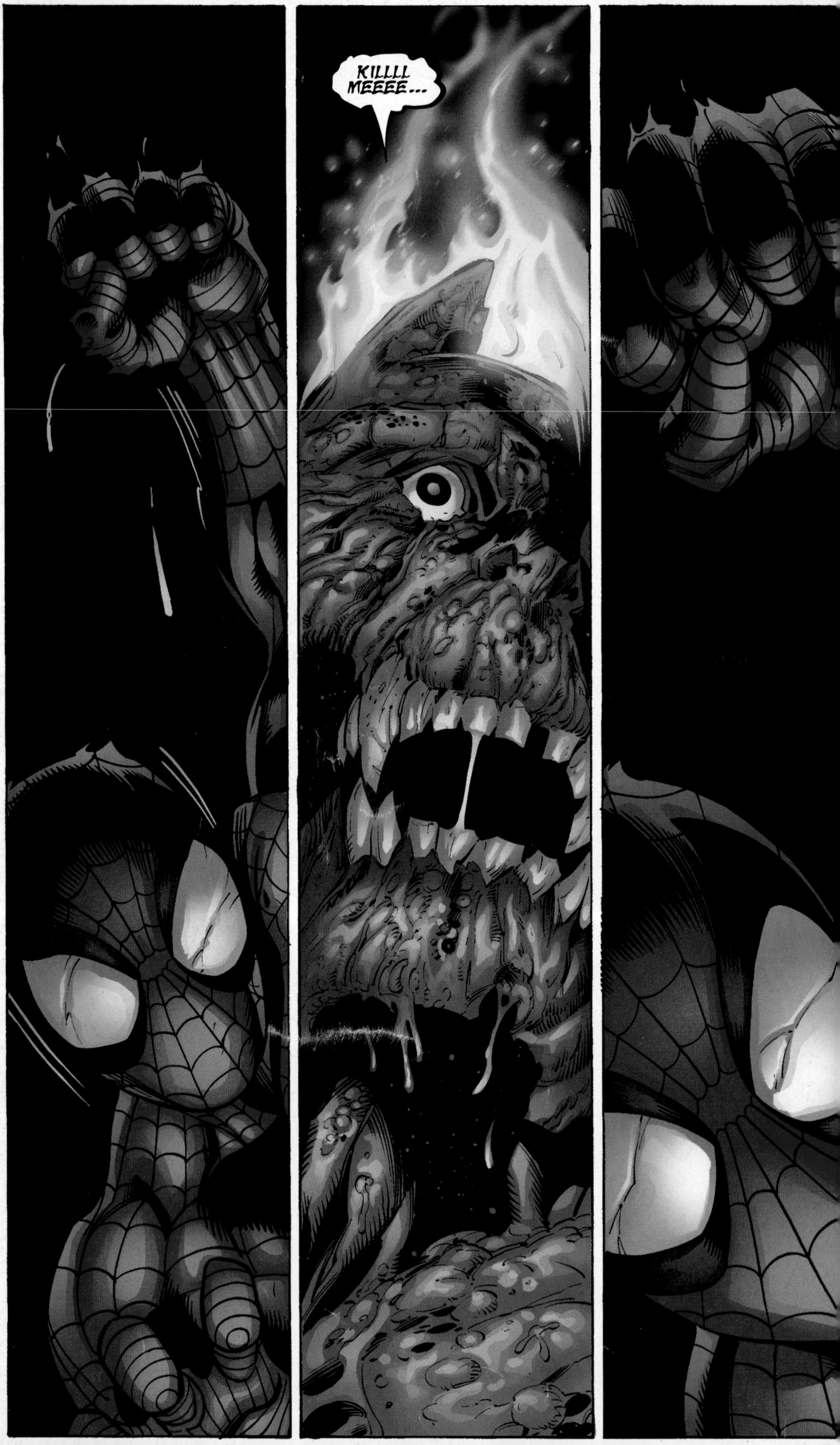
KILLLL MEEEE...

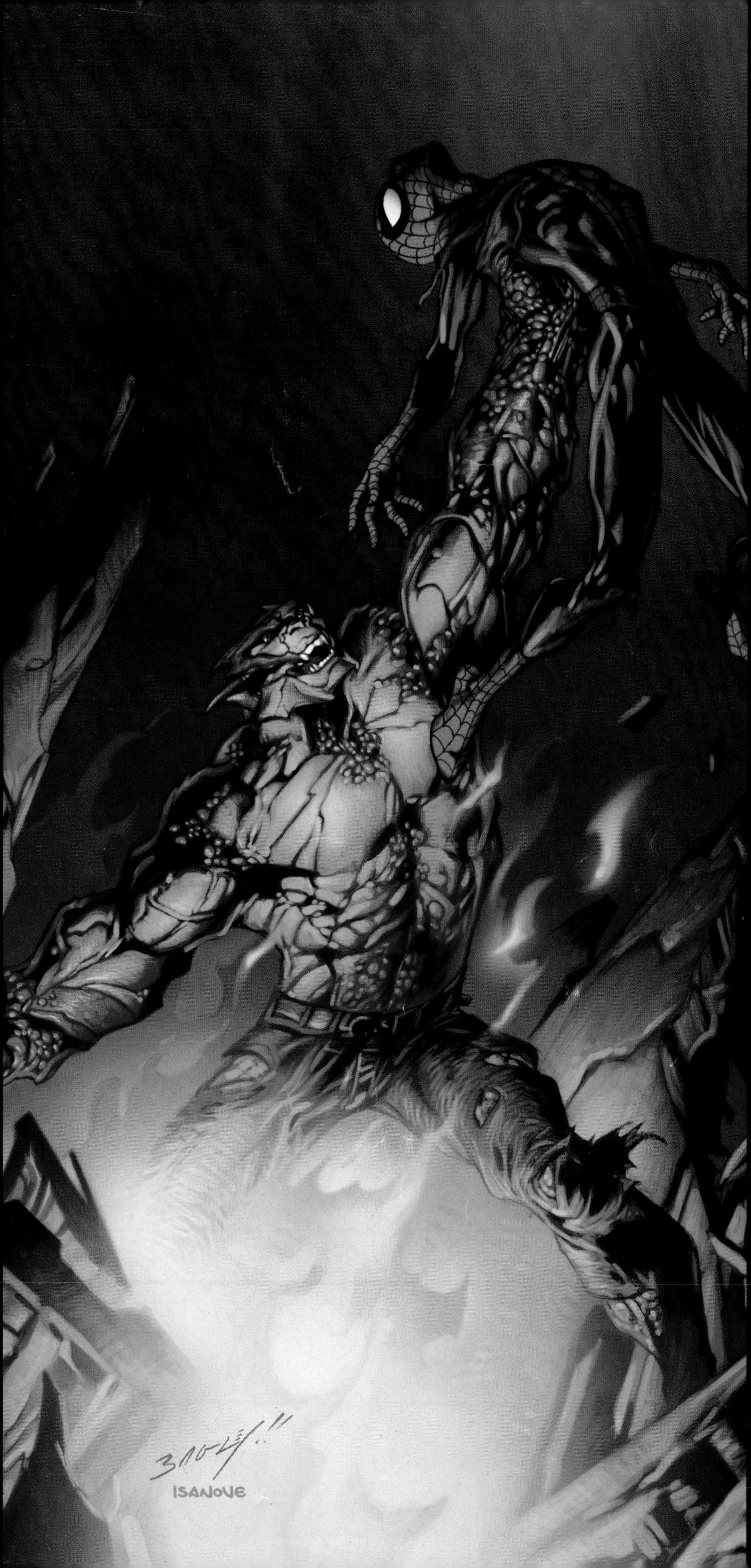
ISANOVE

77

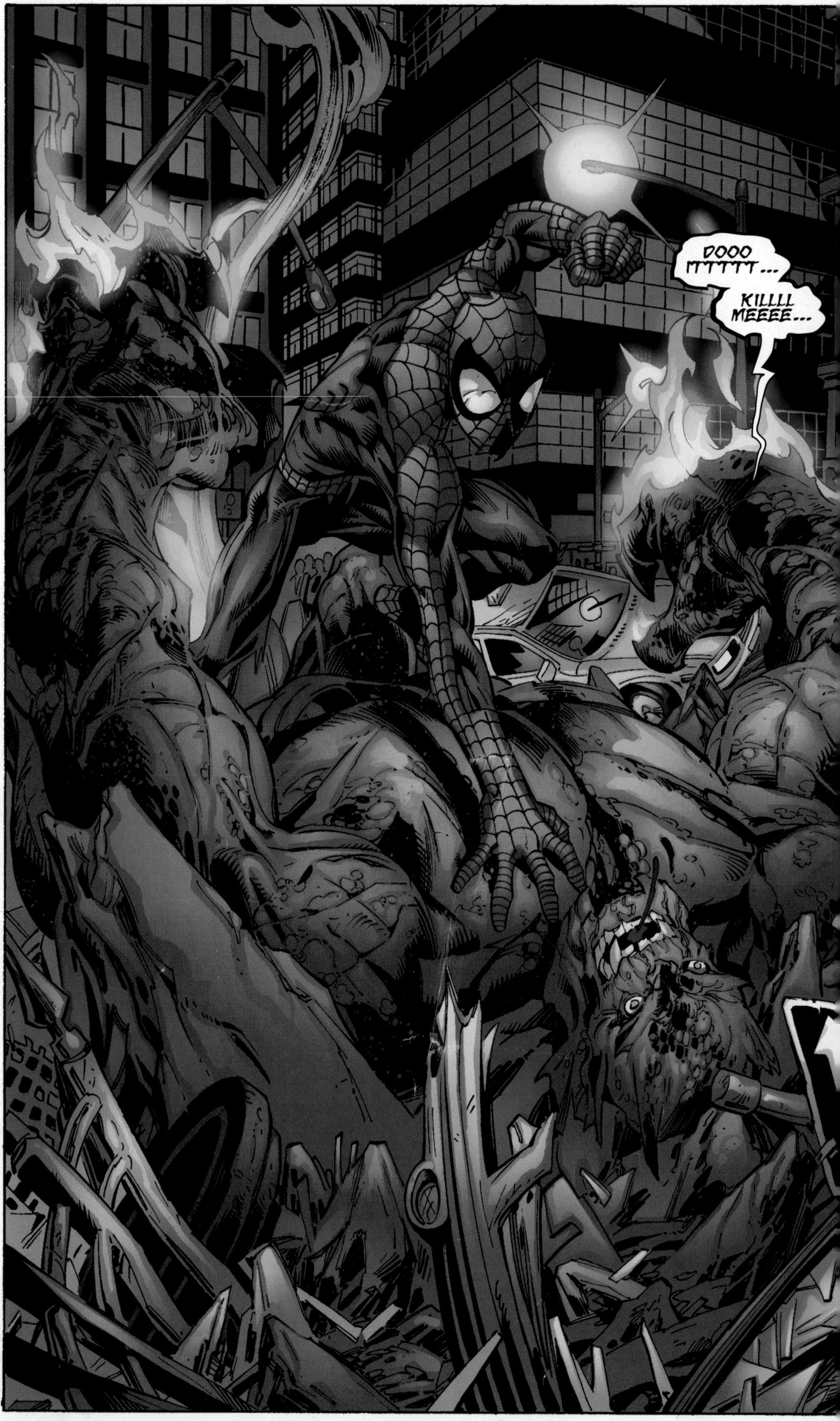
DOOO ITTTTT...
KILLLL MEEEE...

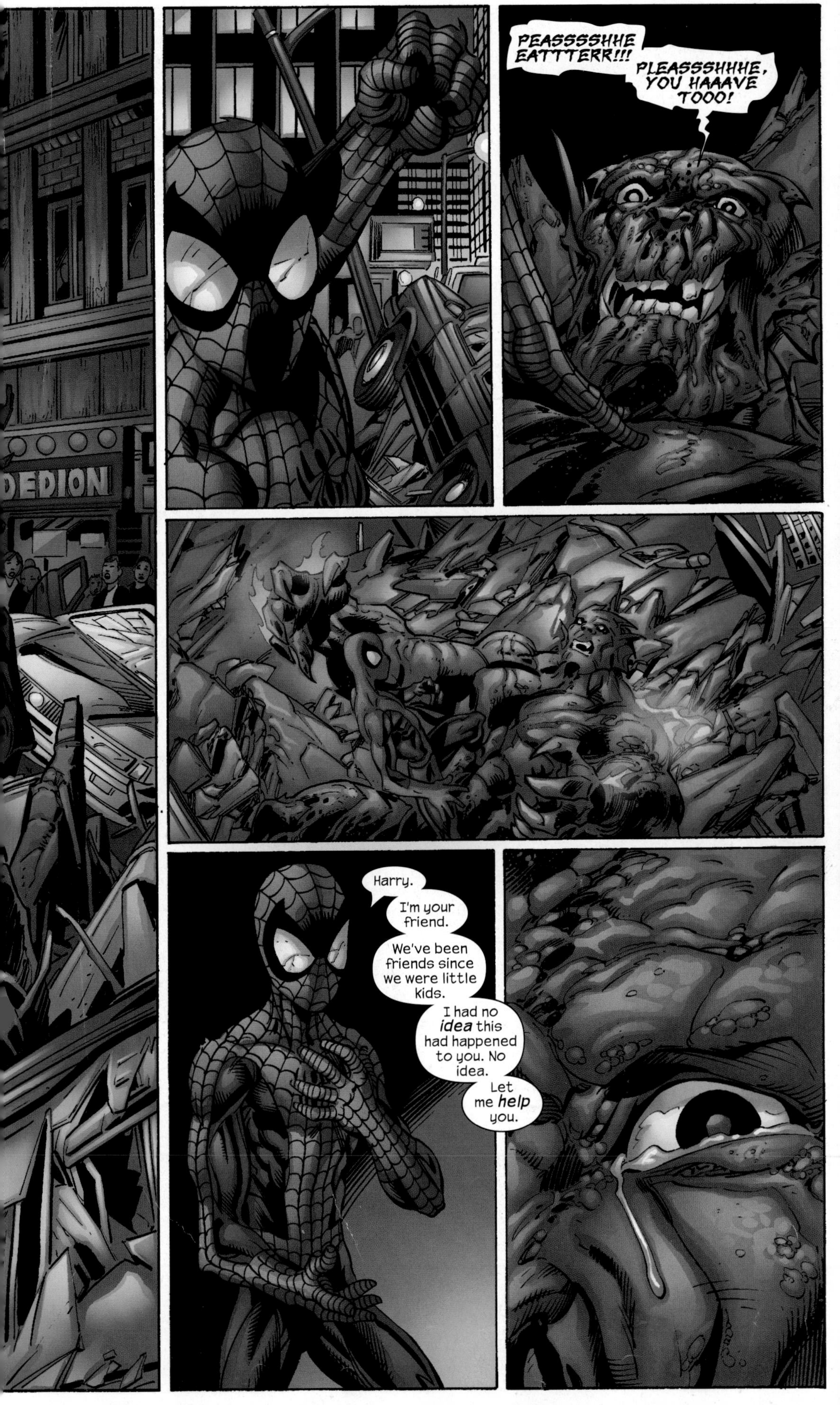

DEDION
PEASSSSHHE EATTTERR!!!
PLEASSSHHHE, YOU HAAAVE TOOO!
Harry.
I'm your friend.
We've been friends since we were little kids.
I had no *idea* this had happened to you. No idea.
Let me *help* you.

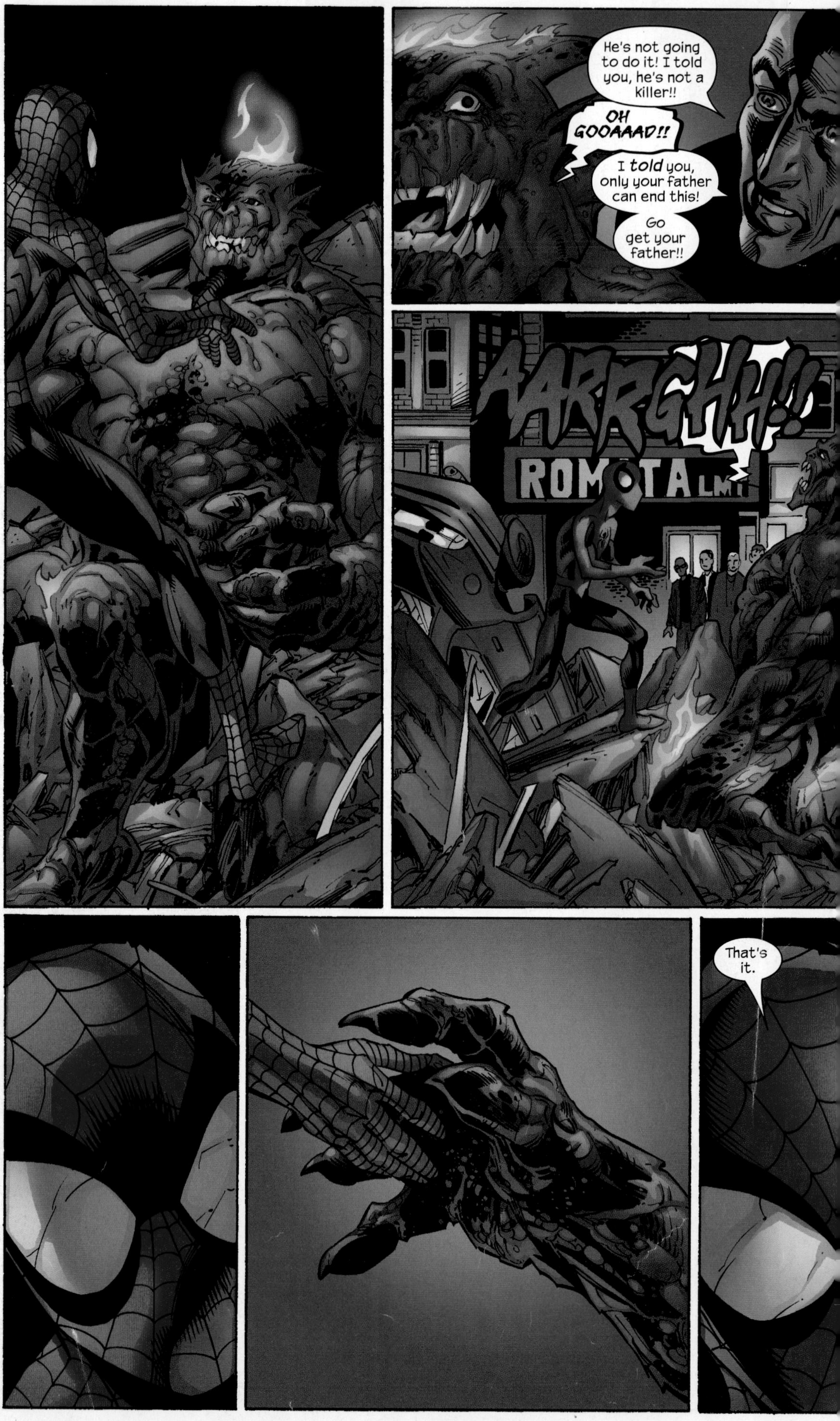

He's not going to do it! I told you, he's not a killer!!
OH GOOAAAD!!
I told you, only your father can end this!
Go get your father!!
AARRGHH!!
ROMOTA LMT
That's it.

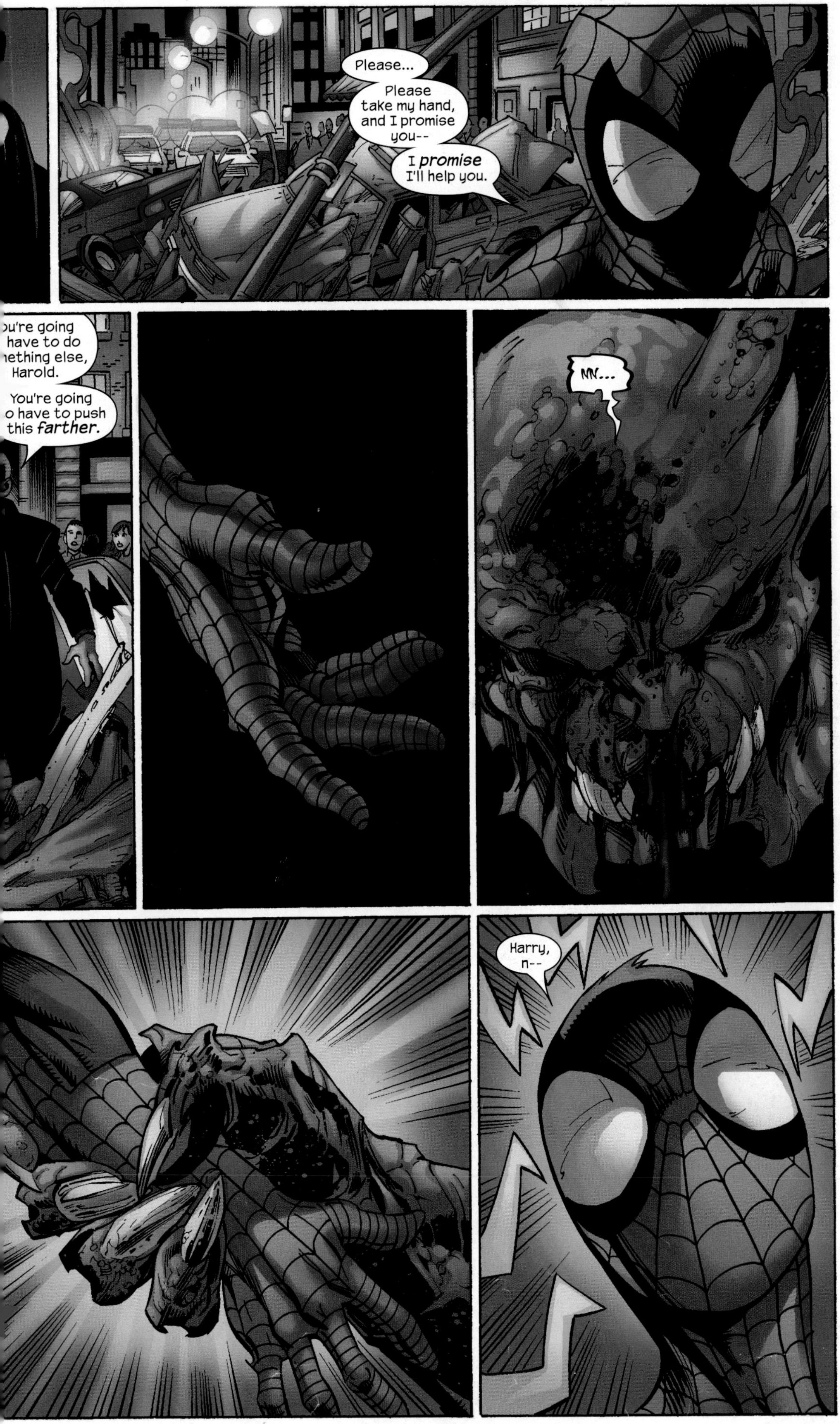
Please...
Please take my hand, and I promise you--
I *promise* I'll help you.
u're going have to do nething else, Harold.
You're going o have to push this *farther*.
NN...
Harry, n--

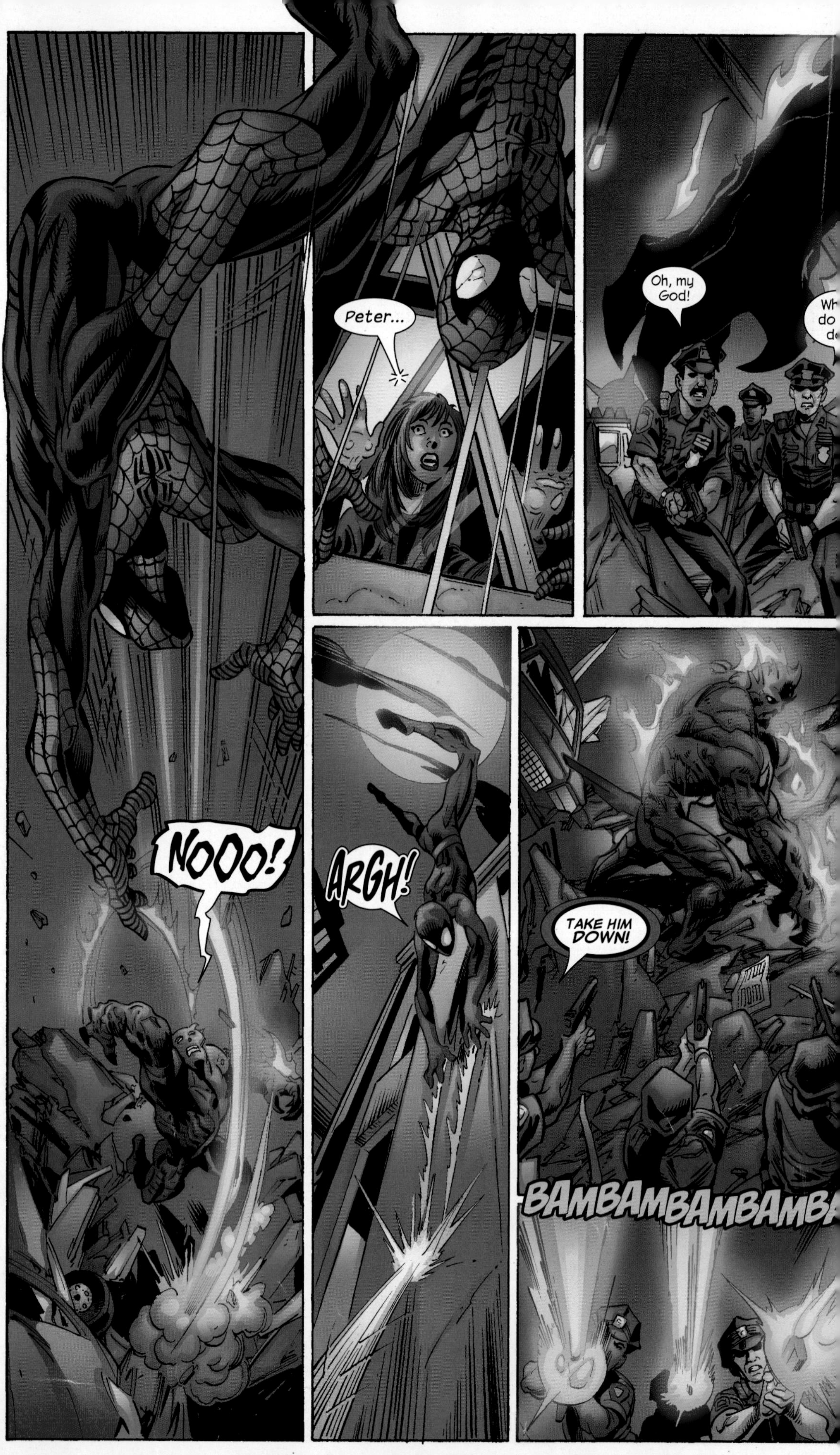
NOOO!
Peter...
Oh, my God!
ARGH!
TAKE HIM DOWN!
BAMBAMBAMBAMBA

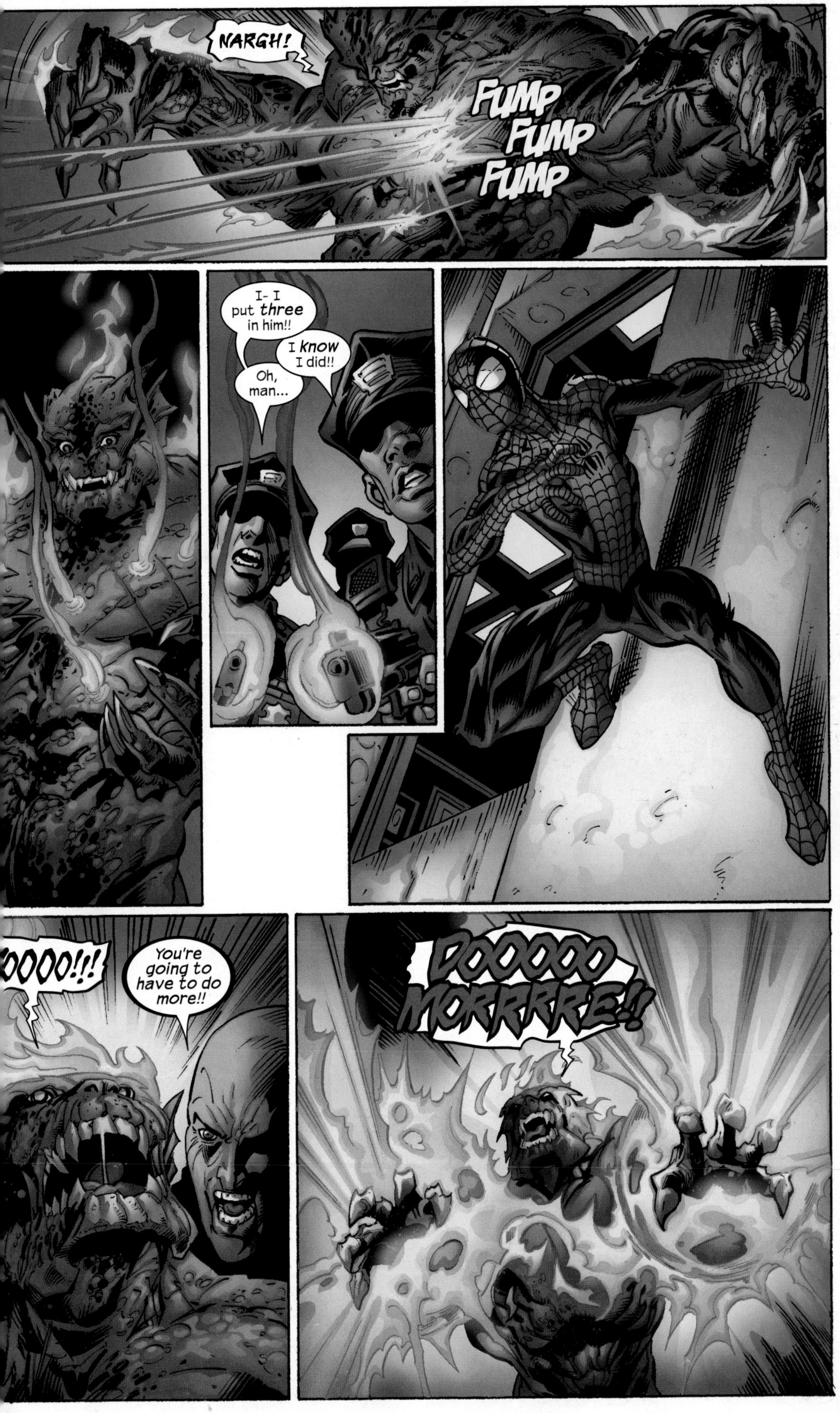

NARGH!
FUMP FUMP FUMP
I- I put three in him!!
I know I did!!
Oh, man...
OOOO!!!
You're going to have to do more!!
DOOOOO MORRRRE!!

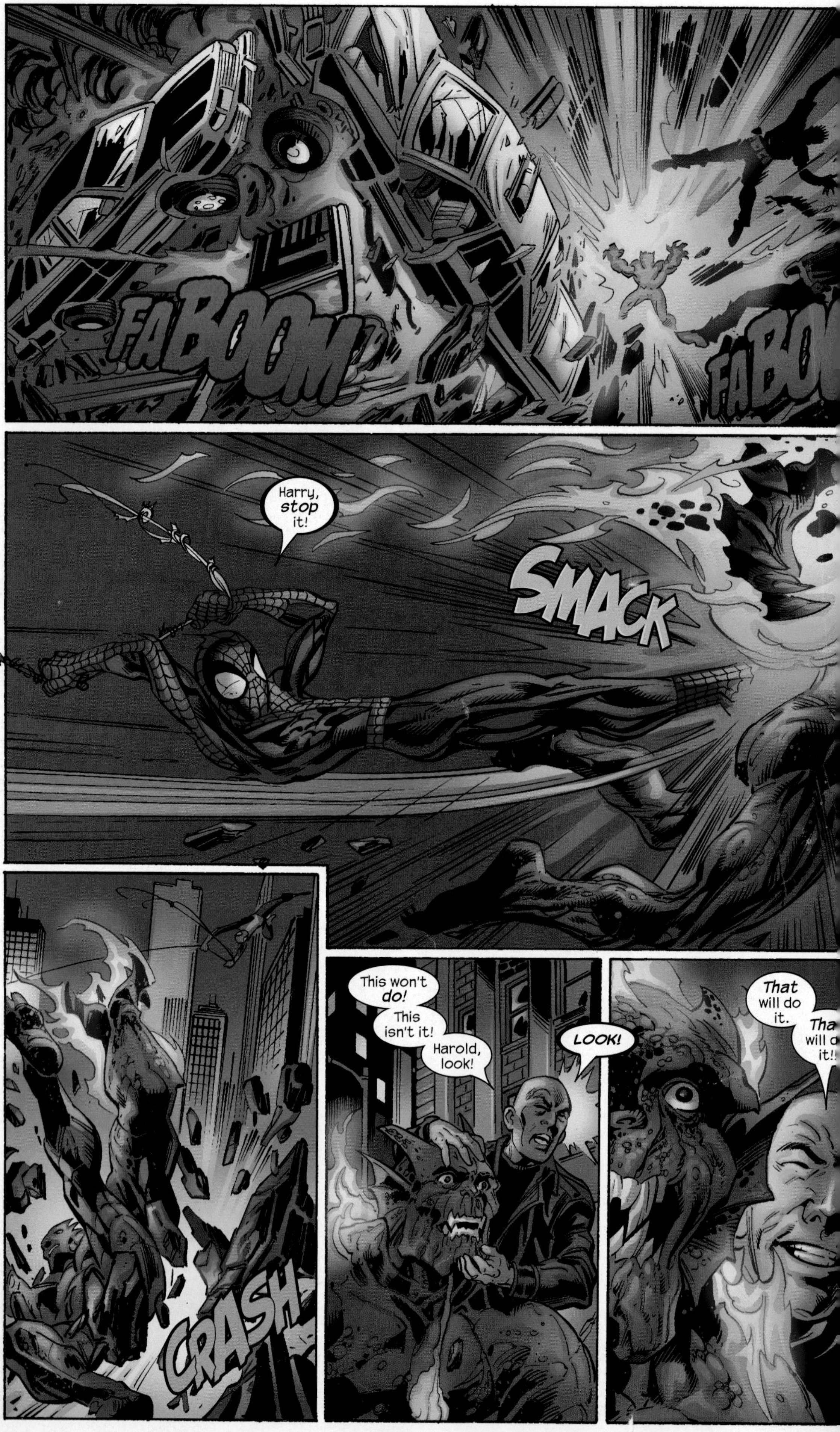
FABOOM
FABOO
Harry, stop it!
SMACK
CRASH
This won't do!
This isn't it!
Harold, look!
LOOK!
That will do it.
Tha
will d
it!!

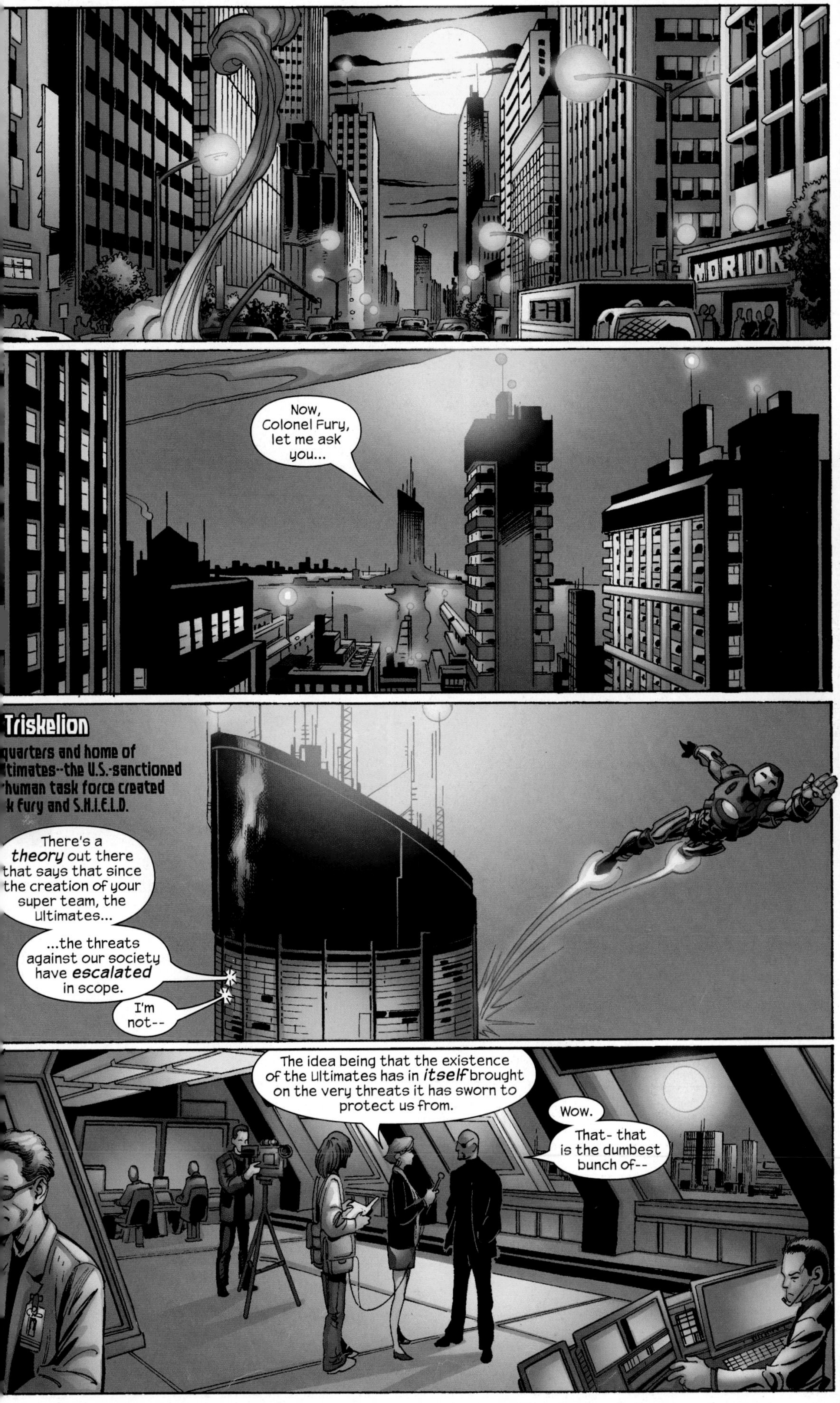

Now, Colonel Fury, let me ask you...
Triskelion
quarters and home of
timates--the U.S.-sanctioned
human task force created
k Fury and S.H.I.E.L.D.
There's a *theory* out there that says that since the creation of your super team, the Ultimates...
...the threats against our society have *escalated* in scope.
I'm not--
The idea being that the existence of the Ultimates has in *itself* brought on the very threats it has sworn to protect us from.
Wow.
That- that is the dumbest bunch of--

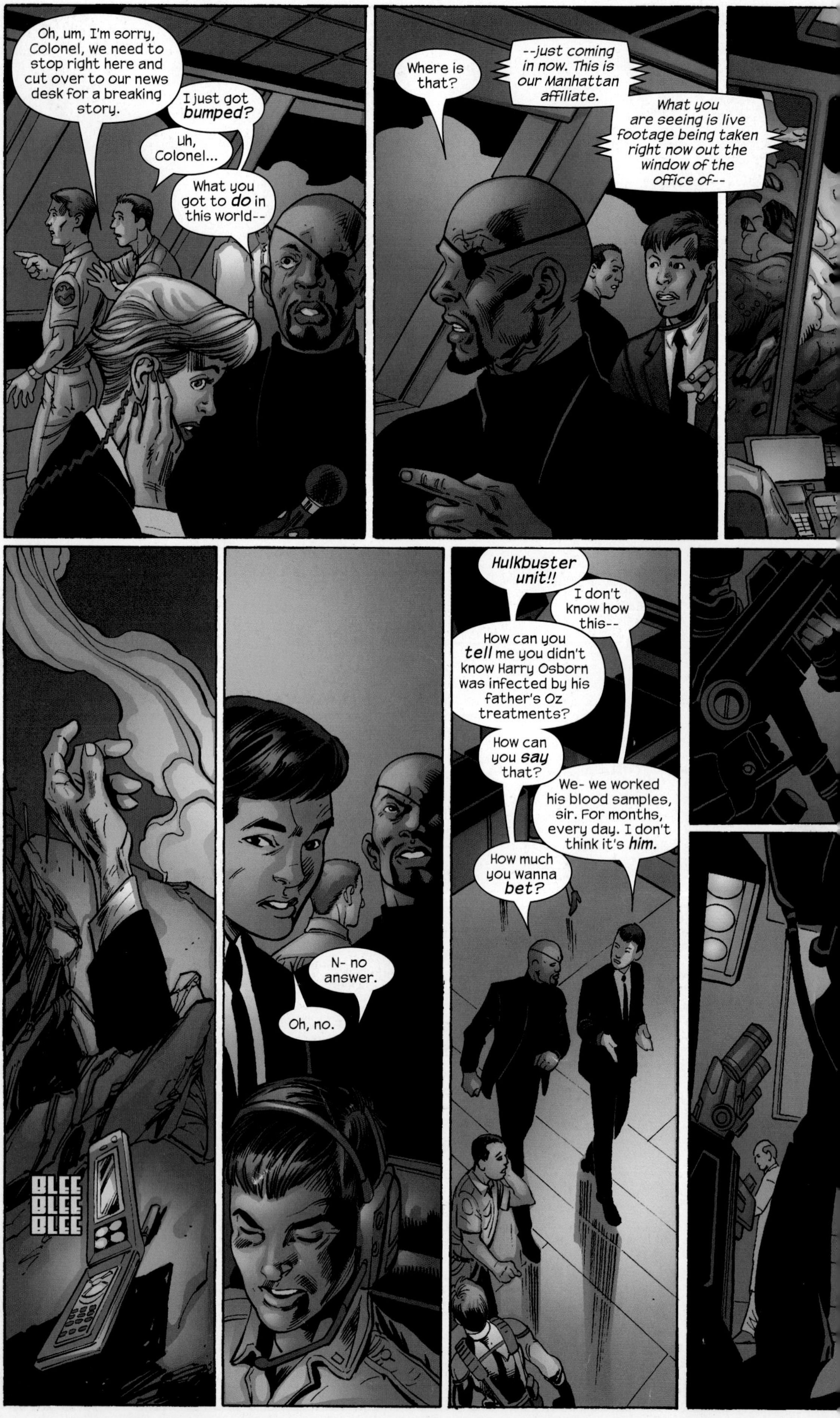

Oh, um, I'm sorry, Colonel, we need to stop right here and cut over to our news desk for a breaking story.
I just got bumped?
Uh, Colonel...
What you got to do in this world--
Where is that?
--just coming in now. This is our Manhattan affiliate.
What you are seeing is live footage being taken right now out the window of the office of--
BLEE BLEE BLEE
N- no answer.
Oh, no.
Hulkbuster unit!!
I don't know how this--
How can you tell me you didn't know Harry Osborn was infected by his father's Oz treatments?
How can you say that?
We- we worked his blood samples, sir. For months, every day. I don't think it's him.
How much you wanna bet?

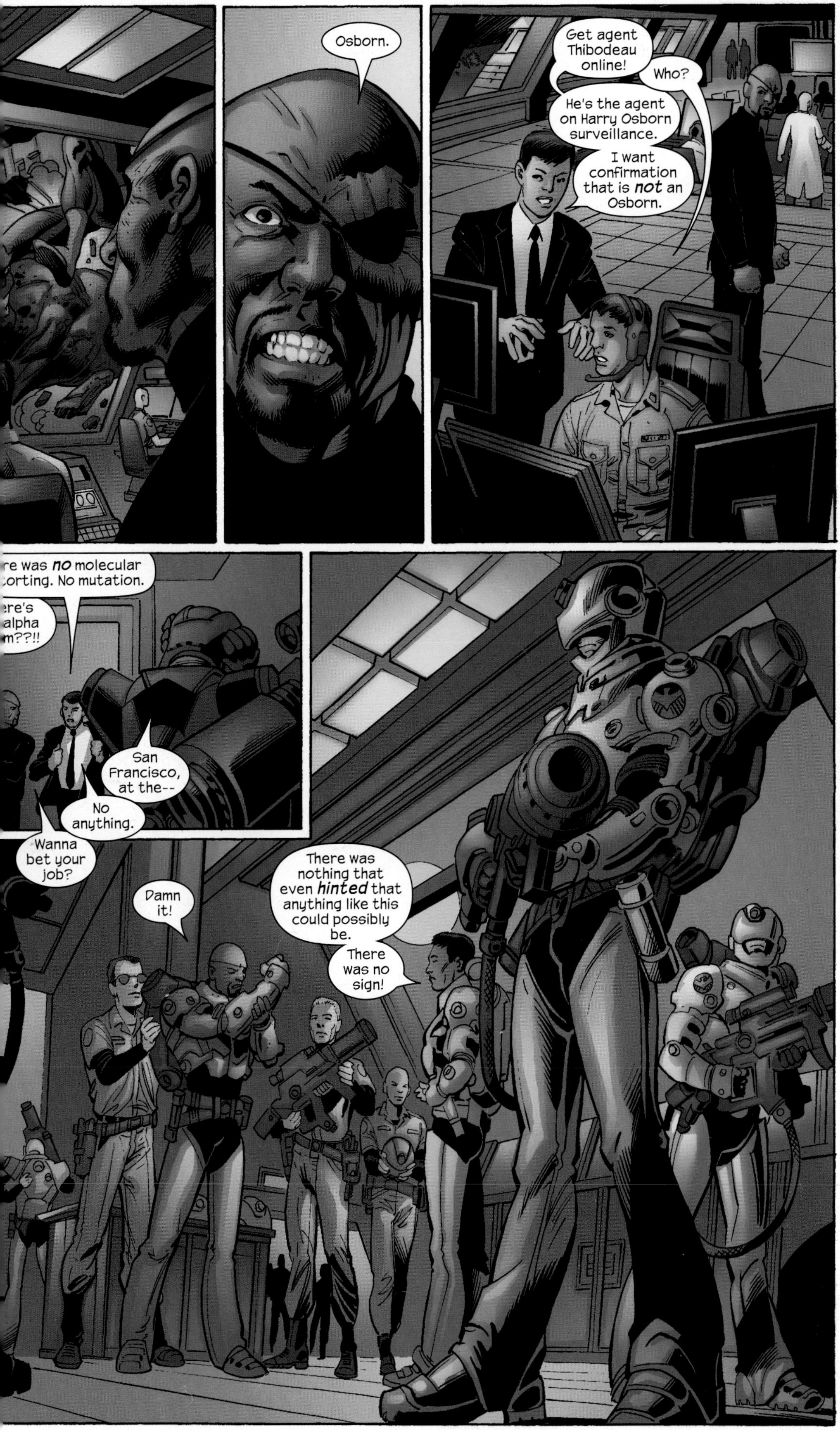

Osborn.
Get agent Thibodeau online!
Who?
He's the agent on Harry Osborn surveillance.
I want confirmation that is *not* an Osborn.
re was *no* molecular orting. No mutation.
ere's alpha m??!!
San Francisco, at the--
No anything.
Wanna bet your job?
Damn it!
There was nothing that even *hinted* that anything like this could possibly be.
There was no sign!

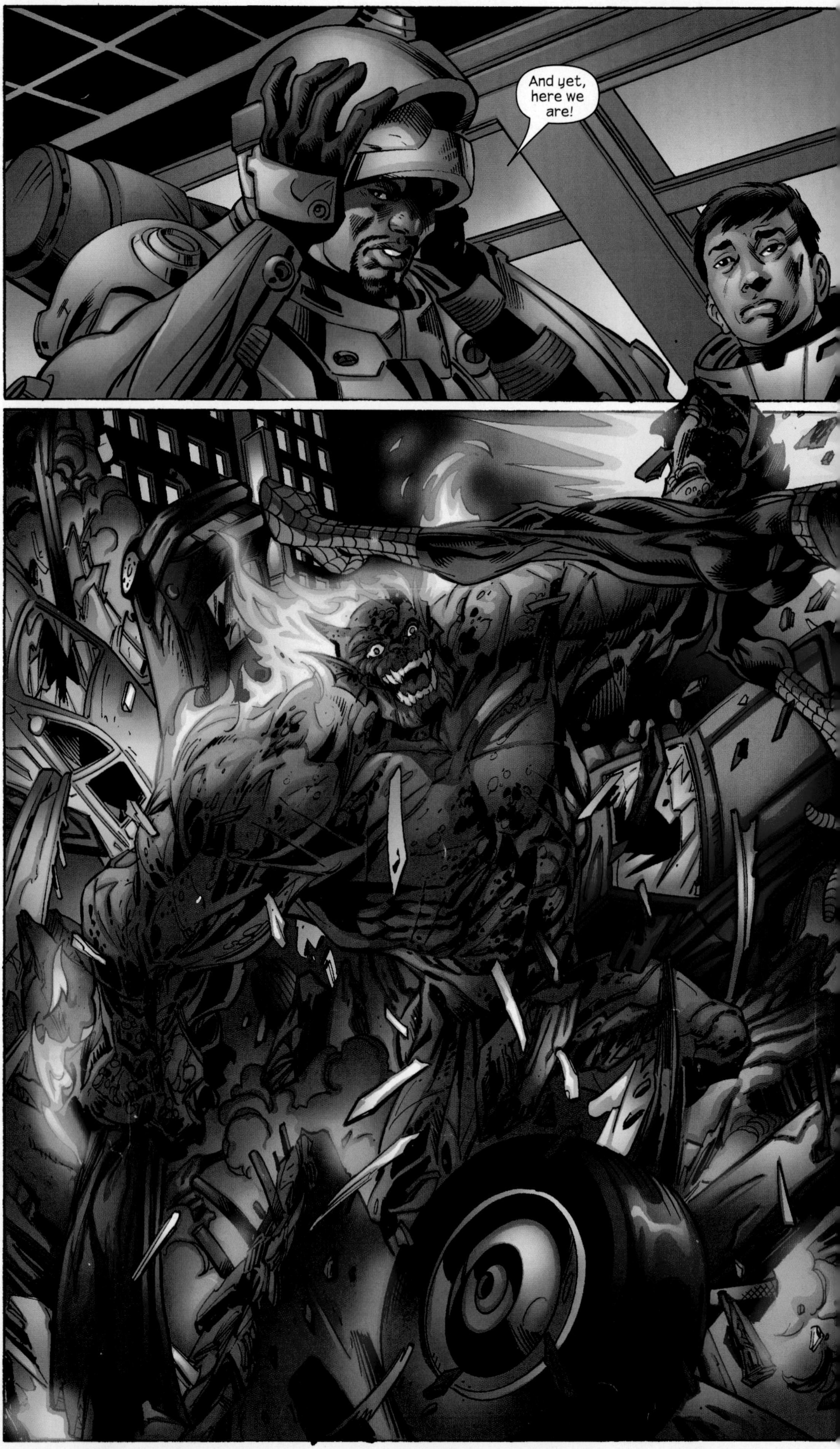
And yet, here we are!

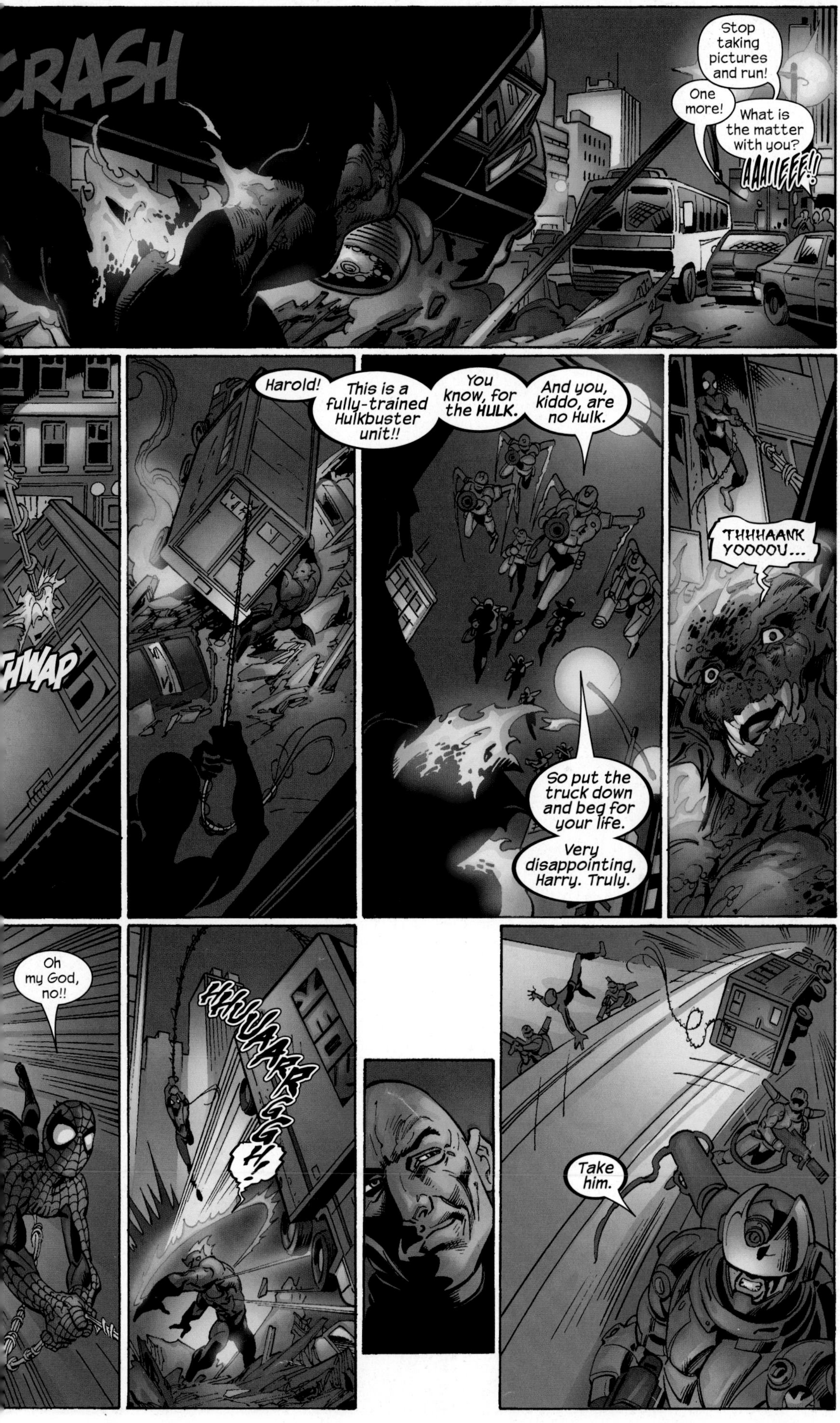
CRASH
Stop taking pictures and run!
One more!
What is the matter with you?
AAAIIEEE!!
THWAP
Harold!
This is a fully-trained Hulkbuster unit!!
You know, for the HULK.
And you, kiddo, are no Hulk.
So put the truck down and beg for your life.
Very disappointing, Harry. Truly.
THHHAANK YOOOOU...
Oh my God, no!!
HHUAARRGGGH!
Take him.

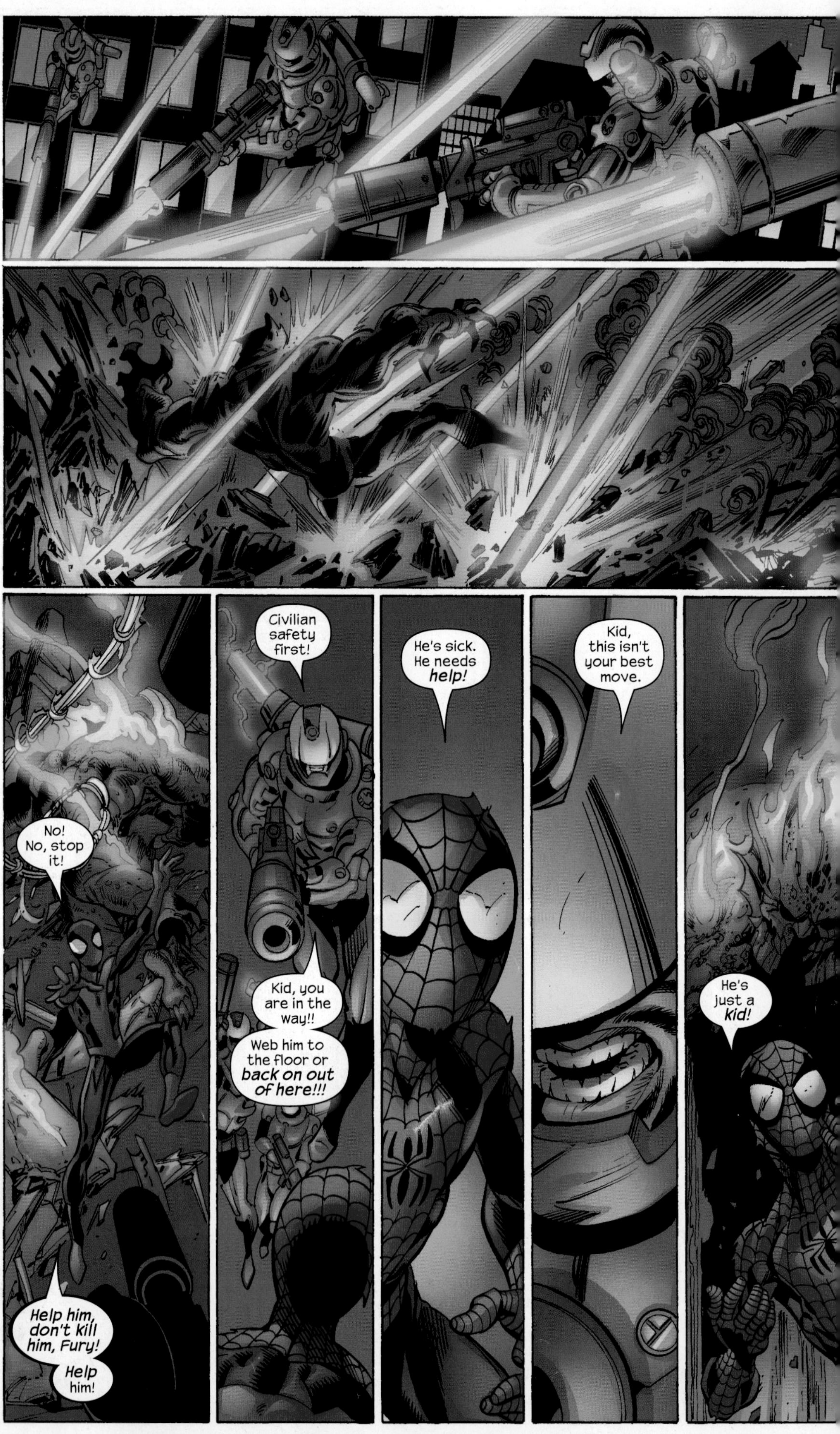

No! No, stop it!
Help him, don't kill him, Fury!
Help him!
Civilian safety first!
Kid, you are in the way!!
Web him to the floor or back on out of here!!!
He's sick. He needs help!
Kid, this isn't your best move.
He's just a kid!

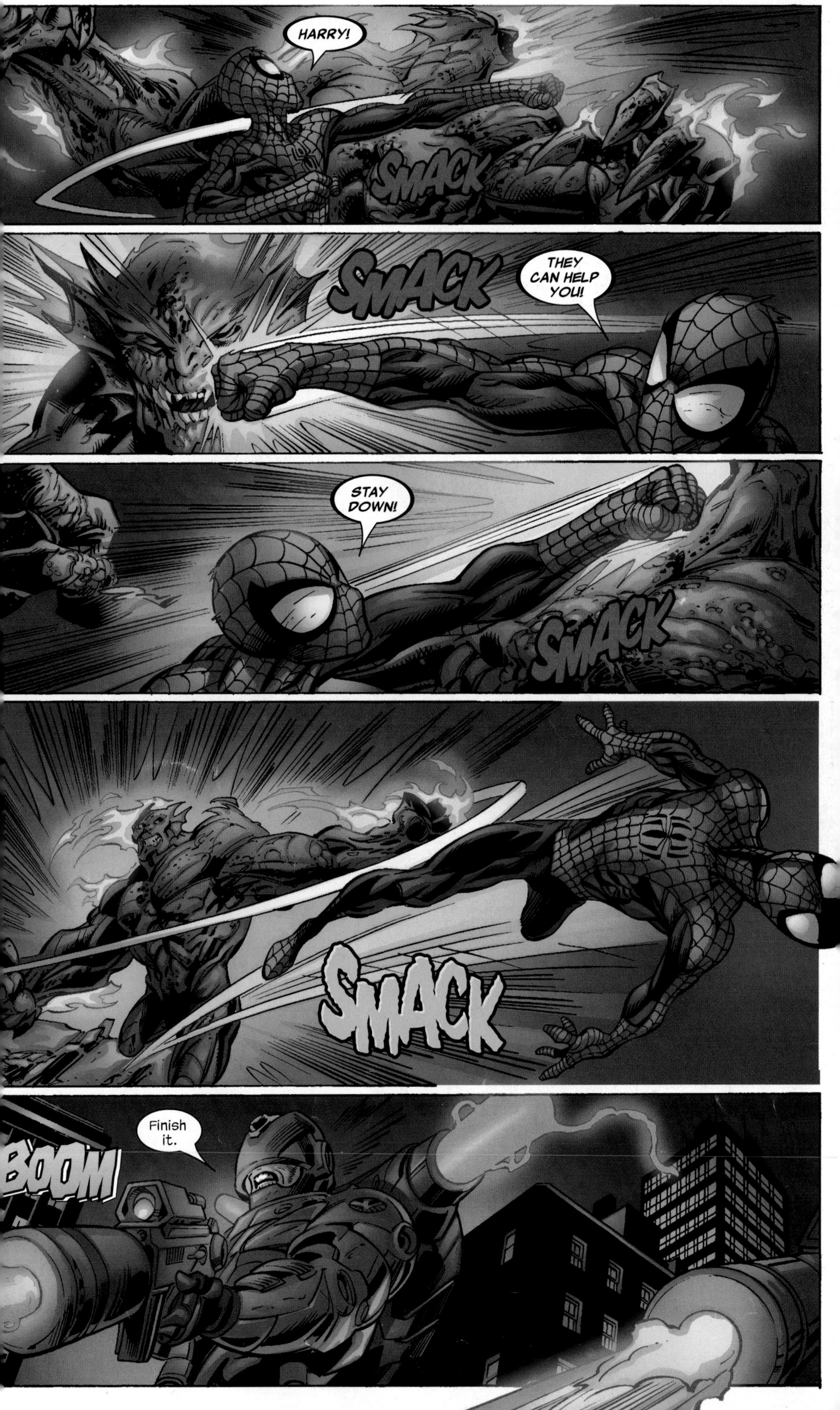
HARRY!
SMACK
SMACK
THEY CAN HELP YOU!
STAY DOWN!
SMACK
SMACK
Finish it.
BOOM

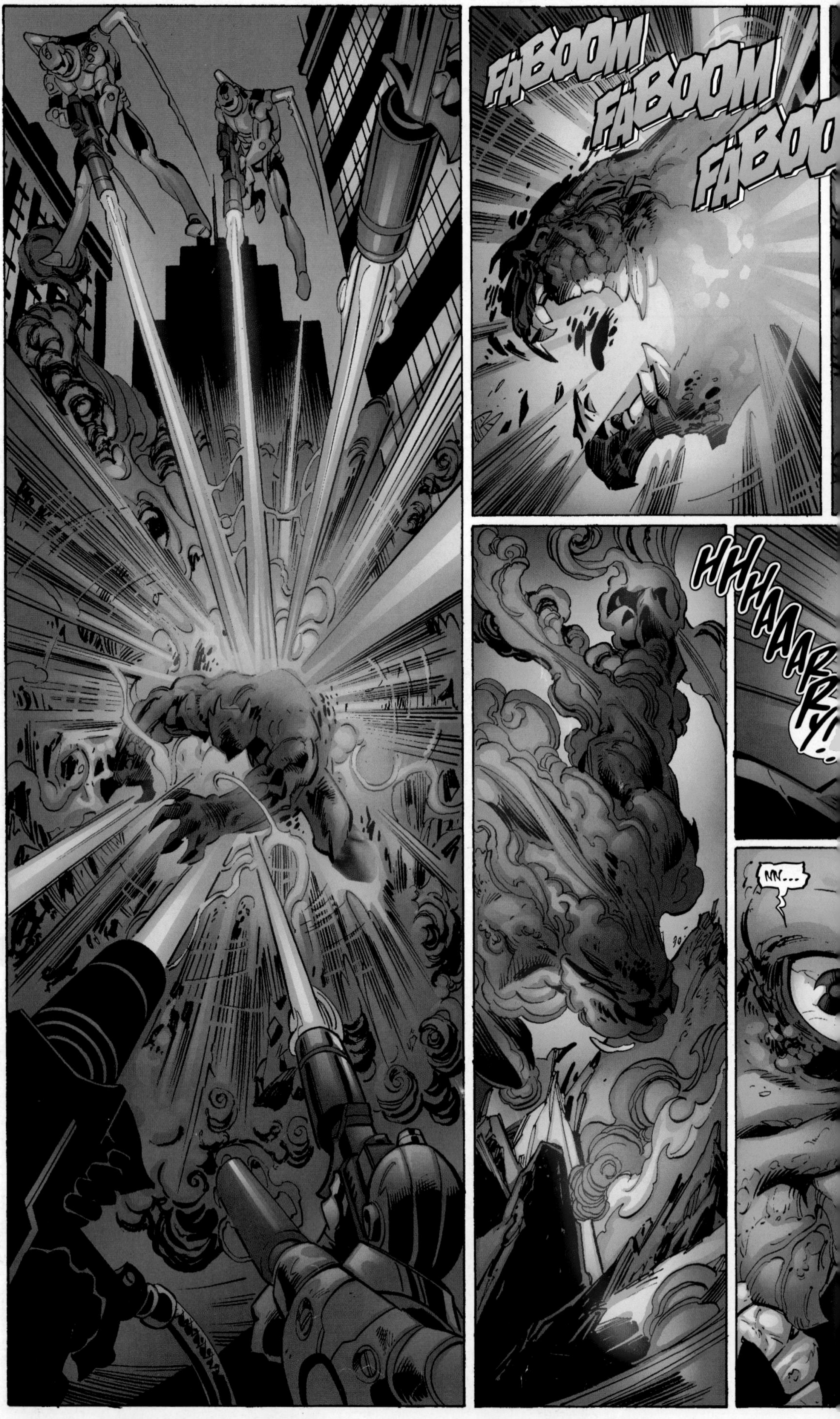
FABOOM
FABOOM
FABOO
HHHAAAARRY!
MN...

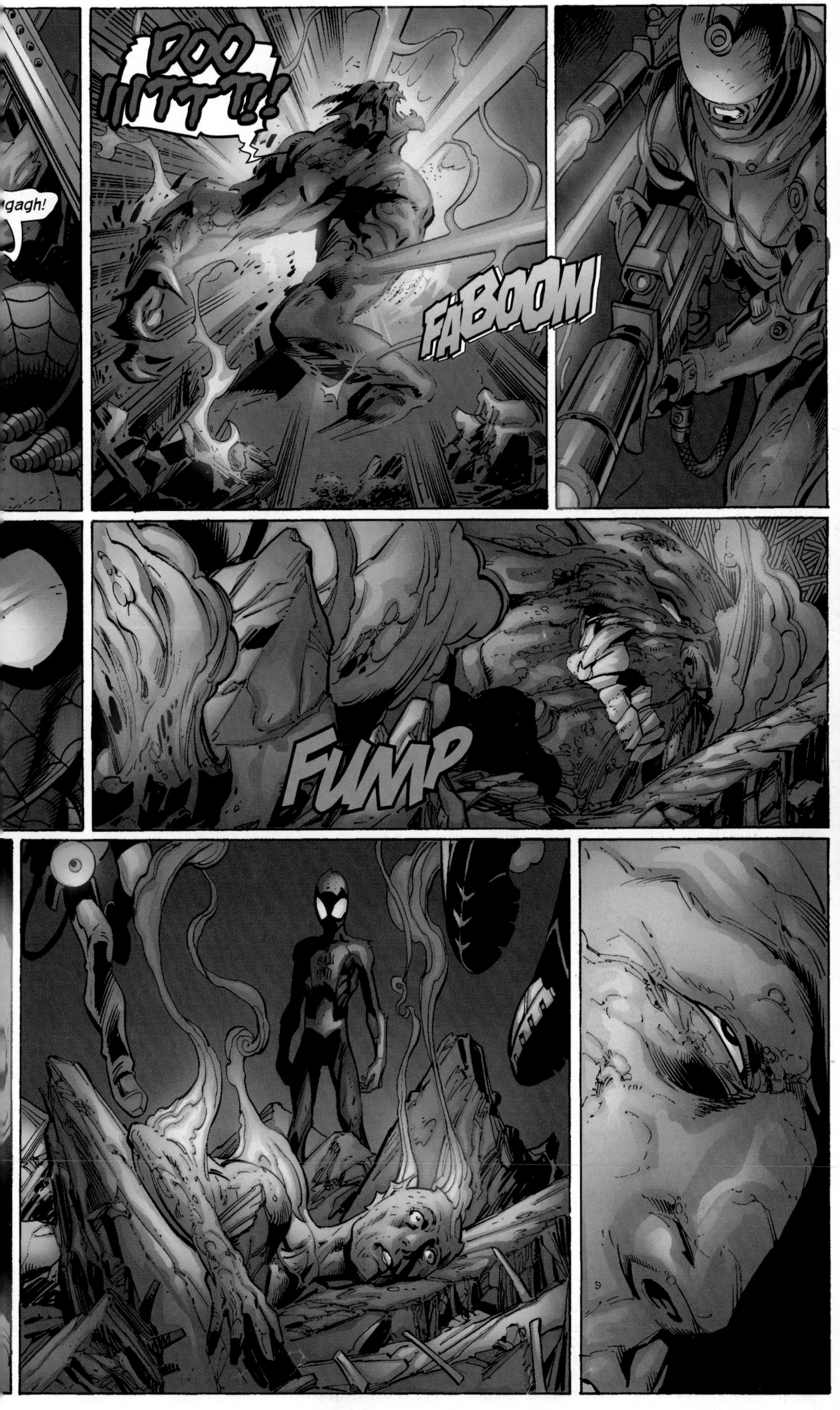
DOO IIITTT!!
gagh!
FABOOM
FUMP

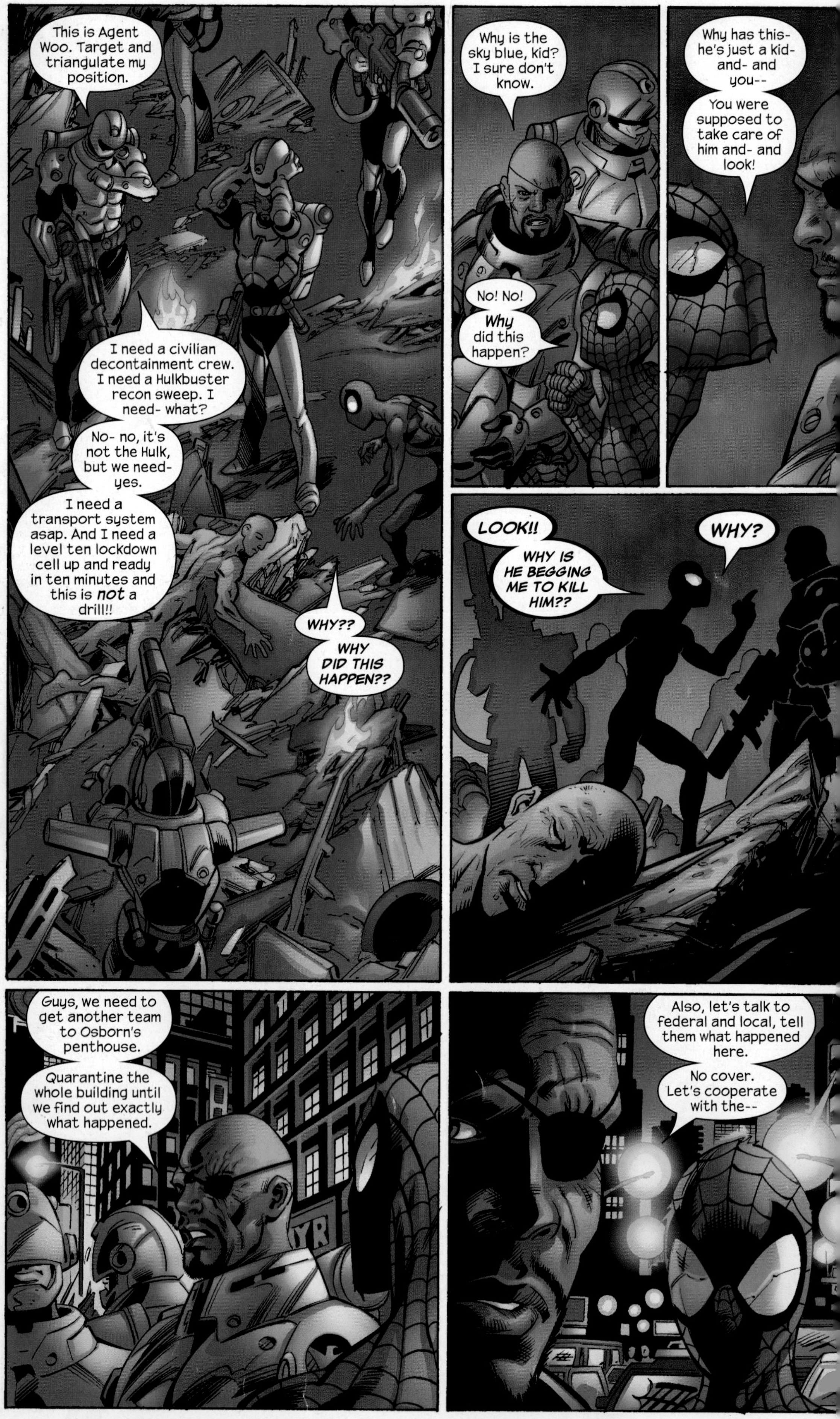

This is Agent Woo. Target and triangulate my position.
I need a civilian decontainment crew. I need a Hulkbuster recon sweep. I need- what?
No- no, it's not the Hulk, but we need- yes.
I need a transport system asap. And I need a level ten lockdown cell up and ready in ten minutes and this is not a drill!!
WHY??
WHY DID THIS HAPPEN??
Why is the sky blue, kid? I sure don't know.
No! No!
Why did this happen?
Why has this- he's just a kid- and- and you--
You were supposed to take care of him and- and look!
LOOK!!
WHY IS HE BEGGING ME TO KILL HIM??
WHY?
Guys, we need to get another team to Osborn's penthouse.
Quarantine the whole building until we find out exactly what happened.
Also, let's talk to federal and local, tell them what happened here.
No cover. Let's cooperate with the--

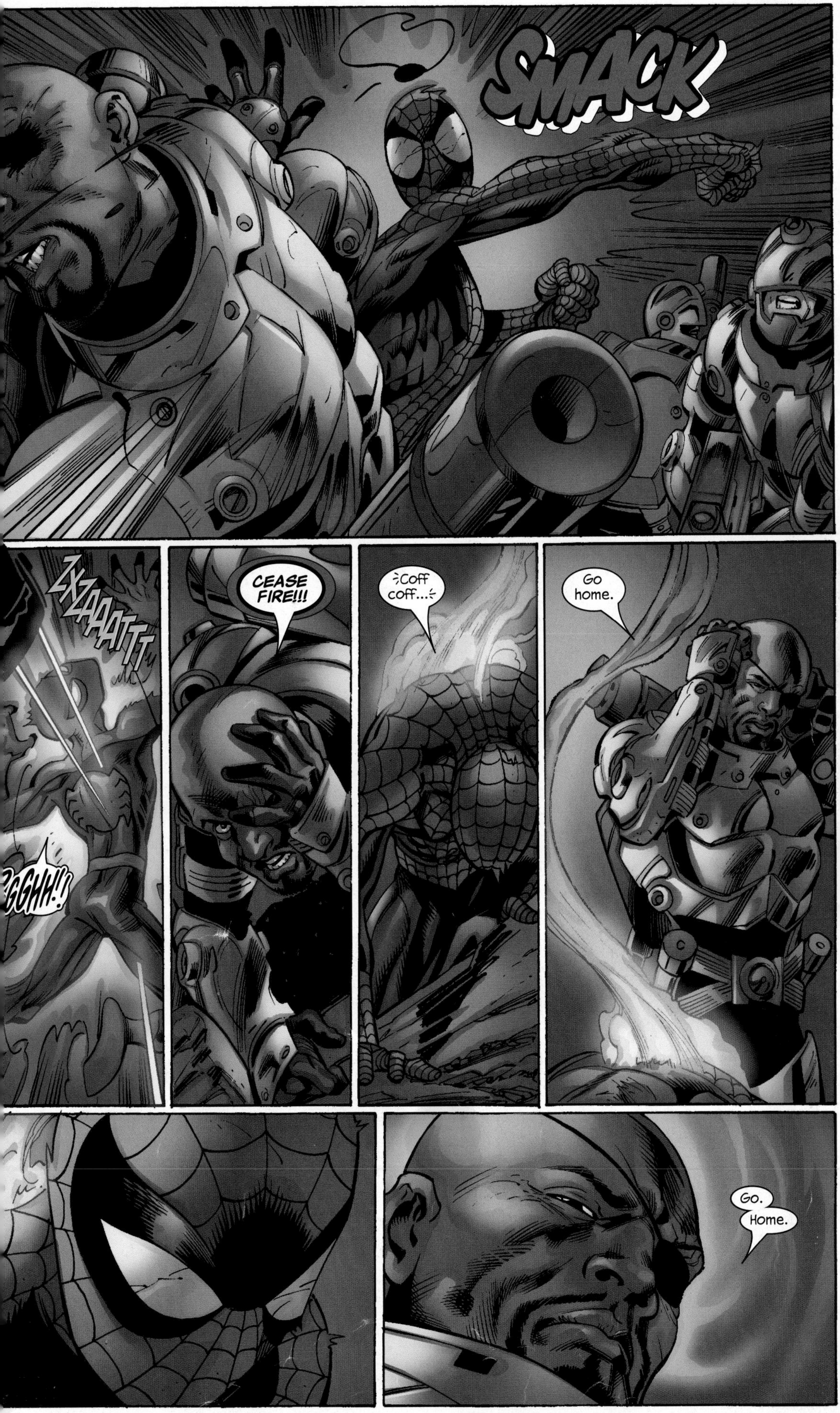

SMACK
ZXZAAAATTT
GGHH!!
CEASE FIRE!!!
Coff coff...
Go home.
Go.
Home.

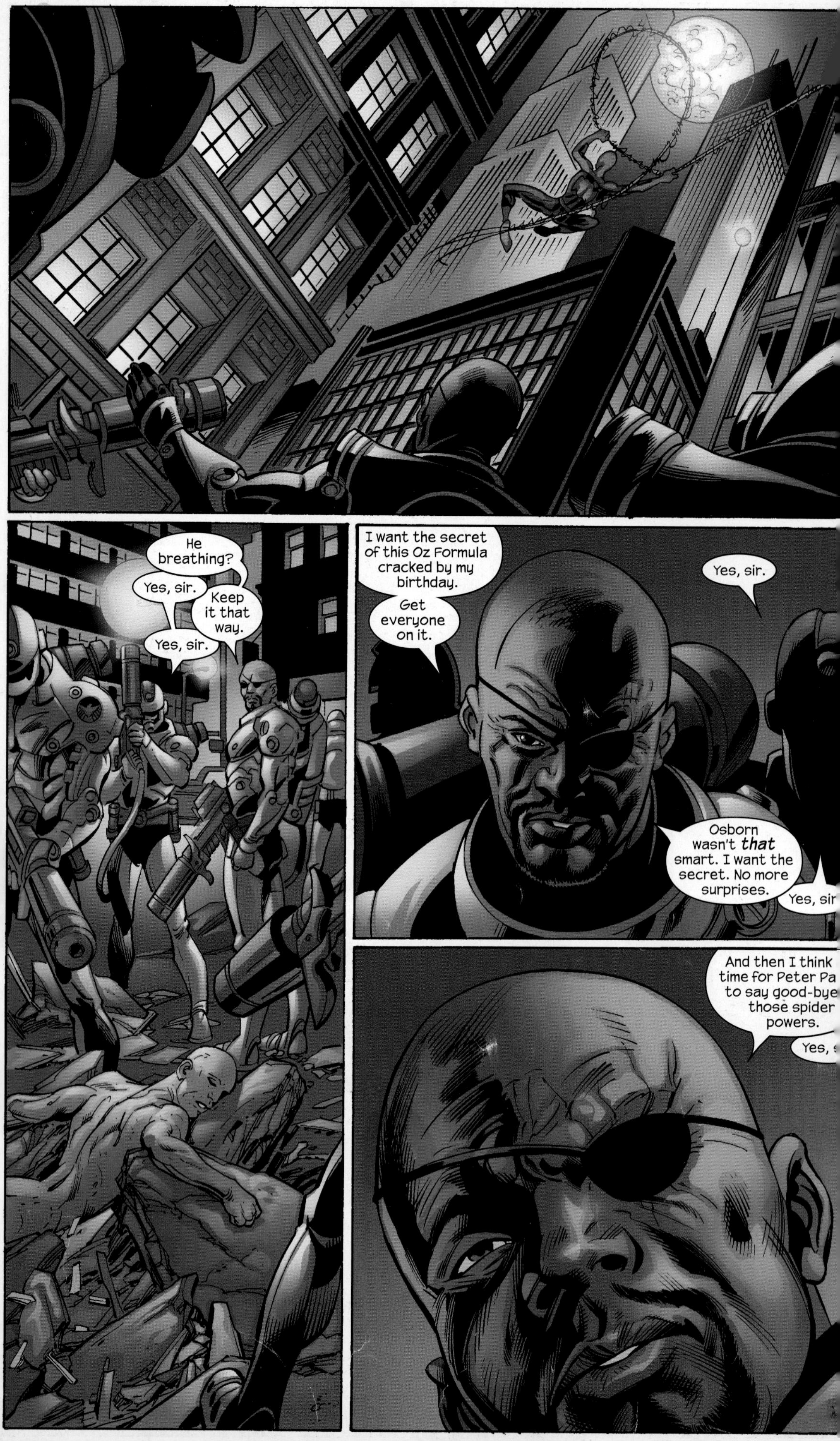
He breathing?
Yes, sir.
Keep it that way.
Yes, sir.
I want the secret of this Oz Formula cracked by my birthday.
Get everyone on it.
Yes, sir.
Osborn wasn't *that* smart. I want the secret. No more surprises.
Yes, sir
And then I think time for Peter Pa to say good-bye those spider powers.
Yes,

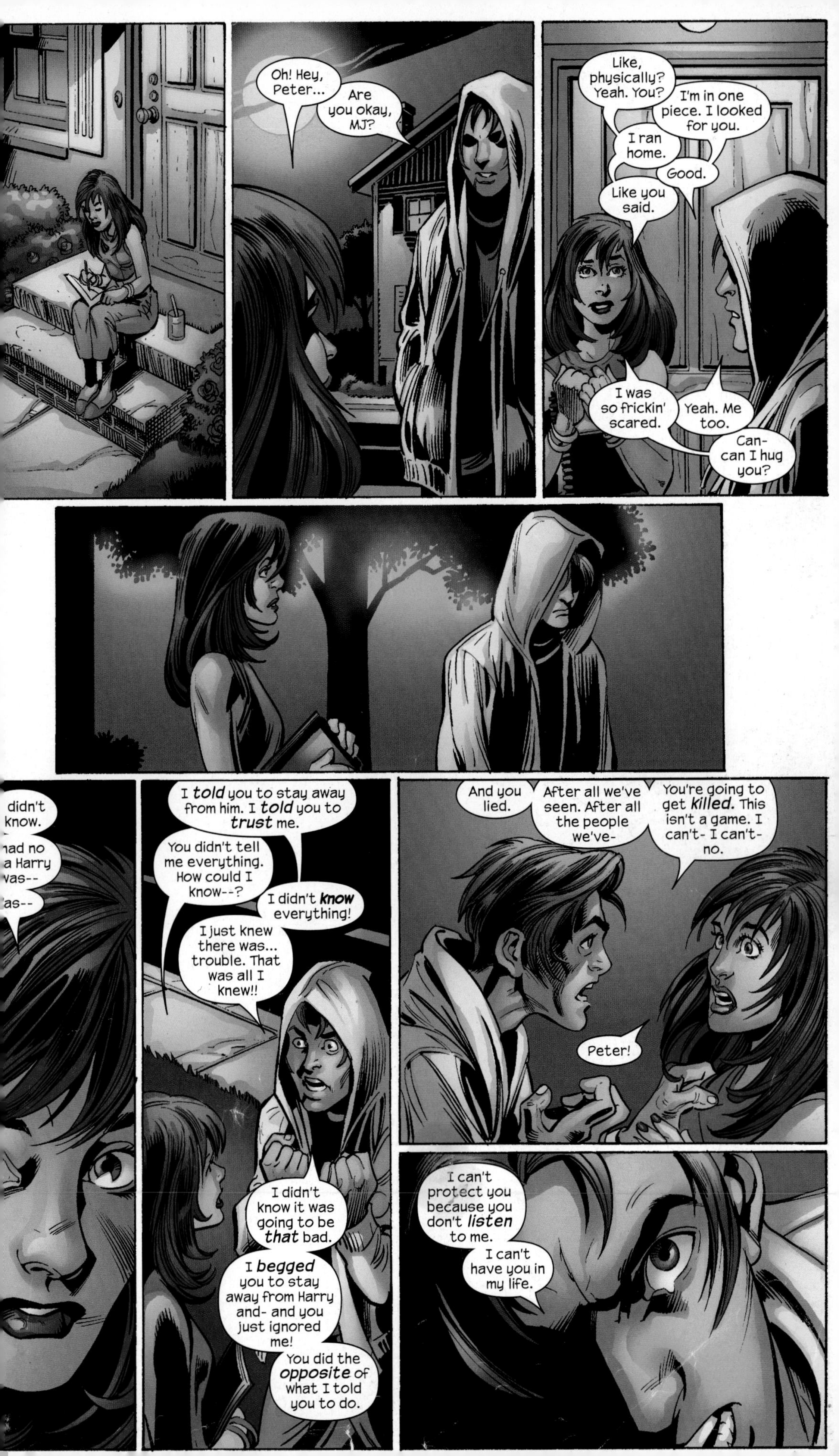
Oh! Hey, Peter...
Are you okay, MJ?
Like, physically? Yeah. You?
I'm in one piece. I looked for you.
I ran home.
Good.
Like you said.
I was so frickin' scared.
Yeah. Me too.
Can-can I hug you?
didn't know.
I *told* you to stay away from him. I *told* you to *trust* me.
You didn't tell me everything. How could I know--?
I didn't *know* everything!
I just knew there was... trouble. That was all I knew!!
I didn't know it was going to be *that* bad.
I *begged* you to stay away from Harry and- and you just ignored me!
You did the *opposite* of what I told you to do.
And you lied.
After all we've seen. After all the people we've-
You're going to get *killed.* This isn't a game. I can't- I can't- no.
Peter!
I can't protect you because you don't *listen* to me.
I can't have you in my life.

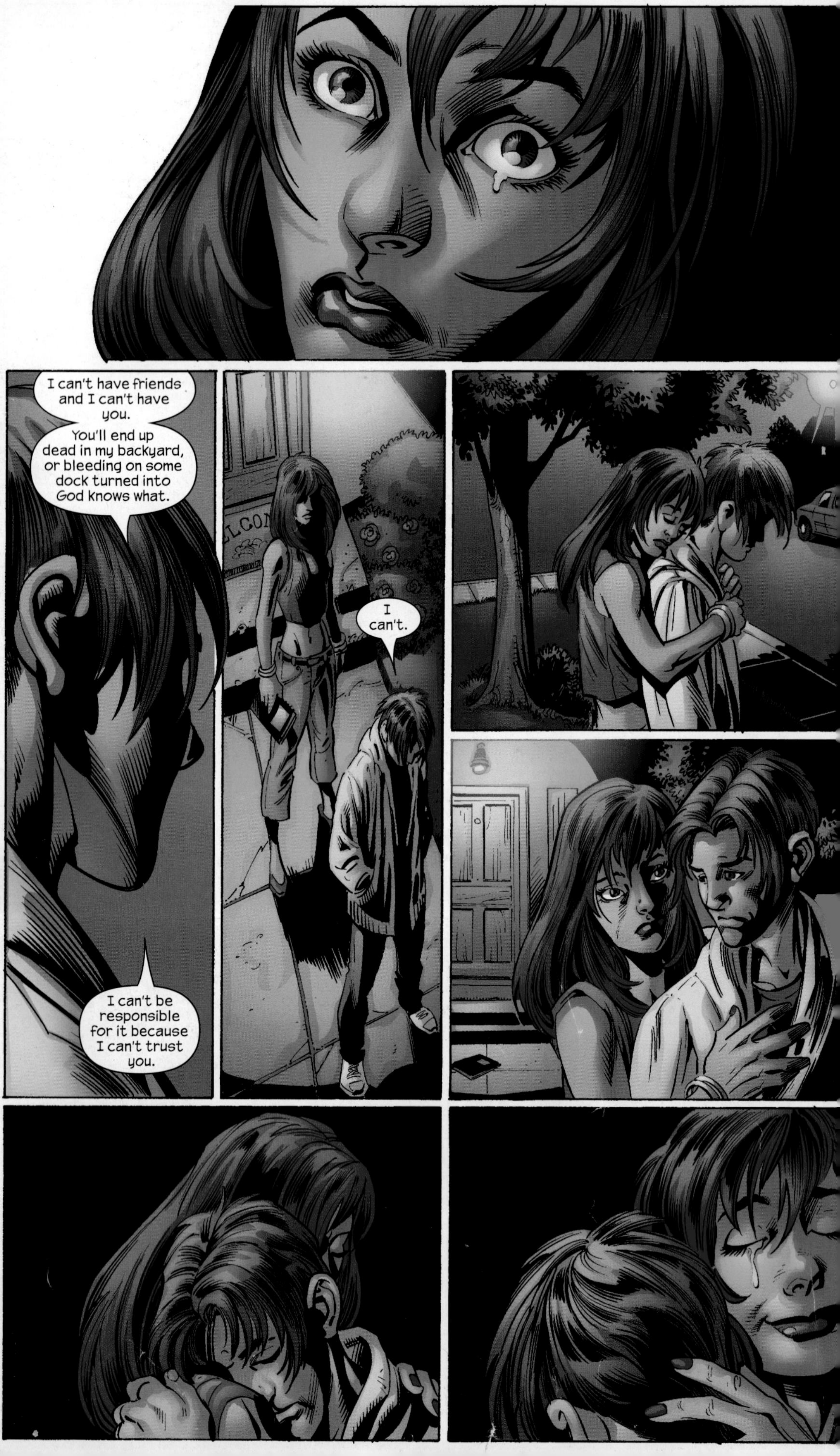
I can't have friends and I can't have you.
You'll end up dead in my backyard, or bleeding on some dock turned into God knows what.
I can't be responsible for it because I can't trust you.
I can't.

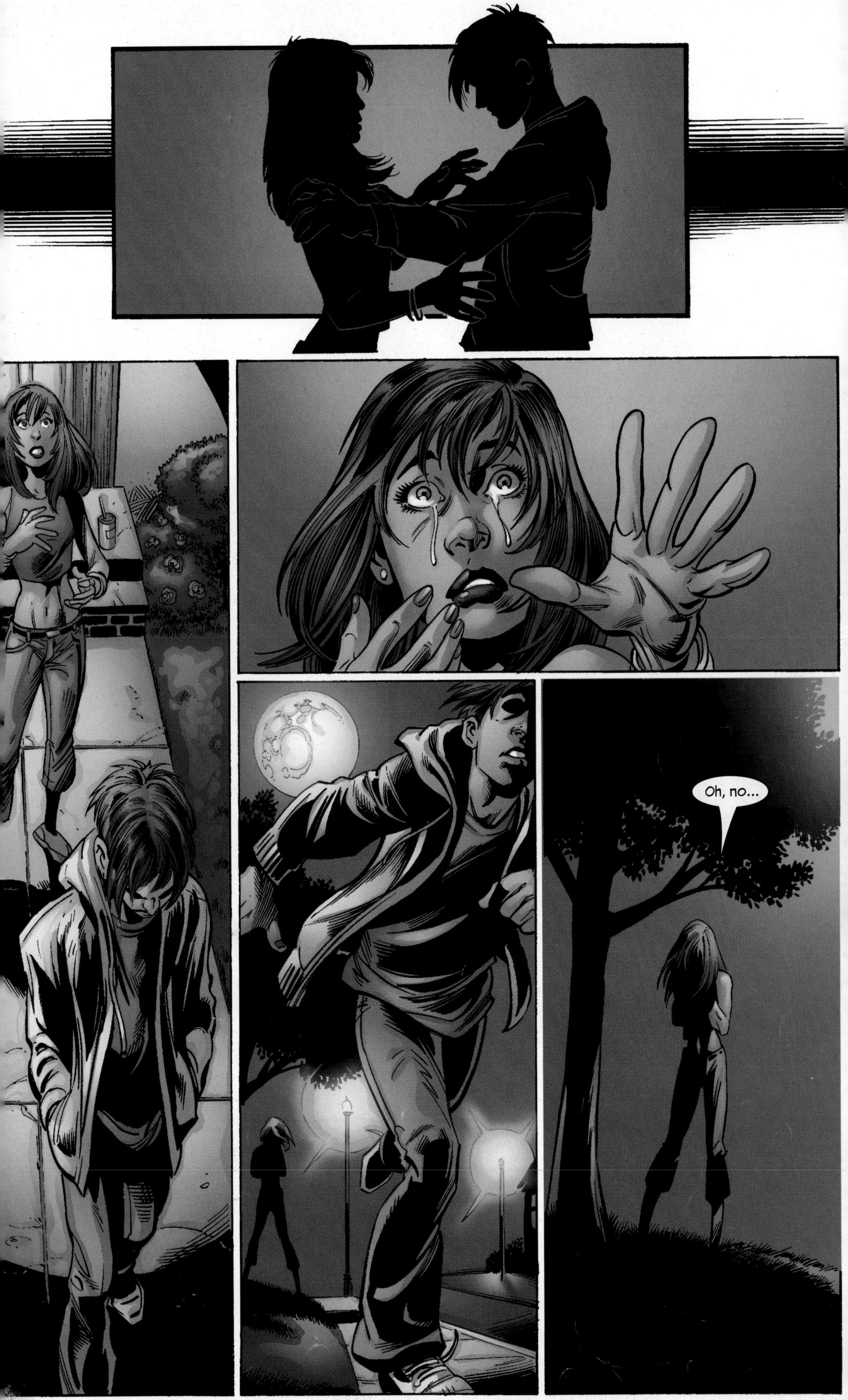
Oh, no...

78

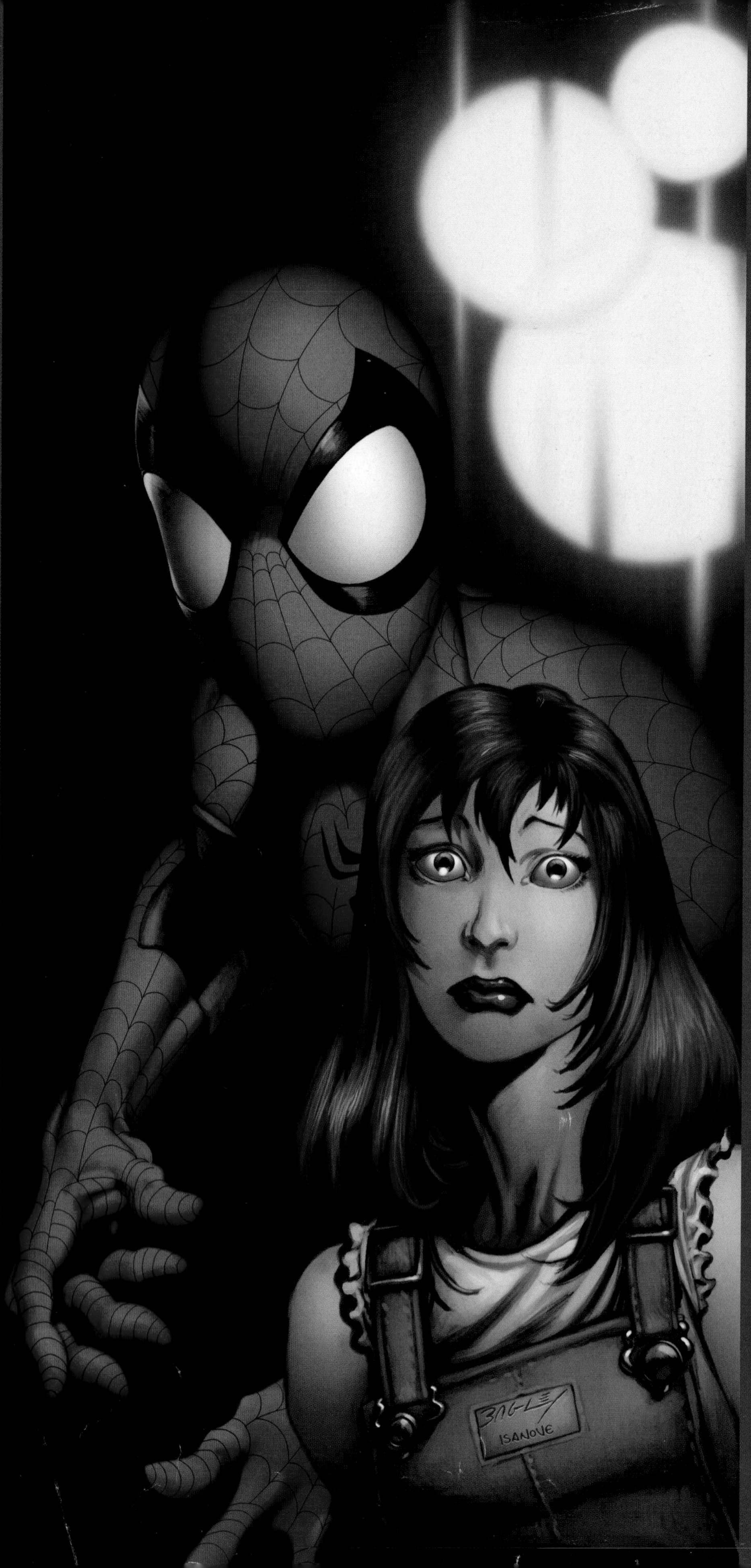
BAGLEY
ISANOVE

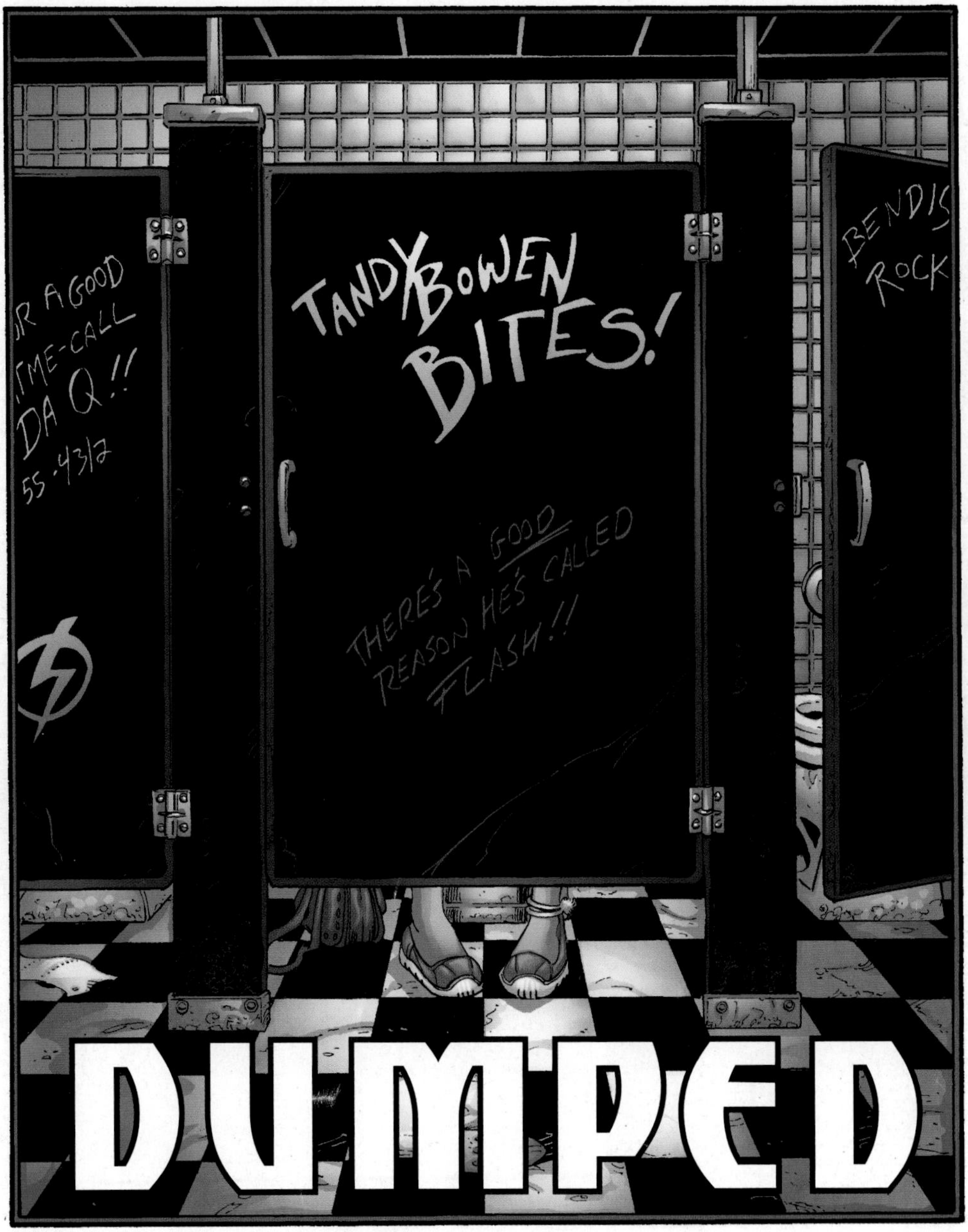
R A GOOD
TIME-CALL
DA Q !!
55-4312
TANDY BOWEN
BITES!
BENDIS
ROCK
THERE'S A GOOD
REASON HE'S CALLED
FLASH!!
DUMPED

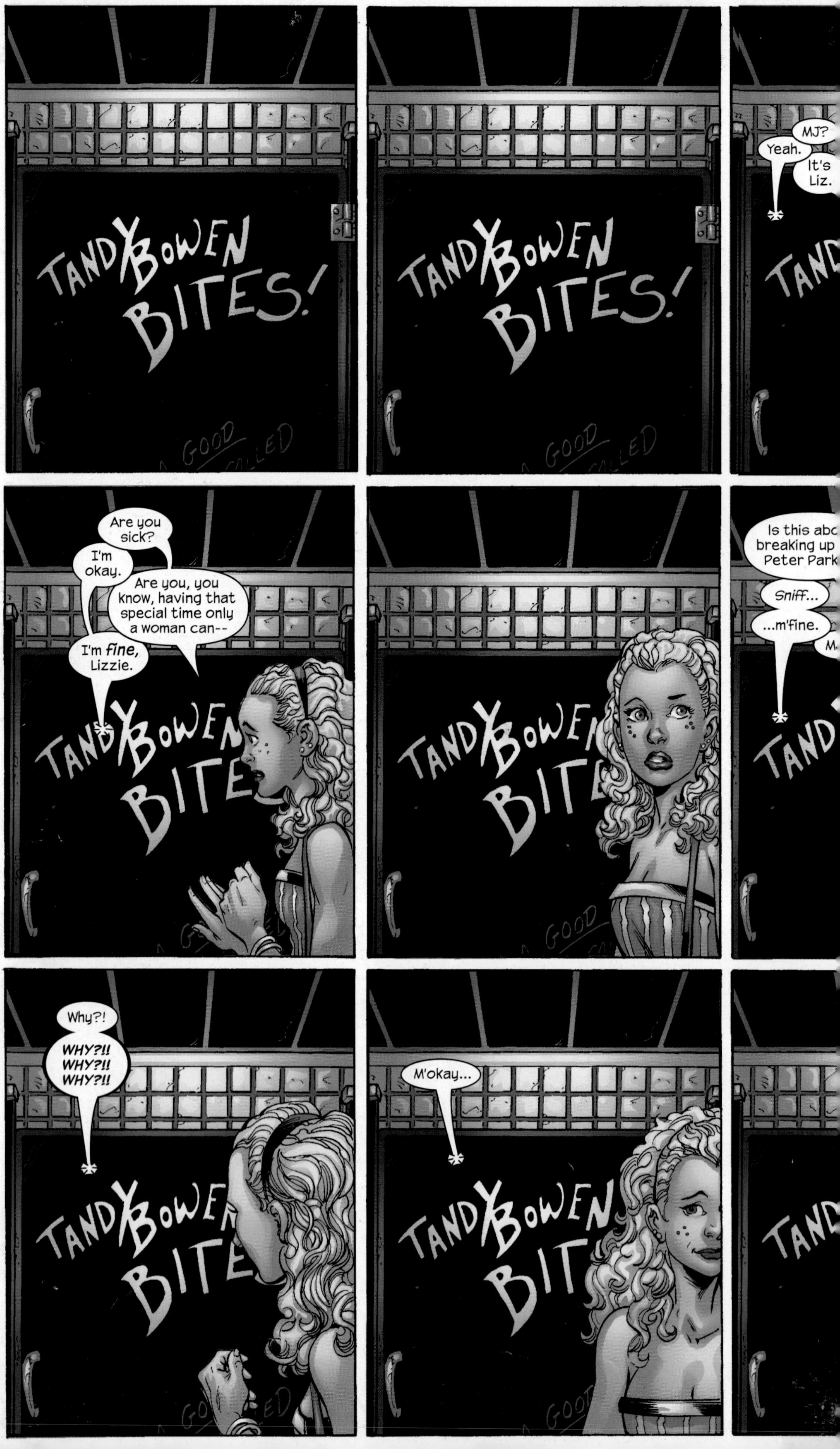
TANDY BOWEN BITES!
MJ?
Yeah.
It's Liz.
Are you sick?
I'm okay.
Are you, you know, having that special time only a woman can--
I'm *fine*, Lizzie.
Is this abo breaking up Peter Park
Sniff...
...m'fine.
Why?!
WHY?!! WHY?!! WHY?!!
M'okay...

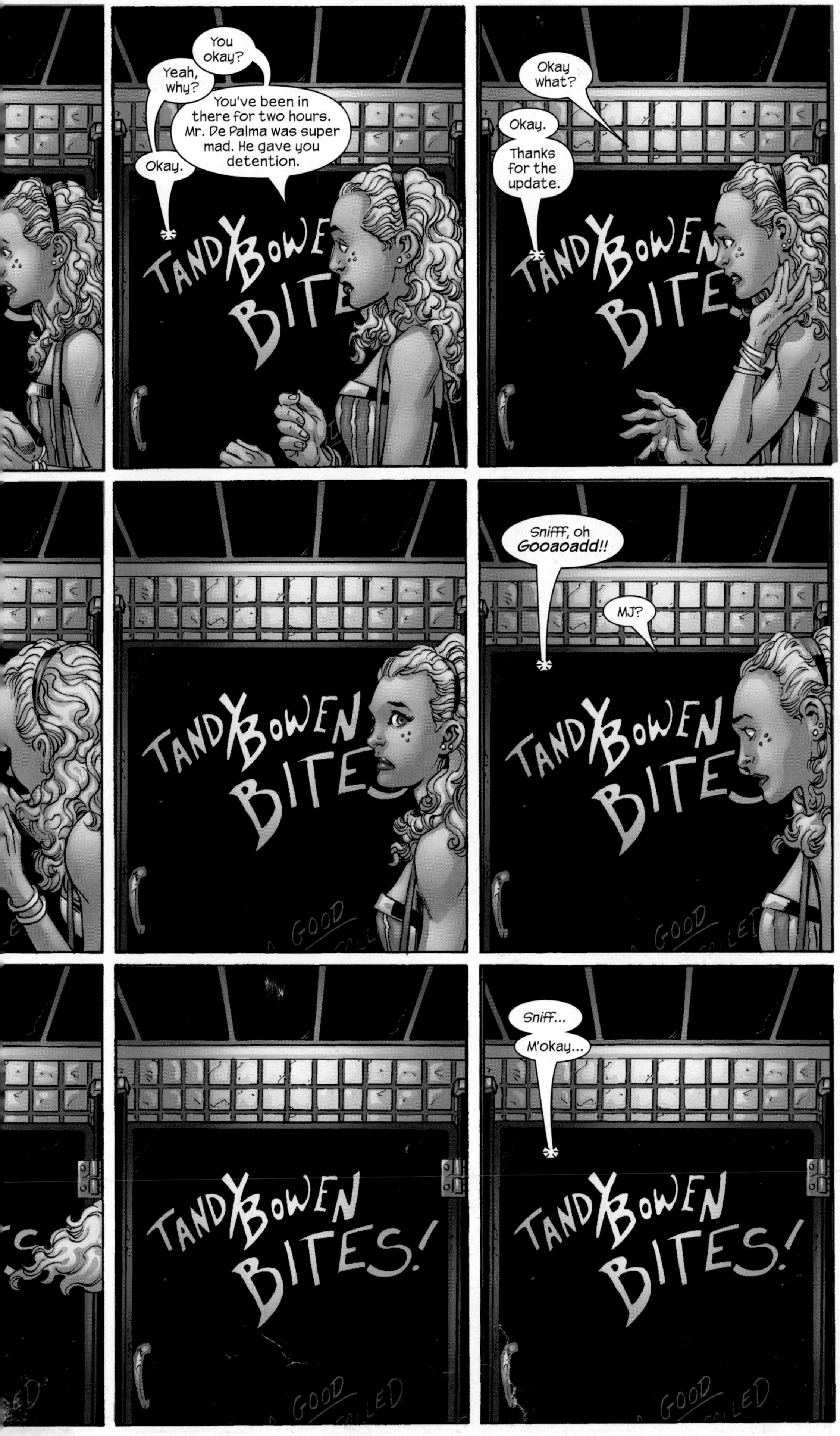

You okay?
Yeah, why?
You've been in there for two hours. Mr. De Palma was super mad. He gave you detention.
Okay.
TANDY BOWEN BITES
Okay what?
Okay.
Thanks for the update.
TANDY BOWEN BITES
TANDY BOWEN BITES
Snifff, oh Gooaoadd!!
MJ?
TANDY BOWEN BITES
GOOD
TANDY BOWEN BITES!
GOOD
CALLED
Sniff...
M'okay...
TANDY BOWEN BITES!
GOOD
CALLED

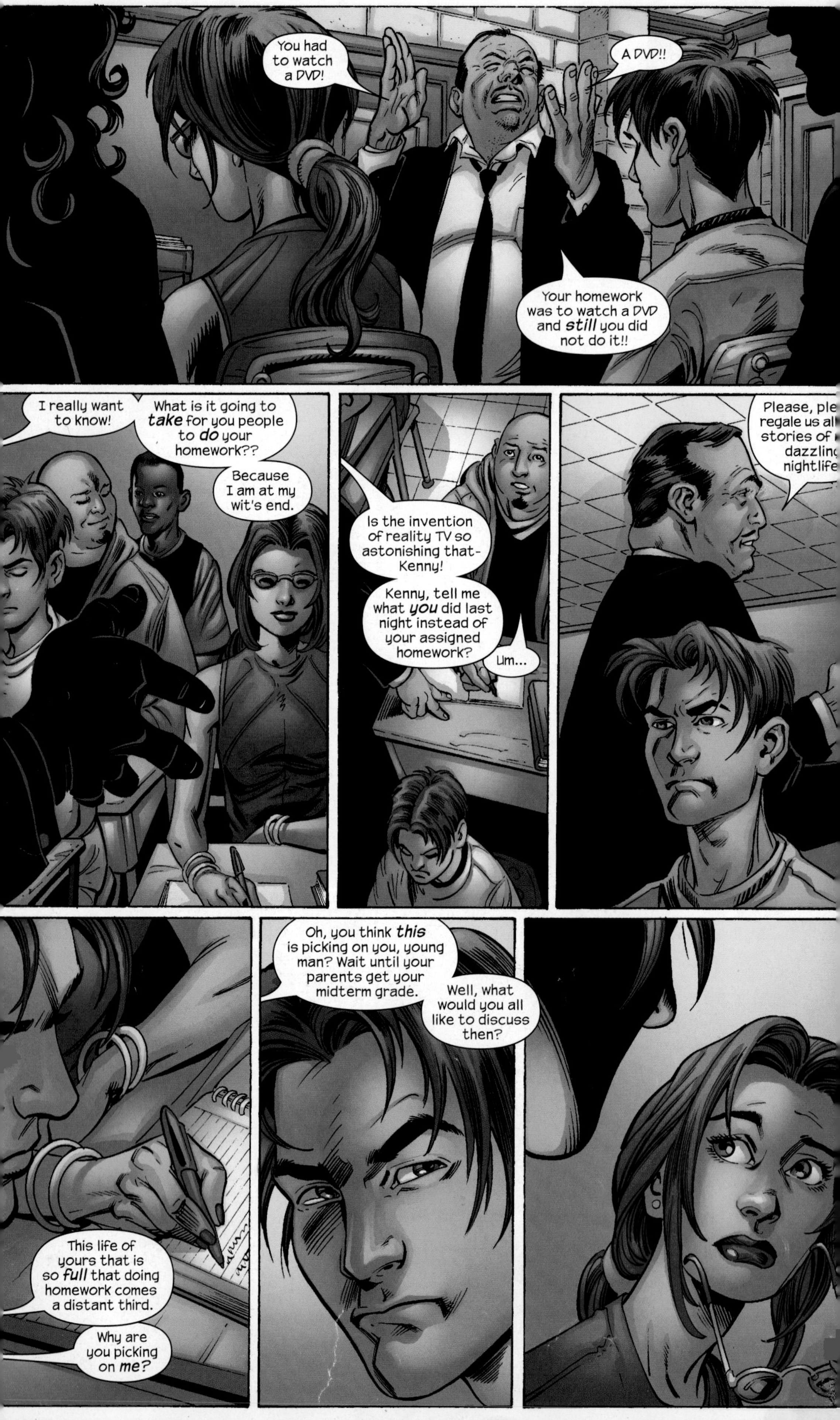

You had to watch a DVD!
A DVD!!
Your homework was to watch a DVD and *still* you did not do it!!
I really want to know!
What is it going to *take* for you people to *do* your homework??
Because I am at my wit's end.
Is the invention of reality TV so astonishing that- Kenny!
Kenny, tell me what *you* did last night instead of your assigned homework?
Um...
Please, ple
regale us al
stories of
dazzlin
nightlife
This life of yours that is so *full* that doing homework comes a distant third.
Why are you picking on *me*?
Oh, you think *this* is picking on you, young man? Wait until your parents get your midterm grade.
Well, what would you all like to discuss then?

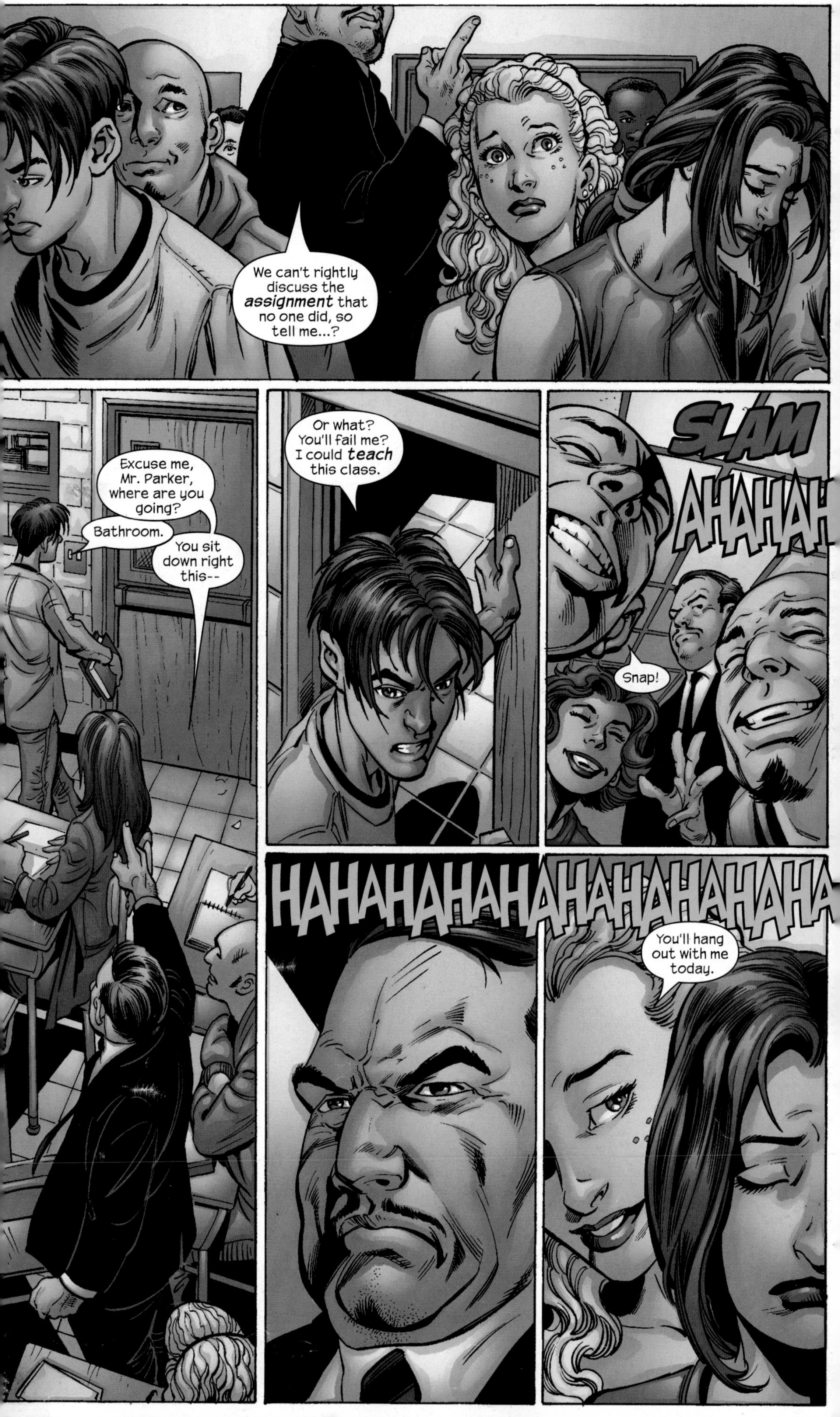
We can't rightly discuss the ***assignment*** that no one did, so tell me...?
Excuse me, Mr. Parker, where are you going?
Bathroom.
You sit down right this--
Or what? You'll fail me? I could ***teach*** this class.
SLAM
AHAHAH
Snap!
HAHAHAHAHAHAHAHAHAHA
You'll hang out with me today.

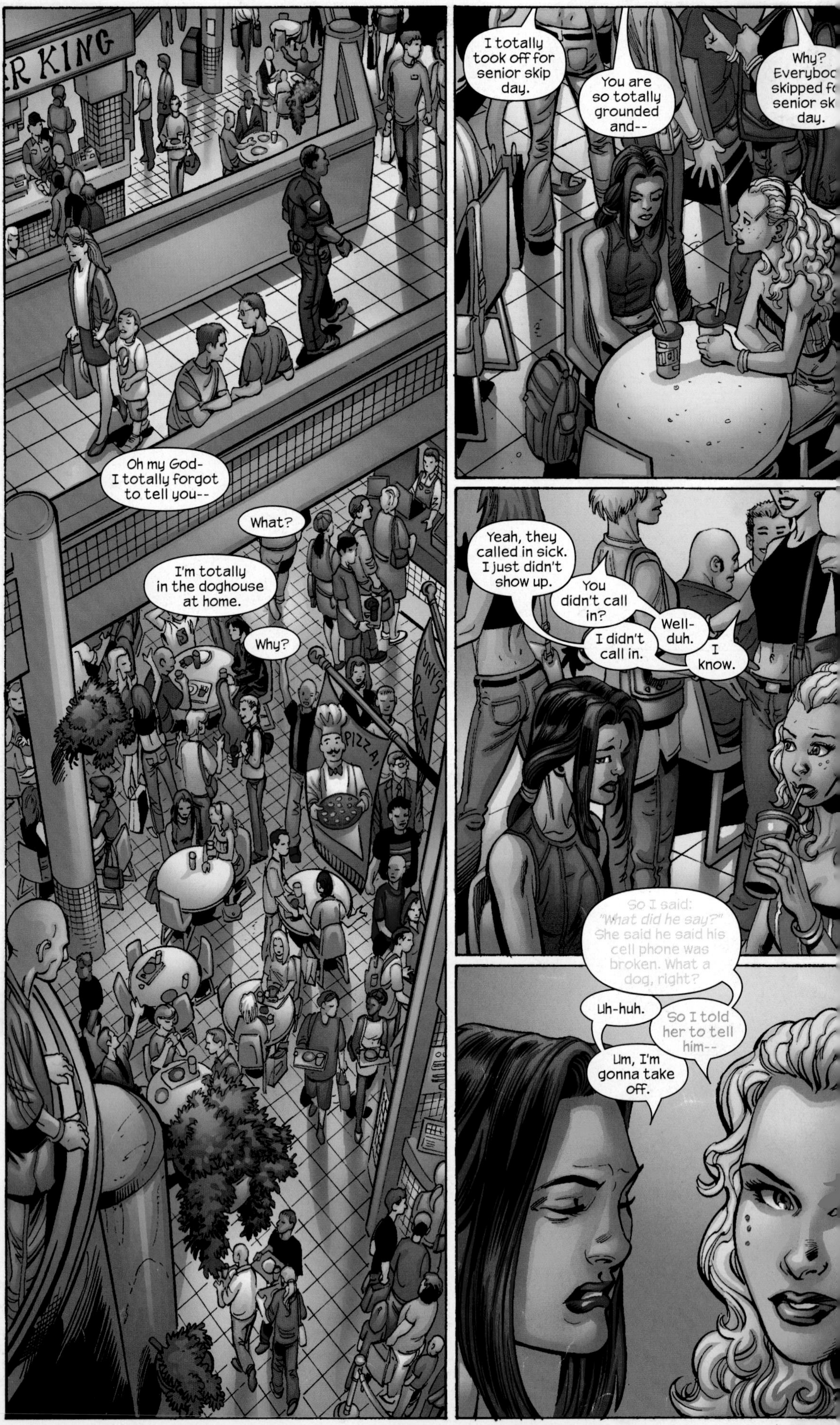
ER KING
Oh my God-
I totally forgot
to tell you--
What?
I'm totally
in the doghouse
at home.
Why?
PIZZA!
I totally
took off for
senior skip
day.
You are
so totally
grounded
and--
Yeah, they
called in sick.
I just didn't
show up.
You
didn't call
in?
I didn't
call in.
Well-
duh.
I
know.
So I said:
"What did he say?"
She said he said his
cell phone was
broken. What a
dog, right?
Uh-huh.
So I told
her to tell
him--
Um, I'm
gonna take
off.

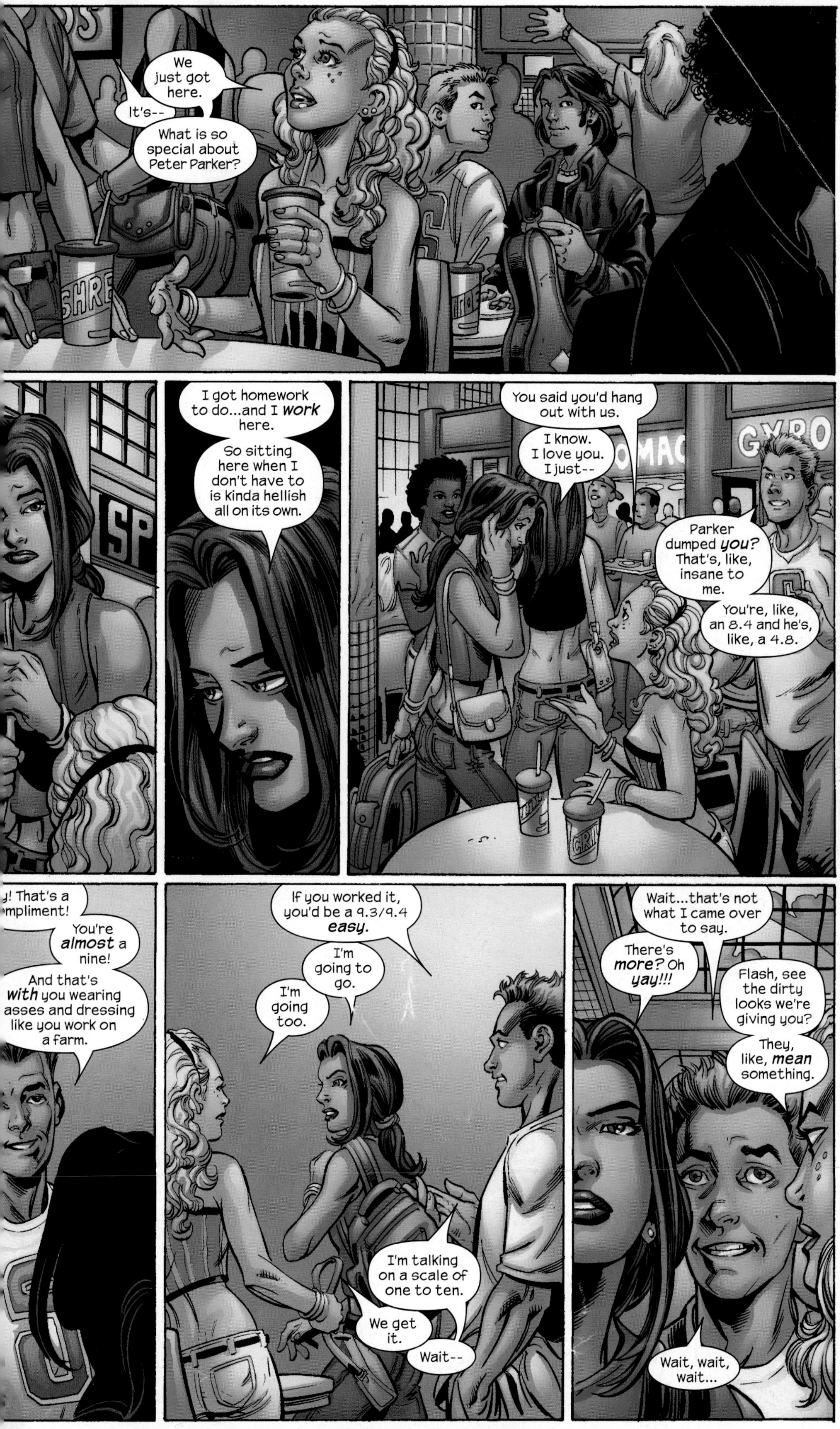

We just got here.
It's--
What is so special about Peter Parker?
I got homework to do...and I *work* here.
So sitting here when I don't have to is kinda hellish all on its own.
You said you'd hang out with us.
I know. I love you. I just--
Parker dumped *you*? That's, like, insane to me.
You're, like, an 8.4 and he's, like, a 4.8.
y! That's a mpliment!
You're *almost* a nine!
And that's *with* you wearing asses and dressing like you work on a farm.
If you worked it, you'd be a 9.3/9.4 *easy.*
I'm going to go.
I'm going too.
I'm talking on a scale of one to ten.
We get it.
Wait--
Wait...that's not what I came over to say.
There's *more?* Oh *yay!!!*
Flash, see the dirty looks we're giving you?
They, like, *mean* something.
Wait, wait, wait...

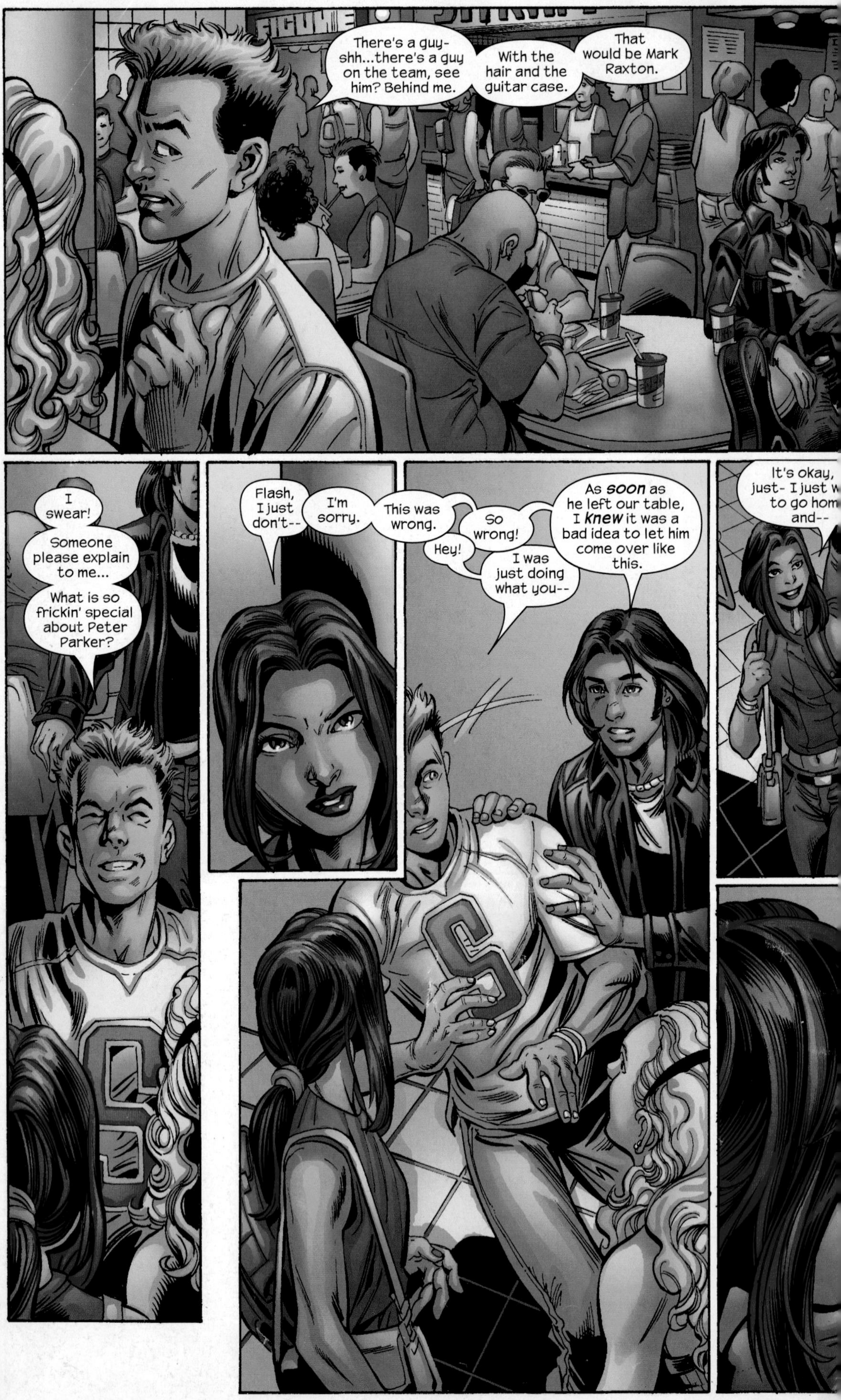
There's a guy-shh...there's a guy on the team, see him? Behind me.
With the hair and the guitar case.
That would be Mark Raxton.
I swear!
Someone please explain to me...
What is so frickin' special about Peter Parker?
Flash, I just don't--
I'm sorry.
This was wrong.
So wrong!
Hey!
I was just doing what you--
As SOON as he left our table, I KNEW it was a bad idea to let him come over like this.
It's okay, just- I just w
to go hom
and--

Keep talking.

He's on the basketball team. Senior. He's got a band.

He's a good guy.

So he- he sorta said he *likes* you.

I mean, he likes what he sees. You know?

(Got a thing for redheads...)

He asked me to come over here...

That's okay.

No, he's not like me, he's--

A nice guy.

I'm not looking for--

Well, yeah, I mean, he's a good guy.

Seriously?? Because of Parker?

Flash!

He's a senior!

I was working the magic.

You go sit.

But--

Go, sit.

But--

Sit!

But--

Sit!

...ew...

He heard me say-- he wants to be my buddy or something and he heard me talking about you and he said he was friends with you- and- and I let him come over.

That was my ...ot with you and ...blew it. I just ...anted to come ...ver here and apologize.

I'm sorry.

It's okay.

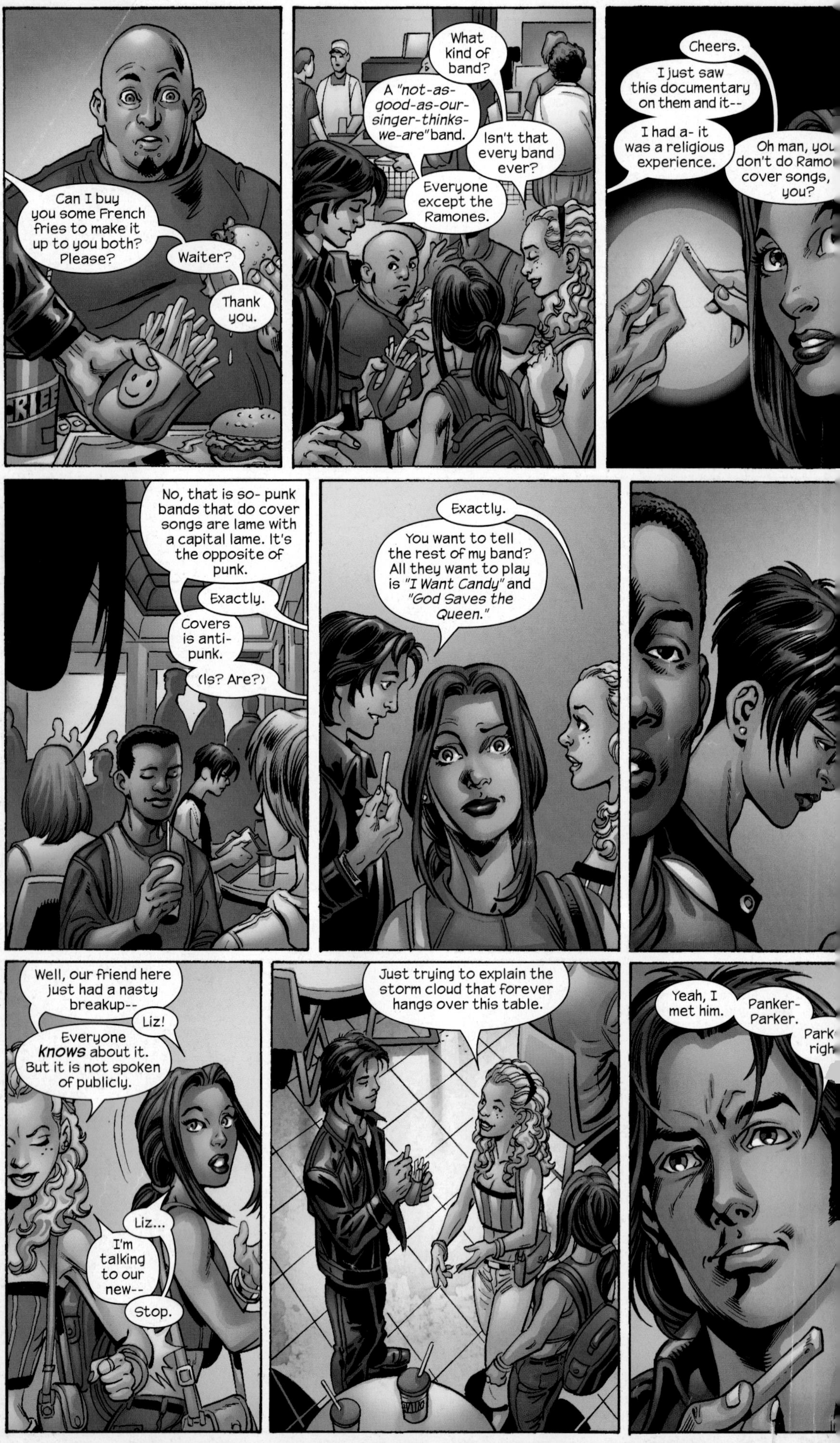
Can I buy you some French fries to make it up to you both? Please?
Waiter?
Thank you.
What kind of band?
A "not-as-good-as-our-singer-thinks-we-are" band.
Isn't that every band ever?
Everyone except the Ramones.
Cheers.
I just saw this documentary on them and it--
I had a- it was a religious experience.
Oh man, you don't do Ramo cover songs, you?
No, that is so- punk bands that do cover songs are lame with a capital lame. It's the opposite of punk.
Exactly.
Covers is anti-punk.
(Is? Are?)
Exactly.
You want to tell the rest of my band? All they want to play is "I Want Candy" and "God Saves the Queen."
Well, our friend here just had a nasty breakup--
Liz!
Everyone KNOWS about it. But it is not spoken of publicly.
Liz...
I'm talking to our new--
Stop.
Just trying to explain the storm cloud that forever hangs over this table.
Yeah, I met him.
Panker-Parker.
Park righ

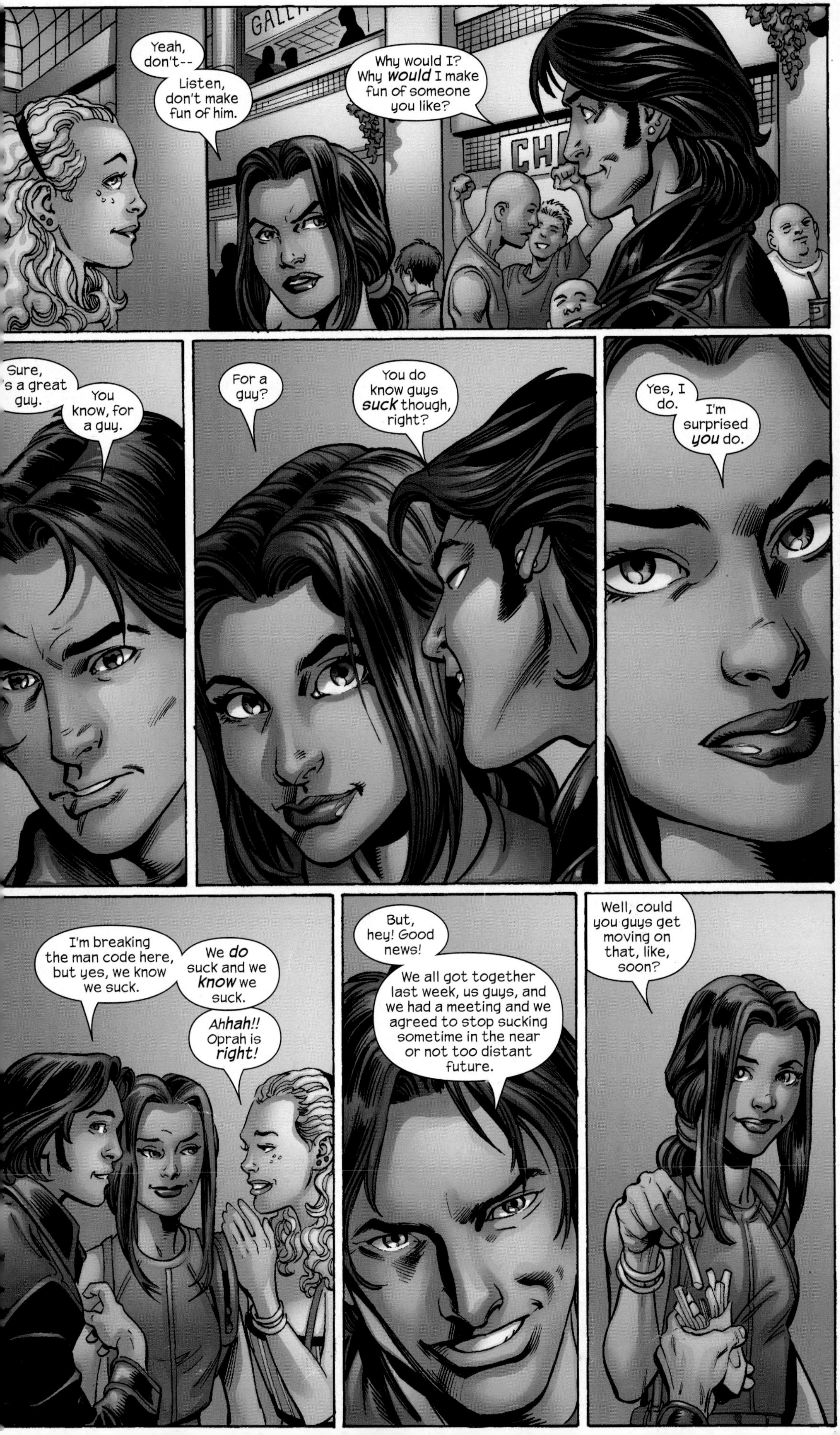

Yeah, don't--
Listen, don't make fun of him.
Why would I? Why *would* I make fun of someone you like?
Sure, 's a great guy.
You know, for a guy.
For a guy?
You do know guys *suck* though, right?
Yes, I do.
I'm surprised *you* do.
I'm breaking the man code here, but yes, we know we suck.
We *do* suck and we *know* we suck.
Ahhah!! Oprah is *right!*
But, hey! Good news!
We all got together last week, us guys, and we had a meeting and we agreed to stop sucking sometime in the near or not too distant future.
Well, could you guys get moving on that, like, soon?

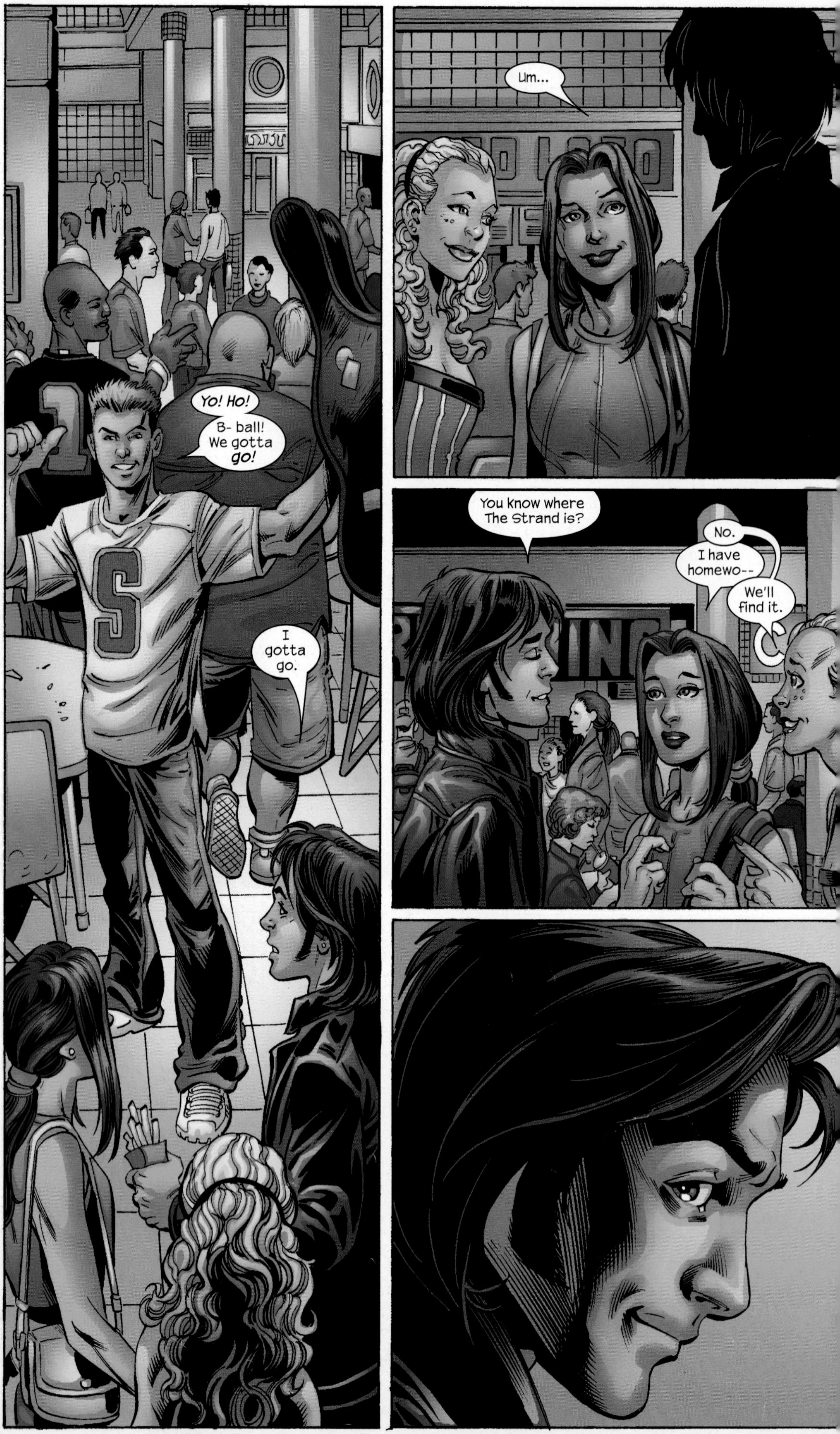
Yo! Ho!
B- ball! We gotta go!
I gotta go.
Um...
You know where The Strand is?
No.
I have homewo--
We'll find it.

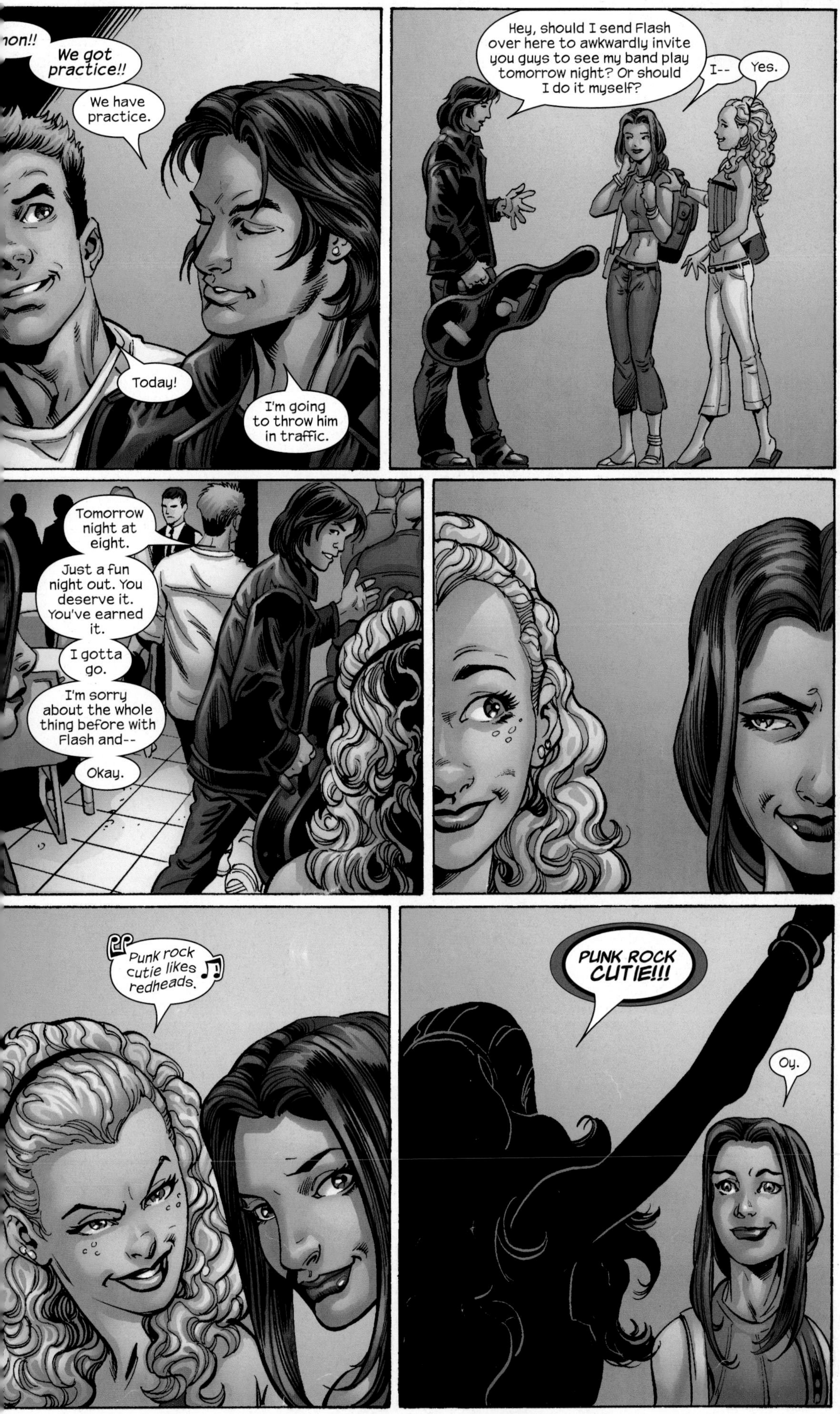
non!!
We got practice!!
We have practice.
Today!
I'm going to throw him in traffic.
Hey, should I send Flash over here to awkwardly invite you guys to see my band play tomorrow night? Or should I do it myself?
I--
Yes.
Tomorrow night at eight.
Just a fun night out. You deserve it. You've earned it.
I gotta go.
I'm sorry about the whole thing before with Flash and--
Okay.
Punk rock cutie likes redheads.
PUNK ROCK CUTIE!!!
Oy.

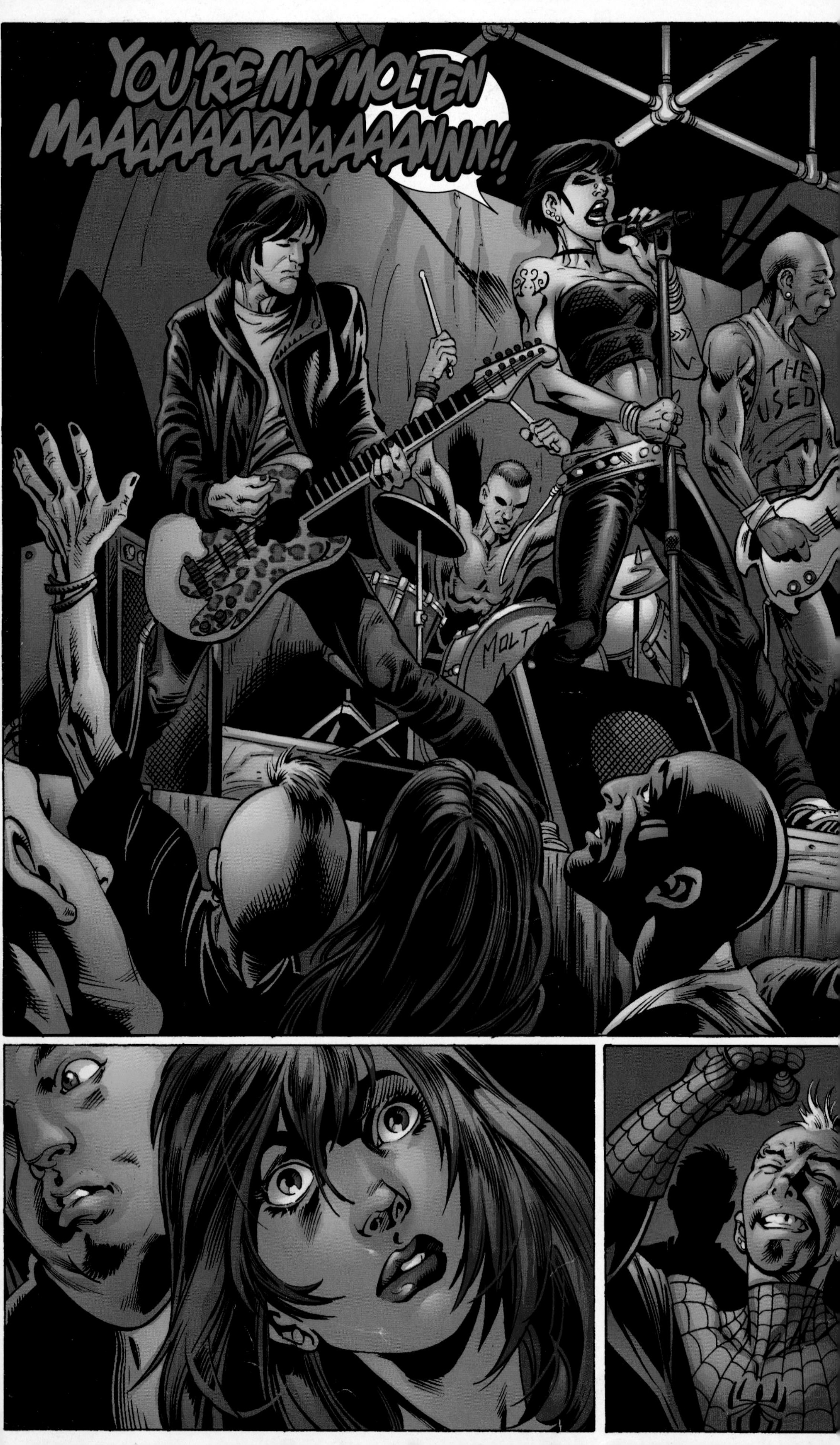
YOU'RE MY MOLTEN MAAAAAAAAAAAANNNN!!
THE USED
MOLTA

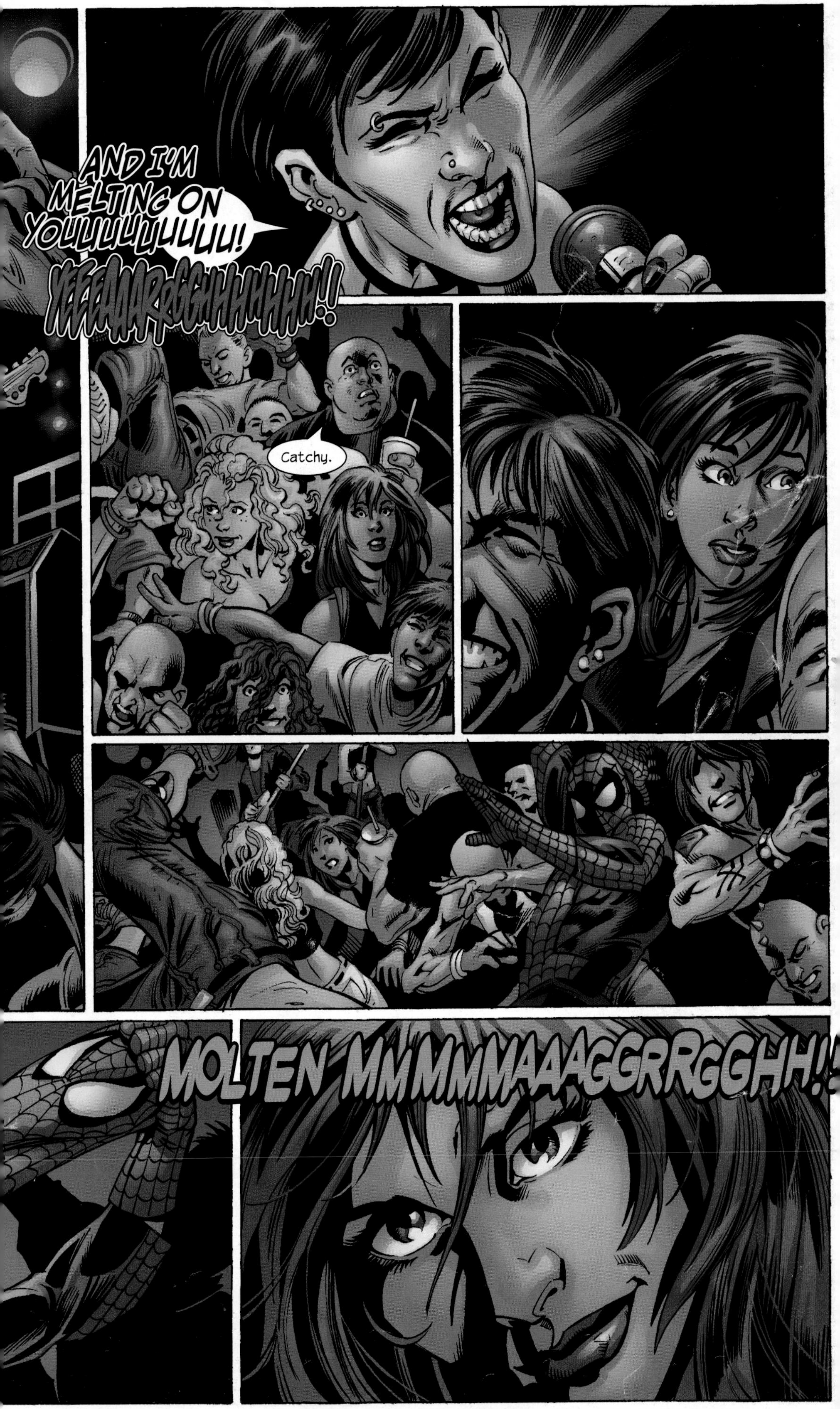
AND I'M MELTING ON YOUUUUUUUUU!
YEEEAAARRGGHHHHHHH!!
Catchy.
MOLTEN MMMMMAAAGGRRGGHH!!

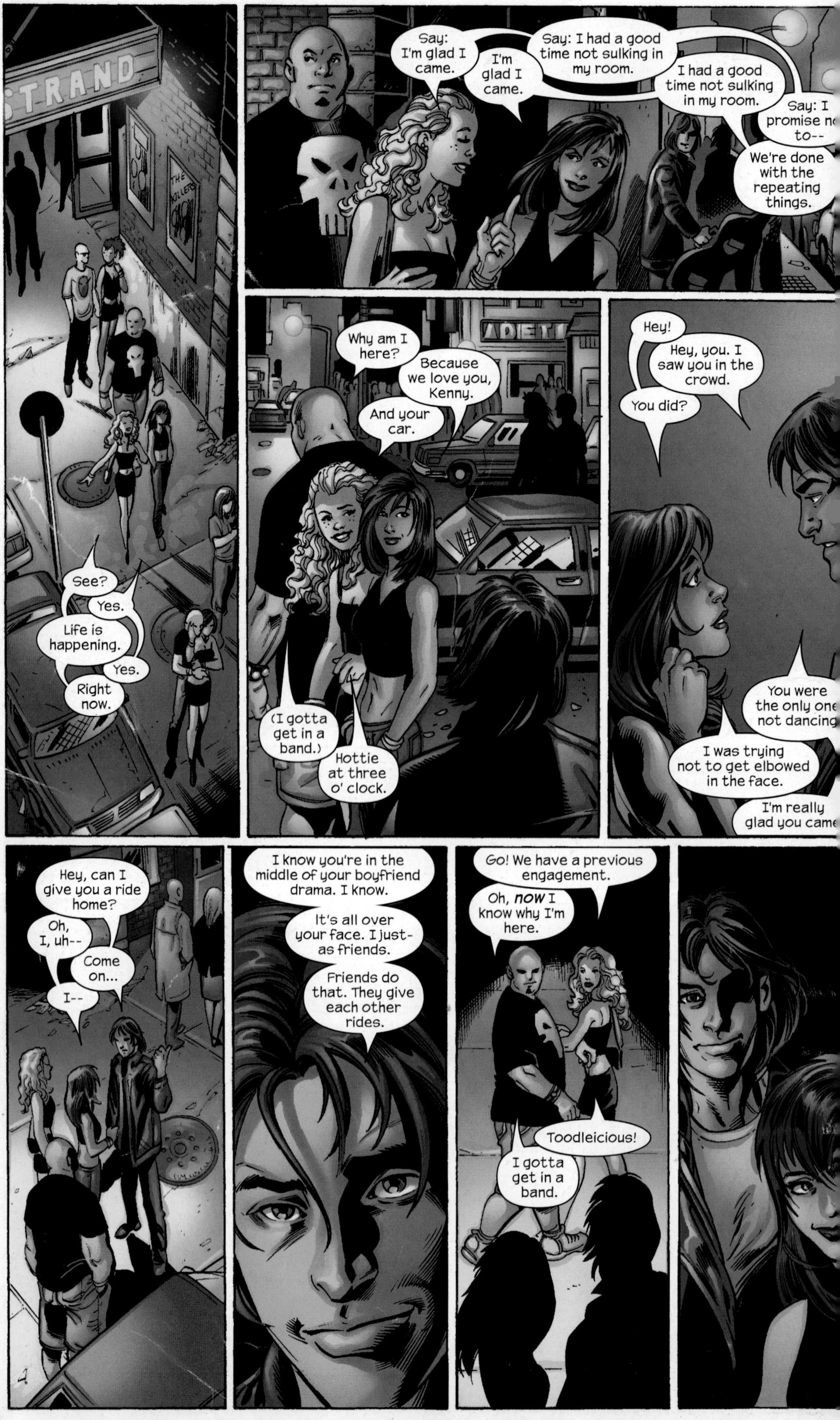
STRAND
THE KILLERS
See?
Yes.
Life is happening.
Yes.
Right now.
Say: I'm glad I came.
I'm glad I came.
Say: I had a good time not sulking in my room.
I had a good time not sulking in my room.
Say: I promise n
to--
We're done with the repeating things.
Why am I here?
Because we love you, Kenny.
And your car.
(I gotta get in a band.)
Hottie at three o' clock.
Hey!
Hey, you. I saw you in the crowd.
You did?
You were the only one not dancing
I was trying not to get elbowed in the face.
I'm really glad you came
Hey, can I give you a ride home?
Oh, I, uh--
Come on...
I--
I know you're in the middle of your boyfriend drama. I know.
It's all over your face. I just- as friends.
Friends do that. They give each other rides.
Go! We have a previous engagement.
Oh, *NOW* I know why I'm here.
Toodleicious!
I gotta get in a band.

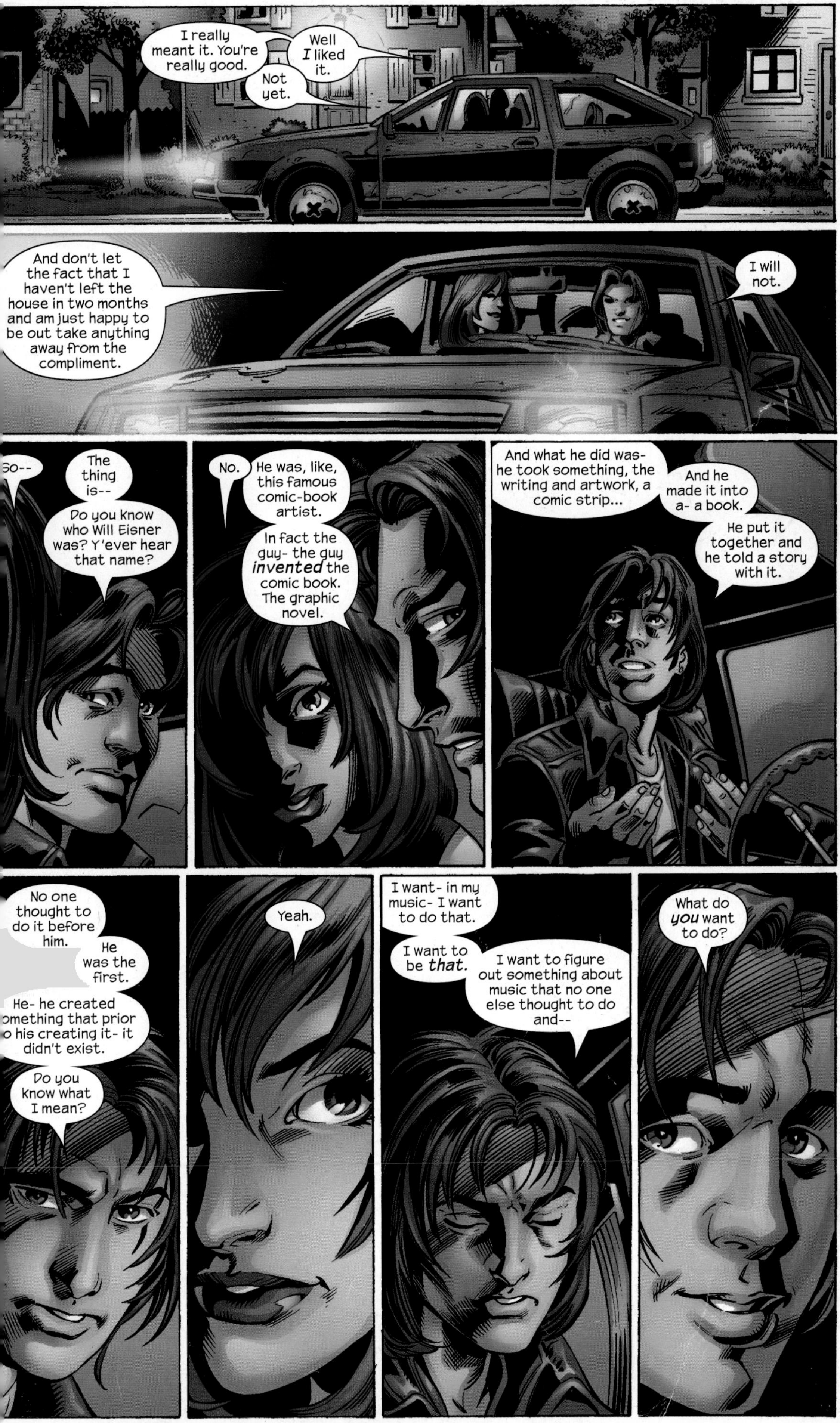

I really meant it. You're really good.
Well I liked it.
Not yet.
And don't let the fact that I haven't left the house in two months and am just happy to be out take anything away from the compliment.
I will not.
So--
The thing is--
Do you know who Will Eisner was? Y'ever hear that name?
No.
He was, like, this famous comic-book artist.
In fact the guy- the guy invented the comic book. The graphic novel.
And what he did was- he took something, the writing and artwork, a comic strip...
And he made it into a- a book.
He put it together and he told a story with it.
No one thought to do it before him.
He was the first.
He- he created omething that prior o his creating it- it didn't exist.
Do you know what I mean?
Yeah.
I want- in my music- I want to do that.
I want to be that.
I want to figure out something about music that no one else thought to do and--
What do you want to do?

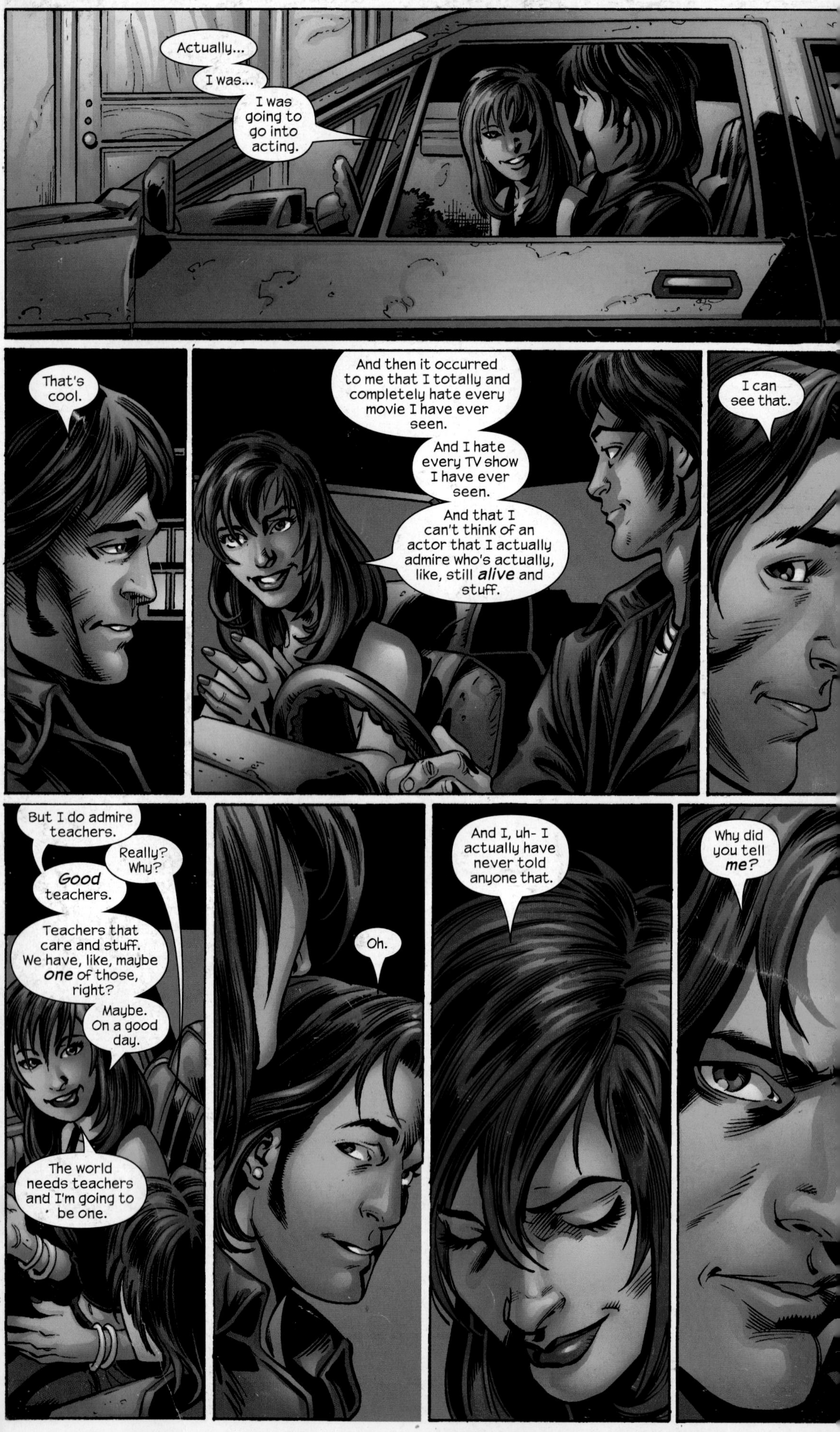
Actually...
I was...
I was going to go into acting.
That's cool.
And then it occurred to me that I totally and completely hate every movie I have ever seen.
And I hate every TV show I have ever seen.
And that I can't think of an actor that I actually admire who's actually, like, still *alive* and stuff.
I can see that.
But I do admire teachers.
Really? Why?
Good teachers.
Teachers that care and stuff. We have, like, maybe *one* of those, right?
Maybe. On a good day.
The world needs teachers and I'm going to be one.
Oh.
And I, uh- I actually have never told anyone that.
Why did you tell *me*?

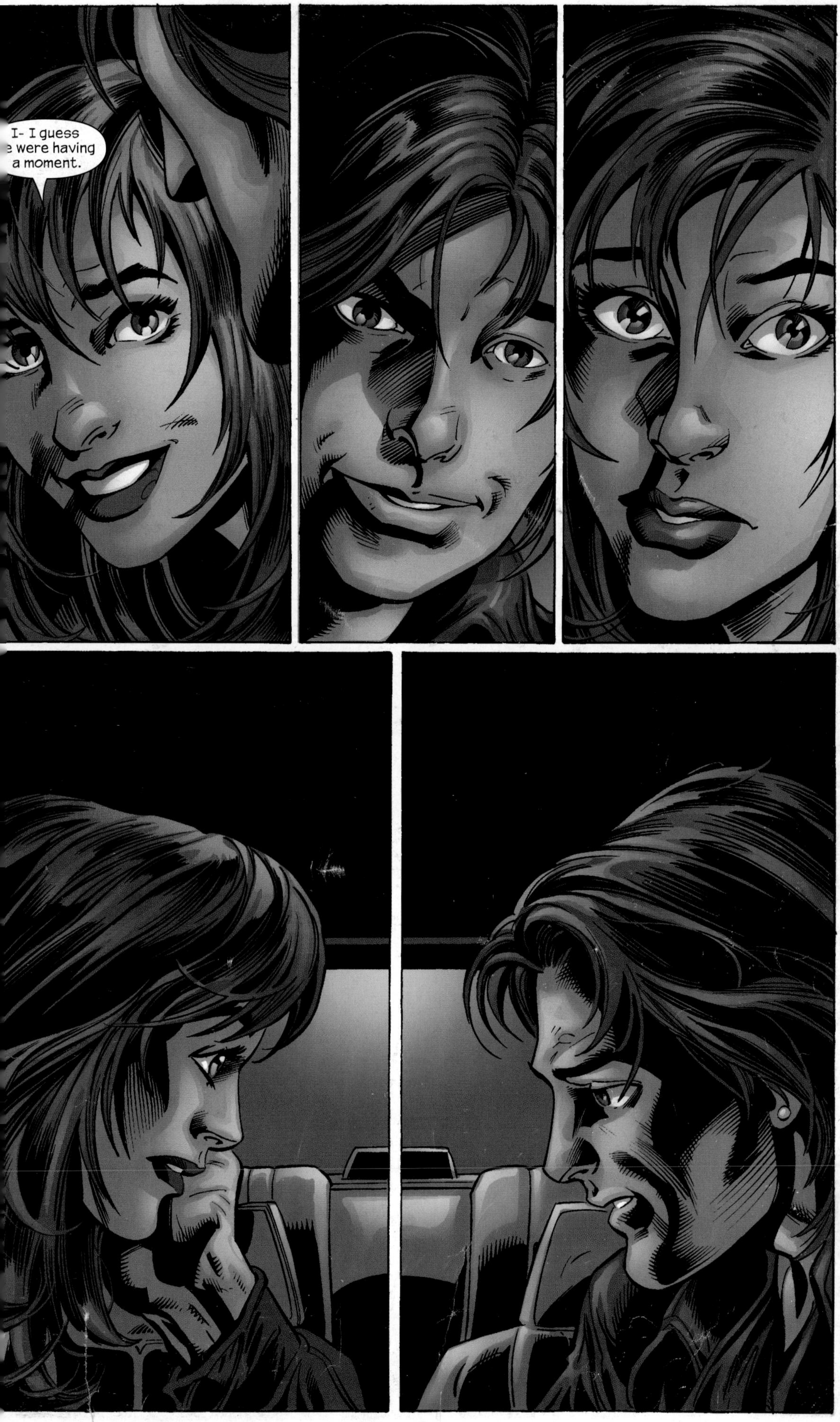
I- I guess
e were having
a moment.

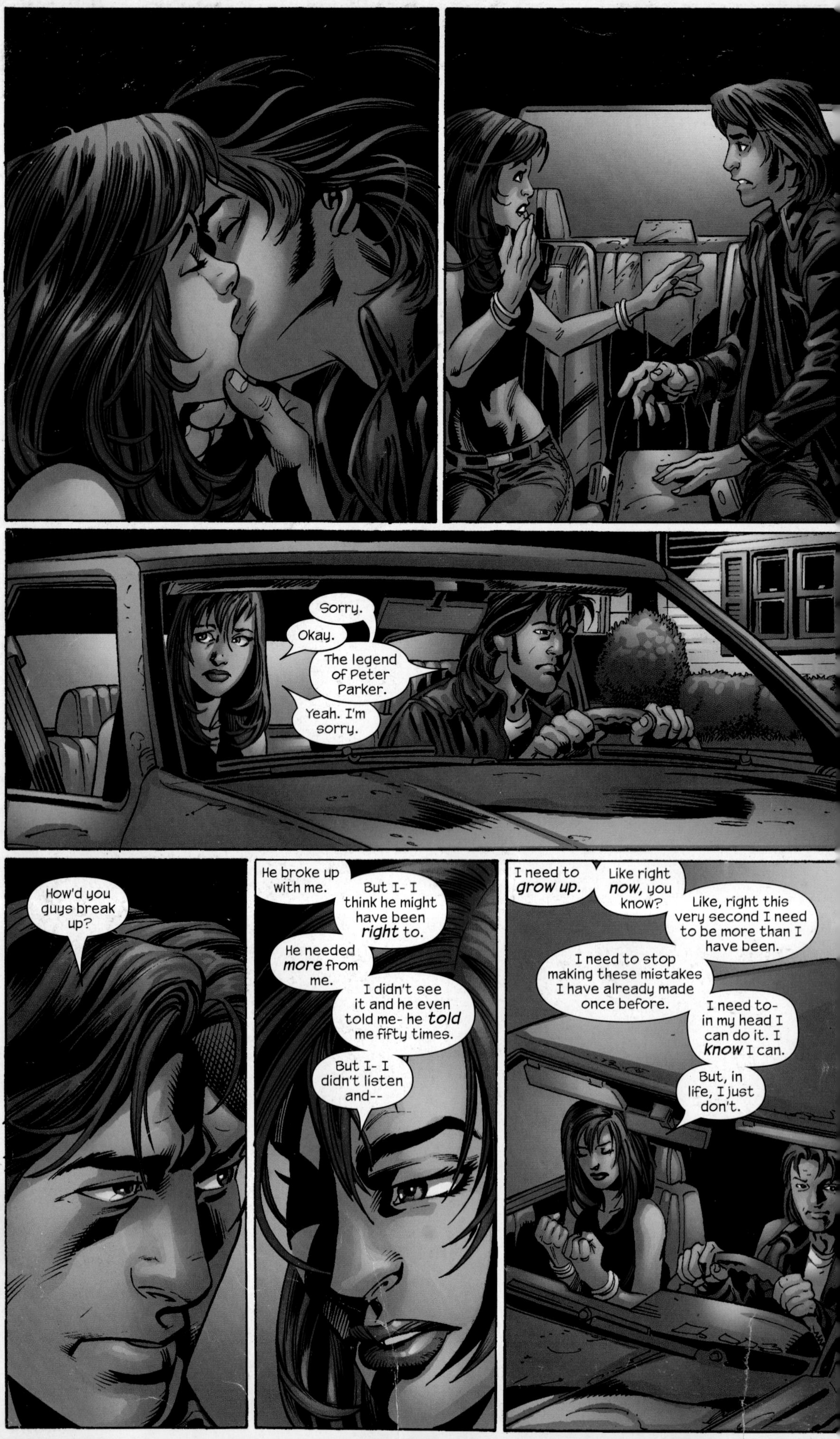
Sorry.
Okay.
The legend of Peter Parker.
Yeah. I'm sorry.
How'd you guys break up?
He broke up with me.
But I- I think he might have been *right* to.
He needed *more* from me.
I didn't see it and he even told me- he *told* me fifty times.
But I- I didn't listen and--
I need to *grow up.*
Like right *now,* you know?
Like, right this very second I need to be more than I have been.
I need to stop making these mistakes I have already made once before.
I need to- in my head I can do it. I *know* I can.
But, in life, I just don't.

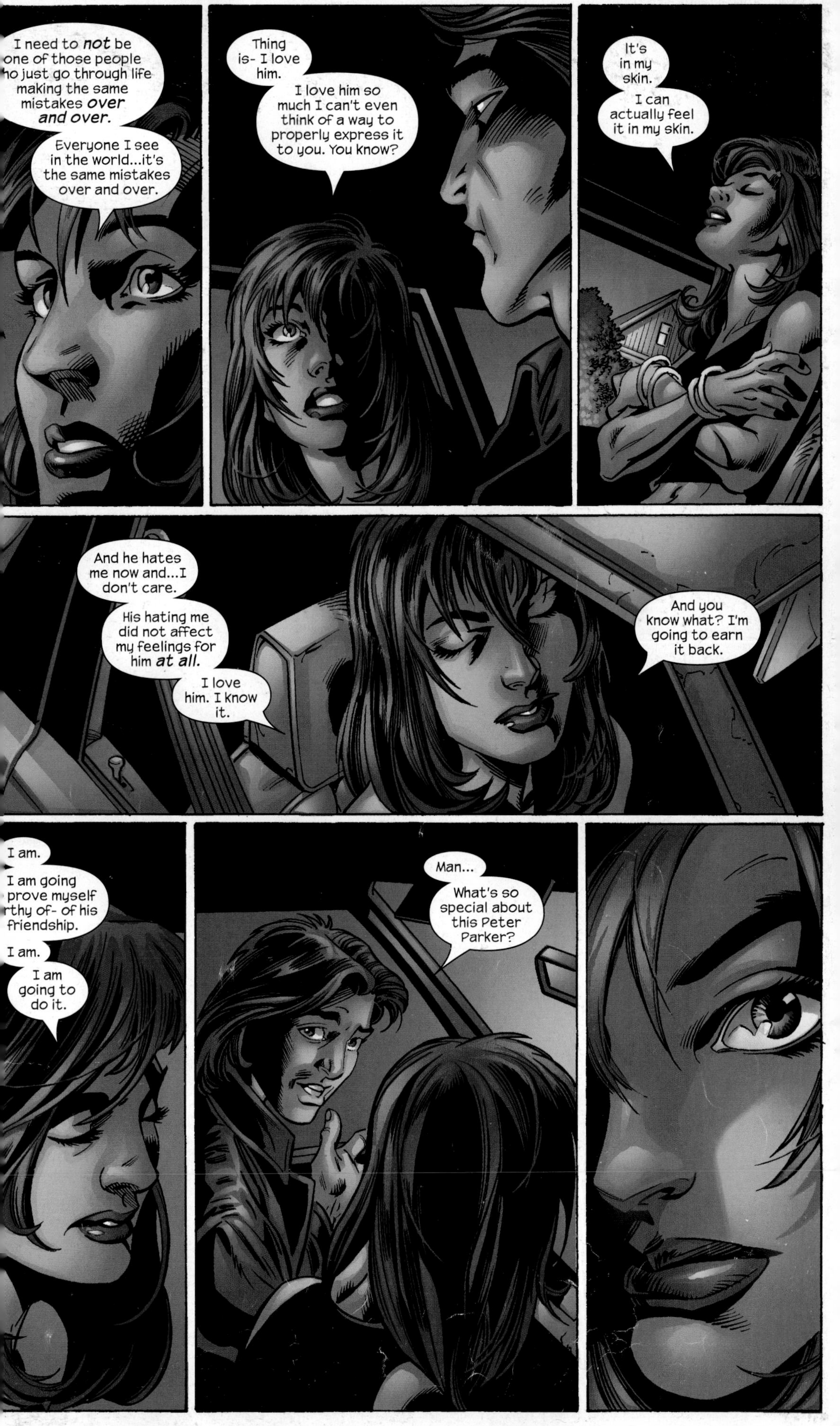
I need to *not* be one of those people ho just go through life making the same mistakes *over and over.*
Everyone I see in the world...it's the same mistakes over and over.
Thing is- I love him.
I love him so much I can't even think of a way to properly express it to you. You know?
It's in my skin.
I can actually feel it in my skin.
And he hates me now and...I don't care.
His hating me did not affect my feelings for him *at all.*
I love him. I know it.
And you know what? I'm going to earn it back.
I am.
I am going prove myself rthy of- of his friendship.
I am.
I am going to do it.
Man...
What's so special about this Peter Parker?

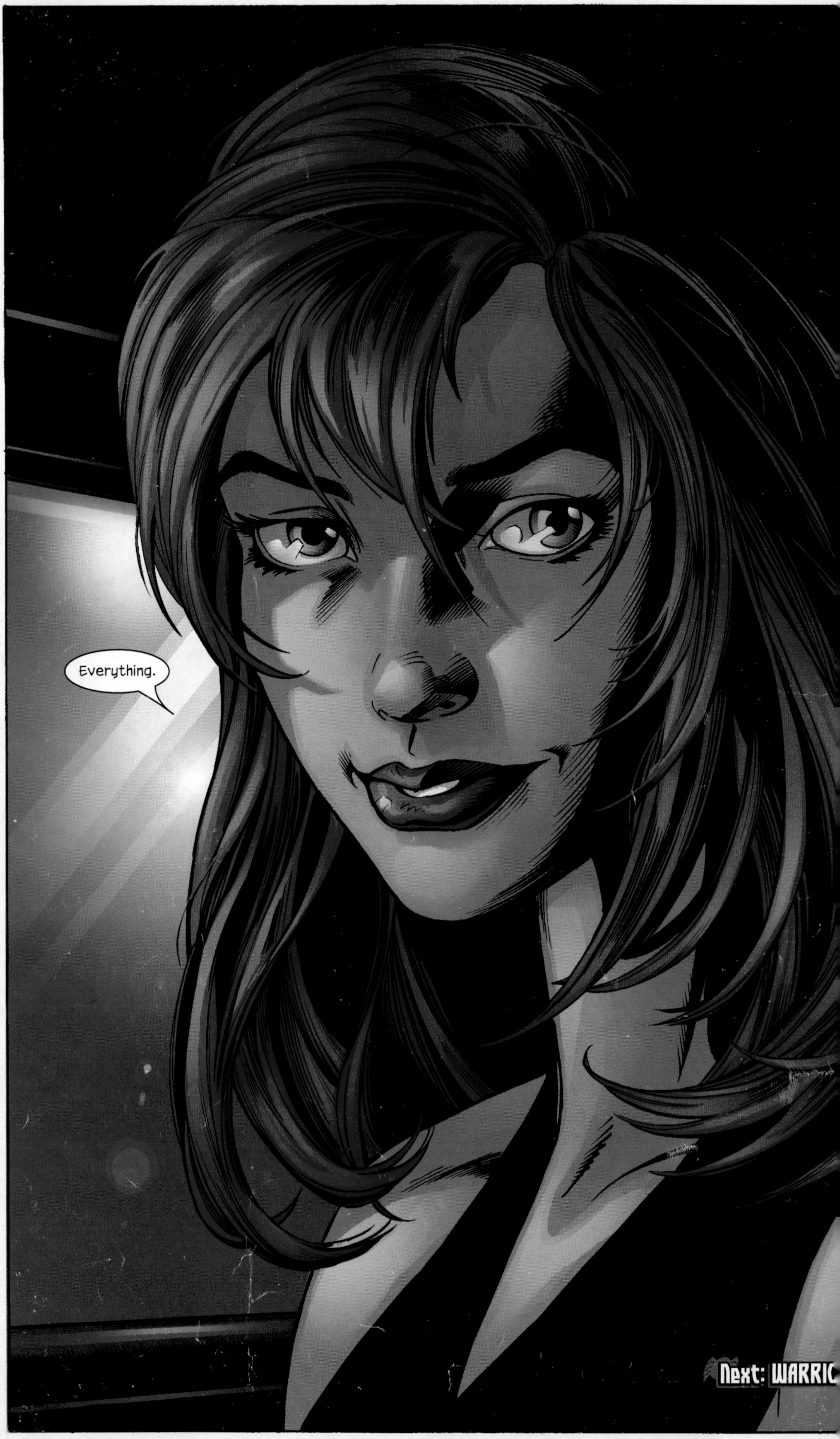
Everything.
Next: WARRIC